St. Paul for the Perplexed

Making sense of the man:
his life
his letters
his story

(Revised Edition)

Charles P. Anderson

DEDICATION

To Patricia whose constant love and encouragement until
death did us part made this book possible.

ACKNOWLEDGEMENTS

My gratitude to my family for their contributions: my daughter Diane who, despite my many requests for revisions, persevered to create the covers of both the first and the revised editions of this book; my daughter-in-law, Maureen who challenged me in fierce but friendly debate over style from which (some) changes were made; my present partner, Ardy, who walked the second (and third) mile in protecting my writing time; my son Dave for motivating me to put my thoughts about Paul on paper and for our numerous subsequent conversations; my other son John who, like Paul, worked with his hands and became a teacher to help others to grow; my daughter-in-law Laura and my son-in-law Harry who willingly shared their computer savvy when I most needed it. Each of you has left your mark on my life and my writing. Thank you.

My thanks also to three scholars who read the revised manuscript and offered helpful suggestions for improvement, and who have been kind enough to write brief comments for the book cover: Drs. Rob Cousland, Paul Newman, and George Johnson.

Cover by Diane C. Nicholson

CONTENTS

THE PRIMARY SOURCES

PREFACE TO THE REVISED EDITION

During the intervening years since the publication of the first edition of this book five years ago, continuing reflection on Paul's letters and the Acts of the Apostles have convinced me that a second edition is necessary. Consequently, numerous revisions have been made in this edition. The number of scriptural quotations of the original edition has been reduced by about a third to make room for more expansive commentary on Paul's own thoughts, both in the text and in the notes. In particular, Chapter 13 has been rewritten as a result of my attempts to understand better the reasons for the survival and flourishing of the communities Paul engineered. Chapter seven has been expanded in order to explain more thoroughly the rationale of atoning sacrifices as background for Paul's use of that imagery. In order to make the notes more easily accessible to the reader, they have been converted from endnotes to footnotes, and an index has been added.

More importantly, my appreciation of Paul as a person who has much to say to our time has continued to deepen. Today's mantra of "spiritual but not religious" provides a new vantage point from which to engage Paul's own emphasis on "Spirit." I have come to feel that too much emphasis is often placed on Paul's religion and his theology at the expense of his values and his understanding of what it means to be a viable human being. The story of his conversion from opposing to promoting the teachings of Jesus is widely known. Less appreciated is Paul's analysis of the forces that changed his life and their implications for humanity in general. He found in the life and teachings of Jesus an archetype of "the good life" perennially sought by humanity. That vision led him to develop a strategy and a story for aiding others in their own transformation.

His strategy developed from his understanding that to achieve and maintain release from destructive thoughts and behavior, a supportive community was necessary. So he formed and mentored face-to-face communities (life-schools) in which participants were taught to practice the saving graces: empathy, kindness, non-judgmentalism, generosity, gratitude, and respect—all summarized in the phrase "love of neighbor." Gender equality, openness to other ethnicities, and empathy for all were embedded in the community's entry ritual and founding story.

To facilitate and emphasize the importance of both personal and social transformation, Paul created a universalizing story about the human condition in its worst and best manifestations, beginning with Adam and concluding with Jesus. Each personified an alternative way of living—Adam self-absorbed egotism, Jesus self-giving, non-conditional love. Paul's favorite term for guidance in thought and behavior was the "imitation of Christ."

The conventional view of Paul as an advocate of patriarchy, uncritical subservience to government, and condemnation of non-heterosexual gender identities is not supported by his own authentic writings, but only by appeal to writings attributed to him by later members of "Pauline" churches.

Against the backdrop of the current extremism, divisiveness, corruption, self-promotion, hatred, xenophobia, racism, mistreatment of women, anti-LGBTQ propaganda and actions, greed, lying and disregard for truth and facts, Paul offers a breath of fresh air. He deserves to be revisited in this perplexing time.

Readers should not feel compelled to read this book from start to finish. If the portions dealing with Paul's life seem daunting, turn to Chapter 13 to gain a sense of his character, message, and importance. Then perhaps the details of his life will take on more significance.

FOREWORD

Why another book on St. Paul? Dr. Charles Anderson notes that Paul's legacy continues into our time. Indeed, it is generally accepted that Paul played a vital role in the development of Christianity. Much of Christian doctrine is rooted in Paul's thought. In fact, as Samuel Sandmel, a Jewish scholar, has concluded: "Paul was a religious genius."

In order to keep Paul's legacy relevant, it is critical to express it in contemporary thought forms. Using the vehicle of story/narrative, Dr. Anderson succeeds in making Paul come alive for our day. For example, rather than presenting the trajectory of thought leading up to Paul in abstract terms, it is personalized by focusing on Adam, Abraham, Moses and Jesus. Also Paul's own views are discussed in close relationship to his life. The use of story/narrative is not artificially imposed on Paul but woven into the fabric of the entire book.

Using the concept of healing, Paul's story is presented in a captivating manner. The first two parts of the book deal with the story of Paul's own healing and the healing of the nations. Why do I find the language of healing so refreshing? I like to view the church as a hospital. We are all there to help each other to get well.

The introduction to the book exudes a global perspective that grows out of a mature reflection on a lifetime of research and teaching. Dr. Anderson provides a comprehensive and direct account of his approach to Paul. He specifically asserts that his book is not an attack on faith but endeavors to be faith neutral. Paul's story, life and letters are to be presented from an objective academic perspective. The discussion of the authenticity of Paul's letters and the issue of their inspiration is representative of the views of many New

Testament professors. My teaching career is based in conservative Canadian theological seminaries and follows a more traditional approach. I do, however, find this book to be an excellent resource to understand the view espoused by various other scholars.

I have appreciated Dr. Anderson's expertise in the field of the academic study of the New Testament. In fact, the first course I ever had on the New Testament was from him at the University of British Columbia in the 1960s. Then Dr. Anderson served as my M.A. thesis supervisor at UBC in the early 70s. I especially owe a debt of gratitude to "Chuck" for giving me a fabulous recommendation so that I was awarded a 4-year Canada Council Doctoral Fellowship to pursue Ph. D studies.

The word "Perplexed" in the title of the book is intriguing. It is used in two significant ways. First of all, by avoiding the use of technical language, Dr. Anderson has definitely succeeded in presenting Paul in a non-perplexing form to the reader. The numerous summaries also help the reader to focus on the main thrust of the book.

However, I'm more intrigued by the other aspect of "Perplexed." The "book is also written for those who may be perplexed about themselves and are seeking resolution." In other words, the book is not only about the healing of Paul and the nations in general but also about personal healing. The aspect of personal healing was not as evident in Dr. Anderson's teaching when I was his student at UBC. What brought this more "pastoral" element into play? Is it Dr. Anderson's greater church involvement since I knew him as a student? After all, for quite a while he has been an active member of the United Church of Canada. It appears that for "Chuck" Paul's impact has moved ever more beyond academic circles into everyday life and the community of the church.

In chapters 1–12 the relevance for personal healing is implicit. One has to search for it among a wealth of other details of Paul's life and letters. In chapter 13 the relevance to personal healing becomes more explicit. While Professor Anderson has in no way resorted to "preaching," the content of this chapter definitely can be applied to his goal of personal healing. The twelve reasons for Paul's missionary success are as relevant today as they were then. In fact, they could serve to initiate dialogue in both religious and secular settings. For example, Paul can assist us in striking "a workable balance between a high morality and personal freedom." Working in a non-condemnatory manner on this balance is a major challenge in North American society today.

The "Final Comments" in chapter 13 are especially powerful. With Paul "The law of Christ, love, was now the one commandment of God for all." And how does this apply to our time? I am challenged by Dr. Anderson's conclusion: "Love is a sturdy foundation for a community. To build a world on it is perhaps an impossible dream. Achievable or not, that was Paul's vision."

Professor Anderson stresses that Paul imitated Christ. Reading between the lines it appears to me that "Minister" Anderson also encourages us to follow Paul's example. Let's chip away at the impossible dream!

Benno Przybylski, Ph.D.
Retired Biblical Studies Professor

INTRODUCTION

This book is written for those who find Paul perplexing. Many who try to read his letters give up in despair. Apart from a few memorable passages quoted at weddings or funerals, his writings do not resonate with most of us. There are good reasons for that disconnect. By their very nature, letters tell only half the story; in Paul's case the reader is left wondering about the recipients, their point of view, their issues, and their responses to what he wrote. In addition, his terminology, concepts, and assumptions come from a different world than ours. Much of his writing is argumentative, and it is not always clear what he is arguing about and why. It is no wonder his letters often leave the reader bewildered.

This book is also written for those who may be perplexed about themselves and/or the world we live in. Paradoxically, the same Paul who can be so perplexing also offers an understanding of human existence and a mode of living that has empowered incalculable numbers who were seeking a more satisfying life, or, to change the image, who were looking for healing of their wounded selves and their world. Paul's letters were all written after he himself had unexpectedly found a new meaning and purpose for his life and was in process of sharing his story with others. His life goal had become the furtherance of a revolution in human thinking and acting which had begun with a Jewish teacher in Galilee. Paul's special calling was to take the revolution which had encompassed him into the larger Roman world. Persuasion by word and deed consistent with the values and principles of the Galilean teacher was the primary tool to bring about the radical change Paul sought. Persuasion can take various forms; Paul was particularly adept at argumentation but his personal character gave substance to his verbal and written presentations. Underneath and imbedded in all his communications was his story of the healing of humanity. It is this story that is the subject of this book.

Paul as Storyteller

Paul has a story to tell. He told it in city after city throughout the eastern Mediterranean for at least a quarter of a century. He told it in synagogues, workshops, on the street, in at least one lecture hall, wherever he could find someone to listen. Though some of his audiences may have found his story entertaining, and Paul was not above humor, his purpose was deadly serious. Paul's experience had led him to the conclusion that a profound illness had descended upon humanity. Its symptoms are observable everywhere: gossip, jealousy, factionalism, boastfulness, lying, selfishness, hostility, hatred, murder, idolatry, and moral degradations of all sorts—to which we today could add our own examples and illustrations. The malady is not confined to individuals; it has infected social and cultural structures, through which it propagates itself. It is the original socially transmitted disease to which no person, no society, no religion, and no nation have immunity. The whole world has fallen victim to an insidious and destructive virus. Where was healing to be found?

Paul's story is his answer to that question. He had a vision of a remade world—a new creation—in which empathy, kindness, caring, and sharing had become the norm rather than the exception. His experience of his own healing, despite his determined resistance to the healer, provided the proof of his story's validity. Finally, his mystic vision of the healer compelled him to take his emerging story on the road to "the nations," i.e., the Gentiles.

Although Paul's story draws on themes and characters from the Jewish scriptures and the emerging Jesus movement, it had to be applicable to the non-Jewish world. It was a formidable task that Paul took on, both in formulating such a universal narrative and in communicating it. To be credible and effective, it had to touch those who heard it in their deepest being, and Paul's own speech and behavior had to be consistent with it. Only when those conditions were met would his audiences be likely to find their own reflections in his story. Only then could it become the healing narrative of their lives and their communities.

Paul's Place in the Jesus Movement

Paul lived at a time when a new worldview and a new way of living were emerging; he was to play a key role in their development. It may not be too much to claim that next to Jesus, Paul was the most important figure in the earliest period of Christianity, perhaps in its entire history. Without his energy, commitment, and ability to forge a credible rationale for bringing others besides Jews into the new faith, it is possible that the Jesus movement would have remained a Jewish sect. How long, or even whether it would have survived, the Gentile[1] world might not have been a part of it. The trajectory championed by Paul eventually led to a new world religion, which, while owing much to its Jewish parent, nevertheless took on its own distinctive identity.

Paul joined the Jesus movement within a few years, almost certainly no more than three or four and possibly only one or two, after the death of Jesus. By the year 50 of this era the fruits of his missionary labors had become extensive enough that Paul turned to the letter format to keep in touch with the communities that he had founded. Except for part of the final personal greetings which he himself sometimes wrote, the contents of his letters were dictated to a secretary. They were then delivered by trusted colleagues or friends and read to and discussed with their intended audiences.

---

[1] Gentile: A non-Jew; in the Bible, someone who belongs to a people or ethnic group other than Israel, i.e., one of the "nations."

Some decades after Paul's death his letters were collected to form the earliest part of the Christian additions to the Jewish Bible used by the new faith.[2]

Paul's version of the developing Christian story was not the only one being told. Various interpretations of Jesus arose in the formative period of the new faith. The presence of writings in the New Testament[3] attributed to Peter, Matthew, John, and James suggests that each represented a different arena of thought and practice. However, Paul's letters preceded these and all other Christian writings in articulating a truly universal form of the Christ story. The influence of Paul's "gospel," as he calls it, on the later writings which became known as Gospels is substantial.

Thus two essential aspects of the Christian faith–an identity including but moving beyond its Jewish roots and a distinctively Christian scripture–owe much to Paul's endeavors. It is ironic, therefore, that so many people today, including Christians, and even some of their clergy, know so little about Paul himself. In recent decades a veritable flood of Pauline studies for other specialists and many written for the general public have been published. Yet misunderstanding and misinterpretation of this seminal figure continue to abound in the general public. His importance demands continued attention.

Sources

The literary sources for our endeavor will be explored more thoroughly in the final two chapters, but a few preliminary comments are appropriate here. This book is based primari-

[2] Trobisch argues that Paul himself published the first collection of his letters, which consisted of Romans, 1 and 2 Corinthians, and Galatians. *Paul's Letter Collection: Tracing the Origins.*

[3] From this point on, New Testament will be abbreviated as NT and the Jewish Bible (the Christian Old Testament) as OT.

ly on the seven undisputed letters authored by Paul: Romans, 1 and 2 Corinthians, Galatians, Philippians, 1 Thessalonians, and Philemon. The Acts of the Apostles will also be used, but secondary to Paul's genuine letters.

The other six letters attributed to him will not be employed because many scholars, myself included, do not regard them as authentically Paul's. This conclusion is based on substantial evidence, such as differences in vocabulary, different meanings of terms, different social situations, and many other considerations which we shall not go into here. By using only the seven undisputed letters as a control, we can justifiably compare the picture of Paul derived from them with the representations found in the other six letters. We shall have occasion later to comment on some of the disparities which validate excluding them from our data base.

Paul's authentic letters tells us a great deal about the kind of person he was. They reveal a remarkable man deeply immersed in his life-mission, motivated by a calling for which he was willing to suffer and die if necessary. He could be tender and sarcastic, refined and crude, brilliant and opaque, congenial and controversial. The scope and depth of his thought are impressive; his vision of a new kind of society was far ahead of his time—and in many ways our own. On the other hand, his letters reveal little about the externals of his life. At most, they record memories of selected events, and sometimes a brief summary or evaluation of a whole period of his life. His focus was not on himself, but on the story he was compelled to narrate. His lack of attention to the details of his own life may make the biographical task appear questionable if not impossible. That said, we must also recognize that his letters provide a wealth of primary personal sources seldom equaled in the ancient world. In the case of early Christianity, Jesus left no writings; we know very little about the author(s) of any of the other Christian writings (or for that matter, any of the authors of the Jewish Bible or extra-canonical[4] literature). Only regarding the authentic letters of Paul can we be confident that we are dealing with the literary output of an identifiable person within the Jesus movement whom we can locate in a specific period and geographical area.

In addition to his letters, we possess a valuable though not infallible secondary source in the Acts of the Apostles. Over half of this writing is about Paul, his missionary travels, his contacts with other leaders of the Jesus movement, the congregations he founded, and numerous other topics of interest to the student of Paul. The jury is still out—and may never be in— regarding how much of what the author[5] of Acts writes about Paul can be taken at face value. Different scholars evaluate Acts on a scale of often unreliable to nearly totally trustworthy. But that is a matter to be considered later as particular points relative to Paul's life are discussed.

Reading Paul

Now, allow me to lay my own cards on the table. Though I do not agree with everything he wrote or did, I count myself among Paul's admirers. He developed a rationale and a program aimed at bringing about a radical change in human behavior, thought, society and culture. He articulated, practiced, and promoted a culture of empathy based on compassion, equity, and concern for the well-being of others. He founded numerous urban communities in which traditional divisions between peoples, genders, and classes were replaced by egalitarian relationships. He

---

[4] Originally designating a reed, "canon" came to be used of a measuring stick, then a rule or standard in various areas, and was applied to literature, people, teachings, etc. The canon of the Bible is the accepted writings it contains. A closed canon is one that is no longer open to the addition of other writings. Extra-canonical writings are those from roughly the same period and places as the later canonical writings but not accepted into the canon.

[5] The author is commonly thought to be Luke, supposedly Paul's companion, on the basis of Philemon 24, Colossians 4:14, and 2 Timothy 4:11.

had the courage to live by the principles he taught and the story he told, even though he thereby exposed himself to potential risks and dangers.

Some who read the last paragraph may be thinking, "That is not the Paul I know or have heard about!" The reality is that in modern times Paul has not had a sympathetic press among the general public. Indeed, he has often been portrayed as uncritically accepting some of his society's worst practices such as slavery, oppressive government, and male dominance, and as one who disapproved of marriage. However, when what he actually wrote is delineated from what has been falsely attributed to him, and contextually interpreted, such accusations are exposed for what they are, half-truths and inaccuracies. Paul's own letters reveal a person whose life was radically rechanneled by a profound mystical experience, whose all-consuming goal was not only to be a faithful interpreter of the one about whom he preached, but to become as Christ was, obedient to the love commandment in which all other commandments find their perfection. His vision, when rightly understood, of humanity's erroneous course of thought and behavior and its resolution is not to be easily dismissed. Once we get beyond the many misunderstandings and misrepresentations of Paul and allow him to inform us about himself, his life, his vision, and his ideas, we discover what an extraordinary person he was and what a powerful story he told.

We who would journey into the first Christian century in search of Paul and his story need to pay special attention to two matters. First, we must be open to the objective body of knowledge about Paul and his environment, and to the scholarly methods which give access to that knowledge. A valid approach to Paul requires an evidence-based procedure. That means this book will not simply be "telling it like it is." Rather, it is my intention to lead the reader through the evidence in order that he or she may make reasoned judgments about its meaning, and ideally, to get excited about the process itself. To put it differently, the reader should be prepared to learn something about the ways scholars work through the sources in search of Paul and his story. We shall be making copious use of quotations from his letters and the Acts of the Apostles as they relate to the subject immediately under discussion. The reader is also urged to read Paul's authentic letters and Acts in their entirety, hopefully more than once, in order to gain first-hand familiarity with their contents.[6] In a way, seeking meaning in these writings, especially Paul's, is like reading detective stories. Things are not always as they seem; one must often look below the surface, ask the right questions, and then search for that combination of clues that answers them. Make no mistake: there is much in Paul that is difficult to comprehend. But that only adds to the challenge.

Second, there is a subjective dimension to the study of Paul which must also be given due attention. What we bring to Paul's letters and Acts greatly influences what we find there. To understand these ancient writings, our knowledge of and attitude toward Christianity as it exists today, including its vocabulary, need to be set aside. That holds for believers and non-believers alike. The biblical writers have the right to define their own terms; modern readers must not impose on them preconceptions. Further, translations from these Greek writings into modern languages such as English are necessary, but we must continually enquire about their original meanings. Otherwise, there is danger of reading our assumptions into them.[7]

---

[6] A Bible Atlas is highly recommended in order to familiarize the reader with the location and relationship of the many place names in Paul's letters and Acts. A good multi-volume Bible dictionary is also an important aid. A Bible concordance enables the reader to locate other uses of a term, both in Paul's writings and elsewhere. The internet contains much information, but must be used carefully and critically; it can be very misleading.

[7] One set of terms particularly relevant for this book concerns names by which early Christian communities are designated. The common Greek word for such a community meeting as a group was *ekklēsia,* an assembly or gathering of people. Paul takes this word from the Greek version of the Jewish Bible, the Septuagint, where it commonly refers to the people of God. "Church," "congregation," "fol-

Among contemporary assumptions requiring attention may be one that can especially complicate matters for some readers: the fact that Paul's and Luke's writings are considered "scripture" and therefore may be considered to be "inspired." These two terms have different connotations for different people. For some it may imply that those whose writings became scripture were exempted from the intellectual and creative processes to which human beings are normally subject. According to this perspective, biblical writers were not really authors in control of what they wrote, inspiration somehow bypassing human input or placing limits on the human writer in favor of the divine author. If that is your belief, then you need to set it aside while reading this book. One must have full freedom to appreciate Paul the man in all his complexities and the range of his character and thought, as revealed by his own writings. Freedom from uncritically accepted cultural assumptions was one of Paul's most cherished values, and it should be practiced when reading his letters.

That is not to say that the category of "inspiration" must be omitted from an approach to Paul's letters and Acts. But that particular form of inspiration which declares scripture to be infallible is incompatible with the historical/literary method assumed in this study of Paul. From my perspective, inspiration is something to be derived from biblical or other writings, not attributed to them be-

---

lowers of Jesus" as well as "believers" and "converts" will be used in this book to translate *ekklēsia,* despite the risk of suggesting associations not appropriate to that time. *Ekklēsia* can also designate all the Christians living in a certain area, just as the word "church" can today. Another set of terms involves naming those who worked to spread the message about Jesus. The basic Greek term was *apostolos,* i.e., "one who is sent" on a mission as a representative or envoy. Later, this term acquired specific meanings related to the founders of the Christian movement, i.e., the twelve Apostles. But in Paul's time the term was still fluid. *Apostolos* will sometimes be translated as "missionary" in this book, but with no intention to draw a parallel with the missionary movements closer to our time. These are only examples of the necessity of setting contemporary meanings aside as we read Paul. Marcus Borg's book, *Speaking Christian,* is recommended as an introduction to rethinking our understanding of Christian terminology in general.

forehand. That is, if one finds things in them inspiring, well and good. But that is not a prerequisite. There is much in scripture that is less than inspiring, representing ideas and practices that belong to an earlier time and should be left there, as Paul himself believed. That does not detract from those parts of scripture, including parts of Paul's letters and Acts, which evoke wonder and awe in the reader, and consequently are convincingly inspiring. We recognize they express truths about ourselves as human beings and point to a transcendent dimension of our lives of which we are not always aware. In other words, they inspire us. It is therefore entirely appropriate to approach these writings in the hope that one may find inspiration in them.

It should go without saying that Paul's letters and Acts are not to be used to justify or validate preexisting opinions or values. These writings deserve the same respect as any person. Although it has limitations, some of us have found it helpful to consider biblical writings as conversation partners. In Paul's case, the conversation model is especially appropriate. His letters were written as communications for the purpose of promoting beliefs and actions consistent with the message he proclaimed. If his letters were not immediately understood, his representative who delivered them could help explain Paul's intent.

Of course, our situation is vastly different from that time. Modern readers lack the advantage of knowing Hellenistic Greek as a first or second language and of participating in one of Paul's communities including entering into dialogue with him or one of his colleagues. Since we are reading someone else's correspondence, our task as a conversation partner with Paul requires a different approach from that of their original recipients. Dealing with Paul, a person of a different time, place, language, culture, assumptions, and experience, can be arduous. This is where biblical scholarship comes in; scholars have made available to us resources to help us discover what Paul probably meant to say to his immediate readers.

Finally, our contemporary worldview is as far removed from Paul's as our world is from his. During the last few centuries, we heirs of the so-called Enlightenment have become believers in a worldview shaped by modern science. Paul's apocalyptic[8] terminology now seems strange and outdated. His experience of visions and revelations is no longer as credible as it once was. His expectation of the early return of Christ to finish the work he had begun proved mistaken. So how do we relate to Paul and his belief structure?

There are those who want modern people to jettison religious faith and live by a totally secularized worldview. The implication for the study of Paul would be that, even if Paul were still regarded as worth reading, which is doubtful, we would judge him from our perspective and our standards today, since we "know" our scientific worldview is the right and true one. But that would do Paul, and most persons studied historically, a disservice.

Words and ideas exist at a secondary level of experience; at the primary level is a mystery which seems to reveal itself to us according to the questions we ask. Language and its constructions are human creations, not the reality they are intended to describe. Our definitions are not the same as the reality itself. If we can no longer accept Paul's apocalyptic picture of reality, we still need to inquire about what was behind that worldview, what its participants were trying to express. Our own mental pictures of the universe, what-

---

[8] This word refers both to a literary genre (e.g., The Apocalypse of St. John, i.e., the book of Revelation) and to a worldview. Apocalypse means "disclosure" or "that which is revealed," in particular of something that had been hidden or kept secret. As a literary genre, over a dozen Jewish or Christian apocalypses originating from the third century BCE to the second century CE are extant, ostensibly written by a biblical figure. As a worldview, apocalyptic provided a vocabulary and a set of concepts through which Jesus and his followers expressed their convictions. Apocalyptic features include a dualism between heaven and earth and good and evil, expectation of a perfected world to come under the control of God, and divine disclosures to human beings about God's acts, past and future.

ever they may be, are just as relative as we judge Paul's to be, and one day will fall under the same judgment that we may lay upon his worldview. Therefore, we need to enter this journey with a healthy dose of humility. As far as possible, let us allow Paul his beliefs and not impose our concepts or our biases on him. Our goal is to understand him and the reality he is striving to articulate.

This book would be greatly misunderstood if taken as an attack on faith. It is my intention to make it as "faith-neutral" as I can, relying on an approach accessible to all regardless of their own faith stance—or lack thereof. My intention is to hang as close to the biblical texts as possible, and to give them a voice that can be heard today. Therefore, biblical quotations are extensively used in order that the reader may have them at hand and see how they and their interpretation are related. This is not a book to tell how it was, but to show how it might have been, and where the evidence warrants, how it probably was. Throughout, I hope the reader will be encouraged to engage the biblical texts relating to Paul, including those with which he was engaged.

Different interpretations of Paul abound. This book expresses mine, though I hasten to add that I cannot begin to name all those from whom I have learned and to whom I am grateful beyond words. I have tried throughout this book to draw on responsible scholarship, but this is not a book for other scholars. In no sense is it a report of research. Rather, it is written for anyone with a curious and open mind who might appreciate an overall introduction to Paul, his writings, his ideas, and especially his "gospel"—college and university students, pastors and other church folk, and the curious in the general public. It may also be helpful to those who wish to explore biblical writings in a serious and disciplined way, taking advantage of modern literary and historical tools.

In line with that broad purpose, my original intention was to avoid footnotes. In practice I found them indispensable, mostly to provide further information on particular topics. References to scholarly works are intended both to give credit and for the reader to pursue further a topic if so desired.

One important topic is not covered in this book, the manuscripts of Paul's letters from which modern scholars derive the texts deemed to represent most accurately what Paul wrote. Over 800 of these manuscripts, whole or partial, exist and no two of them are exactly the same. The most ancient extant copy of Paul's letters was made 150-200 years after he died. The textual history of these manuscripts is a fascinating study in itself, but it is beyond the scope of this book.

PAUL'S STORY OF BEING HEALED

CHAPTER 1: "My Earlier Life in Judaism"

You have heard, no doubt, of my earlier life in Judaism,
how I was violently persecuting the church of God and trying to destroy it. I advanced in Judaism beyond many
among my people of the same age, for I was far more zealous for the traditions of my ancestors. (Galatians 1:13-14,
NRSV)

If anyone else has reason to be confident in the flesh, I have
more: circumcised on the eighth day, a member of the people of Israel, of the tribe of Benjamin, a Hebrew born of
Hebrews; as to the law, a Pharisee. . . .(Philippians 3:5,
NRSV)

Jesus was born a Jew, lived as a Jew, and died a Jew. Paul, it
might be thought, was born and raised as a Jew, but left his traditional faith and became a Christian.[9] From a Jewish point of
view, Paul could be, and has been, regarded as an apostate. However, Paul insists that his Jewish identity remained intact even after he
became a believer.

A large part of this chapter will be spent unpacking the
phrase, "my earlier life in Judaism." But some preliminary observations are in order. First, we should recognize that when Paul
pens his letters in which he looks back to his pre-Christian period,

---

[9] This term is rare in the NT. It appears only in three places: Acts 11:26; 26:28; 1
Peter 4:16. The more common term in Acts for the path followed by the disciples
of Jesus is just that: "the Path" or "the Way," which is used in a technical sense six
times (Acts: 9:2; 19:9, 23; 22:4; 24:14, 22). Paul never uses either term in any of
his letters.

he has already had at least two decades of a radically changed life. His view of that earlier period is no longer what it was when he was walking that path. Modern studies demonstrate that memory is not fixed, but can change over time, even if there is no disruption of fundamental life values and goals. How much more would that be the case when goals and values are radically altered? Our interpretation of Paul's words about his former life should recognize his intervening experiences and the vantage point from which he now remembers that earlier time.

Second, we should not confuse what Paul has to say about "Judaism" with how other Jews would have experienced their religion. Paul's reassessment of his life prior to joining the Jesus movement was based on a new set of convictions not shared by most of his Jewish compatriots.

Third, we need to take into account Paul's definition of Judaism. I will argue that he distinguishes between being a Jew, which he remained for the rest of his life, and practicing "Judaism" which he gave up after meeting Jesus. We shall go into this in more detail later, but the distinction may help us be more sensitive to the precise significance of the words with which he describes his earlier life.

Saul/Paul

With those preliminary comments behind us, let us turn to what we know about Paul's life before he met Jesus. We start with Paul's name on the assumption that one's name and self-definition are wrapped up together. Names matter! In his letters, he consistently identifies himself as "Paul." This name appears 18 times in the seven undisputed epistles. "Paul" is not a Jewish name but Roman. No other person known to us in the NT bears that name except the Roman proconsul of Cyprus, Sergius Paulus (Acts 13:7).

In contrast, according to Acts, in which Paul's name appears seven times as frequently as in his letters (127 versus 18), he had a Jewish as well as a Roman name. His Jewish name was Saul, found 21 times in Acts (*Sha'ul* in Hebrew, *Saulos* in Greek).[10] This name was undoubtedly derived from the Hebrew King Saul, who, like Paul's family, was from the tribe of Benjamin (1 Samuel 9; Philippians 3:5; Romans 11:1). Only two other persons mentioned in the Bible bear the name Saul.[11] However, nowhere in his letters does Paul ever refer to himself by his Hebrew name; he exclusively uses only the Greek version (Paulos) of the Latin Paulus. Does that mean that Luke is wrong about his being named "Saul?" Not necessarily; Paul himself verifies his tribal roots as Benjaminite and what better name for parents of that heritage to give a male child than that of the first king of Israel? It was not uncommon for Jewish men to bear both a Jewish and a Greek or Roman name.[12]

Why then does Paul avoid using his Jewish name? Perhaps the association in Greek slang of *saulos* with a peculiar kind of walk or gait, including the way prostitutes walked, swinging their hips, is the explanation.[13] In his capacity as a missionary to the Gentiles, Paul could hardly live with a name that likened him to a (male) prostitute! It is possible that his parents gave him both names, one to be used in a Jewish context, the other among Gentiles. Or perhaps with the acceptance of his new non-violent way of life he no longer wanted to be associated with the mentally unstable king who tried to kill David, the ancestor of the Messiah. It is also possible that Saul deliberately chose this particular name as a personal

[10] The spelling *Saoul* also appears in Acts in passages where Saul is addressed.

[11] One was not an Israelite (Genesis 36:37-38); the other was the son of a Canaanite woman married to Simeon, one of the children of Jacob (Genesis 46:10; Exodus 6:15).

[12] For example, "John called Mark" (Acts 12:12, 25; 15:37).

[13] T. J. Leary, "Paul's Improper Name," *NTS*, 38 (1992), 467-469, referenced in Akenson, *Saint Saul: A Skeleton Key to the Historical Jesus*, 61. See also Murphy-O'Connor, *Paul: A Critical Life*, 42, n. 79.

statement about himself and the message he proclaimed. The Latin adjective "paulus" means "little" or "small." Whether or not he was actually a small man,[14] by identifying himself as such Paul pointed to the power of God being made perfect in human weakness and insignificance. His new name was one more demonstration of the power of his gospel manifesting itself even though mediated through a vessel of clay (2 Corinthians 4:7).

Home Town

AT the time of his birth, according to Acts, Paul's family lived in Tarsus, a highly respected university city and prosperous trade center in the northeastern corner of the Mediterranean. Earlier, Tarsus had been the capital of the Roman province of Cilicia, but in Paul's time the eastern part of Cilicia where Tarsus was located was administered by the proconsul of Syria. Paul himself writes of going to Syria and Cilicia as if they were a unit (Galatians 1:21). His statement has a counterpart in Acts: he was escorted to Caesarea and shipped off to Tarsus by the believers in Jerusalem (9:30). Caesar Augustus had earlier granted Tarsus free city status, a significant honor as well as privilege. The Paul of Acts names his home city twice (21:39; 22:3).

---

[14] The second-century *Acts of Paul and Thecla* contains a purported physical description of Paul which in fact follows a conventional stylized pattern portraying the character or personality of a person through an imagined physical description. Paul is given a physiognomy appropriate to the personal qualities the author (a presbyter of Asia Minor, according to Tertullian, writing in ca. 160) wanted to convey about Paul, namely that he was a righteous and all-around admirable person. He is described as being small, bald, with a hooked nose, heavy eyebrows, and crooked legs. In other writings from the Roman world, the hooked nose indicated royalty, the meeting eyebrows either beauty or manliness, and the crooked legs courage, and so on. It is the symbolism behind the "description" that determines its significance. Whether or not the author intended precisely those meanings, there can be no question here of an extra-biblical tradition of what Paul actually looked like. See Malina and Neyrey, *Portraits of Paul: An Archaeology of Ancient Personality*, 127-152.

This placing of Paul's birth in Tarsus, since it is not verified by Paul himself,[15] might be questioned. However, in my opinion, there is no substantial reason to believe that Luke is wrong about this detail. Tarsus does not play a key role in the development of the narrative in Acts, nor is it part of Luke's agenda in the spread of the church. Indeed, no Christian congregation in Tarsus is ever reported either in Acts or by Paul. Nothing in Paul's writings or in any other source contradicts his being born in Tarsus. While absolute certainty is out of the question, there does not seem to be a good reason to doubt that Acts is correct on this point.

Roman Citizenship

Another questioned bit of information from Luke is Paul's Roman citizenship. The claim that he possessed it surfaces several times, always in relation to one of his arrests or imprisonments. It first appears when Paul is in Philippi of Macedonia (Acts 16:37-38), is repeated when he is arrested by the Roman army in Jerusalem (Acts 22:25-28), and finally is found in a letter from the Roman tribune, Claudius Lysias, to the procurator Felix[16] (Acts 23:27).

On the one hand, Paul's Roman citizenship could be considered the creation of the author of Acts. Paul himself never claims it. Neither is there any other corroborating evidence beyond Acts. Roman citizenship for Paul would serve Luke's purpose well. In

---

[15] There is perhaps an indication of a connection with Tarsus when Paul writes that after leaving Jerusalem following his flight from Damascus, he went into Cilicia (Galatians 1:21). We have ample evidence, both from Paul and from Acts, of his reason for going to Syria, but nothing about his motivation for a trip to Tarsus. According to Acts, he was fleeing once again for his life, which may explain a Tarsus destination which could offer him sanctuary in familiar surroundings.

[16] Antonius Felix was procurator of Judea from 52 to 59 or 60 CE. According to Acts 24:27, Paul had been in prison for two years when Felix was replaced by Porcius Festus. That would place Paul's arrest in 57 or 58 CE.

contrast to Paul's time, Acts was written when Roman authorities were well aware that Christians and Jews were two different groups. When the emperor Claudius expelled the Jews from Rome in 49 CE because of their continued inner conflicts, probably over the proclamation of Christ in the Roman synagogues, he made no distinction between Jews who believed in Jesus and Jews who didn't. But 15 years later, Nero targeted not Jews but Christians to blame for the fire that razed much of Rome. From then on, Jewish Christians were unable to claim the legitimacy that had been accorded the Jewish people by the Roman government for the previous century. One of Luke's goals was to persuade Roman officials that the Jesus movement was not only Jewish, but actually the true Jewish religion. Further, he wanted to demonstrate that the new movement was neither contrary to Roman law nor did it foment unrest. Whenever Paul was arrested or involved in a riot, the fault lay not with him but with his enemies among the Jews. By claiming citizenship for Paul, Luke could present yet another reason for a favorable treatment of the Jesus movement by Rome.

On the other hand, why would Paul have mentioned in any of his letters his citizenship if he possessed it? What purpose would have been served? When he lists his Jewish qualifications and his achievements as a Pharisee vis-à-vis the Law, he does so in order to counter a criticism from those who reject his law-free gospel for the Gentiles. There is no situation addressed anywhere in his letters in which mention of his Roman status would support one of his arguments or any other purpose.

Luke's account of Paul's arrest and appeal to be tried at the emperor's tribunal presumably makes use of a legal right available to Roman citizens. Unless the entire narrative from Paul's arrest in Jerusalem to his arrival in Rome (Acts 21:27-28:16) is dismissed as a fiction, Paul's appeal to Caesar (Acts 25:11) is the only credible explanation of his being taken to Rome. Of course, none of this is found in Paul's letters. They were all written before his final arrest.

However, Paul does mention having been beaten with rods (2 Corinthians 11:25), a Roman punishment not to be administered to Roman citizens, although exceptions were to be expected. Luke explains the beatings Paul received as the result of official ignorance of his citizenship, which is plausible. Paul may not have wanted to declare his citizenship as it could have led to extended imprisonment while awaiting trial. Further, there is the question of verification. Luke does not inform us if Paul possessed either the cumbersome wooden tablet or the smaller metal plate validating citizenship; Paul's own word is always accepted by Roman officials in Acts.

It is not possible to resolve this issue of citizenship definitively on the basis of available evidence, but it appears to me that scholarly opinion today favors Luke's claim that Paul possessed Roman citizenship, and that it was likely an inheritance from his parents.

Education: in Tarsus and/or Jerusalem?

Where did Paul receive his basic schooling? While Paul is silent on this point, Luke is not:

"I am a Jew, born in Tarsus in Cilicia, but brought up in this city at the feet of Gamaliel, educated strictly according to our ancestral law, being zealous for God, just as all of you are today." (Acts 22:3, NRSV)

The punctuation given to this translation in many English Bibles, with a comma following "Gamaliel," implies not only that Paul was residing in Jerusalem during his upbringing but also that Gamaliel was his custodian who had raised Paul from childhood. However, when that comma is removed and placed after "city," the reading becomes: ". . . brought up in this city, educated[17] strictly at the feet of Gamaliel according to our ancestral law . . . ." Now the meaning is that Gamaliel's role was to educate Paul in the Torah and its interpretation, not to "raise" him. The three verbs in this text correspond to three successive life stages: birth, being nurtured, and being educated.[18]

In either case, there are problems with Luke's story. First, he attempts to make as many connections between Paul and Jerusalem as possible. This could be, though not necessarily, one example. We will note others later. Second, his claim that Paul was a student of Gamaliel (the grandson of Hillel) is not supported by Paul himself. He would almost certainly have mentioned a close connection to this famous scholar as an important part of his status-producing achievements in Galatians and/or Philippians. Third, Paul's biblical quotations are normally from the Greek version, known as the Septuagint (LXX). He does not make his own translations into Greek from Hebrew or Aramaic, the languages we would expect Jewish teachers in Jerusalem to use.

Consequently, some scholars believe that it is likely that Paul received both his primary and secondary education in Tarsus.[19] Being born into an observing Jewish family living in a Greek-speaking environment, he was raised to participate in both worlds.

---

[17] From the Greek paideuō, "to instruct, train, educate, guide, discipline." According to this punctuation (which is supported by Haenchen, *Acts*, 623, and many other commentators on Acts), Gamaliel is represented not as a nurturing parent but only as a teacher who gives Paul advanced training in Torah.

[18] W. C. van Unnik has convincingly demonstrated that these three terms are a "fixed literary unit" widely found in Greek and Roman writings from Plato onwards. (*Tarsus or Jerusalem: The City of Paul's Youth*) As he points out, the same three-term pattern of birth, nurture, and education is also found in Acts in reference to Moses (7:20-22). Luke knows that Greek speakers of his time would recognize its significance and would not confuse Gamaliel's role in Paul's life. See also Haenchen, *Acts*, 624, n. 5.

[19] E.g., Betz, "Paul," *ABD* 5:187; Roetzel, "Paul, the Apostle," *NIB*, 4:506; Murphy-O'Connor, *Paul: A Critical Life*, ch. 2.

Paul would have attended an elementary Hebrew school in Tarsus where he learned to read and write Hebrew, utilizing the Hebrew scriptures. Such a basic education, normally attained during the ages of six to ten, would have been a requirement in order to qualify for his secondary education in which he would have studied oral Torah, i.e., the traditions of interpretation of the legal parts of scripture, starting at the age of eleven or so and continuing for perhaps three years.[20]

Growing up in Tarsus, Paul would also have become well acquainted with the local synagogue(s). Attending synagogue itself would have been an important part of the education of children of observant parents. Not only would it have reinforced the grounding in the biblical tradition Paul received at home and in school, but he would also have observed Gentiles who came to synagogue services. Known as "God-fearers" or "God-worshipers," these Gentiles were motivated by their interest and curiosity regarding the philosophy and ethics of the teaching of Moses. Their questioning of and discussions with the local Jewish intelligentsia would have stimulated the mind of a keen student. Such experiences would have been normal in Greek-speaking Diaspora[21] synagogues where Paul later carried on his missionary work.

Along with his Jewish education, Paul also must have received some Hellenistic schooling. His letters contain images related to various Hellenistic cultural activities, such as athletics, particularly running and boxing, and military weaponry. They reveal a substantial knowledge of Greco-Roman letter-writing and speech-making, especially rhetoric.[22] While they provide no evidence that

---

[20] When Paul mentions "the traditions of my ancestors" (Galatians 1:14, NRSV), he is referring to oral Torah.

[21] *Diaspora* is a Greek word meaning "the scattering" or "the sowing of seeds." It refers to Jews living outside the Jewish homeland, i.e., to their dispersion among the Gentiles.

[22] Tarsus was known for its schools of rhetoric, the "art of persuasion."

Paul knew the classical authors which were part of the normal Hellenistic curriculum, that is hardly to be expected of one who communicated in vernacular Greek.[23] Further, at least his subsequent policy was not to couch his message in "lofty words or wisdom" (1 Corinthians 2:1, NRSV). Paul's facility in letter composition was later recognized even by those who criticized his public speaking:

For they say, "His letters are weighty and strong, but his bodily presence is weak, and his speech contemptible." (2 Corinthians 10:10, NRSV)

Despite his ability to draft persuasive letters, we can be confident that Paul did not excel in his hand writing. His letters were dictated to skilled secretaries. However, following normal letter writing convention, he sometimes, perhaps customarily, took the pen to write his own closing. In one such case, he seems embarrassed by the appearance of his writing:

See what large letters I make when I am writing in my own hand!" (Galatians 6:11, NRSV)

Thus, we have a somewhat blurred picture of Paul's education. His letters demonstrate not only a biblical education but also training in Greek language skills. We know he spoke, read, and wrote Greek in its so-called non-literary form. Since he later joined the Pharisees in Jerusalem, it seems likely that he had at least an elementary knowledge of Hebrew. Possibly his family spoke Aramaic, the language of the Jewish homeland, in their own home.[24]

---

[23] Koinē was the "common" Greek language of everyday discourse. The literary form of Greek was the language of the classics.

[24] Jerome (ca. 347-429 CE) wrote that Paul's family had come to Tarsus from a town or territory in Judea. (Murphy-O'Connor, *Paul*, 37-39.) In Acts, Paul is represented as conversant in Aramaic as well as Greek (22:2, 26:14).

Other scholars, however, accept Luke's statement that Paul was brought up in Jerusalem, on the assumption that Paul's family left Tarsus after his birth. Acts later reports (23:16) that Paul had a nephew living in Jerusalem at the time that Paul was arrested there, so Luke may have had more detailed—and accurate—information about the family than he shares. A childhood Jerusalem setting might also be more consistent with the numerous occasions in Acts where Paul speaks Hebrew or Aramaic. The available information concerning Paul's early life is too sparse to be certain one way or the other, although contemporary scholarship favors the Tarsus setting. Those who maintain a higher degree of trust in Luke's facts may opt for a Jerusalem setting, while those who are more skeptical of Luke's reports will probably find the Tarsus option more convincing.

Paul was also trained in an occupation, which was normal for the later rabbis, and may have been for the Pharisees also. Luke informs us that in Corinth Paul lived and worked with Aquila and Priscilla, because they were all tentmakers, or perhaps, leather-workers.[25] (Acts 18:2-3) Paul occasionally refers to his own physical labor elsewhere as well as at Corinth, though he never specifies his trade (1 Thessalonians 2:9; 1 Corinthians 4:11-12a; 9:6, 12b, 18). One consequence of his trade was the low status it offered; trades were often considered the role of slaves, not of free men.[26] Also, they paid barely enough for free men to live on. When Paul writes to the Corinthians about his deprivation, he is not exaggerating.

---

[25] Different interpretations of the term *skēnopoios* have been offered. While it does contain the word "tent," the prevailing view seems to be that it means not just "tent-making" but "leather-working." Leather was the usual material out of which tents and awnings were made, but canvas was also employed. Both materials also had other uses. See Hock, *The Social Context of Paul's Ministry*, 1. Does Luke suggest that Priscilla was also a leather-worker in Acts 18:3? Or that she was a co-owner of the business?

[26] Manual labor was not valued in Greco-Roman society.

Where, at what age, and how did he acquire this training in a trade? Both in Jewish and Graeco-Roman contexts, it was the common practice for a father who worked at a trade to pass on the knowledge of it to his son(s). Paul's apprenticeship would likely have begun when he was about thirteen or fourteen and continued for two or three years.[27] The leather-worker's tool kit was highly portable, and Paul could have taken his along whenever he moved to a new locale.

Paul's association with the Pharisees probably followed his trade apprenticeship. The Jewish historian, Josephus,[28] who was born ca. 37-38 CE, says he was about nineteen years old when he began his own schooling among the Pharisees,[29] which would normally have taken about twelve months, according to Jacob Neusner.[30]

When Saul is introduced at the stoning of Stephen, he is described as a "young man." (Acts 7:58) That is the only indication Luke gives of Paul's age at any point in his life. Unfortunately, the Greek *neanias* is even more imprecise than our English term "young adult." One classical source suggests it refers to a man in the 24 to 40 year range. The only pointer Paul gives to his age is found in Philemon 9 where he calls himself an "old man." How old must one be to qualify as *presbytēs*, old man?[31] According to Philo,[32]

---

[27] Hock, *The Social Context of Paul's Ministry*, 24.

[28] A Jewish historian (37-ca. 110 CE) who is an important source for Jewish matters relating to the first century CE. He was an eye-witness of (and participant in) the war between the Jews and the Romans (66-73 CE) during which he surrendered to the Romans and provided information to them. Later, he documented its progress in his writing, *The Jewish War*. His subsequent writings were *Jewish Antiquities*, *Life* (his autobiography), and *Against Apion*, all of which are extant.

[29] Josephus, *Life*, 12.

[30] Neusner, *From Politics to Piety, The Emergence of Pharisaic Judaism*, 47.

[31] Some scholars have conjectured that *presbytēs* here should be translated "ambassador." However, ambassador is a term of authority and not appropriate for the context since Paul has just written that he prefers not to appeal to his authori-

who quotes Hippocrates, this term points to the sixth of seven stages of life, fifty to fifty-six years of age. Neither of these two age-indicators is very helpful. Paul could have been born anytime from the turn of the century up to ca. 10 CE, and "his life in Judaism" must have lasted until ca. 34 CE.

Paul the Pharisee

I advanced in Judaism beyond many among my people of the same age . . . . (Galatians 1:14a, NRSV)

Does Paul refer here to his secondary schooling in which he studied oral Torah, starting around the age of puberty? That could be indicated by his mention of people of the same age or generation. Alternatively, he may be pointing to his later affiliation with the Jewish sect known for its strictness in observing and teaching the Torah in all its complexity. He does not identify himself as a Pharisee here as he does in Philippians 3:5, but he seems to be thinking of the same period of his life in both cases. In that case, his "generation" would be other young Jewish males who were studying under a Pharisaic teacher, whether or not it was Gamaliel.

The lack of life details given in Galatians may seem surprising, but we must keep in mind the context of the letter, especially

---

ty. Being both old and a prisoner emphasize Paul's "weakness," not his authority or power.

[32] Philo was a Jewish philosopher living and teaching in Alexandria immediately prior to and during the early years of the Jesus movement. His exact dates are unknown, but his birth is reckoned to be somewhere between ca. 20 to 10 BCE, and his death ca. 50 CE. He employed Greek philosophic categories, especially allegory, to explain the scriptures, focussing especially on the Pentateuch. He was also active in the political life of the Alexandrian Jewish community as seen in his writing, *Embassy to Gaius*. Many of his writings have been preserved.

Paul's intent. He puts a significant part of his past on display for a particular reason: to demonstrate his solid grounding and achievement in "Judaism" so that his readers in Galatia would realize that he is more qualified to speak about the Jewish Law than his critics who have showed up in their churches. He has no need to provide other information about this earlier period of his life.

As we saw above, Luke is more explicit regarding Paul's Pharisaic training, specifying the name of his mentor. Gamaliel was a leading Pharisee of that time, an influential member of the temple council (Sanhedrin). While two of the three points being made in Acts are consistent with information supplied by Paul himself, namely, his zeal and his education in the Jewish Law, his connection with Gamaliel has been doubted, as we have already observed. Before introducing Saul, Luke had already mentioned Gamaliel in connection with the arrest of the apostles and their arraignment before the temple council in Jerusalem (Acts 5:34-35, 38-39). If Paul indeed was a student of Gamaliel, he seems to have ignored the sage's advice to leave the Jesus movement alone. Students do not always follow their teachers' advice!

Since Paul's relationship to Gamaliel has no confirming support in Paul's letters, it is possible that Luke has invented that relationship in order to enhance Paul's prestige and to demonstrate further his connection to Jerusalem. However, even without having been a student of Gamaliel, Paul's training in Pharisaism is well attested by his own stated claims of being an enthusiastic Pharisee. That leads to the question, where did he go to join the Pharisees? We have no evidence that they conducted schools outside of Jerusalem, even if their influence may have been felt in the larger Roman world. From the sparse existing sources, their primary sphere of activity was Judea, the Jewish homeland.[33] Luke's placing of Paul in Jerusalem during his Pharisaic period is probably accurate, even if there is doubt about his connection with Gamaliel.

---

[33] Saldarini, "Pharisees," *ABD* 5:289-303.

Paul's Jewish Identity, his Pharisaism, and "Judaism"

We return to the question, what does Paul mean when he uses the term "Judaism?" In his letter to the Galatians, he indicates it is related to the life which he gave up when he met Jesus. Does he mean he has given up his Jewish identity? To this question Paul answers with an emphatic NO! In his final letter, Paul leaves no doubt that he continues to count himself as a member of the Jewish people:

> . . . I have great sorrow and unceasing anguish in my heart. For I could wish that I myself were accursed and cut off from Christ for the sake of my own people, my kindred according to the flesh. They are Israelites, and to them belong the adoption, the glory, the covenants, the giving of the law, the worship, and the promises; to them belong the patriarchs, and from them, according to the flesh, comes the Messiah . . . . (Romans 9:2-5, NRSV).

Paul's last sentence almost reads like a schoolboy's recitation of a memorized list of items comprising the heritage of the Jews. A bit later in the same letter he affirms his identity as an Israelite, a child of Abraham, and as a Benjaminite (11:1b). The same note is similarly sounded in Galatians where Paul recounts a confrontation with Peter over table fellowship between Jews and Gentiles in the church at Antioch:

> We ourselves are Jews by birth and not Gentile sinners. . . .
> (Galatians 2:15, NRSV)

Finally, in a list of the dangerous circumstances he has faced as a servant of Christ, he includes a telling phrase:

> ... in danger from rivers, danger from bandits, danger from
> my own people, danger from Gentiles, danger in the city,
> danger in the wilderness, danger at sea, danger from false
> brothers and sisters . . . . (2 Corinthians 11:26, NRSV)

"My own people"—Paul's identity as a Jew cannot be erased or
forgotten. His Jewishness is not something he has given up at
his conversion. We cannot read Paul's words to mean that he
converted from being a Jew to being a Christian, a term with
which he appears unfamiliar. Therefore, we must exercise special care in interpreting the following:

> Yet whatever gains I had, these I have come to regard as loss
> because of Christ. . . . I regard them as rubbish, in order that
> I may gain Christ . . . . (Philippians 3:7, 8c, NRSV)

On the one hand, Paul continues to be a Jew. On the other,
he no longer practices Judaism. How can Paul make that sharp separation of Jewish identity from practicing Judaism? In his earlier
period the two were welded together. To be Jewish implied the
practicing of Judaism as best modeled in the way of the Pharisees.
As the strictest interpreters of the Jewish Law, they offered the
keys to the kingdom. If one intended to be as certain as possible of
obeying God's commandments, then one listened to the Pharisees,
or better yet, became one. When Paul writes:

> I advanced in Judaism beyond many among my people of
> the same age, for I was far more zealous for the traditions of
> my ancestors. (Galatians 1:14, NRSV)

He is saying the same thing as "to the law, a Pharisee" (Philippians
3:5). Paul's dedication to the Pharisaic path is the key to understanding his life before his revelation of Jesus.

38

In a letter to his congregation at Philippi, Paul characterizes his pre-Christian life in a series of curt phrases, introduced as a comparison with certain opponents:

> If anyone else has reason to be confident in the flesh, I have more: circumcised on the eighth day, a member of the people of Israel, of the tribe of Benjamin, a Hebrew born of Hebrews; as to the law, a Pharisee; as to zeal, a persecutor of the church; as to righteousness under the law, blameless."
> (Philippians 3:4b-6, NRSV)

This seven-fold summary of his "life in Judaism" is laid out like the painting of an impressionist. With only a few strokes Paul creates a self-portrait that contains the essence of his former life, as he now sees it. He has at the ready this review of his pre-Christian life, which his readers already know, as he explicitly says in Galatians. No doubt it was formulated originally as part of his missionary presentations. Indeed, one can hardly imagine Paul proclaiming his message without referring to his life before meeting Christ. Paul's gospel needed that context in order to demonstrate the radical healing that Christ had wrought in his own life. It was available for him to draw upon here and elsewhere to counter threats to his message and to his own status as an apostle. The direction of his former life also provided an insight into the opposition his gospel currently encountered from his own people.

Paul's statements about his past situate him in an enviable, high-status Jewish environment. He is an Israelite,[34] a Hebrew,[35] and a child of Abraham. Paul thereby makes it clear he was not a proselyte, a Gentile convert to Judaism, a matter of some im-

---

[34] 2 Corinthians 11:22; Romans 11:1. "Israelite" is the preferred, honorific term of self-designation, while "Jew" is the term others applied to Israelites (Jewett (*Romans: a Commentary,* 562).

[35] Philippians 3:5; 2 Corinthians 11:22. It has been argued that the term "Hebrew" was an indicator of language, i.e., that Paul is saying he spoke Hebrew or Aramaic.

portance in the contexts in which the topic is brought up. His family were observant Jews, illustrated by their following the Torah, and in giving him a Jewish education in which he excelled as a student.

There are still more details in Paul's description of his "life in Judaism." In the relevant passages in both Philippians and Galatians, his self-description moves inexorably toward persecution of the church. That is the high point of his former life, and its memory the low point of his present one. Indeed, this feature of his life in Judaism should have deprived him of being considered an apostle:

> For I am the least of the apostles, unfit to be called an apostle, because I persecuted the church of God. (1 Corinthians 15:9, NRSV)

The route by which he traveled to opposing the church went through Pharisaic territory. It is not clear whether he attributed his zeal to his Pharisaism, or to his own natural inclination. In any case, it is not an accident or fortuitous that Paul calls attention to his zeal. It had been at the core of his convictions,[36] and at the opposite end of the spectrum from apostasy, of which he had accused the Jesus movement. His zeal had found expression in two goals; first in his dedication to the "traditions of my fathers," and second in attempting to destroy the Jesus movement.

The first goal led Paul into the way of the Pharisees, the strictest of the Jewish sects, the one which interpreted the Law

---

[36] "Zeal" should not be confused with the later Jewish Zealots who provoked the rebellion against Rome in 66 CE. However, Saul and the Zealots were both exclusivistic: those who didn't share their particular commitments had no right to be considered faithful to God. This form of zeal easily morphs into extremism in the name of God, as Paul admits had been true of him. Ironically, his zeal for God led him into opposing God, according to his later perspective.

most faithfully, and the one most highly regarded by the people.[37] Paul's second goal also had a Pharisaic grounding. To appreciate this, we need to look more deeply into this expression of Judaism.

The beginnings of Pharisaism are unknown, but its guiding ideology can be traced to the early post-exilic period, i.e., to the late sixth and fifth centuries BCE when Jews taken from their homeland by the Babylonians were allowed to return home by the victorious Persians. The major concern of that time was the re-establishment of a faithful national life and its future survival. The biblical books of Ezra and Nehemiah reveal the measures taken toward that end. Building on the conviction that the exile befell Israel because of its failure to maintain its identity as God's people, Ezra and Nehemiah set in place a mind-set and practical structures to assure that the past would not be repeated. Mixed marriages were annulled, purity regulations (found especially in Leviticus and Numbers) were enforced, and temple worship was re-established. Undergirding those measures was the notion of separation from the impure, whether in food, people, or in any aspect of daily life. At stake, it was believed, were the identity and survival of the people of Israel.

These goals and attitudes are also evident in the later Pharisees. Both Jewish sources and the NT Gospels show that the Pharisees emphasized purity regulations, tithing, and observance of the Sabbath. The term "Pharisee" is probably derived from a root meaning "to separate" and refers to separating from anything unclean or unholy. Paul and Josephus are the only known persons to identify themselves as Pharisees. The name, like the term "Christian," may have originated among outsiders.

Pharisees justified their interpretation of Jewish Law by citing a "chain of tradition" from their own time back through earlier sages and prophets (collectively, the "fathers") all the way back to Moses and finally to Abraham in an unbroken succession. They

---

[37] Josephus, *Jewish Antiquities* 13:297; 18:12-15.

held that Moses gave the Law at Mount Sinai in two forms. One was the traditional written Torah, known in Greek as the Pentateuch.[38] The other was the oral Torah. The written Torah required interpretation and application. Pharisees believed that Moses had delivered the oral Torah at Sinai to serve as the guide to the written Torah. Another metaphor for the oral Torah: it is a hedge or fence for the written Torah, to protect both the Torah and those who might transgress unknowingly against it. The oral Torah incorporated the growing body of discussions and decisions regarding particular laws in the written Torah.

It is not difficult to see why the Pharisees and the followers of Jesus clashed. The Pharisees were focused on the Law as the revelation and full expression of God. Their purpose was to define precisely and in great detail the behaviour necessary to observe the Law, and to bring about that obedience as much as possible. While the followers of Jesus accepted the importance of the written Law, they, like Jesus, rejected the oral Law, regarding it as a human invention and not divinely given. Further, Jesus himself came to be regarded by his followers as the revelation and expression of God. This posed the problem of the relation of Jesus and the Law, but that is a topic to be considered later, in Chapter 7.

Given Pharisaic convictions and the teachings of the Jesus movement, it is not surprising that Paul the Pharisee felt justified in working toward the destruction of this new messianic sect. Any dedicated Pharisee would have been convinced that Jesus' followers were teaching a path contrary to the Torah, both oral and written. Since that path not only constituted apostasy but involved misleading others, it needed to be eliminated. False prophecy was not to be tolerated. In Paul's thinking, this was really only the other side of

---

[38] Literally, the "five scrolls." This word refers to the first five books of the Jewish and Christian Bibles, traditionally attributed to Moses, i.e., Genesis, Exodus, Leviticus, Numbers, and Deuteronomy.

the coin: pro-Pharisee on one side, anti-Jesus movement on the other.

While Paul never reveals the specific points of his quarrel with the followers of Jesus, the three key points of disagreement mentioned above between Jesus and his disciples, on the one hand, and the Pharisees on the other, probably set the agenda.

First, the two parties held different views of what it meant to honor the Sabbath. The Torah commands the cessation of all work on the Sabbath, but it does not specify what constitutes work. Great attention was given by the Pharisees to the definition of work so that the conscientious Israelite could truly keep the Sabbath. The Pharisees probably would have agreed completely with the detailed listing of the thirty nine classes of work later found in the Talmud (Mishnah *Shabbat 7:2)*; indeed, they undoubtedly contributed to it.

Jesus and his followers, on the other hand, dismissed this approach to the Sabbath. While the Jesus of the Gospels agreed that the Sabbath was to be honored and was a time to attend synagogue (Luke 4:16), he defended his disciples against Pharisaic condemnation when they were accused of breaking the Sabbath by "harvesting" grain on that day to satisfy their hunger (Matthew 12:1-8 and parallels). The primary area of dispute, however, was his practice of healing on the Sabbath (e.g., Matthew 12:9-14 and parallels; John 5:2-18; 9:13-16). Healing was allowed on the Sabbath only in special circumstances; e.g., if there was danger to life. None of the reported healings by Jesus met that criterion. The conflict revolved not around obedience of the written Torah as such, but of the validity of oral Torah. Jesus and the Pharisees had differing interpretations of the authoritative written Torah.

Second, tithing, which involves presenting to the temple priests a portion of vegetable and animal products (or their cash equivalents), is a commandment in the Torah (Numbers 18:21-32; Leviticus 27:30-33; Deuteronomy 26:1-15). In the period with which we are concerned, tithing had been extended to include all increase of wealth, as portrayed in the parable of the tax collector and the Pharisee, where the latter boasts of his fasting and giving a tenth of his income (Luke 18:12).

Comparatively little is found in the Gospels regarding tithing, but what does exist is roundly criticized in Matthew and Luke:

> Woe to you, scribes and Pharisees, hypocrites! For you tithe mint, dill, and cummin, and have neglected the weightier matters of the law: justice and mercy and faith. It is these you ought to have practiced without neglecting the others. (Matthew 23:23, NRSV; see Luke 11:42)

The issue here is priority. It is not that tithing is wrong, but that in Pharisaic hands it has displaced the more important commandments.

The third main point of disagreement between the Pharisees and the Jesus movement, and perhaps most contentious, concerns ritual purity:

> Now when the Pharisees and some of the scribes who had come from Jerusalem had gathered around him, they noticed that some of his disciples were eating with defiled hands, that is, without washing them. (For the Pharisees, and all the Jews, do not eat unless they thoroughly wash their hands, thus observing the traditions of the elders; and they do not eat anything from the market unless they wash it; and there are also many other traditions that they observe, the washing of cups, pots, and bronze kettles.) (Mark 7:1-4, NRSV)

This passage gives a fairly accurate, though general, description of some of the purity practices of the Pharisees. Mark correctly grounds them in the "traditions of the elders," or, in Paul's words, the "traditions of my fathers." The Pharisees developed an extensive code governing in great detail the actions to be taken in observance of the purity commandments. Especially important was the purification of food utensils, the ritual washing of hands prior to eating, and careful tithing of the foods they ate to make them ritually acceptable.

In his rejoinder to those who had criticized his disciples Jesus quotes a passage from the prophet Isaiah:

> "Isaiah prophesied rightly about you hypocrites, as it is written, 'This people honors me with their lips, but their hearts are far from me; in vain do they worship me, teaching human precepts as doctrines.' You abandon the commandment of God and hold to human tradition." (Mark 7:6-7, NRSV; see Isaiah 29:13)

Further critiques of Pharisaic teachings follow, concluding with the sweeping pronouncement by Jesus:

> "Listen to me, all of you, and understand: there is nothing outside a person that by going in can defile, but the things that come out are what defile." (Mark 7:14b-15, NRSV)

A key area of ritual purity involved those with whom one shared food. Pharisees were known to practice table fellowship only with other Pharisees. They refused to sit at table with those who did not observe the Pharisaic purity practices. Specifically excluded were tax collectors. Jesus and his disciples, on the contrary, practiced open table fellowship, including tax collectors. The two different approaches are represented in the story of the dinner in Levi's house, where Jesus replies to the criticism directed at himself:

> "Those who are well have no need of a physician, but those who are sick; I have come to call not the righteous but sinners." (Mark 2: 17, NRSV)

Here we have an instance of the Pharisees' avoidance not only of things but also of persons who would compromise their purity. Naturally, that placed serious restrictions on the company with whom one could eat. This issue will be revisited in Paul's experience in the church at Antioch in Chapter 8.

The writers of the Gospels go considerably beyond an objective depiction of the Pharisees, as we have seen above where they are called "hypocrites" or play-actors.[39] Behind this name-calling, which unfortunately became normative in Christian practice, is the historical context in which the Gospels were written.[40] The developing church was finding itself in competition with the Pharisees for the loyalty of the Jewish people. The war between the Judean Jews and Rome left the temple destroyed and the priestly class without a power base. Both the Christians and the Pharisees sought to step into the vacuum. As it turned out, the Pharisees, or their successors, won, thereby setting the stage for the final separation of Judaism and Christianity. Consequently, the church increasingly turned toward other pastures and found in Paul a model of thought and direction.

When Paul writes about the Judaism in which he had advanced beyond his peers, it is apparent that he refers to the central role of the Law as seen through his Pharisaic point of view. While he no longer believes in the efficacy of the Law as the path to remedying a world gone wrong, Paul still recognizes its importance in

---

[39] "Hypocrite" is derived from a Greek verb with a root meaning "to judge," and applied to an actor (who makes judgments about the character he or she is portraying) on a stage. The term was then extended into non-theatrical areas where pretence or inconsistency is perceived.

[40] The Gospels were compiled after the destruction of the Temple in 70 CE. The Pharisees or their descendants sought Roman agreement that they would have the right to lead the Jewish nation in religious matters; in turn they would support Roman political rule. At the same time, the Christians were attempting to win Jewish converts. In those circumstances, it was inevitable that the two groups would clash. This may account for some of the vilification of the Pharisees in the Gospels.

the plan of God. As we saw above (p. 30), it is included in his list of items belonging to his own Jewish heritage. A second list also contains the Law:

> They are Israelites, and to them belong the adoption, the glory, the covenants, the giving of the Law, the worship, and the promises. To them belong the patriarchs, and from them, according to the flesh, comes the Messiah . . . . (Romans 9:4-5, NRSV)

Each element is part of God's plan for remaking the world. But one important item is missing from both lists—the "promised land." Why would Paul omit this essential part of Jewish history and culture? Even if as a Pharisee he had held the homeland in special regard, his vision now encompasses also—perhaps even primarily—the world of the Gentiles. It should be noted that for Paul the lists are not about "Judaism," but the building blocks of God's plan for healing humanity, which came to the Jews first but now to the nations also. One suspects that Paul considered that the Promised Land, like the Torah, was time sensitive. Their era was now over, replaced by the new age decreed by God in which the former walls between Jew and Gentile are being torn down. Geography is no longer a primary consideration; indeed, it may be a hindrance.

Although included in the Romans list, "the worship," i.e., the cultic activity carried out in the Jerusalem temple, is also effectively ignored by Paul. Only once in his letters does he specifically mention the Jerusalem temple and its priests, and then only as an illustration of the principle that laborers deserve their pay (1 Corinthians 9:13).[41] However, Paul does transfer temple terminology and symbolism to the church. Luke, on the other hand, includes Paul's

---

[41] Paul also once refers to the central piece of furniture in the sanctuary, the "mercy seat," which symbolized the throne of God (Romans 3:25). More on this in Chapter 7.

participation in temple activities as part of his documentation of Paul's Jewish orthodoxy (Acts 22:17; 24:18; 25:8; 26:21).

Paul's silence regarding the temple may seem strange inasmuch as the Pharisees' dedication to ritual purity was based on extending the temple purity regulations required of priests to the laity in everyday life. The temple was the de facto center of Jewish life in the homeland. Every Jew, whether living in the homeland or in the Diaspora, was required to pay an annual temple tax. The economy of Jerusalem depended on the temple.[42] To ignore its importance borders on the incredible. But Paul does precisely that. What is the explanation?

Paul's identity as a Diaspora Jew may be part of the answer. Jewish life in the Diaspora was largely oriented to the local synagogue. The temple was geographically too remote to be a significant part of life for many Jews. An occasional pilgrimage to the temple might be envisioned, but only by those whose financial means allowed it, or whose trading business took them to Jerusalem. The synagogue was a place of study and prayer, not sacrifice and priestly ritual. It had very little in common with the Jerusalem temple.

This excursion into the nature of Pharisaism has been undertaken to convey what being a Pharisee probably meant to Saul. The path he walked during "his life in Judaism" was specifically the Pharisaic way of being Jewish. What the Gospels writers narrate about the Pharisees would have applied to Saul the Pharisee. He was living the life of a Jewish puritan, avoiding those regarded as sinners, observing in detail what the oral Torah regarded as "work" so as not to break the Sabbath, and tithing as required by the Pharisaic teaching. But his zeal did not stop there; he went the second mile in joining those who vigorously sought to eliminate this new sectarian movement which threatened the very foundation of Judaism.

---

[42] Jeremias, *Jerusalem in the Time of Jesus.*

Paul the Enforcer

The remaining element in Paul's picture of his "life in Judaism," is his persecution of the Jesus movement. Luke tells us that while Paul was in Jerusalem, he encountered the followers of Jesus and their "good news" which he found so objectionable. The relationship of Paul and Jerusalem during his pre-Christian period has been the subject of numerous uncertainties. Saul is first mentioned by the author of Acts in connection with the stoning of Stephen:

> Then they dragged him out of the city and began to stone him; and the witnesses laid their coats at the feet of a young man named Saul. . . . And Saul approved of their killing him. (Acts 7:58; 8:1a, NRSV)

Paul provides no verification of this event; he never mentions either Stephen or a Jerusalem locale for his persecution of the Jesus movement. He does seem to rule out one particular geographical area, Judea, which of course would include Jerusalem. He writes that when he went to visit Cephas[43] three years after his conversion, the Judean churches only knew him by word of mouth as the former persecutor who had now joined their movement, but had never actually seen him (Galatians 1:18, 21-23). However, Paul mentions the churches of Judea not to deny that he had persecuted them, but to claim that his gospel was not dependent on them. They only knew about him from hearsay.

Luke represents Paul not as taking an active role in attacking the followers of Jesus in Jerusalem but as passively agreeing with

---

[43] The Aramaic name of Peter. It is usually spelled Cephas in English translations, but the "C" needs to be pronounced with a hard sound, i.e., as a "K." Thus Kēphas would be the better spelling in English.

the stoning of Stephen. We are not in possession of enough information about this apparently brief period of Paul's life to definitively sketch out his attitudes and actions regarding Stephen or others who were opposed for their beliefs.

Acts contains another uncertain claim. Luke and Paul agree that his conversion took place in or near Damascus while he was engaged in pursuing or persecuting Jesus' followers (Acts 9:3; Galatians 1:17). Paul does not inform us how or when he came to be in Damascus. Luke's narrative has Paul sent there by the high priest in Jerusalem as an envoy to the synagogues of Damascus with specific directions to arrest any who "belonged to the Way." (Acts 9:2, NRSV)

On the one hand, there is no evidence that the Jerusalem council had any such power over the synagogues in Damascus, which was not in Jewish-controlled territory, and it is inherently unlikely. Even Luke makes no similar connection between the high priest and the synagogues in other cities. It looks like his claim is part of his picture of Paul's rampage against Christians in the Jerusalem area which is then extended to Damascus. Luke apparently possessed information that Paul was in the Damascus area when he joined those he had previously persecuted. So he explains to the reader how Paul came to be in Damascus. Luke's connecting link became indelibly imprinted in the subsequent Pauline hagiography right down to our own time. But it may not have happened that way. Paul was in Damascus persecuting Christians, but his letters do not reveal how he came to be in Damascus.

On the other hand, Paul must have been in Jerusalem during his training with the Pharisees, and it is reasonable that he was involved in resistance to the followers of Jesus at that time. Further, even without official oversight of Diaspora synagogues, the Jerusalem Sanhedrin could have given Paul a letter of recommendation to use his persuasive powers to counter the teaching of the Jesus followers in Damascus. That he could actually arrest and transport people to Jerusalem does stretch credulity, but Luke gives a reason-

50

able account of the larger picture. In the absence of evidence to the contrary, there seems to be no convincing reason to doubt that he was correct regarding the main facts.

The Jesus movement had obviously made inroads into the Jewish community in Damascus. We know the city contained a large Jewish population. For example, during the Jewish revolt against the Romans less than three decades after Paul was there, more than 10,000 Jews were murdered by other Damascenes, according to Josephus.[44]

What were the tools Paul would have used against the followers of Jesus in Damascus? Although he says nothing specific about his tactics or even what he found objectionable about "the Way," we can offer reasonable suggestions about both. His opposition no doubt would have included heated and acrimonious debates in the synagogues, especially about the meaning of specific scriptural passages. Paul would have pointed out key concerns of the Pharisees about the followers of Jesus. Their leader had rejected the teachings of the Pharisees. He had been executed as a criminal by the Roman procurator. The followers of Jesus were calling their crucified leader the Messiah, a very serious matter which could lead to violent repression by the Romans.

If the Christians in the synagogues of Damascus were as convinced as Paul later became of the message driving the Jesus movement, the conflict was too profound to be settled by argument. Paul was as zealous for the oral Law as they were for Jesus. Certain formal procedures were available to synagogue officials to deal with recalcitrant and disruptive Jews. If persuasion did not suffice, then the next level involved physical punishment, the "forty lashes minus one."[45] Paul later reports that he himself had been subject to

---

[44] Josephus, *Jewish War* 2:561.

[45] "Forty lashes may be given but not more; if more lashes that these are given, your neighbor will be degraded in your sight." (Deuteronomy 25:3, NRSV) For the tradition of "forty less one" see Mishnah, Makkoth 3:10—"How many stripes do

that discipline no fewer than five times (2 Corinthians 11:24). There was one final level, witnessed in the NT Gospels, particularly in the Fourth Gospel, namely, exclusion from the synagogue. But this may have been a later development that was not yet in force in Paul's time.

This leads to the question, how shall we understand Paul's words when he writes he was "persecuting the church of God?" The Greek *diōkō* can mean "run" or "press on" toward a goal, or "pursue" in a literal or metaphorical sense. In this passage Paul means it to be taken literally, and therefore "persecute" is an appropriate translation. He was pursuing the Jesus movement in order to destroy it as a movement.

In Acts, persecution can include stoning and death. The classical case is Stephen, who is killed following his tirade against the temple and his testimony to Jesus. Stephen's execution is seemingly presented as the outcome of a legal decision by the high court, but the description of his death appears more like a mob lynching, leaving doubts about Luke's information, or his use of that information. Most likely Stephen's death was the result of a riot. Saul enters the story at the stoning of Stephen and participates in the general persecution of believers, including their imprisonment and sentencing to death (Acts 22:4; 26:10-11). Luke's statements here are surely an exaggeration. Paul could have had no such official standing in the Sanhedrin. He never mentions it as part of his "life in Judaism." Whether the Sanhedrin possessed the right to impose capital punishment is doubtful; Rome normally reserved that power to the Roman procurator, as shown in the trial and execution of Jesus.

How then shall we interpret Paul's statement that he "was violently persecuting the church of God and was trying to destroy it?" (Galatians 1:13, NRSV) What content do we give the word

they inflict on a man? Forty save one, for it is written 'By number forty'; [that is to say,] a number near to forty." (Danby, *The Mishnah*, 1933.)

"violently," the translation of the Greek *kath hyperbolē* in the NSRV? While "hyperbole" could suggest physical violence in certain contexts, it primarily means to do something "to excess," or "to an extraordinary degree." We should not understand it on the basis of Luke's description of Paul's activity against the Christians, but look to Paul's own circle of discourse. He employs this term six other times.[46] In every case the meaning is something like "to an extreme degree." When Paul employs this term in Galatians 1:13 he does not provide details. Therefore, rather than positing something like "violently" which may conjure vivid images of bodily damage approaching or even including death, it is better to retain its basic meaning when translating "hyperbole." Thus, what Paul is saying is that "I pursued the church of God to the utmost," or, "I gave it all I had." His actions could have involved physical violence against followers of Jesus, such as the 39 lashes, but Luke's implications of imprisonment, Sanhedrin trials, and death go beyond the evidence supplied by Paul.

Likewise, the term translated "destroy" (Greek *portheō*) does not indicate the annihilation of individuals, but of the "church," a social entity, a movement. There is no reason to believe Paul was responsible for the death of any follower of Jesus, either by legal or extra-legal means. Even Luke who develops this motif of Paul's persecution of Christians and claims he did major violence against them, has no specific examples of Christians who were martyred, apart from Stephen and James, the son of Zebedee who was executed by Herod Agrippa[47] I (Acts 7:60; 12:2). Perhaps there were not others.

---

[46] Romans 7:13; 1 Corinthians 12:31; 2 Corinthians 1:8; 4:7, 17; 12:7a.

[47] Two descendants of Herod the Great bore this name, both given the title of king of parts of Jewish areas and other nearby territories ruled by Rome in the first century CE. Agrippa I (10 BCE-44CE) was the grandson of King Herod and the king mentioned in Acts 12:1-4 who was responsible for the death of James, the son of Zebedee. His son, Agrippa II (ca. 27 CE-100), mentioned in in the extended narra-

Paul calls himself a "zealot" (Greek *zēlōtēs*) regarding his enthusiasm for "the traditions of my fathers," the flip side of his persecution of the Jesus movement. It is tempting to interpret this word as referring to one prepared to use violence against those perceived to threaten the institutions of the Jewish people.[48] Josephus applies the term both to a revolutionary contemporary of Jesus named Judas, and to the extremists who ignited the war between the Jews and the Romans in the late 60s CE.[49] However, Paul employs the word not in regard to his persecution of the Jesus movement but to his high level of dedication to the traditions. This is in keeping with other examples of his use of "zeal" where it always refers to a positive action or attitude. I see no reason to consider Paul a zealot out to do violence against the members of the Jesus movement. He sought rather to destroy the movement itself. The means that Paul employed to achieve that end were likely verbal.

Summary

Paul offers very little information about the externals of his life, so we have to combine the few general references in his letters, especially in Galatians and Philippians, with a critical reading of Acts to make informed judgments. That leads to the following conclusions.

Paul was born into a traditional and pious Jewish family which likely possessed Roman citizenship. He received both a Jewish and

---

tive of Acts 25:13-26:32, along with his sister Bernice and the Roman procurator, Porcius Festus, gave Paul a hearing before he was sent to Rome.

[48] The chief biblical model of the violent zealot is Phinehas who killed the Israelite Zimri and his Midianite wife (Numbers 25:5-15; see also Psalm 106:30-31)). In more recent times the Hasmonean rebellion against the Seleucid government was also understood as an expression of "zeal for God."

[49] Josephus writes that a certain Judas initiated the zealot movement that resulted in the war. (*Jewish Antiquities* 18:3-10, 23)

a Greco-Roman education in his home city of Tarsus. There he also attended a Greek-speaking synagogue where he observed the interest of Gentiles in the Jewish philosophy traced to Moses. Paul probably spent two or three of his teen-years apprenticing in a trade there, perhaps under the tutelage of his father.

He became exceedingly enthusiastic about living according to the Law of God, which led him to join the Pharisees in Jerusalem. He subsequently became an active participant in the Pharisaic opposition to the Jesus movement and travelled to Damascus to publicly oppose the followers of Jesus in the synagogues there. We do not know the details of how he came to be in Damascus, but it is not unlikely that he took it upon himself to follow there some proponents of the Jesus movement who had fled Jerusalem with the intention of opposing them and their teaching. Luke's account of official backing for this enterprise may be fundamentally correct, but it is not corroborated by Paul himself.

Paul regarded the Jesus movement as a threat to Judaism and to the people. Being a holy people required separation from the unholy in all its manifestations. Those who proclaimed Jesus as a crucified Messiah and practiced table fellowship with sinners were in violation of the oral Torah and a threat to the nation. Paul was implementing his intent to destroy this sectarian movement when an unexpected mystical event happened. It radically altered the course of his life and through it, history.

CHAPTER 2: "God Revealed his Son to Me"

Perhaps no aspect of early Christianity is more foreign to western people of the 21st century than the subject of this chapter. Visions, revelations, ascents to heaven, and appearances of one who had died are not the stuff of our contemporary experience. But they played an important role in the Jesus movement following his death. His teachings may have been attractive, but the stories placing them in a transcendent context were equally compelling. Visions of the risen Messiah are both the climax and the foundation of the NT Gospels. The interpretations given to Jesus' death arose in context of belief in his resurrection. An appearance of the resurrected Jesus was a prerequisite for apostolic status. Paul's endurance of the hardships and dangers he faced when taking his story of God's corrective plan for humanity to the Greco-Roman world is inexplicable apart from his own confidence in the truth of the story.

That era was open not only to stories of the sacred and the miraculous, but also to experiences interpreted as manifestations of divine presence. It is hardly surprising, then, that Paul's entry into the Jesus movement is marked by a story of a revelation given to him. Unlike some others, he had been neither a follower of Jesus nor persuaded by claims of Jesus' resurrection. The critique of the oral Torah by Christians disturbed Paul the Pharisee and made it clear to him that the Jesus movement was not authentic Judaism. It took a mystical experience to change his mind and his life. As Job had said, "I had heard of you by the hearing of the ear, but now my eye sees you." (Job 42:5, NRSV) Paul's mystical experience was foundational for his self-understanding, his new vocation, and the story he told, i.e., his gospel.

Paul's letters do not include a single, clear, and full description of the dynamics of his inaugural revelation. Numerous passages from different letters give clues, but they require careful examination before being combined to create a picture of this event in Paul's life. They are all brief, highly condensed and not a little opaque. None is written to satisfy the biographical questions we are asking. The book of Acts, on the other hand, demonstrates interests closer to our own. It tells a more complete story, with variants, of the resurrected Jesus confronting the persecuting Paul. Luke's narrative is popularly regarded as the standard account of what is often called Paul's "conversion."

The Stories in Acts of Paul's Conversion

Luke's accounts of Paul's conversion are found in three places in Acts: the event as it happens and twice later as it is recounted in speeches attributed to Paul. Each has differences from the others. In the first two versions, the narrative unfolds in two scenes, beginning on the road near Damascus and concluding in the city. The third version combines the two locations into a single scene which has its setting exclusively on the road.

Scene One: The Vision on the Road

Meanwhile Saul, breathing threats and murder against the disciples of the Lord, went to the high priest and asked him for letters to the synagogues at Damascus, so that if he found any who belonged to the Way, men or women, he might bring them bound to Jerusalem. Now as he was going along and approaching Damascus, suddenly a light from heaven flashed around him. He fell to the ground and heard a voice saying to him, "Saul, Saul, why do you persecute me?" He asked, "Who are you, Lord?" The reply came, "I am Jesus, whom you are persecuting. But get up and enter the city, and you will be told what you are to do." The men who were traveling with him stood speechless, because they heard the voice but saw no one. (Acts 9:1-7, NRSV)

The story is repeated in Paul's address to the Jewish authorities when he was being arrested toward the end of his career (22:4-11). It is told once again in Paul's speech before the Roman procurator Porcius Festus, King Agrippa II, his sister Bernice, and prominent Jews in Caesarea (26:9-18).

The three accounts of Paul's experience differ in several details. In the first, his travel companions hear the voice, but nothing is said of their seeing the light. On the other hand, it is not denied. In the second, only Saul is said to have seen the light, but his companions nevertheless react by falling along with him. Saul alone hears the voice, which contradicts the first narrative. In both, Jesus gives no information about Saul's future other than to direct him to go into Damascus where he will be told what to do.

The third account is substantially longer and contains new details, but it compresses the road and city scenes into one. The light appears at a specific time, midday. Jesus addresses Saul in the Hebrew (Aramaic) language. But rather than commanding Saul to go into Damascus where he will be informed what to do next, Jesus immediately tells Saul about his commission, specifically that he will become a missionary to the Gentiles, and that his safety is ensured.

Scene Two: Revelation in Damascus

In the first two accounts, the scene now shifts to Damascus, where Saul, blinded by the bright light from heaven, has been led by his companions. At this point in the first narration of the event (chapter 9), a Jewish Christian named Ananias assumes the lead role. He is directed in a vision to go to the house of Judas, located on the "street called Straight" (the main east-west thorough-fare in Damascus) where he will find Saul whose sight is to be restored. Ananias objects for fear of this persecutor of whom he has heard, but is informed that Saul has been chosen to be a witness to Gentiles, kings, and Israel. Ananias obeys; Saul regains his sight, is baptized, and proclaims Jesus in the local synagogues (Acts 9:10-22).

In the retelling before the Jewish authorities in Jerusalem (chapter 22), Paul relates his experience from his own point of view (Ananias' vision is absent). Ananias had come directly to Saul, healed him, and informed him of his chosen role in God's plan, which included hearing the voice of and seeing God's Righteous One of whom he will bear witness to all the world. A ministry in Damascus is not mentioned (Acts 22:12-16).

The third account incorporates Ananias' role into Saul's visionary experience on the road, i.e., Jesus himself informs Saul about his upcoming Gentile mission. Afterward, Saul proclaims Jesus in Damascus, then in Jerusalem and Judea (Acts 26:19-20). As the accounts progress, Ananias has a diminishing role until in the final narrative he disappears completely.

There are still more inconsistencies. In the first two accounts, Luke has included a new and surprising detail. First, in the speech of Ananias to Saul in Damascus:

"Brother Saul, the Lord Jesus, who appeared to you on your way here, has sent me so that you may regain your sight and be filled with the Holy Spirit." (Acts 9:17b, NRSV)

This declaration that Jesus has appeared to Saul contradicts the preceding narrative. There Luke had emphasized that Saul saw a light and heard a voice (Jesus'), but none of the party, including Saul, saw anyone. But Ananias now says to him, "Jesus, who appeared to you. . . ." This point is repeated in the Jerusalem speech in which Paul says that he has seen and heard Jesus:

"After I had returned to Jerusalem and while I was praying in the temple, I fell into a trance and saw Jesus saying to me . . . ." (Acts 22:17-18a, NRSV)

These admissions in Acts that Jesus has appeared to Paul are particularly surprising because they are not only contrary to the first narrative of Paul's vision in which Jesus is heard but not seen, but also to Luke's schema of forty days of appearances of the resurrected Jesus (Acts 1:3), which are brought to a close by Jesus' ascension.

Which account is to be accepted, that Paul did or did not see Jesus? The story of Jesus' appearance while Paul was in an ecstatic state in the temple may easily be designated as Luke's own creation, but even so it implies that Luke believed Paul saw Jesus. Ananias' assertion is not so easily dismissed as the result of Luke's imagination. Even if it were a Lucan creation, it still suggests that despite the inconsistencies in his three accounts, Luke was convinced that Jesus had appeared to Paul. The inconsistencies could be attributed to different sources used by Luke, but since those sources are not independently known to us, that explanation must remain no more than a possibility.

However the inconsistencies be explained, it should be obvious to the modern reader that Luke was not trying to meet the standards of accuracy we expect of history writing today. It will not do to read these accounts as straightforward factual reports. Luke could hardly have been oblivious to the differences between them, but for his own reasons he chose not to harmonize them. He felt free to shape his stories to fit the occasion and to include new details when it suited him, even to the point of literal contradiction.

Since Luke was a participant in the movement about which he was writing, we should not expect an objective observer's perspective. As a believer, he was promoting the faith. He wrote to convince and persuade, to edify and encourage. In preparation for his task, he had assembled a wide array of information, much but not all of it credible. Some of his "facts" are suspect when they conflict with a statement of Paul's, or clearly have been influenced by one or more of Luke's underlying motifs.[50]

On the other hand, the author of Acts demonstrates substantial knowledge of municipal, provincial, and imperial administration, police and trial procedures, nomenclature, and geography. He often connects events to known political figures, provincial or pre-Roman ethnic regions, or publicly known happenings.[51] He tells his readers that he was not the first to write an "orderly account" or narrative of the beginnings of the faith, but he appears to have in mind primarily materials relating to Jesus, rather than the subsequent Jesus movement.[52] Luke's sources for the latter were probably mostly oral, although he incorporated at least one written source.[53] To obtain his sources Luke would have had either to travel extensively or otherwise contact the many communities covered in Acts, perhaps through letters or conversations with travelers.

At least one of the communities which play an important role in Acts no longer existed. The Jerusalem church did not survive the war between the Judeans and the Romans (66-73 CE). That conflict had also affected many Jewish communities outside Judea. One of

---

[50] See Chapter 15.

[51] On occasion, Luke gets it wrong. Perhaps his best known error is his dating of the birth of Jesus in relation to the Roman census of Quirinius in 6 CE (Luke 2:2). That date is internally inconsistent with Luke's connecting the births of Jesus and John the Baptist, and his dating of John's birth to the reign of Herod, who died in 4 BCE (Luke 1:5, 39-41).

[52] The prologue to the Gospel According to Luke mentions other writings, one of which we know to be the Gospel According to Mark, and another the Sayings Source, also known as Q.

[53] The most obvious, and perhaps the only written source, are the four "we-passages" (or Travel Document), so called because the narrative switches from the third person plural voice (they) to the first person (we) in Acts 16:10-17; 20:5-15; 21:1-18; 27:1-28:16.

those was in Damascus. Its Christian community also may have been scattered or even decimated, being considered Jewish. Yet, Luke has managed to find some stories about Paul from his Damascus period, particularly relating to Paul's vision and to the Jewish Christian Ananias who figures prominently in Luke's account of Paul's conversion. The church at Antioch had survived the war and was still active. Traditions about both Paul and the Jerusalem church were probably accessible to Luke in Antioch as well as elsewhere.

Of the churches that Paul had founded in Galatia, Macedonia, Achaia, and Asia, Luke has stories relating to the last three. He has no traditions from the Galatian churches; they are not even mentioned in Acts.[54] Finally, Luke may have retrieved some material relating to Paul from the churches in Rome, perhaps Luke's home community. A determined investigator could locate at least some of what he was after, but we should not expect a critical sifting of the gathered information in order to create an "objective" history according to modern standards.

Why Paul's letters are not among Luke's sources remains a mystery, especially since he claims to have thoroughly researched his topic. In a writing of which so much is dedicated to Paul's missionary activities, one would expect Luke to rely on Paul's own writings as much as possible. At least some of them were surely accessible to Luke.[55] Yet there is no evidence in Acts that the author was familiar with the contents of any of Paul's letters.

We do not know the details of how Luke arrived at the chronological and geographical framework of Acts, apart from his use of the Travel Document. Some of Acts' framework was almost certainly Luke's own creation. For example, the number of Paul's

---

[54] This assumes that Paul's letter to the Galatians was not written to the four churches he and Barnabas founded on the so-called first missionary journey, a matter to be discussed in Chapter 9.

[55] Gamble, *Books and Readers in the Early Church*, 58-63, 95-101.

trips to Jerusalem, when they occurred, and for what reason are not consistent with evidence from Paul's letters. Luke narrates five visits, but Paul only two, plus his final anticipated trip to Jerusalem to deliver the collection for the poor.

Luke's story of Paul's conversion was composed about sixty or seventy years after the event. We are not privy to the route(s) by which the elements of that story traveled from Damascus to become part of Luke's account in Acts. The lack of consistency in his three accounts suggests he picked up oral reports from different sources. He could have harmonized them, but choosing to honor each he wove elements from various reports into his "history." Some of these sources no doubt came from circles favorable to Paul, but others from less friendly believers. Since we do not have access to the sources on which Luke drew it is problematic to speculate on how he might have modified them in producing his own narrative. However, we shall see that there are some common elements between Luke's account of Paul's conversion and Paul's story of his call, and some which cannot be reconciled.

Paul's Account(s) of his Revelation

Paul's letters contain four passages in which he refers specifically to his revelatory experiences. One is designated a "revelation of Jesus Christ," two refer to "seeing" Jesus, and one is an account of an "ascent to heaven." A fifth does not contain divine disclosure vocabulary, but nevertheless is a valuable aid in understanding the others. In addition, we shall examine other passages, both from Paul and from Acts, which may also contribute indirectly to our quest.

Galatians 1:11-17

We begin with the basic passage in which Paul, a couple of decades after the event, recounts the origin of his gospel and his experience which convinced him that the Jesus movement was of God's doing:

> . . . the gospel that was proclaimed by me is not of human origin; for I did not receive it from a human source, nor was I taught it, but I received it through a revelation of Jesus Christ. . . . But when God, who had set me apart before I was born and had called me through his grace, was pleased to reveal his Son to me, so that I might proclaim him among the Gentiles. . . . (Galatians 1:11b-12; 15-16a, NRSV)

Paul's letter to the Galatians was prompted by a dual challenge; first, to his claim to have been commissioned by God as a missionary of Christ, and second, to the master story he was telling his Gentile converts. The two were inseparable. His formulation of the Christ story brought Gentiles into the household of God with no commitment to observe the Law of Moses other than to love the neighbor (which Paul claimed summarized all the commandments). His critics denounced his policy as contrary to their gospel. Anyone who taught Gentiles that they did not need to observe the Law could not be a faithful representative of God. Paul's practice of not circumcising male Gentile converts was a human innovation contrary to the requirement of the Law. By making it easy for Gentiles to convert, to "please people," Paul demonstrated his lack of concern for his converts' wellbeing. By not speaking the whole truth to them, he had jeopardized their salvation, which required observance of the Law, beginning with their circumcision.

Paul's response goes beyond a counter-claim ("you say, but I say"), although he begins there. He denies with two arguments that he had corrupted a preexisting gospel which he had been taught.

The first is intended to counter the claim that his gospel came from a human source, perhaps particularly a source located in Jerusalem. He points out that he had been in Jerusalem only twice since joining the movement, the first only after three years following his conversion, the second a decade after that. Each visit was for a specific purpose, and for a brief time. He had no contact at all with other churches in Judea.

His second argument demonstrates that the authorities in the Jerusalem church had originally accepted the validity of the gospel he proclaimed among the Gentiles. But later they changed the ground rules and issued regulations for Gentiles in Antioch and other churches with a mixed population of Jews and Gentiles. He alone among the Jewish Christians in Antioch had opposed that imposition in order to maintain the truth of the gospel for the Gentiles, the truth that came by revelation.

The cornerstone of Paul's argument is his mystical experience in which he received enlightenment. He calls it a "revelation of Jesus Christ." After pointing out his previous extreme opposition to the church, he then writes that "God was pleased to reveal his Son to me, so that I might proclaim him among the Gentiles." He twice employs this loaded term indicating divine disclosure. While the passage may seem straightforward and clear, it raises several matters to ponder.

First, Paul's description is extremely brief. While Luke describes Paul's conversion at length, and then twice repeats the story, Paul gives the reader very little detailed information. What he writes has the character of a summary, not a story.

Second, is Paul describing a particular event such as is found in Luke's account, or is he only saying that his gospel came _via_ revelation and not necessarily by _a_ revelation which could be dated and geographically located? The Greek language does not have an indefinite article, so either interpretation is grammatically possible. However, in view of his other references to having seen Jesus, it is more likely that Paul is pointing to a single event.

Third, what is the nature of his "revelation of Jesus Christ?" Mystical experiences can come in either or both auditory and visual forms. We saw earlier that Acts emphasizes the auditory, words spoken by the unseen Christ and later by the prophet Ananias, while belatedly admitting also a visual appearance of Jesus. What does Paul mean by a "revelation of Jesus Christ?" Do these words indicate a vision of Christ, a hearing of Christ, both, or a mental process by which Paul comes to a new understanding?

Finally, what is the relation between Paul's revelation of Jesus Christ and Paul's gospel, the main issue under discussion in Galatians? Did his experience(s) include a verbal reception of what he was to proclaim, or did he arrive at the latter on the basis of inference from the former? These are questions to keep in mind during the remainder of this chapter.

Paul next turns to his pre-Christian life and focuses on two features of it. Both demonstrate that during his "life in Judaism" he was not preparing to join the "church of God." On the contrary, he was advancing in the former and persecuting the latter. His conversion was not a gradual process, but a sudden unexpected event to be explained only by divine intervention.

It is widely recognized that Paul's description of his revelation incorporates terminology from two biblical prophets:

The Lord called me before I was born, while I was in my mother's womb he named me. . . . he says, "It is too light a thing that you should be my servant to raise up the tribes of Jacob and to restore the survivors of Israel; I will give you as a light to the nations, that my salvation may reach to the end of the earth." (Isaiah 49:1b, 6, NRSV)

Now the word of the Lord came to me saying, "Before I formed you in the womb I knew you, and before you were born I consecrated you; I appointed you a prophet to the nations." (Jeremiah 1:4-5, NRSV)

66

Paul combines the two passages in formulating his story of his prophetic call. Each speaks to his situation. Their main features include the prophet being chosen before birth and a summons to address the nations, specifically as a prophet in Jeremiah and as a servant in Isaiah.

Paul's description of his own commissioning repeats those features but modifies one and inserts a new element:

> Paul had been <u>set apart</u> before he was born,
> God <u>called</u> Paul ("the word of the Lord came"),
> God <u>revealed</u> his Son in order that...
> Paul might <u>proclaim him among the Gentiles.</u>

The third element, the revelation of God's Son, provides Paul with his unique gospel and the fourth element gives him the right to be called an apostle of Christ. Everything that Paul is, teaches, and does from this point on proceeds from that revelation of the Son and his call to proclaim him to the Gentiles.

This passage in Galatians introduces the reader to two sets of assumptions fundamental to Paul. First, God speaks through scripture to the present generation.[56] Nearly 90 scripture quotations are found in his letters where they provide divine guidance for contemporary concerns. It appears that for Paul the function of scripture was not primarily predictive but prophetic, i.e., the communication of God through human representatives. Since prophecy was not just a past but also a present phenomenon, scripture was on a continuum with the present. Past and present prophets all speak to

---

[56] Two examples: Paul writes that Abraham's faith was considered by God to be righteousness (See Genesis 15:6), and that those words were written not only for Abraham but also for Paul's generation (Romans 4:22-24a). Second, Paul refers to Deuteronomy 25:4 (an ox was not to be muzzled while treading out the grain) and infers that this passage supports the practice of giving contemporary missionaries financial support for their services (1 Corinthians 9:9-10).

the generation living in Paul's time, giving guidance and encouragement. One of the most important functions of earlier prophets was to mediate God's promises concerning the gospel of Christ. The opening of Paul's letter to the churches in Rome is an example:

> Paul, a servant of Jesus Christ, called to be an apostle, set apart for the gospel of God, which he promised beforehand through his prophets in the holy scriptures, the gospel concerning his Son. . . . (Romans 1:1-2, NRSV)

Second, Paul finds in Isaiah and Jeremiah a dual prophecy about himself. It was not Isaiah who was appointed to be a light to the nations and take the Lord's salvation to the end of the earth, but Paul.[57] Likewise, he rather than Jeremiah was the one appointed to be the "prophet to the nations." Paul has been given this supporting role in the unfolding of the divine drama in which Christ has the leading part. Paul is the prophesied prophet to take the proclamation of the revealed Son to the nations. No human being chose him for this role, but God.

Paul's interpretation of the passage from Jeremiah is the key not only to his mission but also to his self-understanding. However, he needed to change one of Jeremiah's terms to bring the passage more fully into line with his own role as a missionary of the gospel. Paul's contemporary context and experience required the use of the term "apostle" (one who is sent as a representative) instead of "prophet" (one who speaks for God). Even though he no doubt considered himself a contemporary prophet who mediated

---

[57] Note that Luke incorporates the "ends of the earth" phrase into the outline of Acts (1:8).

the word of God, the term was insufficient for his calling. Only "apostle" conveyed both his role and his authority.[58]

The Galatians passage compresses into a few sentences a verbal picture of Paul's former life and the revelation which commissioned him to tell the Gentiles the story contained or implied in his revelation. The passage reveals his conviction of being a latter-day representative of God with a special mission to tell others what God had revealed to him regarding God's action plan. Everything in this passage revolves around the hub of Paul's "revelation of Jesus Christ."

2 Corinthians 12:1-4

The second text in which Paul refers to a personal revelation points to a specific event which he introduces with the ambiguous phrase "visions and revelations:"

It is necessary to boast; nothing is to be gained by it, but I will go on to visions and revelations of the Lord. I know a person in Christ who fourteen years ago was caught up to the third heaven—whether in the body or out of the body, I do not know; God knows. And I know that such a person— whether in the body or out of the body I do not know; God knows—was caught up into Paradise and heard things that are not to be told, that no mortal is permitted to repeat. (2 Corinthians 12:1-4, NRSV)

The context of this passage shows that Paul is once again in defensive mode. This time his critics have claimed, among other things, that Paul is inferior to other missionaries, perhaps also in

---

[58] Luke has it the other way around, giving Paul the title of prophet and teacher (Acts 13:1) but not apostle of Christ. Acts 14:4 and 14:14 refer to Barnabas and Paul as apostles or missionaries of the church of Antioch.

experiencing visions and revelations. In response, he recounts a vision—or is it a revelation?[59] Perhaps the combination of "visions and revelations" is simply a literary convention or a common expression.

Second, although Paul introduces what follows by "visions and revelations" in the plural, and afterward repeats the word "revelations" (v. 7), he relates only a single event. Why not more? And why not the story recounted in Galatians 1:11-16?

Third, the topic is not visions and revelations in general, but of "the Lord" in particular. Is the Lord (i.e., Jesus) the object of a visual experience, or is the Lord the one who speaks mysteries not to be repeated? Since there is no visual terminology employed, the second option is more likely.

Finally, giving the event a temporal location—fourteen years ago—indicates that Paul is not thinking of the event(s) of the Galatians passage. When 2 Corinthians was written, considerably more than fourteen years would have elapsed since Paul's inaugural revelation.

The account in 2 Corinthians 12 stands apart from the others considered in this chapter. Even though identified as a vision and/or revelation "of the Lord," it contains no reference to Paul's calling or his gospel. Neither the "Son" nor Jesus is mentioned. Apocalyptic in form and content, it is about an ascent to the "third heaven" or "paradise."[60] In such visionary ascents the seer often

---

[59] For a similar "revealing" account, see The Revelation to John, which also involves visions of heavenly things, some of which cannot be told. That writing is also identified as a prophecy (Revelation 1:3).

[60] Stories of ascents into heaven were not uncommon in this period. The NT book of Revelation, written by a Christian, incorporates such a story. It was preceded not only by Paul's account but also, among others, by the Jewish apocalypses of 1 Enoch and the Testament of Moses (also known as the Assumption of Moses). In the Jewish Second Esdras (also known as 4 Ezra), Ezra ascends to heaven 30 years after the destruction of the Temple (i.e., ca. 100 CE) where through visions and oracles and dialogue with an angel he receives understanding and consolation regarding God's ways and their historical manifestations.

receives divine communications but is forbidden to repeat them. A vision of this sort stands in contrast not only to the "word of God" which comes to prophets on the OT model, but also to Paul's account in Galatians. While his revelation in Galatians is the source of his gospel, his vision in 2 Corinthians contains no revelatory content. It makes no reference to features often found in similar ascent stories, i.e., the composition of the cosmos, angelic guidance, or why God permits evil. Like a visual form of speaking in tongues, it is a private experience which yields only esoteric knowledge of no value to others.

Then why does Paul report this vision in 2 Corinthians? As usual, the explanation is in the context. Paul has stepped outside his normal role as a representative of Christ (11:17) in order to play the part of a fool (11:1-12:10). His purpose is to neutralize his opponents' arguments on the grounds that from the perspective of the gospel, they are fools. His critics proclaim a different Jesus, a different spirit, and a different gospel from Paul's. They denigrate Paul's speech and point to his humility as a lack of status and honor. He is no more than a volunteer who doesn't even receive recompense for his labor. Finally, their own Jewish heritage contributes to their status as missionaries.

Paul counters that the gospel is not about human advantages, but the revelation of divine power in human weakness. So Paul boasts not about his strengths but about the things that show his weakness (11:30). He reminds his audience of the dangers and hardships that he had faced in bringing them the true gospel. He points to his flight from the governing authorities in Damascus as a fugitive. Further, he was sent some sort of bodily illness as an antidote to his temptation to boast about his "visions and revelations." (12:7b) Finally, he admits that his repeated prayers for healing of his sickness lacked power to persuade God, which might demonstrate his lack of faith. On the contrary, it was another learning experience for Paul. God's answer was, "My grace is sufficient for you, for power is made perfect in weakness." (2 Corinthians 11:9a, NRSV) Paul then summarizes his argument:

So I will boast all the more gladly of my weaknesses, so that the power of Christ may dwell in me. Therefore I am content with weaknesses, insults, hardships, persecutions, and calamities for the sake of Christ; for whenever I am weak, then I am strong. (2 Corinthians 12:9b-10, NRSV)

Paul considers his vision of paradise and what he heard there to be irrelevant to his gospel. Visions may be important to those who boast about their achievements and badges of honor. But for Paul, such visions do not contribute to the gospel of Christ. On the contrary, they may be detrimental to the gospel of the one who did not promote himself but gave his life for others. Like his advantages and accomplishments in Judaism, unless his visions validated his gospel, they were not worth talking about.

1 Corinthians 15:3, 5-9

In the third passage Paul claims both to have seen Jesus and to be an apostle:

For I handed on to you as of first importance what I in turn had received . . . . that he appeared to Cephas, then to the twelve. Then he appeared to more than five hundred brothers and sisters at one time, most of whom are still alive, though some have died. Then he appeared to James, then to all the apostles. Last of all, as to one untimely born, he appeared also to me. For I am the least of the apostles, unfit to be called an apostle, because I persecuted the church of God. But by the grace of God I am what I am, and his grace toward me has not been in vain. (1 Corinthians 15:3, 5-10a, NRSV)

Paul is in the midst of mounting arguments for the reality of resurrection in general against those who have doubts. He counters doubts or denial of resurrection by pointing to the particular example of Jesus. He follows with a second point; the truth of the proclamation of Christ's resurrection is demonstrated by his appearance to many witnesses, including himself. He then admits his unworthiness to be called an apostle, since he had persecuted the church, but justifies his status in terms of God's grace.

The introduction to the four-fold repetition of Jesus' appearance is instructive. By using the technical terms for the transmission of tradition—Paul passes on the tradition he has received—he appeals to the authority of those who preceded him in order to place his own vision of the risen Christ into the same context. Paul contrasts the period of his life when he persecuted the church to the later time when he was called to be an apostle.

This passage illustrates that seeing Jesus was a necessary but insufficient qualification for apostleship. Many persons besides apostles had been granted appearances of the resurrected Jesus—Paul mentions over five hundred. Clearly, for him the category of apostles encompasses more persons than Peter and the twelve.[61] What was needed in addition to seeing Jesus to qualify to be an apostle? Although not expressly stated here, the very definition of apostle contains the answer. In addition to the vision, one needed to be called and sent by God or Christ to be an apostle. Paul main-

---

[61] Luke, on the other hand, understands the group of apostles, in the technical sense, to be coterminous with the twelve (Luke 6:13-16; Acts 1:26). His application of the term to Barnabas and Saul in Acts 14:4 and 14:14 is likely due to the source he was using—it either contradicts his own conception of apostleship, or, more likely, it simply means "missionaries" sent out by a congregation. In Paul's time, "apostle" still had the general meaning of one who was sent by another or others for a specific purpose. Narrowing the term to the twelve was a later development, found not only in Luke 6:13, but also in Matthew 10:2 and Mark 3:14. The passage from Mark also has an alternative reading in which the words "whom he also named apostles" are missing.

tains that he had all the prerequisites for the title, even though he had not seen Jesus in the flesh.

The same association of persecution and call as in the Galatians passage is found here in 1 Corinthians 15. In both cases, persecution and call stand as opposites. In 1 Corinthians, however, Paul makes explicit the reason he mentions his persecution of the church—it calls attention to the generosity of God. It is this undeserved favor magnifying the momentous reality of his calling to be an apostle to the Gentiles that explains his reference to persecuting the church in both letters.

1 Corinthians 9:1

The fourth passage finds Paul once again defending his authority and his gospel:

> Am I not free? Am I not an apostle? Have I not seen Jesus our Lord? Are you not my work in the Lord? If I am not an apostle to others, at least I am to you; for you are the seal of my apostleship in the Lord. (1 Corinthians 9:1-2, NRSV)

A necessary item in apostolic qualifications is having seen Jesus. Paul may have been reminded of his deficiency by some of his Christian opponents who questioned his claim to be an authentic apostle of Christ. The immediate disciples of Jesus had a built-in advantage which Paul could never match: they had unquestionably seen the earthly Jesus. Paul's rebuttal that he <u>had</u> seen Jesus implies that the important "seeing" of Jesus was his post-resurrection appearance to selected persons, of whom Paul is one. This passage leaves no doubt that Paul has had one or more visions of the risen Jesus. "Seeing Jesus" may have nuances beyond a mere appearance:

> From now on, therefore, we regard no one from a human point of view; even though we once knew Christ from a

human point of view, we know him no longer in that way. (2 Corinthians 5:16, NRSV)

"From a human point of view" translates a common phrase of Paul's, *kata sarka,* literally, "according to [the] flesh." As a preliminary step toward understanding this passage, it is necessary to consider the meaning Paul often gives to the Greek word *sarx* used here and elsewhere in his writings. Paul abbreviates the Semitic idiom "flesh and blood," i.e., a human being or a mortal, to the single word "flesh." Thus, the word does not normally refer to the material attached to the bones of a physical body, but to a person as such. Paul often narrows "flesh" to mean human values in opposition to God's values, and thus to an attitude, a mode of thinking and behaving in tune with the "world" rather than with God. "Flesh" can therefore point to a wide range of meanings associated with being a human being out of synch with the Creator's intention. Those who live according to the flesh relate to each other in a selfish, competitive, suspicious, hurtful, and destructive way. They incorporate this paradigm into their psyches and hearts, live it, and thereby reinforce its persuasive power. To live according to the flesh is the way of the world, which Paul identifies as the way of death rather than the way of life. It is this mode of existence that Paul saw as the result of the virus infecting humanity.

The human point of view, according to Paul, can even be—and has been—the lens through which Jesus has been seen. Paul includes himself among those who once knew Jesus according to the flesh, from a human point of view. That was his perspective when he was opposing the Jesus movement. But his eyes have since been opened. The change occurred when it was revealed to Paul that Jesus was not one to be opposed and persecuted, but the "Lord" to be served. Knowing Jesus according to the flesh is not to know Jesus at all, since only those who have the Spirit of God, or the mind of

Christ (1 Corinthians 2:16; Philippians 2:5), can confess him as Lord, his true identity.[62]

Apart from this statement in 2 Corinthians, Paul never refers to his thoughts about Jesus during his pre-Christian period. We can only conclude from the fact that Saul zealously dedicated himself to eradicating the Jesus movement that he knew enough about its proclamation to see it as a contradiction of his Pharisaic convictions. In particular, he knew it denied the validity of the oral Torah, the life-blood of his Judaism. As the martyr behind this heretical movement, Jesus symbolized to Saul the betrayal of the Jewish heritage. Jesus had corrupted his followers and was potentially endangering Israel.

But since then, Paul has "seen Jesus." There can be no doubt that a visionary experience is implied by Paul's statement. It also implies that "seeing is believing" and that seeing implies enlightenment.

Philippians 3:4b-9a

While this passage is not technically about revelation, it bears on Paul's life prior to and after coming to know Christ, i.e., Paul's attitudes, commitments, and activities on both sides of his revelation:

If anyone else has reason to be confident in the flesh, I have more: circumcised on the eighth day, a member of the people of Israel, of the tribe of Benjamin, a Hebrew born of Hebrews; as to the law, a Pharisee; as to zeal, a persecutor of the church; as to righteousness under the law, blameless.

Yet whatever gains I had, these I have come to regard as loss because of Christ. More than that, I regard every-

---

[62] Borg and Crossan aptly speak of a "Spirit transplant." *The First Paul,* 161, among other places.

thing as loss because of the surpassing value of knowing Christ Jesus my Lord. For his sake I have suffered the loss of all things, and I regard them as rubbish, in order that I may gain Christ and be found in him. . . . (Philippians 3:4b-9a, NRSV)

This passage includes several of the same elements as the Galatians text. It begins with Paul's dual emphasis on his dedication to the Pharisaic way or the traditions of the fathers, and his zealous persecution of the church. It concludes with his rejection of all that gave him confidence before encountering Christ. While no revelatory event is mentioned, "loss" and "gain" assume some such pivotal experience.

There is no mention in this passage of Paul's calling. In contrast to Galatians, he is not responding to challenges to his gospel and authority. In warning his audience to be on guard against those who insist that male Gentile converts must be circumcised, he points out that though he can match or even exceed all the Jewish qualifications of his critics, such claims are misguided. Those who want his converts to be circumcised have missed the point:

Beware of the dogs, beware of the evil workers, beware of those who mutilate the flesh! For it is we who are the circumcision, who worship in the Spirit of God and boast in Jesus Christ and have no confidence in the flesh—even though I, too, have reasons for confidence in the flesh. (Philippians 3:2-4a, NRSV) [63]

---

[63] The identity of those whom Paul warns about is not clear. On the surface it appears that he has three different targets in mind: the "dogs,' those who "do evil," and those who cut or "mutilate" the flesh. Those who work evil is too general to speculate about. "Dog" was a highly pejorative term, with a long history of metaphorical application in the Bible (e.g., Mark 7:27-28 and Matthew 15:26-27). For millennia it had designated male prostitutes, both in and beyond the Bible, and that likely is the meaning here (Townsley, "Paul, the Goddess Religions, and Queer Sects: Romans 1:23-28"). Regarding the third term, Paul may be drawing a deroga-

A gospel with conditions, particularly the requirement of circumcision, is contrary to Paul's universal and unconditional gospel. Salvation depends entirely on God's grace, not human status or ethnic identity, a motif emphasized in Deuteronomy (e.g., 7:7-8; 8:17-188:4-6). Paul's litany of his human advantages (which include circumcision) is followed by considering them junk. Refusing to value them is part of faith in Christ. Paul reminds his readers of his own example, his loss and gain, in order to encourage them to make the same decision by imitating his own example (Philippians 3:17). In contrast to Galatians, his calling to be an apostle was not relevant to his purpose in Philippians. Apostleship was something his readers could not imitate.

The Media of Revelation

If revelation is communication from the divine arena, then in principle it can come in many ways. In the broadest sense, the cosmos itself reveals God (Romans 1:20). However, certain modes are emphasized by Paul, especially those activities of the Spirit which have an effect on the inner person:

. . . these things God has revealed to us through the Spirit; for the Spirit searches everything, even the depths of God. . . . so that we may understand the gifts bestowed on us by God. (1 Corinthians 2:10, 12b, NRSV)

---

tory parallel between the "circumcisers" and priests or male worshipers of Cybele, the Mother Goddess, who in an ecstatic state castrate themselves (Martyn, *Galatians*, 478). Compare Paul's rude statement in Galatians 5:12, "I wish those who unsettle you would castrate themselves!" (NRSV) Note the sarcasm involved in Paul's drawing a parallel between those who insist that Gentile converts must be circumcised and pagans who engage in practices condemned by Jews (Deuteronomy 23:17-18).

The gifts Paul refers to (see also Romans 12:6-8) are also called the "fruit of the Spirit" (Galatians 5:22-23, NRSV) and the "manifestation of the Spirit" (1 Corinthians 12:7-11, NRSV). Their purpose is to enhance the common good and validate the truth of the gospel. But what is the Spirit? If it searches the depths of God, it is God's Spirit acting just as the human spirit which alone knows itself. If the Spirit is not an entity separate from God, in what sense is the Spirit a medium of revelation rather than the source of revelation? For Paul, at a minimum the Spirit is the divine energy which carries out God's intentions and the divine presence which dwells in the community of believers. It is the present connection between God and human beings who are open to the Spirit.[64]

Paul also regards at least parts of scripture as communication from God. Through certain words of scripture God or the Spirit speaks, but the revelation is complete only when it is understood. To those who do not have the Spirit, scripture is veiled. Scripture reveals the nature of the human problem, i.e., the power of sin to corrupt human life, plus God's promises to release humanity from the bonds of sin, the manner in which that will be achieved, and the new creation. In other words, scripture points to Paul's story.

Telling the Christ story is of course a major vehicle of revelation. It is only through hearing and responding to the story of salvation that people participate in it:

"Everyone who calls on the name of the Lord shall be saved." But how are they to call on one in whom they have not believed? And how are they to believe in one of whom they have never heard? And how are they to hear without someone to proclaim him? And how are they to proclaim

---

[64] The Word in the prologue to the Fourth Gospel is similar to the Spirit in Paul's thought in the sense that the Word is both God and with God.

him unless they are sent? (Romans 10:13-15a, NRSV; see Joel 2:32)

The proclamation of the gospel is the open declaration of what had been hidden in scripture but now revealed in Christ.

Another manifestation of the Spirit is the ecstatic experience of believers. Paul distinguishes two forms: prophecy and speaking in tongues. Each was commonly practiced, as we shall see especially regarding Paul's churches in Corinth. Each form had its own value, but the spiritual potential of prophecy exceeded that of speaking in tongues:

"And God has appointed in the church first apostles, second prophets, third teachers, then deeds of power, then gifts of healing, forms of assistance, forms of leadership, various kinds of tongues." (1 Corinthians 12:28, NRSV)

This list is by no means exhaustive, as 1 Corinthians 12:8-10 shows, but illustrative. It is not accidental that the list begins with apostles and concludes with those who speak in tongues. The list is arranged, at least at the beginning and the end, according to the relative value and importance of its elements.[65] Apostles are naturally first; without them, no one would hear the gospel. Prophecy and teaching follow in that order. Each is expressed in intelligible speech, each involves the mind, and each needs to be tested. While speaking in tongues also comes from God, and can be revelatory, in and of itself it lacks power to communicate to others. It is a private spiritual conversation with God, whereas prophecy is a gift from God to the community, a revelation by which others than the speaker benefit.

---

[65] Acts 13:1 retains the same relative order between prophets and teachers.

80

Following the lyrically praised "more excellent way" of love in chapter 13,[66] Paul continues his comparison of speaking in tongues and prophecy:

> Pursue love and strive for the spiritual gifts, especially that you may prophesy. For those who speak in a tongue do not speak to other people but to God; for nobody understands them, since they are speaking mysteries in the Spirit. On the other hand, those who prophesy speak to other people for their upbuilding and encouragement and consolation. Those who speak in a tongue build up themselves, but those who prophesy build up the church. Now I would like all of you to speak in tongues, but even more to prophesy. One who prophesies is greater than one who speaks in tongues, unless someone interprets, so that the church may be built up. (1 Corinthians 14:1-5, NRSV)

The phrase "unless someone interprets" introduces a caveat to Paul's relatively low estimation of speaking in tongues. Interpretation changes the situation by making accessible in plain language what the speaker is saying in non-intelligible sounds. Interpretation gives speaking in tongues the potential of benefitting others. Paul doesn't go so far as to say that interpretation transforms speaking in tongues into prophecy, but one wonders what the difference would be.

The purpose of prophecy is for the "upbuilding and encouragement and consolation" of others. While intended for the church, prophecy can also be instrumental in converting outsiders insofar as it reveals their inner thoughts:

---

[66] For a similar focus on love, but from a different tradition of the Jesus movement, see 1 John 4:7-21.

But if all prophesy, an unbeliever or outsider who enters is reproved by all and called to account by all. After the secrets of the unbeliever's heart are disclosed, that person will bow down before God and worship him, declaring, "God is really among you." (1 Corinthians 14:24-25, NRSV)

This is a truly remarkable statement. In Paul's thought contemporary prophecy does not predict the future as much as it reveals the contents of human hearts. That alone sets it apart from speaking in tongues, an unproductive sign to outsiders leading them to believe that those who emit such sounds are "out of their minds." Prophecy, while uplifting for believers, also has power to convert the outsider who may enter the assembly because it discloses the secrets of his/her heart. In that sense, there is an overlap between prophecy and proclaiming the gospel. Both are forms of revelation.

Like speaking in tongues, prophecy is not without its problems, chief of which is how to distinguish between authentic and inauthentic prophecy. While a biblical precedent existed of which Paul was certainly aware (Deuteronomy 18:22), he ignores it, perhaps because it assumes that prophecy is basically predictive. Paul's solution is that other prophets should reflect on prophetic utterances and test them (1 Corinthians 14:29, 32). The one prophesying is thereby removed from a potential conflict of interest.

Paul never identifies himself as a prophet, as he does regarding being a speaker in tongues (14:18). However, he also never names himself as a teacher, and mentions his teaching only once (1 Corinthians 4:17), but his letters contain a great deal of teaching and no doubt he previously had given much teaching to those to whom he now writes. Indeed, a large part of his letters consists of his teaching. Perhaps Paul understands the role of the apostle to include most of the functions mentioned in 1 Corinthians 12:28-30.

Paul's Vocabulary of Revelation

The terminology employed by Paul for divine disclosures comes primarily from three word groups:[67] *phaneroō* [68] ("reveal," "manifest," "show"), *apokalyptō* [69] ("uncover," "reveal," "disclose"), and *horaō*[70] ("appear"). The first two are virtually synonymous in Paul's letters. The third is found only in 1 Corinthians (9:1; 15:5-8) where it refers to appearances of the resurrected Jesus. It had already become a technical term by Paul's time as part of the tradition he had received and passed on.

Paul's references to what is manifested (*phaneroō*) by God cover a large field: the knowledge of God available to Gentiles (Romans 1:19-20); God's righteousness disclosed through faith for all who believe (Romans 3:21); the purposes of the heart at the day of judgment (1 Corinthians 3:13; 4:5); the gifts of the Spirit (1 Corinthians 12:7); and the life of Jesus evident in his missionaries (2 Corinthians 4:10-11).

Paul employs *apokalyptō* to indicate the revelation of: the righteousness of God (Romans 1:17); the wrath of God (Romans 1:18); God's righteous judgment (Romans 2:5); the coming glory (Romans 8:18); the children of God (Romans 8:19); the wisdom and the Spirit of God (1 Corinthians 2:10); faith (Galatians 3:23); thoughts of believers (Philippians 3:15); Jesus Christ at the last day

---

[67] The one exception is *optasia* ("vision") found only in 2 Corinthians 12:1. This word is employed three times in Luke/Acts: of the appearance of an angel to Zechariah in the Temple (Luke 1:22), of angels to the women at the tomb (24:23), and of Jesus' appearance to Paul (Acts 26:19).

[68] *Phaneroō*, in either its verbal or nominative form, is found 14 times in Paul's letters.

[69] *Apokalyptō* appears 19 times in Paul's writings.

[70] Paul never employs the noun, *horama* ("vision"). On the other hand, it is a favorite of Luke's, being found 11 times in Acts, regarding Moses (7:31); Ananias (9:10, 12); Peter (10:3, 17, 19; 11:5; 12:9); and Paul (16:9-10; 18:9).

(1 Corinthians 1:7); personal disclosure of the gospel (Galatians 1:12); a directive given to Paul (Galatians 2:2); and divine communications spoken in the assembly for its upbuilding (1 Corinthians 14:6, 26, 30).

As is evident from the above references, most instances of Paul's employment of divine disclosure terminology have no connection with visionary events. However, as we saw earlier, there are two occasions in which he specifically says that he has seen Jesus or that Jesus appeared to him (1 Corinthians 9:1, 15:8). While Paul does not actually employ visual terminology in Galatians 1:16, there can be little doubt that this passage also refers to an appearance of Jesus, probably the same one mentioned in 1 Corinthians. Otherwise, in Paul's writings revelatory terminology refers to some aspect of the larger story he told which came to him via a variety of means, but through other than visionary experiences. Yes, Paul was a mystic, but he was also an intellectual who was mapping out a new cosmic perspective as it was unfolding before him. The only vision that counted was the revelation of Jesus as the Son of God. That event provided the perspective for everything else. It initiated a worldview in which revelation was the key concept. Paul dared to believe that the divine plan was being revealed to and through him. He was called to cooperate with the Spirit of Jesus to overcome worldly divisions and destructive attitudes and actions, and facilitate the creation of a new empathic community embracing all people. That deep conviction was reinforced by the transformation of those who heard—really heard—Paul's story.

The "Conversion" Accounts Compared

While there are notable differences in detail in the three versions in Acts, they have a common core: (1) in carrying out his opposition to the Jesus movement, (2) Saul has an experience near Damascus in which he hears Jesus addressing him by name. (3) Jesus identifies himself as the one being persecuted, and in the first two versions, through Ananias, (4) Jesus announces his plan for Saul that includes proclaiming Jesus to the Gentiles. Saul's transformation from the persecuting Pharisee[71] to an enthusiastic evangelist for Jesus begins with his vision outside Damascus and concludes with his baptism by Ananias in Damascus. The whole comprises a conversion story intertwined with a call to mission.

Traditionally, Paul's story of his revelation in Galatians has been read as a variant of Luke's account, as if Paul were remembering his own conversion as told in Acts. That approach is understandable, given the power of the detailed story in Acts, and the fact that in Galatians Paul's revelatory experience is immediately preceded by his persecution of the church as it is in Acts. The reader naturally assumes that Paul is narrating his transition from opposing to joining the church, as a single event. However, we saw earlier that the core of his story is not so much about his conversion to the faith as his call to proclaim his gospel to the Gentiles.[72] But emphasis upon call and recognition of conversion are not mutually exclusive. When Paul's descriptions of his attempt to destroy the church are taken into account, both in Galatians 1:13-14 and 1 Corinthians 15:9, his call also takes on features of a conversion. In each case Paul moves directly from persecution to the sequel, from his life in Judaism to his apostolic calling. The two are not to be separated.

Acts both unifies and distinguishes between Saul's revelation and his conversion. A sequence of events is presented which includes a mystical encounter between Jesus and Saul on the road, and an account with a setting inside the city. The latter looks very much like a conversion story. Its focus is a visit to Saul from Ananias: Ananias lays his hands on Saul, heals him, mediates the Holy Spirit, and has him baptized (9:17-18). The two accounts are

---

[71] Luke identifies Paul as a Pharisee explicitly in Acts 23:6 and 26:5.

[72] See also Stendhal, *Paul Among Jews and Gentiles,* 7-23.

stitched together by Jesus' directive to go into the city, and by Ananias' reference to the prior appearance of Jesus.[73]

The laying on of hands in Acts has two significations: it can indicate an appointment to a task (6:6; 13:3), or a ritual whereby the converted receives or is filled with the Holy Spirit. (8:17, 19; 19:6). In Saul's case, it conveys both the healing of his blindness[74] and his reception of the Holy Spirit (9:12, 17). In addition to being a healer, Ananias performs a prophet's role[75] according to the pattern described by Paul in 1 Corinthians 14:24-25. Ananias receives a revelation, provides comfort and encouragement (and healing), and most important, plays a key role in the conversion of an outsider.[76]

It is possible that Luke—or his source—has combined two originally separate accounts into a single story of Paul's revelation leading to his conversion and call. It is intriguing that Luke's ac-

---

[73] "Appeared" (ophtheis) is the same term Paul uses to indicate an appearance of Jesus.

[74] The word used here (anablepō) can have more than one meaning. It may indicate a person who earlier had sight, lost it, and then regained it, but it may also mean "to look up" (Luke 19:5; 21:1), "to look up to heaven," (Luke 9:16), or simply "to see" (Acts 22:13—in this verse the first use means "to regain sight," the second means "to see." It may also suggest "to see" in a spiritual sense.

[75] Several persons are identified as prophets in Acts: the five at Antioch (Barnabas, Simeon, Lucius, Manaen, and Saul; 13:1); Agabus, one of a group of prophets that came from Jerusalem to Antioch (11:27-28) and later to Caesarea (21:10-11); Judas and Silas at Antioch (15:32); the four daughters of Philip the evangelist (21:8-9); and the disciples in Ephesus who had been baptized by John the Baptist who spoke in tongues and prophesied when Paul laid his hands on them (19:6). Agabus gives two specific prophecies, both predictive, one regarding a famine, the other Paul's imprisonment. Otherwise, specific prophecies are not mentioned. However, without naming Paul as a prophet (other than in 13:1), Luke describes several visions which clearly identify Paul in prophetic mode. Through prophets Paul is appointed as a missionary, given directions, assured of his safety, and encouraged.

[76] Ananias plays a role similar to Peter's in the conversion of Cornelius (Acts 10). In each case, both the converted and the converter had prior visions leading to the conversion event, i.e., they act as prophets in the way described by Paul in 1 Corinthians 14:24-25.

count of Ananias' activity matches Paul's description of the role of a prophet. Paul's high valuation of prophecy and his peculiar explanation of its power to convert seem to match his experience with Ananias according to Acts. However, nothing in Paul's letters points to a conversion independent of his call, and the present form of the Acts account agrees.

There is one more similarity between Luke's and Paul's accounts. Both connect the beginning of Paul's proclamation of Jesus as the Son of God with Damascus. Paul writes that immediately after his revelatory experience,

> . . . I went away at once into Arabia, and afterward I returned to Damascus. (Galatians 1:17b, NRSV)

> For several days he was with the disciples in Damascus, and immediately he began to proclaim Jesus in the synagogues, saying, "He is the Son of God." (Acts 9:19b-20, NRSV)

Since this is the only place in Acts where the phrase "the Son of God" appears, apart from a quotation,[77] it may be derived from one of the sources used by Luke in his account of Saul's call/conversion story. Luke's account differs from Paul's in that Paul associates his Damascus revelation with his Gentile mission, while Luke connects Paul's revelation to his proclamation to Jews in Damascus.

It is sometimes maintained that Paul's account rules out the role of Ananias in Luke's story. Since Paul denies any human input into his gospel, it is held that Luke's account of Ananias' role in Saul's conversion must be fabricated. But the two accounts address different issues. Ananias is instrumental in Saul's conversion, but not in formulating the content of his gospel to the Gentiles. Apart

---

[77] The only other example is in the quotation from Psalm 2:7, "You are my Son," in the speech attributed to Paul at Phrygian Antioch (Acts 13:33).

from his report of Saul's proclamation of Jesus as the Son of God, the content of his preaching is not treated here by Luke.

Finally, we should take notice of a dimension of Saul's conversion specified only in Acts, but consistent with Paul's account of his revelation and his master story of Christ. In the concluding scene in Acts 9, Saul is healed of his blindness through the agency of Ananias.[78] Receiving sight can have a metaphorical as well as a literal meaning. Both are probably intended in Luke's account of Paul's conversion; Saul's healing coincides with his reception of the Holy Spirit. In Paul's letters, "seeing Jesus" or having the Son of God revealed to him is not represented as a physical event. It was an inner experience, transforming him and resulting in peace with God, himself, and others. It was a healing experience at the deepest level of Paul's being. It enabled a reassessment of his perspective, values, and life-course resulting in radical changes in all three. It also led to a new and definitive insight into the infectious and debilitating disease which had spread to all humankind. Through his own experience, Paul realized that the missing link for human well-being was not the Law but the Spirit of non-violence, kindness and compassion; in a word, love. The common policy of bringing peace through violence does not heal; on the contrary, it exacerbates the symptoms of the disease. Healing can only come through a new way. That new way is the kernel of Paul's story.

---

[78] The healing of Paul's temporary blindness in Luke's account of Paul's conversion of course suggests Paul's experience of enlightenment, but it also makes one wonder if Paul in fact suffered from a chronic eye malady. His work among the Galatians was prompted by his physical ailment (Galatians 4:13-14). Their goodwill toward him at that time was such that they would have given him their own eyes (4:15). However, this may be explained as an allusion to a common saying; eyes were considered the most precious treasure one possessed. Paul is simply pointing to the depths of the Galatians' affection for him then as contrasted with their doubts about him now. (See Betz, *Galatians*, 228.)

Summary

Both Acts and Paul's letters contain accounts of Paul's call to missionize. Whereas Acts envisages first a mission to the Jews, Paul represents his call as exclusively to the Gentiles. Both base his call in a revelation of Christ. Although in his original narration of Saul's vision Luke denies that Saul saw Christ, Ananias' speech to Saul claims otherwise. This latter version agrees with Paul's claims to have seen Jesus.

In addition, Acts contains a story of Saul's conversion through the agency of the prophet Ananias. When stitched onto the account of Saul's vision, it creates a single narrative in which vision and conversion converge and complement each other. It is this combined story which has become the normative account of Paul's "conversion" from an enemy of the Jesus movement to its proponent who will take the gospel throughout the Gentile world all the way to Rome.

Paul's emphasis, on the other hand, is on his calling and the source of his unique gospel. This is made most clearly in his incorporation of prophetic call terminology in describing the revelation of God's Son. Paul understands that he is the one prophesied to proclaim the message of Christ to the nations. In none of his letters does he refer to the actual event of his conversion. However, when his account of his call is seen in light of his opposition to the church, his call is also his conversion to a new life.

In the end, both Acts and Paul tell essentially the same story regarding Paul's calling and conversion. Their differences in detail should not be surprising when we consider the different routes the stories traveled before being written down. Both authors relate the uniqueness of Paul's entry into the Christian community, how he turned directly from persecuting the church to proclaiming its message. Both base Paul's call in a vision or revelation in which Jesus appears to Paul. Both include a mission to proclaim Jesus as God's Son. Both include the Gentiles in that mission. Paul alone emphasizes that his gospel emerged from his revelation. In large part, there is no more divergence between the accounts in Acts and Paul's letters than there is between the three accounts in Acts.

THE HEALING OF THE NATIONS

CHAPTER 3: Paul Formulates his New Story

We know intuitively how important stories are in daily life.[79] We encounter them wherever we turn—stories in the newspaper, stories on the various screens we sit in front of or carry around, stories of events in our lives that we tell each other, stories of cultural and national origins, stories enacted on the stage or put to music—stories fill our lives. Our personal experiences are automatically translated into story form, not only to be shared with others, but first to identify meaning for ourselves. We look upon our lives as a story composed of stories. We are the main character, the antagonist on a quest for something: possessions, knowledge, wisdom, recognition, belonging, answers, redemption, etc. There is a plot to our lives in which we encounter various forms of adversity, challenges, and risks which require courageous responses. We experience guilt and shame; we search for love and acceptance. We may or may not develop that objectivity about ourselves that enables us to critique our own lives. And we enjoy what has been called the "story trance," namely, that experience of surrendering ourselves to a meaningful tale well told, which for a time takes us out of ourselves and our immediate situation and perhaps even gives us a taste of ecstasy. It is not possible or desirable to avoid the story format which pervades our individual lives.

In a larger sense, we are part of communities and nations which have their own stories, especially those which narrate begin-

---

[79] As Richard Kearney puts it, "Telling stories is as basic to human beings as eating." *On Stories, 3.*

nings and values. Stories are more than chronicles about events, information, and data; they have purpose. Some of them rise to special prominence; they may be called "master stories" which define an identity for collectives and set a course for them to follow.

The Christian faith is based on such a story. Though Jesus is the spring feeding its headwaters, the narrative cannot be traced to any one individual or group, but like a folk song it emerged as an anonymous social entity with numerous variations. Many of the details of the formation of the Christ narrative are lost to us, but one thing is certain: Paul did not originate it. His public denunciation of and active opposition to those who told that story before he came to believe it are sufficient evidence of that.

The event we call Paul's conversion can also be considered as his embracing of an early rendering of the Christian story. Subsequently, Paul developed his own version of that story which he called his "gospel," i.e., his proclamation of good news. His story grew out of his knowledge of the scriptures and his own experience. His narrative played a key role in the formation of communities of Jesus-followers throughout the eastern Roman Empire. It was because of his ongoing contact with those communities that we have access to his letters from which we are attempting to reconstruct his story. Paul has sometimes been accused of creating a new interpretation of Jesus which developed into a new religion, in particular of dressing the human Jesus in the mythical costume of the Son of God, thereby changing Jesus' message. As one 19th century wit put it, and I paraphrase, "Jesus preached the coming of the Kingdom of God, but what we got was the Church" with its worship of Jesus as God. Paul's importance in the development of the Christian faith is not in doubt. That it was he who transformed the human Jesus into a divine figure is quite another matter. Paul claimed that his gospel of the crucified and resurrected Messiah was continuous with that of the leaders of the Jerusalem church, which included at least three or four immediate followers of Jesus (Galatians 1:18-19; 2:6-9). Paul tells us that he was one link in the chain

92

of transmission of the core story constructed around the death and resurrection of Jesus (1 Corinthians 15:3-7).

On the other hand, Paul insisted that following his revelation he had no contact with the Jerusalem apostles, nor did he consult any other believer regarding his gospel (Galatians 1:16b-17a). It sounds like he is saying that his gospel came immediately from God, and owed nothing to Jesus' followers. That is not the case.

Paul's revelation may be considered a tri-partite process. The first stage is his realization that Jesus and his followers were not God's enemies but God's agents for the healing of humankind. As a result he accepted their story of Jesus as Messiah and joined them in spreading it.

The second part of his revelation concerns his special commission to take the gospel to the Gentiles. Having grown up in the Greek-speaking Jewish Diaspora, Paul was aware that for Gentiles to understand the gospel story it would have to be dressed in different garb than it had for Aramaic-speaking Jews in the homeland. Fresh models would need to be explored, new arguments developed that would appeal to non-Jews. His call required a reformulation of the Christ story in order to emphasize its universality.

Finally, his revelation included his own transformation. It was an inner healing which brought clarity to his mind and unlocked his heart. It disclosed his dark side and enabled the integration of his self, energizing him to walk a new path, and to compose a new narrative about his own life and humankind in general. This would be a narrative not learned from his predecessors in the Jesus movement, but largely his own. The story line would move from the onset of the "sickness unto death"[80] still afflicting humankind to the healing measures disclosed in Christ and his Spirit.

Paul was not the only missionary to the Gentiles, or even the first. But he was the only one whose letters were retained and pub-

---

[80] The title of a book by Søren Kierkegaard; the phrase signifies despair, which he identifies as the most basic of all sins.

lished. While some elements of his story might have been derived from prior or contemporary missionary activity in the Gentile world, they were given his own unique stamp. Such borrowing is sometimes difficult to trace, but we can identify five areas from which Paul drew to formulate his version of the Christian story designed specifically for Gentiles.

First, being an educated Jew, he knew intimately the scriptures, no doubt many by memory. Here we must be careful not to project our image or definition of what constitutes scripture onto Paul. In fact, his "Bible" was very different from ours. Of course it contained no Christian writing, so there was no New Testament. Further, Paul knew of no single book containing all the Hebrew scriptures, or what Christians came to call the Old Testament. In his time, the many writings of the OT existed only as a multiplicity of separate scrolls. In addition, the very idea of a Bible or an authoritative scripture had not yet resulted in a closed canon. The boundaries of scripture were still fluid. Many if not most modern Bibles contain the Apocrypha,[81] a number of Jewish writings dating from ca. 250 BCE into the first century CE which were especially valued by the early Christians. However, modern Bibles do not contain many other Jewish writings from the same period or later, to which scholars have given the overall name Pseudepigrapha.[82]

---

[81] Technically, this term refers to "The Old Testament Apocrypha," a collection of Jewish writings originating from the third century BCE to the first century CE. Most of them were included in the Septuagint (LXX), the Greek translation of the Hebrew scriptures which was produced in the third century BCE. After the destruction of the Jerusalem temple in 70 CE, these writings continued to be valued by Christians but no longer by Jews. The number of writings in the Apocrypha varies from 13 (Roman Catholic) to 17 (Orthodox). Protestants designate them the Apocrypha (the Greek word means "hidden"), and non-canonical, while the Roman Catholic Church refers to them as Deuterocanonical (and canonical) writings. The Orthodox churches also consider them as scriptural.

[82] This term is based on two Greek words meaning "false writings," i.e., writings falsely attributed to someone else. That is, the author assumes the name of an ancient biblical figure such as Enoch, Ezra, Adam and Eve, Solomon, Moses, or the Twelve Patriarchs (sons of Jacob). Such writings are Jewish in origin, composed in

Many of these were in circulation during Paul's time and he was probably aware of them. So when we say that Paul intimately knew the Jewish scriptures, we must leave open the possibility that scripture was a broadly and somewhat ill-defined concept. Nevertheless, the core of Paul's scripture was composed of the writings of the Hebrew Bible in its Greek translation, known as the Septuagint (LXX). This was the primary source from which he drew much of the material for his new story. It would be instructive to identify which parts of scripture he doesn't mention as well as which parts he does. For example, he refers to the wilderness wandering of the Hebrews, but not their assault on the Canaanites or their wars with the Philistines. Is the reason merely coincidental/accidental, or does he avoid such violence as contrary to his understanding of the loving God he portrays in his gospel? In any case, stories of new beginnings are inevitably selective regarding their connections to the past.

The Jewish scriptures were considered the archives not only of ancient wisdom and testimony to Israel's past, but also of God's communication through his prophets, especially Moses, regarding what God required of Israel. The scriptures explained to Jews who they were, gave them behavioural guidance, defined their place in the larger world, and pointed to their destiny. For the new Paul, steeped as he was in the biblical tradition and energized by mystical experiences, the scriptures were alive; the Spirit of God spoke through them and gave him guidance for interpreting the momentous events of his time.[83] In these writings he and other members

---

Hebrew, Aramaic, or Greek; some contain Christian additions. They are an important source for Jewish thought over several centuries beginning in about 300 BCE.

[83] Paul employs several formulas to introduce scriptural quotations (all in Romans, 1 & 2 Corinthians, and Galatians). In addition to "as it has been written," or "thus it is written," which indicate a divine origin by using the passive voice, we find direct attribution to God in "as God said" and "the Lord says." In one case Paul writes, "The scripture says," as if it were a person speaking.

of the Jesus movement found clues to the divine drama being enacted in their midst. It is possible that in Paul's time there were oral or even written collections of scriptural quotations ("testimonia") created for missionary and teaching purposes on which he and others could draw.

Second, being a Jew committed to the Jesus movement, Paul had a second set of resources, a body of oral traditions about Jesus. These he learned from contacts with those who had known Jesus personally and from others who passed on traditions about him. There may have been written collections of those traditions in Paul's time; for example, two of the Gospels (Matthew and Luke) incorporated an earlier collection of traditions about Jesus, now known as "Q,"[84] which may have been a written document. However, Paul's letters show no evidence that he utilized or even knew of any such collection. The writings we know as Gospels were still over the horizon; they originated from 15 to 40 years or so after Paul's death. He does quote or allude to a few of the sayings of Jesus known to us from the Gospels. Indeed, Paul is our earliest witness to some of those sayings. One reason more of them are not found in his writings is simply that he was sending letters to address immediate needs in his congregations; he was not publishing a collection of the words and deeds of Jesus.

In addition to traditions about the historical Jesus, Paul knew accounts of appearances of the resurrected Jesus to early followers of the risen Christ (but apparently not the stories about the empty tomb) and the interpretation of his death "for our sins." Further, he knew the earliest traditions about the Lord's Supper. Undoubtedly, in his conversations and debates with other members of the Jesus movement, including his two weeks with Peter three years after his conversion, Paul had come to know a great deal about Jesus. One might be tempted to say, "as much as anyone of his time."

---

[84] Q is an abbreviation of the German "Quelle," i.e., "source" or "spring." It designates a hypothetical oral or written collection of Jesus' sayings common to Matthew and Luke but not found in Mark.

That temptation must be resisted because there were likely numerous sets of traditions about Jesus' sayings and actions, his identity, the meaning of his death, and his appearances circulating in different communities. Nobody knew them all. On the other hand, Paul's missionary trajectory from Damascus to Jerusalem to Antioch to Galatia, Macedonia, Achaia, Asia, and finally to Rome must have brought him into contact with a wide range of other believers and traditions.

Third, being a Jew committed to the Jesus movement because of his encounter with the risen Christ, Paul possessed another set of resources, his own personal mystical experiences. Paul identified so deeply with Jesus that he could say that Christ had replaced his own ego (Galatians 2:20). That conviction drove him to dedicate his life to sharing his story and made it possible for him to withstand almost unbelievable physical and emotional suffering in the process. Paul's personal experiences of Christ, including the profound awareness of his spiritual presence, reinvented him and gave him a new outlook on his world. It would be difficult to exaggerate their importance.

Fourth, Paul was familiar with prophetic pronouncements arising from spiritual experiences in the early church. Some of those may have been included in his story. One possible example is the scenario found in his letter to the Thessalonians regarding the events to be expected on the day of Christ's return (1 Thessalonians 4:15-17). It is possible that the very prospect of Christ returning to the earth at the end time was also the result of prophecy.

Fifth, Paul's life in the Gentile world was another experiential source for his view of the world drama, both positive and negative. On the positive side, he found elements of the philosophical teachings of the Stoics useful for proclaiming the gospel among Gentiles. The emphasis of Stoicism[85] upon a cosmos[86] governed by divine

---

[85] A philosophical school founded in the late fourth century BCE. By NT times it had become the most popular philosophy in the Roman Empire. One of its most effective proponents was Epictetus, who was born about the time that Paul wrote

reason shared by human beings was widely known in Paul's time. His belief that God's requirements for right living were revealed in the natural environment and should have been apparent to Gentiles may also have been derived from the Stoics (see Romans 1:19-20). Also attractive to Paul, Stoicism taught that the good of the whole community overruled individual self-interest. The importance placed by the Stoics and other intellectuals on right thinking and right speech for perceiving the truth and for persuading others of it was also highly valued by Paul. Of course, he put his own particular interpretation on what he borrowed.

On the negative side, Paul would have observed daily some of the darker aspects of life in Gentile society as his missionary work took him into various cities. In particular, the many religious cults commonly regarded by Jews as examples of idolatry and their aberrant sexual manifestations no doubt confirmed Paul's conviction that the Gentiles needed to hear his story.

Finally, Paul inherited a biblical worldview. It covered the interplay between the divine and the human realms since the beginning of time, from the creation of the world and the first human beings, their disobedience of God and subsequent exclusion from God's presence, the execution of God's judgment on evil at the time of Noah, the call of Abraham and God's promise to raise up numerous progeny to him and to give them a land, their slavery in Egypt and liberation under Moses, the giving of the Torah at Mt.

---

his letter to the Thessalonians. Stoicism taught that virtue consisted in accepting life with equanimity, and in harmonizing personal life with the life of nature or the cosmos.

[86] *Kosmos* is a Greek term indicating the organized universe, in contrast to chaos (e.g., Genesis 1 portrays chaos being transformed into the cosmos). The term has multiple variations and nuances, especially when used in relation to God: it may refer to the world in opposition to God, the world being transformed by divine action, the world in contrast to heaven, etc. Nevertheless, its primary meaning is the totality of the created order.

Sinai, Israel's wandering in the desert and entry into the promised land, the rise of the Judges and then the monarchy under David and Solomon and their successors, the activities of prophets in the affairs of the nation, the building of the first temple, exile(s) and return, the building of the second temple, and so on. Accompanying the written story of Moses and the Torah were the oral stories and interpretations passed on by Paul's Pharisaic mentors.

Out of these sources, and no doubt others, came Paul's version of the divine drama. Believers before him may have provided earlier drafts, but if so he had a major role in editing, redacting, and fitting them into the larger story of humankind as he came to see it. Paul's experience of Jesus led him to see the old stories in a new light. It was necessary to recast the biblical story and extend it to include Christ and the larger framework of the coming kingdom of God being offered to all humanity. Not of least importance was finding justification in Israel's history for the present inclusion of the Gentiles.

Jesus proclaimed that the kingdom of God is at hand, that the long-awaited day of the Lord is on the horizon. That event was good news for some, bad news for others. God's justice is salvation for the righteous, but "wrath" for the unrighteous. Everyone's deeds will be weighed in the ultimate scales of justice. The present moment is not simply one more time of transition between the past and the future, but a divinely appointed opportunity to participate in the new age now dawning by harmonizing one's life with God's intention for humankind. Salvation was being offered, but it would not be imposed.

Jesus' immediate followers found it necessary to revise his message to take account of his death and resurrection, the fact that the kingdom had not yet arrived in its fullness, and their own experiences of the same Spirit that had motivated Jesus. They continued to address the Jewish people, but with an expanded message. Paul's directive to go to the Gentiles required yet another revision, one that could be understood and embraced by non-Jews. The Christ story was beginning to look like an ever changing drama. It could not have been otherwise. Contexts differ and change; if the ideas and the stories by which people live are no longer believable or even listened to, they fade and disappear from social consciousness. The master story had constantly to be revised and revitalized, and that is what Paul was determined to do for his mission. His story would include the overarching world view of his Jewish heritage, but modified to include the Gentiles as participants.

Paul was not the first Jew to rewrite the biblical story. Perhaps partly in response to the challenge of Hellenistic culture including the Greco-Roman philosophies of that era, numerous Jewish intellectuals had already begun to reflect on their own tradition. Since prophecy was deemed to have ceased, giving way to the primacy of Torah to which nothing could be added, new ways of speaking for God emerged, including apocalyptic, i.e., revelatory, literature. Around 200 BCE, writings began to appear in the names of various biblical figures, e.g., Abraham and Sarah, the twelve patriarchs, Moses, Adam and Eve and their son Seth, Noah, Solomon, Ezra, Isaiah, Jeremiah, Baruch, and Daniel, among others. Some of these writings were later incorporated into the Bible (e.g., Daniel) or the Apocrypha (e.g., Wisdom of Solomon), but many of the others, i.e., the Pseudepigrapha, may also have been widely read.

An older contemporary of Paul, Philo of Alexandria, chose a different path from those who wrote such books in the names of ancient personages; he applied philosophic categories and methods, especially the allegorical,[87] to the interpretation of biblical figures such as Adam, Abraham, and Joseph. The literal was transformed into the symbolic; in the biblical stories were found philosophical teachings, e.g., regarding the virtuous life.

It was a fertile literary period in Hellenistic Judaism. When Paul created his story incorporating certain biblical persons, he was

---

[87] Allegorical interpretation is a technique of finding meaning beyond the literal by treating elements in the text as encoded hidden meanings.

breaking new ground only insofar as he added a new main character, the Messiah, who was the agent of a new creation being proclaimed by his ambassadors.

Paul's story or drama[88] of sickness and healing focuses on four
main characters: Adam, Abraham, Moses, and Jesus.[89] Consequently, I have chosen to divide his story into four acts, each centered on
one of those characters. The next four chapters will trace the plot
of Paul's story from beginning to end, from the original creation to
the new creation.

Each act is presented in two parts, the plot and the background notes. The plots are my attempt to reduce Paul's sometimes
difficult and complex arguments to a form more easily understood
by today's reader. I freely admit to "reading between the lines" in
composing the plots. The background notes address more fully
Paul's understanding of the biblical passages and characters featured
in each act. The plots are presented in a quasi-poetic form, while
the background notes follow a descriptive and discursive style.
Taken as a whole, the plots may be considered as a brief summary
of Paul's "history" of the world, his précis of the biblical story including the Christ figure.

The mixing of poetic and prosaic literary forms in interpreting Paul may at first appear strange. It raises the question of the nature of religious language including the interplay of the literal and
the metaphorical approach to scripture. In particular, how is one to
understand Paul's language? Obviously, much of his writing deals
with the observable world of his era, its ethnic groups, food, work,

---

[88] "Story" and "drama" are being used interchangeably here. Paul employs neither
term. His use of "gospel" is close to what I am calling his "story."

[89] It is noteworthy that the first three characters (Adam, Abraham, and Moses)
are drawn from the five books of Moses, the Torah, which is the centerpiece of
Pharisaic teachings. Prophets, other than Moses and those pointing forward to
Paul's own call, have no part in his story other than as occasional witnesses to the
divine plot. Is this focus on the Mosaic books a result of Paul's Pharisaic background?

travel, cities, and so on. We are right to ask what he is literally writing about when he refers to these and similar topics. But his main concern is with something quite different, the significance of the Christ figure, scripture and prophecy as the voices of God, the new creation now unfolding to replace the old cosmos, and the centrality of compassion and care, i.e., loving the neighbor, in human relationships.

Paul's new cosmos is far removed from our 21st century world. His focus is on a spiritual underpinning of the universe rather than its physical basis, on a new approach to violence rather than relying on it to bring peace, on pioneering a new beginning for humanity rather than perpetuating the old ways of fighting fire with fire. Paul's spiritual cosmos cannot be verified by literal sight and sound and their modern extensions. Whether it has reality beyond his own imagination is a question no one can answer for another, but with which each of us is faced.

CHAPTER 4: Adam and Eve

Setting: A garden somewhere
Characters:
    God
    Adam
    Eve
    Snake

The Plot

God blessed Adam and Eve with life,
God said to Adam, "Go tell your madam,
'That tree is not for husband or wife!'"

So Adam spoke with Eve;
Said he, "Don't touch that tree,
Or you and I will have to leave!"

But Snake sidled up to Eve,
He wanted them out, so he planted a doubt,
With malicious intent to deceive.

Said he, "You can't take God's word,
No point trying, God is lying.
You won't die, that's absurd."

So God's commandment they crossed,
Their vice? They took Snake's advice
And out from the Garden were tossed.

Adam blamed Eve, Eve accused Snake,
"God, you made us doubtable, so we're not accountable!"
But God refused their excuses to take.

Snake was sentenced to eat the dust,
Eve in birth would find her worth,
Equality with the man was now a bust.

Adam was to work the ground now cursed,
Getting burned as the soil he turned,
Until he returned to the dust as at first.

Thus sin and death were born,
Snake lied, and the people died,
And God's creation was asunder torn.

BACKGROUND NOTES

Adam is specifically mentioned in only two of Paul's letters, both written fairly late in his career. However, the motifs drawn from the Adam story as presented in Genesis 2-3 are basic to Paul's teaching, which suggests that he had incorporated Adam into his master story much earlier. We begin with some of the relevant quotations from those two letters:

For since death came through a human being, the resurrection of the dead has also come through a human being; for as all die in Adam, so all will be made alive in Christ. . . . Thus it is written, "The first man, Adam, became a living being"; the last Adam became a life-giving spirit. . . . The first man was from the earth, a man of dust; the second man is from heaven. As was the man of dust, so are those who are of the dust; and as is the man of heaven, so are those who are of heaven. Just as we have borne the image of the man of dust, we will also bear the image of the man of heaven. (1 Corinthians 15:21-22, 45, 47-49, NRSV)

Therefore, just as sin came into the world through one man, and death came through sin, and so death spread to all because all have sinned . . . . Yet death exercised dominion from Adam to Moses, even over those whose sins were not like the transgression of Adam, who is a type of the one who was to come. (Romans 5:12, 14, NRSV)

These passages provide an introduction to two important characteristics of Paul's thought. The first is his binary approach to reality.[90] He is fond of utilizing opposites to which large groups of data may be reduced and then unpacked in imaginative ways. For example, "the first man was from the earth...the second man is from heaven."[91] Earth and heaven are of course parts or levels of the accepted cosmos of Paul's time, but what is important is not their location but what each represents in Paul's view. Earth is the arena of creation handed over to humankind while heaven is God's realm. When Adam is regarded as a man of the earth, and Christ as a man of heaven, they are seen as representatives of their respective realms. Right and wrong, good and evil, yes and no, day and night, life and death, and sickness and health are expressions of that dual way of looking at reality. Like other story-tellers throughout the ages, Paul makes generous use of the opposing binary perspective.

[90] Polar oppositions are common in the scriptures; e.g., Deuteronomy 30:19 refers to "heaven and earth," "life and death," and "blessings and curses." (NRSV) Jeremiah 21:8 speaks of "the way of life and the way of death." (NRSV)

[91] Philo also writes of a man from heaven and a man from earth, but in his thought the heavenly man (Genesis 1:26-27) is an archetype of the earthly in a Platonic sense. The man from earth is the individual created from a lump of clay and enlivened by the divine breath (Genesis 2:7). Paul starts from the earthly man and ends up with the heavenly one in line with his apocalyptic assumptions.

Second, each of the two key players in the above passages has a collective significance. Adam's very name points in that direction. Paul knows that in the Hebrew language, Adam is not a personal name but the common word for "humankind."[92] Paul retains that all-encompassing sense of Adam, but also redefines it to signify those who live in an "Adamic" or earthly way, i.e., according to human rather than godly values. Similarly, but in contrast, "Christ" encompasses those who live in a heavenly way. The pair constitutes a set of dual archetypes, each member representing a different kind of living. On the one hand, Paul speaks of those who bear the image of Adam, and on the other hand, of those who bear the image of Christ. Adam as only a person of the past is not especially important. But as the one whose image is borne by all human beings, he is essential to Paul's story. When Paul writes that "Adam is a type of the one who was to come," it is their contrasting but representative and collective roles to which he points. This is also observable in his phrases, "in Christ" and "in Adam." Adam and Christ are the beginning and end points of Paul's narrative.

The Biblical Story of Adam and Eve

Let us now turn to the story of Adam as Paul finds it in scripture. He starts with the man in the garden. God tells Adam that he has free access to all the fruit trees, perhaps eventually even to the tree of life (immortality), but he is not to eat from the tree of the knowledge of good and evil (omniscience).[93] He is

---

[92] Apart from the original man, "Adam" is never employed as a proper noun in the Bible. Biblical parents did not name their sons Adam. In the Greek version of the Bible (the Septuagint or LXX), the word "Adam" is not transliterated but translated as *anthrōpos*, i.e., man or humankind. In other words, there is no Adam in the Septuagint. Paul imports the Hebrew word "Adam" into his discussions of the first archetypal human being.

[93] The tree is identified as a fig tree in the Apocalypse of Moses 20:5; see Charles, *The Apocrypha and Pseudepigrapha of the Old Testament,* 2:146.

warned that death will be his lot if he disobeys. Recognizing that Adam will have a yearning for companionship, God creates Eve to share life with Adam in this utopia, even to become "one flesh." So far, so good.

In the next scene, things begin to go off the rails. A new character enters, one of the animals created by God, going by the name of Snake. We shall see that while he works his magic on individuals, it is the resulting social consequences with which Paul is concerned. Snake finds Eve alone near the tree of omniscience and engages her in conversation about God's commandment. Bit by bit he wriggles his way into her consciousness. First, he slyly asks her about what God had said (a gratuitous question to which Snake already knows the answer). Next, he questions God's motive and integrity. Then, he flatly contradicts God's warning of death. Finally, Snake brings out the carrot—the forbidden fruit has the power not only to open eyes but to produce equality with God. Unaware of Snake's deception, Eve accepts his arguments and adds her own reasons for eating the fruit (good to look at, tasty), and she and Adam consume it. The immediate result was somewhat less than omniscience, but they did discover they were naked, and they did eventually die. All three parties will receive the consequences of their actions.

Given Eve's importance in the original story, it is noteworthy that Paul barely mentions her. Only once does Eve's name appear in any of Paul's authentic letters:

But I am afraid that as the serpent deceived Eve by its cunning, your thoughts will be led astray from a sincere and pure devotion to Christ. (2 Corinthians 11:3, NRSV)

Eve is regarded as analogous to Paul's readers in Corinth, vulnerable to deception, but not as the one who bears the blame for the woes of humankind. In this depiction, Paul stands in contrast to other evaluations of Eve of that period. Here are three examples, two from Jewish writings and one from a Christian composition:

From a woman sin had its beginning, and because of her we all die. (Sirach 25:24, NRSV)[94]

In the next passage, Eve apologizes to Adam on his death-bed for her error:

". . . it is on my account that this has happened to thee; on my account thou are beset with toils and troubles." (Apocalypse of Moses 8:2)

By the time the third text was written, Paul was becoming increasingly authoritative as an Apostle, and to gain acceptance of his writing its author attributed it to Paul himself:

I permit no woman to teach or have authority over a man; she is to keep silent. For Adam was formed first, then Eve; and Adam was not deceived, but the woman was deceived and became a transgressor. (1 Timothy 2:12-14, NRSV)

Paul's own teaching about equality of the genders will be examined later; for now, it is sufficient to point out that this excerpt from a second-century writing is diametrically opposed to Paul's convictions. In his authentic retelling of the story of Adam and Eve, blame for the transgression is placed on the man, not the woman. If asked to justify his interpretation, Paul would probably rely on his Jewish upbringing and point out that it was not the

---

[94] Sirach is also known as The Wisdom of Ben Sira and Ecclesiasticus (not Ecclesiastes). Originally composed in Hebrew by a Jerusalem scribe in the early 2nd century BCE, it became well known in its Greek translation and was included in the Greek version of the scriptures known to Paul. In form based on the book of Proverbs, Sirach is a classic example of the wisdom genre.

woman but the man who was given the commandment. Adam was thereby responsible for making sure it was also obeyed by his wife:

> And the Lord God commanded the man, "You may freely eat of every tree of the garden; but of the tree of the knowledge of good and evil you shall not eat, for in the day that you eat of it you shall die." (Genesis 2:16-17, NRSV)

Adam's Error

In addition to the collective meaning of Adam's name, Paul sees three things characterizing the man: he was the first human being, the first to disobey God, but most important, he established a pattern of behaviour which leads to death. The divine commandment followed by human disobedience sets in motion the story-line about the alienation between God and humankind which repeats itself throughout time. The Hebraic terms for human disobedience have traditionally been gathered up in Christian thought into a single concept labelled "sin," a word well known to us today, but often given associations foreign to the biblical writers. Both in Hebrew and Greek the main root concept translated sin is "missing the target," which points to a failure of the person to live up to his/her responsibility.

It might be helpful to step completely outside the Christian tradition with the connotations it has added to "sin" and consider a different perspective of what constitutes the human predicament. The Buddhist tradition identifies the root problem facing humanity as *tanha*, often translated as "suffering," but perhaps better, according to a former colleague of mine, "unsatisfactoriness." If the biblical standard or goal of human life is friendship with God, then sin is failure to attain that goal, thereby producing an unsatisfactory state of affairs. Sin disrupts the order of things which give meaning and purpose to life. The intended harmony between creator and creature is fractured and human life at best is less than satisfactory.

Specific consequences of Adam's failure follow in Genesis 3; the most important for Paul are shown here underlined: shame, fear, <u>alienation from the creator</u>, accusation of others rather than accepting personal responsibility, painful childbirth and <u>the woman's subservience to the man</u>, hard work with little gain for the man, and <u>loss of access to the tree of life</u>. These three motifs will be woven into Paul's drama.

Although his starting point is Adam's disobedience of a commandment of God, Paul's concept of sin goes far beyond breaking commandments. He characteristically refers not to sins, but to SIN in the singular. Sin is close to being a character in its own right, a mythological power which exists independently of human beings, but which can invade and control them. In modern terms, it is like an addiction from which one cannot extricate oneself. Paul could have portrayed sin as an evil spirit released by Adam's act of disobedience to plague humankind, a Jewish version of Pandora's box. Likewise, the singular sin bears a striking similarity to Satan, the tempter. But Paul does not treat sin as an evil spirit nor does he introduce Satan into the Genesis account in spite of sin's close association with temptation.[95]

Sin is too much a part of human experience for Paul to simply objectify it or project it onto a transcendent screen. Yet, while present in all human beings, it is not indigenous to humanity. Paul is reaching for an articulation of the human problem which accounts for its universality and explains the enslaving and addicting power of the root cause, while also maintaining human accountability. A big order!

---

[95] Paul uses the word "sin" in one or another form about 70 times. "Satan" is found seven times and "Belial" as another name for Satan once, but neither is explicitly connected to sin. *Diabolos* (the Devil) is not found in Paul's writings. One of the writings included in The Books of Adam and Eve, named The Apocalypse of Moses, has Satan speaking through the serpent's mouth to Eve (xvii:4). See Charles, *Apocrypha and Pseudepigrapha*, 2:146. It is possible that Paul was familiar with this non-canonical Jewish writing.

It may seem curious that Paul never refers to forgiveness of sins.[96] Perhaps he believed that particular sins are only symptoms or manifestations of the underlying disease. Forgiveness of moral lapses would therefore be less important than deliverance from the disease which leads to destructive behaviour. Paul's concern was with the disease or the addiction itself and healing or release from it.

Given Paul's analysis of the human dilemma, his story had to include everybody. It was common knowledge among Jews that the Gentiles were notorious sinners. That is a belief with which Paul agreed. The evidence was all around him. However, he refused to exempt anyone, including his own people, from the power of sin. How does Paul know that sin is universal, even working its power in those considered righteous? First, universality is implied in the Adam story. As a corporate figure representing all human-kind, the disobedient Adam implicates all human beings. Second, Paul found in scripture an explicit affirmation that all people are sinners:

> There is no one who is righteous, not even one; there is no one with understanding, there is no one who seeks God. All have turned aside, together they have become worthless; there is no one who shows kindness, there is not even one. (Romans 3:10-12, NRSV).[97]

Third, sin is observable to any with eyes to see. Paul needed no Augustinian theory of the mechanism by which sin spreads; its presence was observable to any and every person:

---

[96] Contrast the Gospels' emphasis on forgiveness of sins, e.g., "If you forgive the sins of any, they are forgiven them." (John 20:23, NRSV) "But so that you may know that the Son of Man has authority on earth to forgive sins" . . . .(Matthew 9:6)

[97] Paul is quoting loosely from Ecclesiastes 7:20 and Psalm 14:1, 3.

Now the works of the flesh are obvious: fornication, impurity, licentiousness, idolatry, sorcery, enmities, strife, jealousy, anger, quarrels, dissensions, factions, envy, drunkenness, carousing, and things like these. (Galatians 5:19-21a, NRSV)

Thus Paul identifies the basic human problem as literally "living in sin," the state which results from being alienated from the Creator. Sin has become an addiction which renders one powerless to "kick the habit." Resolution of the dilemma requires liberation from the sinful condition. Nothing less is sufficient to remove the virus of sin.

Paul's consideration of sin in the singular, its infectious quality, its hold on human beings even when they are unaware of it, its destructive impact on their lives, and his tendency to treat it more as an addiction than a moral problem lead me to interpret sin in his thought as spiritual sickness. Sin has all the marks of a spiritual cancer caused by a virus communicated through social and cultural channels, and despite its destructiveness, readily embraced like a modern street drug. It enslaves those whom it infects at all levels, including the will, the mind, and the heart. The role of enslaving powers is hidden from the enslaved and the addicted; the truth of their situation is kept secret lest their awareness of that reality break the bonds of their slavery.

René Girard's concept of "mimetic desire"[98] has similarities to Paul's portray of sin. For Girard the human disposition to imitate others leads to competition and rivalry for the same goods, and eventually to potential violence which could destroy the community. He points out that desire is another name for the covetousness forbidden in the 10th Commandment (Exodus 20:17). Girard and

---

[98] Girard's conversation with Steven Berry is a good introduction to his understanding of mimetic desire. See Michael Hardin, ed., *Reading the Bible with René Girard*.

Paul agree that the problem extends beyond the individual—it is communal and therefore affects everyone. The fundamental issue is how people relate to and treat one another. Both Paul and Girard also hold that the only resolution of the problem is to break the stranglehold of desire or covetousness, which is based in egotism and comparison with others.

Sin and Death

There is more to be said about iniquity than its ubiquity. In sin's wake comes death. That is a given both in Genesis and for Paul. In Genesis the connection between sin and death was established when God's commandment was first delivered. Adam was informed that disobedience would lead to death, but he ignored the warning. Death is the ultimate separation between the immortal divine and the mortal human realms. When Adam and Eve are expelled from Eden they lose any hope of access to the tree of life, of sharing God's immortality. Paul weaves that theme into his first act:

> Therefore, just as sin came into the world through one man, and death came through sin, and so death spread to all because all have sinned . . . . (Romans 5:12, NRSV)

Sin and death, the unholy pair, team up to harass and enslave humanity. Both arise from misguided human action. Adam had a choice between trusting the Creator and ignoring the commandment. The second option was too tempting; it promised him a status beyond his life as a creature in relationship with God. Snake's lie defeated and changed Adam. Like all big lies which are repeated or otherwise reinforced, this one took on unquestioned normality.

A variant of this scenario is found in a poem contained in Paul's letter to the Philippians. Although primarily about Christ, some scholars think it also contrasts him to Adam:

> . . . who, though he was in the form of God, did not regard equality with God as something to be exploited . . . . (Philippians 2:6, NRSV)

If this is indeed a comparison of Christ and Adam, the implication is that the first man, created in the image of God, attempted to use his special status for his own benefit. Self-centeredness is the soil in which sin is planted and nourished, leading to alienation and death.

Paul's understanding of death, like some other terms he uses, is complex. Coupled with life, death is half of a binary pair. Sometimes death means to Paul literally the end of life as we know it (e.g., 1 Thessalonians 4:13). But in his interpretation of death as the result of sin, he includes what might be called "living death," i.e., existence in this world separated from God. Such existence does not bring with it the joy of life intended by God. Rather, those who live that way are metaphorically dead to God. For example:

> No longer present your members to sin as instruments of wickedness, but present yourselves to God as those who have been brought from death to life, and present your members to God as instruments of righteousness. (Romans 6:13, NRSV)

Implied in this passage is something we have not yet encountered, namely the symbolism of life and death involved in baptism as practiced in Paul's churches. Earlier in this chapter he has written:

> How can we who died to sin go on living in it? Do you not know that all of us who have been baptized into Christ Jesus were baptized into his death? Therefore we have been buried with him into death, so that, just as Christ was raised

from the dead by the glory of the Father, so we too might walk in newness of life. (Romans 6:2-4, NRSV)

Life and death images are basic to Paul's story. Their literal and metaphorical referents are intermingled and not always easy to disentangle. If we assume for the moment that Paul takes the Genesis account of Adam literally, we also have to recognize that his goal is to derive metaphorical meaning from it. Dying to sin versus living in sin is not a literal statement; as metaphor it points to a mode of attitude, thought, and action. Baptism into Christ's death has both literal and metaphorical dimensions. Converts were literally baptized, but they did not literally die with Christ. Metaphorically, their death with Christ who was raised points to their own "newness of life." The common factor in such interplay between the literal and the metaphorical is Paul's intention that his audience identify with the characters in his story. When it becomes their story, it also becomes their pathway from death to life, from sickness to health, from alienation to reconciliation, from enmity to love, from despair to joy.

Sin and Idolatry

Paul recognizes that sin has multiple manifestations and that there are different degrees of "sinfulness." His most systematic analysis of the roots and consequences of sin is found in his letter to the Roman churches. He begins with a traditional Jewish critique of the Gentiles:

Ever since the creation of the world his eternal power and divine nature, invisible though they are, have been understood and seen through the things he has made. So they are without excuse; for though they knew God, they did not honor him as God or give thanks to him, but they became futile in their thinking, and their senseless minds were darkened. Claiming to be wise, they became fools; and they changed the glory of the immortal God for images resembling a mortal human being or birds or four-footed animals or reptiles.

Therefore God gave them up in the lusts of their hearts to impurity, to the degrading of their bodies among themselves, because they exchanged the truth about God for a lie, and worshiped and served the creature rather than the Creator, who is blessed forever! Amen. (Romans 1:20-25, NRSV)

The vacuum left by alienation from God is filled with human-created substitutes, false gods which came to dominate their makers' cultures and social structures. Refusing to admit the actual transcendent dimension in creation, the Gentiles construct their own gods which they pretend are transcendent and to which they give themselves. Once set in motion, idolatry is self-regenerating, perpetuating the original cognitive error through the actions of those it inspires, "who by their wickedness suppress the truth." Thus the Gentiles are caught in an endless destructive cycle of their own making.

Paul shares with other Jews an abhorrence of the multiple gods and goddesses, their temples, priests and priestesses, rituals and stories found throughout the Greco-Roman world. Paganism's power was manifested in every city in which Paul evangelized.[99] He continues to spell out the consequences of idolatry:

For this reason God gave them up to degrading passions. Their women exchanged natural intercourse for unnatural, and in the same way also the men, giving up natural inter-

[99] Paul wisely refrains from a frontal attack on the state gods and the imperial cult which would have opened himself and other Christians to the charge of atheism, potentially a capital offence.

course with women, were consumed with passion for one another. Men committed shameless acts with men and received in their own persons the due penalty for their error. (Romans 1:26-27, NRSV)

Probably no passage in Paul's letters has provoked as much controversy as this one. It is easy to read back into this passage a topic which has proved divisive in our own time, namely, homosexuality as life-style or identity. There is certainly no mistaking his condemnation of whatever sexual practice he has in mind. But appearances can be deceiving and we must be careful not to project our own assumptions onto Paul. Since his letter was not addressed to us, but to Christian communities in mid-first century Rome, it is important to seek for clues to Paul's meaning which his original audience would have recognized.

The study of this passage by Jeramy Townsley proposes an illuminating interpretation.[100] It is generally recognized that Paul develops a sequence beginning in 1:18 with the refusal to recognize the Creator, moving on (verses 21ff) to the resulting practice of idolatry which suppresses the truth about God. God's response to idolatry (verses 24ff) is to deliver the practitioners over to impurity, degradation of their bodies, and finally, to improper erotic passions.

The key insight for understanding this passage is that it consistently deals with idolatry. Idolatry is the root sin, an inevitable byproduct of alienation from the Creator. Sexual issues are some of the secondary consequences of idolatry. Together, idolatry and sexual aberrations point directly to the practices of the goddess religions which were well known to Paul's readers, as they were to most urbanites of the empire.

---

[100] Jeramy Townsley, "Paul, the Goddess Religions, and Queer Sects: Romans 1:23-28."

Paul had recently come into conflict with adherents of one such cult (Acts 19:23-41). The silversmiths of Ephesus had nearly brought about Paul's death. They anticipated that his critique of idolatry would diminish the market for their figurines of Artemis, whose temple in Ephesus was one of the Seven Wonders of the World.

More germane to Paul's Roman audience were the well-known goddess religions operating in the imperial capital. Cybele or the *Magna Mater* (the Great Mother) had been imported from Phrygia in ca. 205 BCE in an effort to defend Rome against an invasion of the Carthaginians during the second Punic War. A temple had been built for her along with her lover, the castrated Attis, in the center of Rome. Earlier, Venus (Aphrodite), who played a major role in the story of Roman origins, had been enthroned on another of the seven hills of Rome. The two cults were an important part of pagan[101] religious life in Rome.

These and other goddess religions shared certain similarities. Most significantly for Paul, they practiced a particular kind of prostitution, often dubbed "sacred sex." Male worshipers could find in those temples females available for whatever form of sexual encounter was desired. Only one form of sexual intercourse was considered "according to nature" by Paul and others, especially Jews, that which could possibly result in conception. Any other was regarded as "unnatural," perhaps since, for Jews, it ignored the commandment to multiply. Of course, that one form of intercourse was limited to the marriage relationship.

Until recently, modern interpreters have tended to assume that Paul's statement, "Their women exchanged natural intercourse for unnatural," refers to relationships between two females. If so, it

---

[101] As found in the NT, a pagan is one who participated in non-Jewish and non-Christian religious beliefs and practices, sometimes called a polytheist. Both "gentile" and "pagan" are used to translate the Greek *ethnos* (nation).

would be unique in the biblical tradition. Nowhere else in the Bible is there an example of that scenario. That alone should be a red flag against reading lesbianism into this text, as if Paul knew what was going on in the bedrooms of Rome. Rather, he is pointing to heterosexual activity, found in the goddess cults as well as in commercial brothels. In plain language, this text is primarily about the use of females for males in prostitution.

Paul then turns to the males who engage in sexual activity with other males. The passive partners are the effeminate priests or eunuchs who were available to men as prostitutes.[102] Such intercourse was also understandably considered contrary to nature by Paul, as it was also to other Jewish commentators. These priests publicly cross-dressed, engaged in frenzied dancing during parades, and cut their arms with knives or swords to aid in fortune telling.

Throughout this passage Paul is targeting idolatry as publicly manifested in idol temples. The sexual practices which go against nature are those connected to the idolatrous religious cults known to his readers. Both Jews and Christians saw in these Gentile religions aberrations to be denounced.[103]

Having made his point about the most obvious and public results of participation in idol worship, Paul goes on to list further results of idolatry. Once again, those who are alienated from God are allowed by God to proceed to impure and self-destructive behaviour:

---

[102] There is a long history of goddess religions with "gender-variant" priests; they are already found in Sumerian records (Townsley, 719). They fit into neither male nor female categories, another reason why their sexual acts were considered contrary to nature (Romans 1:27).

[103] Elsewhere in passing Paul warns his readers against the behavior here depicted in more detailed and graphic form: in 1 Corinthians 6:9 he mentions prostitutes (*pornoi*) followed immediately by "idolaters," and both partners in male prostitution. See above, note 55.

And since they did not see fit to acknowledge God, God gave them up to a debased mind and to things that should not be done. They were filled with every kind of wickedness, evil, covetousness, malice. Full of envy, murder, strife, deceit, craftiness, they are gossips, slanderers, God-haters, insolent, haughty, boastful, inventors of evil, rebellious toward parents, foolish, faithless, heartless, ruthless. They know God's decree, that those who practice such things deserve to die—yet they not only do them but even applaud others who practice them. (Romans 1:28-32, NRSV)

Thus far Paul has focused on sin as manifested in the idol-worshiping Gentile world. But Paul claims that all people are sinners. What are the sins of the Jews? A reasonable approach to this question is to ask Paul to identify his own pre-conversion sins when he was practicing Judaism. The only one he ever specifies was his attempt to destroy God's church. But what was behind that course of action if not his propensity to judge the followers of Jesus as teaching and acting contrary to the Law and refusing to be open to hearing their own self-definition? Basing his behaviour on what he later deemed to be a lie, he slandered the movement, being convinced of his own righteousness, was heartless and ruthless, invented evil against the disciples, and tried to destroy their movement. While judging others he himself engaged in actions demonstrating his own sinfulness, even though he had considered himself justified in opposing the Jesus movement. He had destined himself to be subject to the wrath of God on the Day of Judgment. Only the grace of God had enlightened his mind, thus saving him. This leads Paul to conclude that God is impartial. If Gentiles sin against the law written on their hearts, they are in the same boat as Jews who sin against the Law. Likewise, if Gentiles obey the law of the heart, they are acceptable to God. Paul's final word regarding the situation of the Jew is based on Deuteronomy 10:16 and 30:6, namely, that Jewish identity is not based on physical but spiritual qualities (Romans 2:29).

No one is exempt from the power of sin. Possessing the scripture is indeed an advantage for the Jew because the scripture imparts knowledge of sin, i.e., it identifies sin, but it does not empowers one not to sin.

Thus the stage is set by Adam and all those who refuse to recognize the transcendent God. Adam's deed becomes the default for all who follow him. The human problem is defined and portrayed, and the audience is now prepared for the next act in Paul's drama.

Summary

The first eleven chapters of Genesis deal with primordial history, that time before time in which the conditions of the world we live in were created. Likewise, in the first act of his divine-human drama, Paul prepared the groundwork for his story of salvation. He found in Adam the archetypal character who exhibits the fundamental problem with humankind, alienation from God. Separation from God renders humanity spiritually handicapped and chronically vulnerable to the sickness which is sin. The door is thereby opened for human attempts to fill the vacuum by making and worshiping idols, creations of their own distorted minds. Humankind was made for life, but sin leads to death, at least metaphorically and probably also literally for Paul. In the next act, the first step toward healing the "sin-sick soul" and recovery of a spiritually healthy life will be taken.

CHAPTER 5: Abraham and Sarah

Setting: On the road from Ur to Canaan
Characters:
    God
    Abraham
    Sarah and her son
    Hagar and her son

The Plot of Act 2

Something was missing from Abram's life.
He had flocks and herds, peacocks and other birds,
And unfortunately a barren wife.

But something more was lacking;
Perhaps travel, exploring history, adventure, mystery?
Yes, all this, but more—specifically, God's backing.

"Abram, this will not be distressing, so do not fear,"
Came a voice from the blue, so convincing and true.
"You will receive my blessing, so move out of here."

Abram packed up and left home,
Took his nephew, and, of course, Sarai too,
It seemed he had been summoned to roam.

"Many descendants you'll have, but you must believe
My promise is sure, and my motives are pure,
Then others, through you, will my blessings receive."

Abram replied, "I do believe you, Lord,
Your blessing I'm confessing;
Sure as I live, you can count me on board."

Then Abram received a gift,
Nothing bling, like a golden ring,
But deep in his heart a discernible shift.

God shared with Abram the divine righteousness,
And Abram became Abraham,
God's beginning to clean up Adam's mess.

Now as Abraham and Sarah grew older,
The chosen pair still had no heir,
So on their own they decided to be bolder.

To Abraham Sarah said, "Take my hand-maiden,
Try with my slave our heritage to save,
But don't delay, your powers are fadin'."

So Hagar bore Ishmael, Abraham's offspring,
But he wasn't the man that God had planned,
Through whom God's blessings to bring.

In God's own time Sarah finally conceived,
Isaac was the one to be known as the son,
Mother and father were truly relieved.

Isaac was the sign that the promise was true.
After all his worry, trying God's will to hurry,
Abraham affirmed what he already knew.

He was the father of those who believe,
Who accept God's grace, and join in the race
To the abundant life lost by Adam and Eve.

BACKGROUND NOTES

Chapter 12 of Genesis introduces a new era, moving from the primeval to the patriarchal age. Abram or Abraham [104] from whose descendants the Israelites came, now steps onto the stage:

Now the Lord said to Abram, "Go from your country and your kindred and your father's house to the land that I will show you. I will make of you a great nation, and I will bless you, and make your name great, so that you will be a blessing. . . . and in you all the families of the earth shall be blessed." (Genesis 12:1-2, 3b, NRSV)

Abraham is mentioned over seventy times in the NT, including about twenty references in Paul's letters. Abraham was a figure to be reckoned with by those in the Jesus movement who sought to persuade others, especially Jews, to join them. Nearly six centuries later, he will also become a seminal figure for a third religious movement, Islam. He indeed was the ancestor of many nations.

Three features of the Genesis 12 passage were of special interest to Paul. First, it is future oriented. The blessing mentioned here comes in the form of a promise of what God is going to do, even though the word "promise" is not used. Paul saw the promised blessing being fulfilled in his time. Second, Abraham himself is go-

---

[104] Abram literally means "father is exalted" or "exalted father." This name is expanded in Genesis 17:5 to Abraham. The meaning given to the new name is explained as "father of many nations." However, the etymological derivation of the name is uncertain.

ing to receive a blessing, both in divine support and numberless offspring in future generations. Third, Abraham is a chosen vessel for playing a key role in God's plan. He will be instrumental in God's blessing of the rest of humankind. In Genesis 12 Paul sees a foreshadowing of good times to come,[105] a change in human destiny from the state Adam had bequeathed. The blessing motif permeates Paul's treatment of the Abraham texts.[106] But the blessings will come in stages, each in its proper time.

The critical issue for Paul revolved around Abraham's promised descendants. Before his call to take the gospel to the Gentiles, Paul had not questioned the assumption that Abraham's descendants were exclusively the Jewish people, those whose relationship to Abraham was traced through his son Isaac (Romans 9:7). But if there was one God of all, then the God of Abraham must also be the God of the Gentiles (Romans 10:12). Believing Gentiles as well as Jews were therefore Abraham's children. The unresolved question among the early followers of Jesus was the process through which Gentiles were to be included in the family of Abraham.

The Abrahamic narrative in Genesis is extensive. While his death is described in chapter 25, the larger story is continued through succeeding generations. Several episodes in the lives of Abraham and Sarah lend themselves to Paul's gospel. For example, the two sons of Abraham and their respective mothers have special significance for his proclamation of Jesus:

> For it is written that Abraham had two sons, one by a slave woman and the other by a free woman. One, the child of the slave, was born according to the flesh; the other, the

---

[105] In his discussion of Abraham, Paul was later joined by other Christian writers. For example, John 8:56, 58; Matthew 3:9; Luke 3:8; Hebrews 2:16; Acts 3:25.

[106] As used here "blessing" signifies God's benevolent or generous attitude toward a person or a people, thereby establishing an intimate, trusting, and enduring relationship with them. To employ another Pauline term, the essential blessing is "peace with God." (Romans 5:1, NRSV)

child of the free woman, was born through the promise. Now this is an allegory: these two women are two covenants. One woman, in fact, is Hagar, from Mount Sinai, bearing children for slavery. Now Hagar is Mount Sinai in Arabia and corresponds to the present Jerusalem, for she is in slavery with her children. But the other woman corresponds to the Jerusalem above; she is free, and she is our mother. (Galatians 4:22-26, NRSV; see Genesis 16:1-16; 21:1-7)

This allegorical interpretation may seem strange and artificial to us, but allegory was at home in certain Jewish circles in Paul's time, as well as in various Greco-Roman traditions. Philo of Alexandria favoured the allegorical over the literal meaning of scripture in a way strikingly similar to Paul's interpretation here. Paul's purpose is to demonstrate that scripture, properly understood, supports his argument that the new and "spiritual" covenant of freedom has superseded the former "fleshly" covenant of slavery. Each of Abraham's wives is taken as representative of a deeper reality than the literal reading would suggest.[107]

Paul finds in the biblical accounts about Abraham's two sons and their mothers the following oppositions: the first covenant under Moses versus the new covenant of Jesus; Gentile freedom from law versus Gentile "slavery" to rules no longer operative now that Christ has come; living "according to the flesh" versus living out the promise to Abraham; the two Jerusalems (a motif appearing only here in Paul's writings), the Jerusalem below versus the one above. Here we are given a hint of the real-life debates in which Paul was involved. Particular scriptures provided the agenda, and those regarding Abraham were among the foremost. Arguments

[107] The NT Gospels also employ the allegorical approach. Two obvious examples are the interpretations given to the parable of the Sower (Mark 4:3-9, 13-20 and parallels in Matthew and Luke) and the parable of the Good and Bad Seed (Matthew 13:24-30, 37-42).

over scriptural interpretation of course were both to convince opponents that his story was true and to persuade prospective converts to believe in his story.

However, the most important Abrahamic passages for Paul precede the Genesis accounts of the birth of Abraham's sons. Key elements of Paul's Christian vocabulary, especially as it relates to his mission to the Gentiles, are introduced in Genesis 15.

The Importance of Abraham for Gentiles

Although Genesis 12 had set the stage, it was in Genesis 15 that Paul found the specific biblical warrant for his new understanding of the role of Abraham in God's drama. Following God's reaffirmation of the promise of many descendants, Abraham objected that God had failed to give him offspring. God then directed Abraham to look at the countless stars of heaven and affirmed:

> "So shall your descendants be." And he believed the Lord; and the Lord reckoned it to him as righteousness. (Genesis 15:5b-6, NRSV; see Galatians 3:6)

The significance of this passage for Paul's understanding of his mission and his message can hardly be exaggerated. The terms "faith" and "righteousness" are two pillars of life under God to which Paul can appeal in any context of discussion and debate, because they have universal application. "Descendants" of Abraham is also a pivotal topic—who are they? In Paul's narrative the idea that Abraham's descendants also include Gentiles is fundamental. Let us begin with this part of his story.

Faith Precedes Circumcision

Abasic conviction of Paul's approach to Gentiles was that circumcision not be required of male converts. He found a biblical warrant to justify his position against opponents in the Abraham story. Abraham was the first person in the Bible to receive the commandment of circumcision, which sealed his covenant with God. But Paul noticed that in the biblical account the promise to Abraham came before his circumcision. Abraham received the dual promise of many descendants and of all the families of the earth being blessed through him first in chapter 12, to be repeated in chapter 15. Circumcision did not yet exist. It came only later, in chapter 17, with the name change from Abram to Abraham. His circumcision in chapter 17 made the uncircumcised Gentile Abram of chapter 15 into a Jew. Therefore, Paul concludes, Gentiles as well as Jews are included in God's promise to Abraham. The category of the "chosen people" is being redefined:

> For not all Israelites truly belong to Israel, and not all of Abraham's children are his true descendants. . . .(Romans 9:6b, 7a, NRSV)

Abraham as a Model of Faith

Having established that God's promise was not limited to the Israelites, Paul can now turn to other aspects of Abraham's persona. First, Abraham was accounted "righteous" by God because he accepted what God was telling him, that he would have a son with Sarah, despite evidence to the contrary. This is an important truth for Paul: God's power is made perfect in human weakness, not in human status or achievements in which one could boast.[108]

Second, Abraham's righteousness was pure gift, an act demonstrating God's graciousness, and was neither Abraham's achievement nor a reward for keeping the commandments, as held by some.[109] The Law was still 430 years in the future, so Abraham could not have observed it. (Exodus 12:40; Galatians 3:17) In other words, Abraham and the Law have no connection with each other.

Third, Abraham's faith was a model for later generations, especially the present one being urged to believe in the crucified and resurrected Jesus as God's blessing. Indeed, Abraham was the first to hear—and believe—the gospel which included the blessing of the Gentiles. That makes him the first believer (in the Christian sense) in Paul's view.[110]

Fourth, Abraham's true descendants were those who imitated his faith, i.e., they were related to him spiritually rather than "according to the flesh." Thus he is the father of all who believe, whether Jew or Gentile. Belief/faith rather than ethnic identity defines Abraham's children.

Fifth, Abraham's experience demonstrates the real meaning of "righteousness," an important concept of Paul's derived from the scripture and inherent in Jewish thought. "Righteousness" in the scriptures relates to the character of God, the relationships God requires between people, and people's relationship to God. It de-

---

[108] See the long section dealing with this theme in 2 Corinthians 11:12-12:10.

[109] For example: Sirach 44:19-21a states that Abraham kept the Law and that his willingness to sacrifice Isaac led to God's assuring him that the Gentiles would be blessed through his descendants. Paul opposes this interpretation on the basis that the Law could not have been known by Abraham and that Abraham was not rewarded, but received a gift. Note the exploration of this reward/gift opposition in the parable of the Workers in the Vineyard (Matthew 20:1-16).

[110] Paul sees in the promise to Abraham a proleptic proclamation of the gospel to Abraham (Galatians 3:8-9), to which Abraham responded with faith. For more on Paul's concept of faith, see below, chapter 13.

rives some of its metaphorical meaning from the law court where justice is to be properly dispensed. It also points to the covenant(s) God had established with Israel. Acting in an unrighteous manner injures the covenantal relationship. Such behavior also dishonors God since it is contrary to God's character as righteous or just. Righteousness is closely associated with faith, truth (that which is reliable), and a Hebrew word often translated as "steadfast love" (*khesedh*). Thus righteousness is a very broad term with many associations.

The text of Genesis 15:6 in which God considers Abraham's belief "righteous" may suggest that either God accounted Abraham as a righteous (or just, or innocent) person, or that God's own divine righteousness was shared with Abraham. Paul seems to opt for the second interpretation. Abraham was the recipient of a gift from God, and it would also be a gift to his descendants, to those who were truly the children of Abraham, whose relationship to God was based on faith as was Abraham's.

Finally, Paul argues that the "seed" (translated as "offspring" or "descendants") in Genesis 17:9 refers to one person, namely Christ, who is the heir of the promise given to Abraham (Galatians 3:16-17). Paul will then extend the notion of heirs to those who are "in Christ."

The Epistle to the Hebrews draws on two stories involving Abraham which are ignored by Paul. In the first, after liberating his nephew Lot and repossessing the goods taken when Lot was captured, Abraham gives a tenth of the goods (a tithe) to Melchizedek, the king of Salem and priest of God Most High.[111] There is nothing in this story which could contribute to Paul's drama.

The second story involves the so-called "testing of Abraham" when he was ordered to offer up his son Isaac as a burnt offering.[112] Abraham obediently complied but was stopped from sacrificing his

---

[111] Genesis 14; Hebrews 7:1-10.

[112] Genesis 22: 1-19; Hebrews 11:8-12.

son by God who supplied a substitute. Abraham's unquestioning obedience is then given as the prerequisite for the blessing to his descendants and the nations. This goes counter to Paul's claim that Abraham's righteousness was entirely a gift from God and not his own achievement on the basis of obeying commandments.[113] However, while Paul does not overtly quote from the passage, Romans 8:32 may contain an echo of that story when he writes that God did not spare his own Son.[114]

These motifs drawn from the story of Abraham give substance to Paul's vision of God's plan to rectify the human tragedy portrayed in Act One. Despite the fact that Paul's interpretations of the Abraham narrative, like the typological juxtaposition of Adam and Christ, are found only in Galatians and Romans, he must have drawn on it frequently in his proclamation, debates, and teaching. It was a treasury he could ill afford to ignore. Indeed, there are too many points of contact between that narrative and his own self-understanding, his justification of his Gentile mission, the centrality of "faith" in his gospel, and the process whereby believers were "justified" or "made righteous," to imagine that it was not part of his thinking from early in his ministry, if not from its beginning.

Summary

The second act signals a new beginning in world history for Paul. The first of two characters intervening between Adam and Christ in Paul's story is introduced. As a faithful servant of God, Abraham initiates the recovery process necessitated by Adam's sin. Abraham receives God's promise of the future blessing

---

[113]The Epistle of James takes a more balanced approach to the interpretation of Abraham's offering of Isaac, arguing that Abraham's act shows that his faith was accompanied by his works, the two complementing each other (2:21-22).

[114]See also Romans 11:21. Hays, *Echoes of Scripture in the Letters of Paul*, 61-62.

of all the peoples of the earth through the authentic descendant, Jesus. By means of identifying with Christ, believers will become children of Abraham and thus heirs of the promise.

The biblical account of Abraham's positive response to God's promise gives Paul a treasury of texts to support his story and his mission to the Gentiles. It will take two more acts to complete what God started in Abraham.

CHAPTER 6: Moses and the Law

Setting: Egypt to Mount Sinai
Characters:
    God
    Moses
    Pharaoh
    The People of Israel

The Plot of Act 3

Moses said to Pharaoh, "Let God's people go."
But Pharaoh's hard heart wouldn't let him part
With those Hebrew slaves, oh no!

But plagued with frogs and flies and all that stuff,
Ten woes in number, what a bummer,
Pharaoh finally cried, "That's enough!"

"Take them and get out," Pharaoh said.
Leaving slavery for freedom took bravery,
But the people from Egypt Moses led.

Under the cloud and through the sea
Into the wilderness, often with bitterness,
To the mountain God's Law to receive.

There God said to Moses, "Here's the thing,
This is the Law, to be obeyed by all;
And my covenant with Israel I bring."

Sternly God warned, "Let the folks below know
That right from the start, you must all keep apart
From the nations; you're my own tell-and-show.

"Unless by my Law you think and act,
Have no doubt, you will be out;
I'm telling you, that is a fact.

"The Law shows what's good and what's bad,
A book of road-maps to avoid life's traps,
What to do whether glad or sad.

"It's intent," God did say,
"Is not to teach math, but to show the path
That my people must walk every day."

"So don't use it to claim you are better,
Or superior and others inferior,
But embrace it to escape sin's fetter."

Moses heard all this as at God he dared not look,
A prophet in name, a scribe he became
To preserve God's words in a book.

BACKGROUND NOTES

If Paul were composing his story before meeting Jesus, this would have been the final act. The giving of the Law through Moses was the pinnacle of Israelite history. Everything that came afterward was related to the Law, whether through disobedience or obedience. As the full and complete revelation of the will of God for Israel, the Law had no equal. It could not be replaced, neither in this age nor in the age to come. There would have been no need for Paul to even think about another act in the divine-human drama.

Paul also would have held Moses in the highest esteem. He had led the Israelites out of slavery from Egypt to the land promised to Abraham. His close relationship to God, with whom he spoke as with a friend (Exodus 33:11), facilitated his role as mediator between God and the people. His wonder-working powers sustained the Israelites in the wilderness. He delivered God's covenant and Law to Israel. The closing words of Deuteronomy eulogize Moses as one of a kind in performing wonders and displaying the power of God (Exodus 34:10-12).

However, Paul's encounter with Jesus challenged the place that Moses and the Law had held in his earlier view of God's plan for the world. The "traditions of the fathers" into which Paul had been initiated as a young Pharisee and which gave him his special perspective on the Law were now questioned. Further, Paul had been called to be an apostle to the Gentiles, whose history and culture did not include Moses and the Law. All in all, a new assessment of Moses and the Law was required, as well as a fourth act in his story.

Adam, Abraham, and now Moses—three successive nodal figures in the divine drama. Paul's view of Adam's character is well-defined: he was the first sinner, releasing sin into the world and in its wake, death. At the other end of the sin/righteousness scale was Abraham, the prime example of faithfulness and righteousness, also clearly delineated. Where does Paul place Moses on that scale? He doesn't. Paul seems uninterested in Moses' character as such, as an examination of his references to Moses illustrates.

Moses' name is found nine times in Paul's letters. Once it appears in a parallel drawn between the Christian sacraments and a passage from Exodus. The ritual of baptism is projected onto the Israelites' experience of following the cloud and passing through the sea. The Lord's Supper provides the lens through which are viewed the food and drink miraculously given to the people following Moses:

> . . . our ancestors were all under the cloud, and all passed through the sea, and all were baptized into Moses in the cloud and in the sea, and all ate the same spiritual food and all drank the same spiritual drink. For they drank from the spiritual rock that followed them, and the rock was Christ. (1 Corinthians 10:1b-4, NRSV; see Exodus 13:21-22; 14:21-31; 16:4-36; 17:1-7)

While this may seem to be a positive way of regarding the Israelites and Moses—they did have "spiritual" moments—Paul sees in these passages a warning. In spite of being nurtured by God's gifts, many of the Israelites subsequently were destroyed because they failed to endure in their commitment to God, falling prey especially to idolatry in the golden calf episode (Exodus 32). Therefore, Paul cautions his readers in Corinth not to repeat the mistakes of Israel.

A second reference to Moses raises puzzling questions about Paul's intended meaning:

> Therefore, just as sin came into the world through one man, and death through sin, and so death spread to all because all have sinned—sin indeed was in the world before the law, but sin is not reckoned when there is no law. Yet death exercised dominion from Adam to Moses, even over those whose sins were not like the transgression of Adam, who is a type of the one who was to come. (Romans 5:12-14, NRSV)

The primary motif in the context is the juxtaposition of Christ and Adam, each representing the realm over which they respectively reign, and each bringing something to humankind. Adam brought condemnation and death, Christ brought justification and life. But Moses cannot be left out of the picture, or more to the point, the Law which he brought.

In this passage Paul begins with the linkage between sin and death and his conviction that sin is universal. He never completes the initial sentence, but interjects two comments about the relation between sin and law, namely that sin preceded law and that sin is not counted where there is no law. If sin is not counted until the Law was given through Moses, one might ask how does sin lead to death? But Adam received a commandment that predated the Law. His disobedience was in a class by itself inasmuch as it led to death for everyone, because he initiated and instituted sin.

Paul argues that if the Law was delivered through Moses, then it was not eternal. If it had a beginning in time, then it also had an ending. Consequently, Paul asserts that the Law of Moses does not change the effect of Adam's sin; it lacks the power to free from sin or to give life. Its purpose is to define sin, to give those who observe the Law knowledge about sin and therefore how to deal with it. Like any law code, religious or secular, the Mosaic Law establishes the parameters of behaviour.

Paul recognizes various grades of violations of the Law. Not all sins are comparable to the trespass of Adam who consciously and with great ramifications disobeyed the original commandment. But in the end, that does not matter. Sin is not limited to legal definition, but exists in its own right as a power transcendent to human beings. As such it is a universal access point for death, whether defined literally or metaphorically. Both sin and death lord it over humanity, the Law notwithstanding. One should not look to the Law for a solution of the human dilemma.

Finally, Paul hints that the figure of Adam is going to be revisited; there is a second Adam whose "type" is somehow related to the first Adam. More on this in Act Four.

Another set of references to Moses is found in Paul's contrast between the new covenant of Christ with the former one brought by Moses:

> Now if the ministry of death, chiseled in letters on stone tablets, came in glory so that the people of Israel could not gaze at Moses' face because of the glory of his face, a glory now set aside, how much more will the ministry of the Spirit come in glory? . . . we act with great boldness, not like Moses, who put a veil over his face to keep the people of Israel from gazing at the end of the glory that was being set aside. . . . Indeed, to this very day when they hear the reading of the old covenant, that same veil is still there, since only in Christ is it set aside. (2 Corinthians 3:7-8, 12b-13, 14b, NRSV)

The context sets the interpretive framework for these statements about Moses. Paul's readers in Corinth have received other missionaries who carried letters of recommendation, from whom we do not know, but the letters did not support Paul's authority. He challenges the assumption that such letters, either to them or from them, are significant. The important letters of recommendation are not the literal ones written on some material external to the person, but the figurative ones written on the heart. Here Paul draws on the prophetic image of the Law written on the hearts of the people in "those days." (Jeremiah 31:33). Written on the hearts of Paul and his companion missionaries is a letter of recommendation from the Corinthians, "to be known and read by all" (2 Corinthians 3:2b, NRSV). The Corinthian church is a living manifestation of the truth of Paul's gospel. Similarly, their existence as a community of Christ shows that Christ has written a letter on their hearts, "not with ink but with the Spirit of the living God." (v. 3, NRSV) Paul and his team are servants taking dictation embodying spiritual substance from their master, Christ.

138

The imagery is taken largely from Exodus 34:27-35, one of several accounts of the Law being written on stone tablets.[115] Paul utilizes this passage to argue for the legitimacy of his own ministry vis-à-vis Moses' ministry. If the Law which brings condemnation (because it defines sin and its consequences but does not liberate from it) was accompanied by glory, how much more glorious is the ministry of the Spirit which brings justification and life? The second is now eclipsing the first. Why does not Israel realize that Moses' glory has faded? Because when they hear Moses read their minds, like Moses' face, are veiled. In a rapidly moving series of arguments, Paul defends his story in which Moses' time is past. There are those who don't understand that a new era has dawned and are still attached to the old era of Moses, i.e., the time of the Law.

It is apparent that the passage we have been considering is not really about Moses as a person, but about his association with the Law. Paul's story is in competition with another Christian story to gain the allegiance of the Gentiles. That other story retains an important and positive role for Moses and the Law in the Christ story; Jesus had not come to destroy the Law, but to bring it to perfection. Those who told that story had not shared Paul's experience of conversion from a Pharisaic enforcer of Law to one whose new perspective placed Christ supreme, even over the Law. The two stories were irreconcilable from Paul's point of view. His letters reflect that conflict.

The final references where Moses' name is mentioned by Paul concern not the man but quotations from writings attributed to him, the Pentateuch.[116] Paul seldom looks to the person of Moses

---

[115] Inscribing the stone tablets is mentioned in Exodus 24:12; 31:18; 32:15-16; 34:27-35. In the first three references, God does the writing, but in the last one, Moses inscribes the tablets. Paul ignores the first three to concentrate on the last since it also includes the motif of "glory."

[116] Literally, the "five scrolls" on which were inscribed Genesis, Exodus, Leviticus, Numbers, and Deuteronomy. Three of Paul's quotations are found in Romans:

when he mentions his name. In contrast to Abraham, Moses is not regarded by Paul as a model of faith. In fact, those two words, "Moses" and "faith," never appear together in any of Paul's letters. What is most important about Moses is not his personal character, but the Law he mediated, the scripture he wrote, and his leading of the Israelites during their exodus from Egypt.

For Paul, Moses' role as a writer of scripture is related to his traditional status as a prophet. As such, the words he writes are not regarded as his own, but the message of God who speaks through the prophet. The scriptures associated with Moses are highly regarded by Paul and other early Christians, as are writings associated with David (the psalms) and the prophets. While a canonical set of writings had not yet been exclusively identified as "the scripture," this singular noun (*hé graphé*) indicates the idea of an authoritative unity. Jews, Jewish Christians, and Gentile God-worshipers alike considered the scripture high up on the scale of authority.

Paul can respect Moses as a mediator of God's authoritative and lasting communications written in the books of Moses, and at the same time consider the Law mediated by Moses as a temporary measure valid only until the revealing of faith in Christ. It is important to keep these two roles of Moses separate; otherwise the reader might be confused when Paul appeals to the books of Moses in order to demonstrate that a relationship with God based on faith rather than on the Law of Moses was already found in Abraham, while at the same time maintaining that the Law is passing away.

9:15 (see Exodus 33:19), 10:5 (Leviticus 18:5), and 10:19 (Deuteronomy 32:21). The fourth is in 1 Corinthians 9:9 (Deuteronomy 25:4).

Summary

Moses plays multiple roles in Paul's story—leading the Israelites from Egypt, delivering the Law at Mount Sinai, and acting as a prophet. However, Paul's main interests in him center on the scripture he wrote, which is both prophetic and legal. The first is a positive contribution inasmuch as it benefits those who came later, especially Paul's generation. The influence of the second is ambiguous; though it provides knowledge of God's requirements, it lacks power to free from sin and to give life. The shadow of Moses continues to fall on Israel and the Gentiles, but the shelf-life of the Law he mediated has expired. It is now time for the concluding act.

CHAPTER 7: Jesus and Paul

We have arrived at the dénouement of Paul's drama. In Act One the human situation was defined by Adam's and Eve's disobedience and subsequent alienation from the source of their being, from each other, and from the rest of creation. Act Two brought God's promise of descendants to Abraham and Sarah, the blessing of those offspring, and God's counting Abraham's faith as righteousness—all signs of hope for humankind. The Law given through Moses in Act Three defined sin but failed to liberate those who observe the Law from sin. But now, life with freedom from sin is available to all, Gentiles as well as Jews. Paul has been called to tell this story to the Gentile world, and to create and nurture healing communities in which the story is lived and passed on.

Setting: Paul's world
Characters:
    God
    Jesus
    Jesus' disciples
    Paul
    Israel
    Gentiles

The Plot of Act Four
(as revealed in a divine soliloquy)

God thought, "It's time to fulfill my blessing,
Long ago I made a start, Abraham played his part,
To show that faith is more than window dressing.

"Next I gathered a people, though with some apprehension,
They weren't all that much, sometimes a tiresome bunch,
For whom my faithfulness seemed beyond comprehension.

"They needed guidance so I gave them a Law,
It wasn't too hard, and not my last card,
But sufficient until the next draw.

"Meanwhile, the nations required attention,
The Law was for Israel to keep, but I had other sheep,
Though in different pastures, I might mention.

"I needed a son of Abraham to pioneer a new way,
So here was my plan, I'd raise up such a man
To model my faithfulness, and my will to obey.

"That one's faith would be supple and strong,
Full of Spirit and fire, he would lead and inspire,
And rectify the first Adam's wrong.

"So Jesus was born and lived and taught,
He followed my will, even onto a hill,
Where a Roman cross had been brought.

"He embraced his calling, my grace to give them
And he sighed as he died,
"Father, forgive them."

"But there was more than this his final breath,
He excelled in living, generous and giving,
Why not in overcoming death?

"He appeared to his followers left in the lurch,
They were amazed when his fire in them blazed,
And they went on to kindle a church.

"Next I sought a visionary for those who were Gentile,
To tell them of the one, who lived as my Son,
And invite them to join my rank and file.

"I needed an Israelite who knew scripture and spoke Greek,
I settled on Saul, also called Paul,
To know my Son, and my Gentiles to seek.

"The problem was, Saul was on the other side,
Thinking my will fit his own bill,
The followers of Jesus he arrested and tried.

"I stopped him one day, while on his way
To Damascus to fight, to prove who was right;
I showed him that I have the final say.

"I revealed to him his prophetic call,
Like a prophet of old, he had to be bold,
To convince the Gentiles my grace is for all.

"Like my first people, they too must learn
How to care and love, trade the eagle for the dove,
And for my kingdom to yearn.

"And Paul, though by the rules he had played
And truly kept the Law, that day he saw
That I had moved on, and a new covenant had made.

"What then was the Law? A temporary child-minder,
Watching the kids, shaming their do's and did's,
Expecting to make them kinder.

"But sadly the Law didn't stop the strife,
Or raise the dead, even though some said
It came to give life.

"Then Paul knew, while the Law had been all the rage,
Its role is now done, it's had its time in the sun
Now I am taking it off the stage.

"So Paul became my messenger to the nations,
Through their cities he went, knowing by whom he was sent,
To tell the story of their salvation.

"The second Adam has come to lead humanity,
Out of retribution, into love's distribution,
Walking in justice, peace, and sanity.

"My righteousness mediated by faith Paul taught,
Leading believers to share, to love and to care,
And to build my community he sought.

"During his mission he formulated this story,
From Adam's mix-up to Jesus' fix-up,
He composed it all for my own glory."

BACKGROUND NOTES

"Never doubt that a small group of thoughtful, committed citizens can change the world; indeed, it's the only thing that ever has." (Margaret Mead)

Before proceeding to the ways Paul formulates his story, let us remind ourselves of the momentous changes underway in which Paul had an important part.

The social change that we identify as the beginning of Christianity was triggered by an individual who convinced others of the priority of thinking and behaving empathetically. His teaching and presence struck his followers as so authoritative and authentic, so life-changing, that only terminology drawn from the divine realm of discourse was deemed adequate to describe the qualities of that person. He taught that God was not only to be the object of love, but more fundamentally its source. The commandment to love God was coupled with the commandment to treat the neighbor according to the same standards desired for oneself. Judgmentalism, retribution and all other forms of hatred and division were forbidden. God was envisaged as a caring parent who was concerned for the best interests of the children who were expected to share that concern, even for their enemies.

Convincing others to join in such a radical change required demonstration of what was being proclaimed, both by personal character and by persuasive verbal testimony and arguments. It was also made urgent by the apocalyptic terminology that accompanied it; i.e., that the long expected close of this age and the introduction of a new era was happening. What was being proclaimed was the way things were soon to be following the present time of preparation through living now the character of the new coming age.

The story to be told had to cover all that, plus an analysis of the human problem, its resolution, and the path to that goal. It also had to be integrated into Israel's sacred narrative as related in the scriptures.

Numerous images of "salvation" emerged among the early Jesus followers as they struggled to find symbols, metaphors, and analogies adequate to express their experience. John Knox identified two stories of salvation in the early church, one based on victory over demonic powers which enslaved humankind, the other on atoning sacrifice to bring about forgiveness.[117] Each is logical in its own context, but the two cannot be combined without contradiction. In a sense that is true, but the fact is, as Knox recognizes, Paul does cite elements from each story, sometimes in close proximity to each other. Was Paul being inconsistent, or simply recognizing and employing different ways of expressing the main truth he wanted to convey without being confined to any particular one?

Paul's citations of sacrificial atonement imagery may be traced to the preexisting Jewish Christian gospel. While the evidence is clear that there are two salvation stories in Paul's writings, one may have been designed mostly for Jewish ears and the other for Gentiles. Paul's own story was composed primarily for the latter, and incorporates ideas easily recognizable to Gentiles. However, Paul's churches included both ethnicities and as a Jew addressing Jews he draws on appropriate imagery for them. His gospel needed to be as comprehensive as possible.

Consequently, several sources are incorporated in his narrative: scripture,[118] contemporary cultic activity and associated sacrificial ideas in the Jerusalem temple,[119] social norms and practices in the Eastern Roman Empire, those, as he puts it, who were in Christ before him, and any other image deemed relevant to the central features of his gospel.

Perhaps the central task in Paul's role as a missionary was to integrate the Jesus story into Israel's historic commission to take God's light to the Gentiles. The Torah, the prophets, and the writings (especially certain psalms) were the library of the early

---

[117] John Knox, *The Death of Christ*, chapter 7.

[118] Paul's letters contain about 90 quotations from the OT.

[119] The first Temple, built by Solomon, was destroyed by the Babylonians. Rebuilding it after return from exile was an extended process, culminating in the Herodian Temple which was barely completed before the Romans demolished it in 70 CE. It was in operation throughout Paul's lifetime.

churches. Quotations from these scriptures provided the assurance of God's hand in the life, teaching, death, and resurrection of Jesus. But explicit references are only part of the picture, the iceberg above the water's surface. The letters of Paul are replete not only with quotations but also with allusions and "echoes"[120] from OT writings which reveal his deep engagement with scripture. One suspects that Paul, as were others, was always on the lookout for more profound understanding of the revelations of God, and especially in scripture. God's word covered everything from the original creation to the new creation. Scripture was a treasury for plumbing the depths of the activity and character of God. It gave him the basic term by which he understood what had gone wrong with humanity, sin.

If the fundamental human problem is defined as "sin," as Paul and others so defined it, then the solution would naturally draw on existing institutions and procedures associated with the removal of sin. But, as we saw in Chapter 4, the particular understanding of "sin" affects the model chosen to portray the resolution of its effects. Paul did not think so much in terms of "sins" but of "sin" as designating a single reality with many manifestations. Sin covered all levels of human wrongness, including the systemic sins of social and cultural life that captivate and mislead people into unproductive paths. Forgiveness of sins of individuals was important, but not the sufficient solution as long as the cultural and social systems were in place.

Paul's story of healing and transformation, like the stories of other early Christian evangelists, of course is centered in Jesus. He

---

[120] Richard B. Hays' insight that Paul's references to scripture go far beyond mere citations to allusions and "echoes" is instructive. Interpretation of Paul's letters requires sensitivity to his imaginative dialogue with and reinterpretation of biblical stories. See Hays' provocative study of Paul's engagement with scripture: *Echoes of Scripture in the Letters of Paul*; also *The Conversion of the Imagination: Paul as Interpreter of Israel's Scripture*. Paul sees in scripture the story of Israel from beginning to end, including its present inclusion of the Gentiles through Christ.

has the lead role in God's drama of putting people onto the right path for finding authentic life. The remainder of this chapter examines the images that Paul drew on to clarify his missionary proclamations about the role of Jesus in God's plan to save people from the mess they had gotten themselves in. We begin with a pre-Pauline creed which Paul quoted as expressing the essence of his gospel.

Isaiah 53

In 1 Corinthians Paul recalls a traditional creed he had received and passed on which suggested a sacrificial interpretation of the death of Jesus:

For I handed on to you as of first importance what I in turn had received: that Christ died for our sins in accordance with the scriptures. . . . (1 Corinthians 15:3, NRSV)

What scriptures does Paul have in mind? There are many scriptural references to sin sacrifices, but the most obvious candidate is Isaiah 53. Despite the fact that this biblical passage is not overtly related to the temple and its sacrifices, it is replete with evocative imagery normally associated with sacrificial atonement:

Surely he has borne our infirmities and carried our diseases. . . . But he was wounded for our transgressions, crushed for our iniquities; upon him was the punishment that made us whole, and by his bruises we are healed. All we like sheep have gone astray; we have all turned to our own way, and the Lord has laid on him the iniquity of us all. . . . For he was cut off from the land of the living, stricken for the transgression of my people. . . . The righteous one, my servant, shall make many righteous, and he shall bear their iniquities. . . . because he poured out himself to death, and was numbered with the transgressors; yet he bore the sin of many, and made intercession for the transgressors.[121] (Isaiah 53:4a, 5-6, 8b, 11b, 12b, NRSV)

These statements are too explicit for Paul's predecessors in the faith, some of his contemporaries, and probably Paul also not to have applied them to Jesus' death. Isaiah 53 must have been an inspiration for many as they tried to make sense of Jesus' violent death. It may not be too adventuresome to find here one of the original biblical sources for the early Christian interpretation of Jesus' death as a sacrifice for the sins of the people.

Isaiah 53 contains other motifs which Paul, as well as others, found especially significant; at least they resurface in the story he was creating: the universality of sin ("All . . . have gone astray"); the alignment of the life and death of the "righteous one" with the will of God; the death of the righteous one as a release from sin for many; and the role of the suffering servant of God in making others righteous.

Some of the references in Isaiah 53 to the sin offering for the community may even suggest that the Day of Atonement ritual (to which we shall return later) is in the background of the author's thinking. In any case, some early Christians may have so perceived it. Sacrificial imagery applied to the death of Jesus points to a reversal of the usual conception of sacrifice. In this case, not humans but God makes the offering on their behalf. This motif bears some resemblance to Abraham's offering his son Isaac (Genesis 22:1-19). In

---

[121] Perhaps in the interests of variety, the NSRV translators of Isaiah 53 rendered the same Greek word, *hamartia*, with different English words. In verse four, *hamartia* is singular but is translated with the plural "infirmities." In verse five, the same singular *hamartia* becomes "transgressions." In verse six, the plural *hamartiai* is translated by the singular "iniquity." In verse 11, the singular *hamartia* is rendered "iniquities," while in verse 12 it is translated as "sin." All these are the same word Paul uses in Galatians 1:4 and 1 Corinthians 15:3 in the plural form, translated there as "sins."

each instance a father offers his son, even though in the biblical story the deed is not completed and the motivation is not the father's.

Also, in Galatians Paul alludes once more to an earlier Jewish Christian creedal formulation based on Jesus' death as a sacrifice for sin:

> . . . who gave himself for our sins to set us free from the present evil age, according to the will of our God and Father . . . . (Galatians 1:4, NRSV)

In this case, however, Paul combines the sacrificial interpretation with a second, namely, Jesus' death as a means of liberation. We shall consider that in detail later. For now, let us turn to the cultic practice known as the "sin sacrifice" which brought about atonement with God.

Atonement

The English term "atonement" is an all-encompassing term for various interpretations of how Jesus brought about the resolution of human wrongness. The word contains in its stem the phrase "at one" and suggests a bringing together or reconciling two or more parties. Paul inherited from his predecessors among the followers of Jesus—and personally experienced—the conviction that the death of Jesus was especially significant. The challenge for all Jesus followers, especially in that initial period, was finding relevant language to express that conviction.

It was the temple's so-called "sin sacrifices"[122] that the early Christians perceived as the most powerful analogue to the death of Jesus. Since sin designated not just breaches of ethical behavior but

---

[122] The Hebrew term translated "sin" is *khatta'th* and the Greek is *hamartia*. Both have similar meanings, "missing the mark." Thus sin is a failure which needs to be corrected. The sin sacrifice removes the residue of past failure.

also the many forms of ritual impurity or uncleanness which were also regarded as offensive to the deity, scholars consider these sacrifices to be more accurately named as "purifying sacrifices." Impurity attached to a wide range of phenomena. While many of the terrestrial, winged, and aquatic creatures were allowed as food sources (clean), others were not (unclean). Impurity was not only toxic to the affected person; it was also dangerous to others because it could be transmitted, like a disease. Intentionality was not necessary; normal and unavoidable situations, such as menstruation and childbirth left a woman in a state of uncleanness, which required purification. Impurity could infect anyone, from the high priest or ruler of the people, to other individuals and the people as a whole. The antidote which reestablished a state of acceptability to God was ritual purification.

Each situation of impurity had its own ritual requirements, including a particular animal to be sacrificed (bull, goat, sheep, or turtle dove/pigeon). The animal itself had to be without blemish. The one who gave the animal to be sacrificed identified with it by placing a hand on its head. The animal was slaughtered primarily for the purpose of making available its blood, which was gathered into a container and sprinkled in prescribed places in the sanctuary. Thereby, "forgiveness of sins" was achieved, but "sins" must be understood as including anything which compromised purity, and "forgiveness" as that which "covered over" or nullified the impurity.

The reader might be wondering about the logic connecting the slaughter of an animal with purification or forgiveness of sin, and what led the early Christians to see Jesus' death as such a purifying sacrifice. There have been many scholarly attempts over the last 150 years to explain the logic of animal (and human) sacrifice, none entirely satisfactory. One way of understanding sacrifice is that it is an offering of life for life. Biblical thought identifies two phenomena as essential for life: breath (Genesis 2:7) and blood (Leviticus 4:1-5:13; 15:31).[123] While breath is non-tangible, blood is physical and symbolic of life itself inasmuch as its loss brings death. However, the death of the animal is of only secondary importance; it is the blood that is primary. Slaughter of the animal is necessary to make the blood available for the atoning ritual which re-establishes the bond between the people and their deity, thus assuring the continuance of their collective and individual lives.

The best example of purifying sacrifices is found in the annual Day of Atonement ritual. We shall look at it more closely later in this chapter.

Sacrifices could only be offered in a particular place, namely the temple in Jerusalem, and by authorized priests. King Herod had replaced the previous temple with a magnificent structure overlooking the city. Construction began in 20 BCE and continued in a minor way almost up to the time of its destruction by the Romans in 70 CE. It was in full operation throughout Paul's lifetime.

The Temple

It takes imagination for modern people to appreciate the religious significance of ancient temples.[124] Temples in the Near East were typically symbolic representations of heaven and earth, and their main purpose was to facilitate communication and good relations between the human and the divine. Temples provided a home on earth for a specific deity (or deities) whose statue was installed in the inner and most sacred part of the building, representing the presence of the deity among the people.

---

[123] Blood is forbidden as a food substance for human beings. Directions for eating meat of animals not slaughtered in the temple require disposal of the blood during preparation. The reason given is that life is in the blood (Deuteronomy 12:23).

[124] Temples had many functions other than what we might consider "religious," depending on time and place: they could serve as treasuries, symbols of national power, funerary chapels (especially in Egypt), centers for food distribution, educational institutions, historical and literary archives, places of healing and sanctuary.

While the Jerusalem temple lacked an image of the God of Israel,[125] God (or his Name) was still believed to be present there, in the "Holy of Holies." As God's abode on earth, the temple was to be treated with the utmost respect. Part of the duties owed any deity was providing daily nourishment, such as cereal, drink, and animal meat. These foods were burned daily on the altar, producing fragrant smoke which ascended to heaven. The cleanliness or purity of the temple, especially its sanctuary, had to be closely guarded. Otherwise, the deity might be offended and even abandon the temple and the people, leaving them without divine assistance.

Temple offerings were of various types and for different purposes.[126] Biblical texts, especially drawn from Leviticus, Numbers, and Deuteronomy, stipulate the details regarding the specific situations which required an offering: priestly qualifications to conduct the ritual; if an animal sacrifice was required, how and where animals were to be slaughtered; what was to done with the materials in each case, etc. Some offerings were voluntary, others mandatory, some were individual, others for the whole community. As Israel's cult center the temple exerted a substantial influence on many aspects of life. Saul's Pharisaic period was probably spent in close proximity to the temple.

To understand Paul's attitude to the temple, we need to keep in mind the larger picture of his situation. From being an ardent Pharisaic opponent of the followers of Jesus to promoting their cause was quite a leap. We have already seen some of the features of Saul's Pharisaism which led him to reject the claims of the early followers of Jesus. We also noted his rejection of that earlier life-pattern following the revelation of God's Son. But to what in particular did the Pharisee Saul object so strenuously?

---

[125] The first of the Ten Commandments prohibit the making of images of God drawn from the created order and worshiping them (Exodus 20:4-5a).

[126] See Gary Anderson, "Sacrifice and Sacrificial Offerings," *ADB* 5:870-886.

Early Christianity was not a monolithic movement. The author of Acts was keenly aware of that, as was Paul. Generally speaking, Luke de-emphasizes or even ignores differences in the Jesus movement because of his goal of uniting its various strands, especially those derived from either Peter or Paul. However, Luke does recognize one significant division in the movement which he locates in Jerusalem in the early days, prior to his introduction of Saul. One group, which he calls the "Hellenists" is distinguished from the "Hebrews." (Acts 6:1-6) While Luke explains the dispute as a complaint over the widows among the Hellenists not being given equal treatment in food distribution, (Acts 6:1) the real issue goes much deeper. Beyond their different languages (Greek and Aramaic), the two groups appear to have very different attitudes toward the Jerusalem temple. The Apostle-led group, called the "Hebrews," continues to pray, heal, and teach in the temple (Acts 2:46; 3:1-4:4; 5:42), though under surveillance from the Jewish authorities. In contrast, the Hellenists are accused of being radical critics of the temple itself, even speaking of its destruction by Jesus who would also change the Mosaic customs (Acts 6:13-14). Stephen, one of the Hellenists, replies to the charge in a speech to the high court, first by reviewing the history of Israel from Abraham to Solomon who built the first temple, and then by quoting Isaiah 66:1 in which God rejects the very idea of human beings building a house for God since God created everything, including God's throne (heaven) and footstool (earth).

Stephen's speech and its aftermath serve as an introduction both to Saul and to the earliest persecution of the church. Together, they imply that Saul's opposition is primarily directed toward the Hellenists who have fled Jerusalem and are taking their message to other cities.

It was bad enough that the Jesus followers disagreed with and acted contrary to Pharisaic concerns about Sabbath, tithing and purity regulations; it was outrageous for them to teach that the temple itself was contrary to God's purposes. While the Essene/Qumran sect was also critical of the temple, their reason was primarily that the contemporary priests and the calendar they used to determine the festival dates were considered illegitimate. They still accepted the temple itself. To spurn the temple implied rejection not only of it but also at least those parts of the Law which established it, its construction, priests, and rituals. Stephen's speech was too far removed from orthodoxy to be tolerated. Any Pharisee would have been outraged by such a critique of the temple. Luke was probably correct in characterizing Saul's response as agreeing with the execution of Stephen (Acts 8:1).

Paul was thoroughly familiar with the purpose, personnel, and operations of the temple. While his writings never refer to its impending destruction as do the Gospels, that event might as well have already happened as far as he was concerned. His story will have no place for it except as part of the past and as a source for metaphors to apply to the present.

Temple and Sacrificial Images in Paul's Writings

Several features of the Jerusalem temple find expression in Paul's letters. First, its inner sanctuary is God's dwelling place on earth. Paul redirects that concept to his communities and individual believers:

> Do you not know that you are God's temple and that God's Spirit dwells in you? (1 Corinthians 3:16, NRSV)

> Or do you not know that your body is a temple of the Holy Spirit within you . . . ? (1 Corinthians 6:19, NRSV)

> For we are the temple of the living God . . . . (2 Corinthians 6:16, NRSV)[127]

The sanctifying Spirit now lives in the hearts of believers and in their common association. That has been made possible by the sacrificial death of Christ. Paul summarizes the thinking behind this transfer of atonement from the temple to Jesus in his letter to the Romans:

> . . . they are now justified by his grace as a gift, through the redemption that is in Christ Jesus, whom God put forward as a sacrifice of atonement by his blood, effective through faith. (Romans 3:24-25a, NRSV)

Paul mixes his metaphors here; "redemption" has no inherent connection with temple sacrifices. It is a common term in the OT where it refers, in general, to making a payment to restore something or someone to the former owner. Both in OT and NT times it also refers to purchasing the freedom of a slave. It is an appropriate metaphor to employ when addressing both Jews and Gentiles, as Paul was doing in this letter. It belongs to what Knox calls the "victory" story of salvation, in which liberation is the major theme.[128]

"Sacrifice of atonement" belongs to the other story identified by Knox. The English phrase is the rendering of a single Greek word (*hilastērion*) which is translated "mercy seat" in the NRSV of Leviticus 16, from which the term is taken. This term literally refers to the cover of the Ark of the Covenant in the holiest room of

---

[127] In all three quotations, "temple" is the translation of Greek *naos, i.e.,* sanctuary or shrine, the inner part (the holiest place) of a temple where the divinity resides. The whole temple precinct is the *hieron*, also translated as "temple."

[128] *The Death of Christ.*

the tabernacle (Exodus 25:21), an arrangement replicated in the temple. The meaning of the underlying Hebrew word is simply "covering"; the verbal form means "to cover over" or "to atone" offenses against God. Paul here identifies Christ as the *hilastērion*, meaning either the place where atonement occurs, or the means of atonement. If the first, then Paul indicates that Jesus is closest to the divine presence (God's throne) and atonement happens in his person. If the latter, then the emphasis is on sacrifice, as the NSRV expresses. It is possible that Paul had both meanings in mind.

The prime NT example of how the imagery of Leviticus 16 was utilized in the interpretation of Jesus' death is found not in Paul's letters but in the Epistle to the Hebrews.[129] Building on the ritual of the Day of Atonement, the author of Hebrews represents the blood of Jesus as the purifying medium of both the inner sanctuary of the heavenly temple and of the earthly people. The author also states that forgiveness of sins requires that blood be shed (9:22b). Jesus is represented as the high priest who takes his own blood into the heavenly temple to purify it, thereby rendering it capable of carrying out its atonement for the sins of the people, or as Hebrews puts it, "cleansing the conscience" (9:14; 10:22).

"Conscience" here translates the Greek *suneidēsis*, which the author understands to be that aspect of a person which needs to be purified. The word could also be rendered as "consciousness," as it is sometimes elsewhere in the NT. "Consciousness" would expand the concept to cover the entire spectrum of awareness, including thoughts and emotions. "Conscience" is limited to that aspect of self-awareness in which one engages in self-evaluation, especially concerning one's moral deeds, and can give one a feeling of either pain or peace. It is this particular focus with which the author of Hebrews is concerned.

---

[129] Paul mentions the *hilastērion* only this one time.

158

Paul seems to agree; he also uses this term primarily in the sense of "conscience."[130] For example, he directs members of his Corinthian congregation to be especially sensitive to the consciences of others who have not yet realized the full implications of Paul's teaching.[131] Behavior must take into account not only one's own conscience, but also those of others. Conscience is where truth and falsity, awareness of guilt and innocence, abide (Romans 9:1). It is located deep within the human core where self-awareness stands on its own, apart from public view. If it is infected by self-accusation, the person can never truly know peace. From Paul's perspective, dealing with sin requires not just purifying the conscience from past misdeeds, but also and even primarily releasing the self from the bondage that sin imposes on it.

The juxtaposition of these two forms of atonement—sacrifice and redemption—should be a reminder that Paul was not attempting to develop a specific theory of atonement. He incorporates and combines metaphors to express in various ways his core conviction that the reconciliation of God and the world was taking place in Christ (1 Corinthians 5:19).

There are numerous other appropriations of temple imagery in Paul's letters, which we can only briefly touch on. For example, while Christ's sacrifice dominated, sacrificial imagery was also employed in regard to believers' renewed lives:

> But even if I am being poured out as a libation over the sacrifice and the offering of your faith, I am glad and rejoice with all of you . . . . (Philippians 2:17, NRSV)

---

[130] For "conscience": Romans 2:15; 9:1; 13:5; 1 Corinthians 1:25-29; 8:7, 10, 12; 2 Corinthians 1:12; for "consciousness": 2 Corinthians 4:2; 5:11.

[131] See 1 Corinthians 8:1-13; 10:25-11:1.

. . . I have received from Epaphroditus the gifts you sent, a fragrant offering, a sacrifice acceptable and pleasing to God. (Philippians 4:18, NRSV)

. . . the grace given to me to be a minister of Christ Jesus to the Gentiles in the priestly service of the gospel of God, so that the offering of the Gentiles may be acceptable, sanctified by the Holy Spirit. (Romans 15:15-16, NRSV) [132]

The first quotation refers to Paul's present imprisonment; he fears it may lead to his death, which he then represents in liturgical terms as a drink offering accompanying the Philippians' offering of their faith to God. The second considers the gifts they had sent him, also envisaged as a temple offering to God. The third portrays Paul as a priest performing a sacred act, in this case proclaiming the gospel as his liturgical commission. A fourth quotation also represents believer's lives in terms of temple sacrifice:

I appeal to you therefore, brothers and sisters, to present your bodies as a living sacrifice, holy and acceptable to God, which is your spiritual worship. Do not be conformed to this world, but be transformed by the renewing of your minds. . . . (Romans 12:1-2, NRSV)

In this brief but densely packed introduction to the following four chapters of moral exhortation, the lives of the believers in Rome are placed in a context of worship of God. Sacrifice is part of that worship, but what is placed on the altar is not something external but the believers themselves. Self-sacrifice is explained as self-transformation.

---

[132] The word translated "minister" is *leitourgos*, used especially of one performing work as a servant of God. The term has various associations, including doing the work at one's own expense. "Priestly service" translates a noun meaning one who performs a holy work.

Sometimes Paul's choice of words, while not directly specifying temple or sacrificial motifs, echoes their presence. For example, his address to the Corinthian church recalls the purification motif:

> . . . to those who are sanctified in Christ Jesus, called to be saints . . . . (1 Corinthians 1:2, NRSV)

Sanctification is the goal of atonement, originally a temple function; those who have successfully undergone cleansing are "saints" (Greek *hagioi*). They have become "holy," i.e., purified so as to be acceptable to God. [133] Paul's congregations are ritually "clean." "Saints" was Paul's usual term for believers; it is found in every one of his letters (17 times) except Galatians. "Sanctified in Christ" indicates that an analogy has been drawn between the atoning power of the temple sin sacrifices and Jesus, focused on his death. For those who accepted the thrust of the metaphor, the atoning role of the temple offering was transferred to Jesus. The corollary is that the temple and its sacrifice for sins were also effectively terminated, even if they were still physically operating.

Acts reports that the followers of Jesus spent much time in the temple (2:46, 3:1-4:4) and that among their converts were "a great many of the priests." (6:7) Perhaps they had some role in drawing connections between Jesus' death and atoning sacrifices.

In transferring the atoning role of the temple to the death of Jesus, the early Christians created an interpretation which was not easily integrated with other interpretations of his life held by his followers. For example, the priestly/sacrificial paradigm did not readily fit the view that Jesus was the Messiah, or that his tribal identity was Judaic, which was associated with kingship but not

---

[133] See also 1 Corinthians 7:14, where children of sanctified (cleansed) parents are considered holy or clean.

priesthood.[134] Nevertheless, the atoning image dominated, as is evident in the Gospels as well as in Paul's letters and the Epistle to the Hebrews.

The Lord's Supper as a Sacrificial Meal

Meals in which meat from a sacrificed animal was consumed were common in both Jewish and Gentile contexts. A potential conflict arose when believers were invited to share in a pagan sacrificial meal, when purchasing meat in the marketplace, or sharing in the distribution of meat by an official. In addressing this concern, Paul draws parallels between both pagan and Jewish meals in which sacrificial meat is consumed, on the one hand, and the Lord's Supper on the other:

> The cup of blessing that we bless, is it not a sharing in the blood of Christ? The bread that we break, is it not a sharing in the body of Christ? . . . Consider the people of Israel; are not those who eat the sacrifices partners in the altar? What do I imply then? That food sacrificed to idols is anything, or that an idol is anything? No, I imply that what pagans sacrifice, they sacrifice to demons and not to God. I do not want you to be partners with demons. You cannot drink the cup of the Lord and the cup of demons. You cannot partake of the table of the Lord and the table of demons. . . . But if someone says to you, "This has been offered in sacrifice, then do not eat it. . . ." (1 Corinthians 10:10:16, 18-21, 28, NRSV)[135]

---

[134] Hebrews solves this problem by finding a connection between Jesus and the priesthood of Melchizedek. (5:6, 10; 7:1-17)

[135] Paul advises that it is permissible to eat meat even though it may have been offered in sacrifice, as long as an observing believer does not know that the meat came from an animal sacrificed in a pagan temple (1 Corinthians 10:27-28). Paul's position is stated in Romans 14:14—"I know and am persuaded in the Lord Jesus

Paul follows other Jewish thinking of his time in identifying pagan deities as "demons."[136] Participation in their ritual meals opens one to the demonic. Likewise, but with opposite consequences, the Lord's Supper is a participation in the death of Jesus in which salvation is found. The two meals are mutually exclusive for believers.

Those who eat the Lord's Supper "proclaim the Lord's death until he comes." (1 Corinthians 11:26, NRSV). The death of Christ is the pivotal event in Paul's story of salvation. It is to be remembered and proclaimed. The cup of wine represents Christ's blood, i.e., his death, and the new era being initiated. Both the Lord's Supper and Baptism point to a participation of believers in Jesus' death (Romans 6:3).

Paul's interpretation goes beyond sacrifice on behalf of others to include them as participants in the sacrifice. That points away from sin sacrifices to those in which meat from the slaughtered animal was eaten. The Lord's Supper is such a ritualistic participation. Paul finds in the practice of eating the Christian sacrificial meal both a proclamation of the death of Christ and a reminder to believers of their call to conform to the image of Christ.

Sacrifice of the Passover Lamb

Up to now Paul's references to Jesus' death have regarded it as a sacrifice for sins, except for the Lord's Supper. The following passage adds another dimension:

---

that nothing is unclean in itself; but it is unclean for anyone who thinks it unclean." (NRSV)

[136] Scriptural warrants for Paul's view are found in Deuteronomy 32:17 and Psalm 106:37. This passage in 1 Corinthians contains Paul's only mention of demons as such, but he clearly believed in supernatural malevolent spirits. His precise understanding of what he thought demons were is not clear, only that they were associated with pagan deities and were antithetical to God.

Your boasting is not a good thing. Do you not know that a little yeast leavens the whole batch of dough? Clean out the old yeast so that you may be a new batch, as you really are unleavened. For our paschal lamb, Christ, has been sacrificed. Therefore, let us celebrate the festival, not with the old yeast, the yeast of malice and evil, but with the unleavened bread of sincerity and truth. (1 Corinthians 5:6-8, NRSV) [137]

The source of the imagery here is the annual Passover Seder and the following Feast of Unleavened Bread. The combined festival celebrates Israel's liberation from slavery in Egypt. It begins with the Passover meal, which requires first killing the lamb which will be consumed at the meal. The Feast of Unleavened Bread then continues for an additional seven days.

Two aspects of this passage are of special interest. First, Paul draws an analogy between his readers and the leaven which is removed from the home before the festival. Yeast here is a negative image,[138] signifying his readers' former way of life which has not sufficiently been cleaned out. In particular, the old leaven is their egocentric "boasting," their practice of elevating their own self-image rather than directing their praise to God. The singular characteristic of leaven is its effect on the dough; it spreads through the whole loaf. The Corinthians had not dealt with the issue of *porneia* (sexual immorality) in their midst (5:1-5, 9-13), yet were self-congratulatory about their spiritual achievements.

---

[137]The Greek word translated as "sacrifice" in this passage can also mean simply to "slaughter" or to "kill."

[138] Contrast the Gospel parable in which the kingdom of heaven is likened to yeast (Matthew 13:33; see also Luke 13:20-21). However, Luke, Matthew and Mark also use yeast in a negative way, comparing yeast to the hypocrisy of the Pharisees (Luke 12:1), to the Pharisees and Sadducees (Matthew 16:6, 11), and to the Pharisees and Herod (Mark 8:15).

Second, in the midst of the yeast analogy Paul introduces the part of the festival concerning the Passover lamb. Jesus' death had occurred at the time of Passover. The synoptic Gospels (Mark, Matthew, Luke)[139] seem to place it on the day itself, though that is not certain, while the Fourth Gospel clearly locates it on the preceding day when the Passover lambs were being slaughtered in preparation for the dinner. Paul picks up on the theme of Jesus as "our Passover lamb" which has been killed or sacrificed.

Several associations can be noted. First, the lamb is not a sin sacrifice,[140] but part of the festival celebrating release from slavery to become the people of God. Second, there is perhaps an allusion here to the time when the letter was being written: "Let us celebrate the festival...." (1 Corinthians 5:8). Third, there is a parallel between celebrating Passover and sharing in the Lord's Supper. As the lamb is eaten at the Passover meal, so the body and blood representing the death of Christ are symbolically consumed, in the forms of bread and wine, at the Lord's Supper. Paul's use of Passover imagery points to the story of freedom from slavery to sin, not to the story of Jesus' death as a sacrifice for sins.[141]

In the same letter Paul argues that temple practices are a model for a common Christian practice. Since temple staff receive their food from the temple resources, evangelists also are to be supported by those who are recipients of the gospel, as Jesus had ordered. (1 Corinthians 9:13-14). Paul goes on to explain why he chose not to

---

[139] The three synoptic Gospels have been given this designation from the fact that they can be placed side by side and "seen together." Such a procedure enables their many similarities as well as differences to be observed and studied.

[140] Elaborate offerings were required on the day of Passover, but they were separate from the slaughter of the Passover lambs (Numbers 28:16-25; Leviticus 23:5-8). Further, in the biblical story the blood of the lamb was not to be smeared on any sacred object in the Temple or poured out at the base of the altar, but to be put on the doorposts and lintels of the people's houses (Exodus 12:7).

[141] It is the author of the Fourth Gospel, not Paul, who employs the image of Jesus as the Passover lamb who removes sin (John 1:29).

avail himself of that opportunity, namely, to make the gospel free of charge to them. The means by which the gospel of freedom comes should be consistent with the gospel itself, seen as the gift of God. Perhaps there is also a hint that the Corinthians should already have recognized his sacrifice.

Sacrificial practice contained many resources for interpreting the death of Jesus and the life of the community of his followers. Paul did not invent the sacrificial interpretation of Jesus' suffering and death, but he embraced it and applied it also to believers as part of their partnership with Christ. For Paul, atonement had happened and was happening; peace with God was being restored, not from anything emanating from the human side but solely from God's side as revealed in the death of Jesus.

Verbal Forgiveness of Sins

While Paul avoids drawing on forgiveness terminology in his salvation story, other early Christian writers did not. Forgiveness of sins is traced in the Gospels to the ministry of John the Baptist, who proclaimed "a baptism of repentance for the forgiveness of sins." (Mark 1:4, NRSV) This ritual had no direct connection to the temple since it took place elsewhere. While Luke's Gospel claims that both of John's parents were of priestly families (1:5), it does not suggest that he was officially authorized to forgive sins. The practice of John's purifying by water is similar to priestly preparation for temple duties. His baptisms could also be associated with the mikveh in common use at this time for certain types of water purification in places other than the temple. [142] Some scholars have also suggested an association of John's baptism with the washing ritual required of all proselytes,

---

[142] Mikvehs (ritual baths) first appeared in the first century BCE. They were often attached to synagogue buildings but were also constructed elsewhere, such as in Herod's palace and at Masada.

male and female. While it is reasonable to assume that John may have created a liturgical formula to pronounce the remission of sins at the time of baptism, the Gospels do not suggest that he used such a formulation. Jesus, on the other hand, was criticized as usurping God's prerogative by pronouncing forgiveness,[143] an "authority" given to him as the Son of Man.

The Lord's Prayer in both its Matthean (6:12) and Lucan (11:4) forms contains a petition for God's forgiveness with no suggestion of an intermediary. Only the Fourth Gospel asserts that the power to forgive sins was passed on to his immediate followers, a result of their having received the Holy Spirit (John 20:22-23). Otherwise, it was only announced that forgiveness came through Christ. Nothing similar to any of this is found in Paul's letters.

Deliverance from Slavery to Sin

We noted above that the Passover story is about liberation from slavery. Like Martin Luther King Jr. nearly two millennia later, Paul considered "freedom" a key concept in his proclamation of Christ to the world of the Gentiles. But unlike King who dreamed of the day in the future when "we will be free," Paul saw freedom as a present reality, though in a personal rather than a political sense. As part of his story, he proclaimed that Christ had liberated believers from slavery to the oppressive regime of sin to be "slaves of righteousness" (Romans 6:18, NRSV).

This passage points up another of Paul's convictions—there is no such thing as absolute freedom. One becomes free from one thing by becoming devoted to another. The counterpart in the Gospels is that one cannot be an authentic slave of two masters at the same time (Matthew 6:24; Luke 16:13). The only question is,

---

[143] Mark 2:5-10; Matthew 9:2-6; Luke 5:20-24; 7:47-49. Jesus' disciples, but not Jesus himself, are represented as forgiving sins in John 20:23. Paul encourages his converts to forgive others (2 Corinthians 2:5- 10), but he never mentions divine forgiveness through or from Christ.

who is the master you obey? Given the degree to which human slavery was practiced in the Roman Empire, it is not surprising that Paul frequently alludes to it, both literally[144] and figuratively.[145] Slaves were found at all levels of society, from those who performed manual labor in the mines and fields to those who held important positions in the government and economy of the state.

Two other factors of slavery in that time provided Paul with significant images for his story. First, a slave was a commodity; he/she could be sold to another owner. The new master then had full authority over the slave who was bound to adjust himself or herself to the will and desires of the new owner. Second, through the practice of manumission slaves could attain the status of a freed person, often through a financial payment. The technical Greek term for the price paid in that transaction is *lytron*. The same term is used for ransoming prisoners, perhaps taken in war or by kidnappers. The basic meaning in all cases is an action which brings freedom to someone. It was a natural image to apply to Jesus' death by those who saw in it liberation from sin. It evokes the same theme as the exodus from slavery in Egypt.

Those who interpret this term sometimes push the ransom image beyond its intended range and impute other meanings to it. For example, to ask about the identity of the recipient of the ransom misses the point. The NT *lytron* is not paid to anyone; it is an image of being freed, not an actual payment in a financial transaction. Nowhere in his letters does Paul suggest that the manumission or ransom image is anything more than a metaphor of liberation.

Unfortunately, for nearly a millennium, a particular theory of the atonement has grown in popularity until today it is commonly accepted in many circles as the standard model of Jesus' sac-

---

[144] 1 Corinthians 7:21-23; 12:13; Galatians 3:28; 4:1; Philemon 16.

[145] Romans 1:1; 6:16-18; 1 Corinthians 9:19; 2 Corinthians 4:5; Galatians 1:10; 4:9; Philippians 1:1; 2:7.

168

rificial death. The fundamental idea is that Jesus died not just for, but in place of human beings. This interpretation was developed by Archbishop Anselm of Canterbury (ca. 1033-1109 CE) in his writing, *Cur Deus Homo* ("Why the God Man"). Anselm was an early proponent of the scholastic method which sought to explain theological doctrines through definition and inference, rather than through analysis and interpretation of biblical texts. His goal in this instance was to demonstrate the truth of the doctrine of the two natures of Christ and its role in Christ's atonement of the sins of humankind.

Reduced to its essentials, Anselm's argument assumes that human sin is a debt owed to God, but incapable of being paid by sinners since nothing they could offer would be enough. The payment therefore must be supplied by God. On the other hand, it must be delivered by a human as payment for human sin. Therefore, the debt can only by paid by one who is both God and man, who stands in for all human beings and satisfies God by paying off their debt to God.

This interpretation of Jesus' sacrificial death is far removed from anything found in Paul's thought. For him, sin is not a debt but an enslaving or addicting power from which humanity is liberated, or which is defeated, by Christ. The theory of substitutionary atonement substitutes Paul's concept of participation of believers in the death and resurrection of Christ for an external quasi-commercial transaction completely foreign to Paul. It ignores the place in Paul's story of God's freedom and grace, making God subject to another force, namely, necessity. Substitutionary atonement is a medieval theological construct, not a biblical category or concept.[146]

---

[146] The theory of substitutionary atonement is also not supported by Gospel passages often employed to demonstrate it, such as Mark 10:45 (parallel in Matthew 20:28) where the Son of Man is identified as a "ransom." When interpreters lose appreciation of biblical imagery as metaphor, analogy, simile, parable, and other literary expressions of imagination, the fundamental meanings of the NT are easily

Belonging to the same root as *lytron* is the Greek word *apoly-trōsis* (redemption). Both words are metaphors of the liberating act or the state of having been freed. Redemption of slaves or hostages was a natural image of liberation from someone or something that exercises power over the captive.

Paul finds the master/slave image a versatile metaphor. It can point to the power of sin over human beings (Romans 6:16-19a), the believer's relationship to righteousness (Romans 6:19b), or the apostles' relationship to Christ (Romans 1:1; Galatians 1:10; Philippians 1:1). Paul also employs it in regard to the believer's relationship to the Law. When Paul addresses Gentile Christians who were considering becoming proselytes to a non-Pauline form of Christianity, following the commandments especially regarding circumcision and dietary laws, he turns to the biblical passages about Abraham having two children, one by a slave woman (Genesis 16:21) and one by Sarah, a free woman (Genesis 21:2). Believers are descendants of the free woman by the act of Christ, and therefore are urged not to become slaves of the Law (Galatians 4:21-5:1).

The dual image of slave/free is applicable inasmuch as Paul's gospel to the Gentiles has no legal strings attached; that is, Gentile believers are already children of Abraham by virtue of their faith. Nothing further is required, despite the insistence of those who have arrived in Galatia with a different gospel. Their teaching, Paul maintains, is a new and illegitimate slavery, and attempts to bring his converts under the Law, denying them their freedom. Christ would thereby also be brought into subjection to the Law, rather than being the inaugural figure of a new covenant of freedom.

In another context, Paul makes a similar point concerning bondage and freedom: marriage law is applicable only until the death of one of the partners. The death of the husband frees the woman to marry again, without being considered an adulteress

---

distorted. When the metaphorical becomes literal, the larger meaning is in danger of disappearing.

(Romans 7:2-3). The common factor in both slavery and marriage is the bond between two parties and the possibility of the exchange of that bond for a new one. This passage leads into Paul's most extended analysis of human bondage to sin—and liberation from it. He proceeds to probe the despondency of the person who has become aware of his/her bondage, but is powerless to break the chains. Three parties are involved: the Law; Paul speaking as a representative of those who obey the Law; and sin:

> What then should we say? That the law is sin? By no means! Yet, if it had not been for the law, I would not have known sin. I would not have known what it is to covet if the law had not said, "You shall not covet." But sin, seizing opportunity in the commandment, produced in me all kinds of covetousness. Apart from the law sin lies dead. . . . the very commandment that promised life proved to be death to me. For sin, seizing an opportunity in the commandment, deceived me and through it killed me. So the law is holy, and the commandment is holy and just and good.
> Did what is good, then, bring death to me? By no means! It was sin, working death in me through what is good . . . . (Romans 7:7-8, 10-13, NRSV)

As in other aspects of human experience, the Law has been hijacked by sin and used for its own purposes, thereby allowing the opposite of the good to triumph. Law itself is a positive phenomenon, but sin dwelling in human beings manages to skirt around the Law's intent and bring not life but death from the human/Law relationship. The inner purpose of the commandments is to guide humanity into mutually beneficial relations, which Paul identifies as love (Romans 13:9), but sin subverts that purpose and exercises dominion over the observer of the Law. Surreptitiously and anonymously, sin disguises itself in a legal costume to achieve its deadly purpose. The result is a divided self who knows and wills the right thing to do, but lacks the power to do it. Paul concludes with a cry of desperation and an exclamation of thanksgiving:

Wretched man that I am! Who will rescue me from this body of death? Thanks be to God through Jesus Christ our Lord! (Romans 7:24-25, NRSV)

Paul has addressed this treatment of sin and the Law to the Jewish Christians at Rome (7:1), but his words apply also to Gentile Christians. Any social convention, any law or moral code, any attempt to regulate can be corrupted in the absence of love. He puts his analysis into the context of the Jewish Law because that was his own personal experience as an observant Jew. His dedication to the Law had led him into persecuting "the church of God." Sin had used his obedience to the Law to deflect him into a path of disobedience of God.

Paul's analysis is closely related to his conviction that all humanity has been infected by the sin virus. Jews by virtue of possessing the Law of God were not immune. Regardless of their ethnic background, all his auditors were expected to accept his logic.

Paul now continues to his main point, which is the antithesis of enslavement to law and sin, i.e., liberation from both:

For the law of the Spirit of life in Christ Jesus has set you free from the law of sin and of death. (Romans 8:2, NRSV)

How is this liberation achieved? While Paul employs numerous images to describe the process, all are based on the foundation of Christ crucified and resurrected. Paul found in that fundamental affirmation of the earliest followers of Jesus the resolution of human slavery to sin and death. While sacrificial and liberation imagery provided two important semantic fields from which to draw for his story of salvation, there was a third which was equally as significant for Paul, perhaps even more so.

Christic as the Second Adam

A s the decisive player in God's drama of salvation given the huge task of rectifying a world gone bad, Christ has a complex role to fulfill. How is he to be scripted? He cannot be simply another human being under the dominion of sin, else how could he save sinners? On the other hand, he needs to be part of humankind with whom other human beings can identify and whose pattern they can imitate. Therefore, he has a unique task, at once representing both the human and the more than human domains.[147] In this capacity Jesus embodies and teaches the divine qualities, and dies an atoning death to purge the sin clinging to humanity. Paul's commission to proclaim this among the Gentiles required a credible model with which his hearers could identify.

Paul's inheritance from his predecessors in the Jesus movement included the interpretation of Jesus' death as a sacrifice of atonement releasing humankind from the effects of their sins. This may have been his starting point in his mission to the Gentiles, but it was not completely satisfactory for his needs. So he turned to an alternative concept, the notion of a primal human which was understandable to anyone, regardless of culture. Further, Adam could readily be portrayed not just as an archetype of humanity per se, but specifically as humankind addicted to sin. Finally, Adam provided Paul with a biblical figure with whom he could contrast Christ as the archetype of the new humanity now being manifested. The pair summarizes the entire range of the human condition, its actual sin and its potential righteousness.

Paul is the only NT writer to develop an interpretation of Christ as an antitype[148] of the original Adam. In early chapters, we

---

[147] This dual identify motif is seen also in the prologue to the Gospel According to John (especially 1:1-14) and in Hebrews 2:9, 14.

[148] Paul does not use the word "antitype" but "type." However, it is clear that his understanding of the relation between Adam and Christ is accurately described by

traced the progression of Paul's story from Adam's introduction of sin and death, to Abraham as a model of faith, on to Moses the lawgiver, and finally to Christ, the one who renews, who re-creates. Paul has a special interest in the first and the last characters. They fit neatly into the dualistic model he favours; there is a right way and a wrong way to be a human being with no compromise between the self-centered disobedience of Adam and the self-giving sacrificial love of Christ. Therefore, the first Adam can now be presented as a foil to the second Adam. Paul's employment of typological and imitative concepts is integral to his focus on the two representatives of humankind.

Since all people are under the power of sin, Adam was a logical choice as an archetype of sin-addicted humanity in Paul's story. At the other end of the scale, Paul sees Christ also as an archetype, but of humanity reconciled to God. Therefore, Paul can refer to Jesus as the "last Adam" or the last Man (1 Corinthians 15:45). Together the first and last Adams provide Paul with a powerful set of images enabling him to reduce to their essentials the complexities of what is wrong with humankind and what it is like in its righted condition. Adam set in motion a movement which has been followed ever since—until a new Adam comes to reverse it. The first symbolizes sin and death, the second their opposite, righteousness and life.

The Adam/Christ model is explicitly expressed in two of Paul's letters written around the middle of the 50s CE:

> But in fact Christ has been raised from the dead, the first fruits of those who have died. For since death came through

---

the term "antitype." Literally, the Greek *typos* is the mark or impression left by pressing one object on another, like a seal on wax. An antitype would be the impression on the wax as compared with the seal; they are opposites of each other while mutually conforming. By extension typos can mean "example" (1 Thessalonians 1:7; 1 Corinthians 10:6; Philippians 3:17), or "pattern" or "form" (Romans 6:17). Only in Romans 5:14 does Paul use *typos* in the sense of an antitype.

a human being, the resurrection of the dead has also come through a human being; for as all die in Adam, so all will be made alive in Christ. (1 Corinthians 15:20-22, NRSV)

Thus it is written, "The first man, Adam, became a living being"; the last Adam became a life-giving spirit. . . . The first man was from the earth, a man of dust; the second man is from heaven. As was the man of dust, so are those who are of the dust; and as is the man of heaven, so are those who are of heaven. Just as we have borne the image of the man of dust, we will also bear the image of the man of heaven. (1 Corinthians 15:45, 47-49, NRSV)

Therefore, just as sin came into the world through one man, and death came through sin, and so death spread to all because all have sinned. . . . Adam, who is a type of the one who was to come. . . . If, because of the one man's trespass, death exercised dominion through that one, much more surely will those who receive the abundance of grace and the free gift of righteousness exercise dominion in life through the one man, Jesus Christ.

Therefore just as one man's trespass led to condemnation for all, so one man's act of righteousness leads to justification and life for all. (Romans 5:12, 14b, 17-18, NRSV)

Paul here moves beyond his portrayal of Adam's role in Act One. The representative of wayward humanity whose deed led to separation from God and to death now prefigures the representative of a righteous people inheriting life with God. Adam and Christ each stand for a collective; first, of those who live and die with Adam as their forerunner; and second, of those who are given life in the new creation.

The Adam/Christ typology with its similarities and opposites provides Paul with the nutshell into which his story is neatly condensed. It allows him to move easily into his key motifs—the universality of sin; its consequences, especially death but also the enslavement of sinners by their sin; the gift of being made right through Christ's righteous act (i.e., his submission to an atoning and liberating death); the universal scope of that gift for all people; resurrection and life in the new order; the conception of the community of believers as the body of Christ; and the nature of righteousness itself. Righteousness is what is missing in Adam and his descendants, those who are dominated by sin. "Rightness" is restored to those who are liberated from their Adamic existence and share in Christ's restored life. This is the intended healthy state of humanity.

Regarding the meaning of righteousness, confusion may result by the English language's lack of a verbal equivalent of the Greek word used by Paul. The verb (*dikaioō*) is translated with the English "to justify" or "to show or do justice," the noun (*dikaiosyne*) as "righteousness,"[149] and the adjective (*dikaios*) as "just" or "righteous." Many contemporary scholars prefer to translate the verb as "make right" or "rectify" instead of "justify," which leans toward a forensic set of meanings. The quotation above from Romans 5:18, "one man's act of righteousness leads to justification and life for all," does not inform the reader that "righteousness" and "justification" are both based on the same Greek root *dikai-*. Righteousness in Paul's thought is not only what is required of human beings, but it is also a gift of God bringing freedom from sin's power. Righteousness means correctness, alignment with original intention or purpose, living in a life-affirming and mature, even perfected, way.

Unfortunately, the terms "righteousness," and even more so "justification," have lost much of their basic meaning for our con-

---

[149] Two other nouns based on the same root carry similar meanings, i.e., *dikaiōma* (Romans 5:16) and *dikaiōsis (Romans 4:25)*. Both are translated "justification" in the NRSV.

temporary world and it is difficult for us to connect with Paul on this point. Considering the massive and constant bombardment of commercial and other cultural claims implicitly carrying a message of the "right" way to live, it is small wonder that Paul's understanding of righteousness has largely faded from view today. Yet Paul would say that it is what we all seek, even though its articulation may be rarely found.

Christ and the Law

Paul's conviction that all people are included in God's drama of bringing the abundant life through Christ leads him into conflict with other Jewish Christians for whom the Law is still a necessary, even the main, player.[150] Paul points to Abraham's faith as the model to be imitated since God "reckoned it to him as righteousness" (Genesis 15:6, NRSV), i.e., God enabled an authentic life for Abraham. Gentile righteousness depends on the same faith that Abraham exhibited. The Law is superfluous once faith and righteousness have become determinative.

That raises the question, why then did God give the Law? Paul's answer is that the Law was a temporary guardian and disciplinarian of Israel from the time of Moses until the time of Christ (Galatians 3:23-26). With the revealing of Christ and faith, Israel is moving into the freedom that accompanies coming of age.

While Paul is convinced that the time of the Law is now past, he still defends the right of Jewish believers in Christ to observe the Law. For example, he cautions Gentile believers not to despise the Jewish members of the churches for keeping the food laws. His most extensive treatment of this topic is found in Romans 9-11, to be considered later. For now it is sufficient to note that Gentiles should not think they need to become Jews to share in the blessing

---

[150] For them the Law was eternal; for Paul it was intended only for a certain period of time, from Moses to Christ.

of Abraham, i.e., in Christ. For Jew and Gentile, male and female, slave and free, civilized and barbarian, and everyone else, faith is the route provided by God to salvation. The only issue for anyone is finding and traveling that path. Faith is trust that Jesus was God's chosen one to usher in the kingdom of God; faith enables the inner transformation of the self into the image of Christ, the second Adam. Since the intent of the Law is thus attained in Christ, the Law is no longer needed.

Some scholars have argued that the preceding paragraph would be an erroneous reading of Paul. Rather, Paul believed that while faith in Christ was the path for the Gentiles, for the Jews the Law was still valid. This is not the place to muster objections to that position, but for me there are too many passages in Paul's letters that argue against it. The notion that Paul accepted two paths to God, one of faith, and one of obedience to the Torah, goes contrary to fundamental elements of his story.

Messiah, Son of God, Lord, Savior

We turn now to a brief consideration of various titles assigned to Jesus. Paul applies all four of the above terms to Jesus. He can use any and all of them, especially the first three, as alternatives to the name "Jesus," and particularly *Christos*, the Greek translation of Messiah, which he often combines with Jesus, either as Jesus Christ or as Christ Jesus. *Christos* is also often found in Paul's writings combined with "Lord," e.g., as "Jesus Christ our Lord." Commentators have often noted that in Paul's writings Christ has become another name for Jesus.

Messiah

As the one anointed by God for the specific purpose outlined in Act Four, the Christian Messiah has come a long way from the Jewish Messiah, so far that it no longer bears the same meaning apart from the saving function evident in both. The term Messiah or Christ would have little religious significance in a non-Jewish context unfamiliar with the anointing tradition in which objects and persons set apart for God's purposes were anointed with holy oil. Although Paul knows the tradition that Jesus was a descendant of David, which placed Jesus in the right lineage to be the Messiah, that formulation is quoted only once (Romans 1:3) and was not part of Paul's own normal representation of Jesus.[151]

The Davidic Messiah also had too many political/military and territorial associations to be of much use in Paul's story. It was also a risky term to use, given Roman wariness of potential insurrection. Paul never applies the term "king" to Jesus, nor suggests any association between that word and "Christ." Further, while he employs the word "Christ" nearly 270 times in his seven authentic letters, not once does he writes that Jesus is the Christ or Messiah, in contrast to all four Gospels. His field of meaning is far removed from the Jewish Messiah. It appears that his employment of the latter term is largely due to the fact that it was already widely used among the followers of Jesus. For Paul, the title had morphed into a name.

Son of God

The title "Son of God" is immeasurably more important for Paul, although he employs it far fewer times than "Christ."[152] Paul's mission began when he came to "know" God's Son, not that he came to believe that Jesus was the Messiah. "Son of God" had numerous nuances in Paul's time, in the Greco-Roman world as well as the Jewish, which we do not need to pursue. Paul's use of

---

[151] Paul immediately follows in Romans 1:4 with the appointment of Jesus as the Son of God, rather than as the Messiah. Both formulations are used in this letter written to congregations containing both Jewish and Gentile believers.

[152] Paul applies "Son of God" to Jesus about 15 times, and identifies those in Christ as sons (and daughters) of God about five times.

the term leaves many questions about his meaning, especially if it is assumed that he meant it in any literal sense. Suffice it to say that "Son of God" emphasizes the uniqueness of Jesus, his close relationship to God, his teaching as authentically the "word of God," his submission to the will of God, and his human character in the sense that he is the ideal human being, most closely fulfilling creation of humankind in the "image of God." (Genesis 1:27, NRSV) It should be noted that the identification of Jesus as "Son of God" predated Paul's use of it.

Some scholars believe that by calling Jesus the Son of God, Paul and other believers were implicitly challenging the authority of the emperor, who was also known by the same title. Co-opting an imperial self-designation by believers certainly would prioritize the Christian path over Caesar's. But of course the application of "Son of God" to Jesus did not imply that the early Christians were suggesting direct political or military action which was both beyond their capacity and contrary to their beliefs.

Further, it is not necessary to move outside the Jewish context to discover sources drawn upon by the early Christians for their application of "Son of God" to Jesus. We have noted earlier the important role of the scriptures in the formulation of the Christian gospel.[153] Two such passages utilized by the Jesus followers contain explicit father/son terminology:[154]

---

[153] Luke 24:27 traces the practice of looking to scripture for understanding Jesus, especially his identity and role in God's plan of salvation, to the resurrected Jesus himself: "Then beginning with Moses and all the prophets, he interpreted to them the things about himself in all the scriptures." (NRSV) Paul's carefully worded introduction to his letter to the believers in Rome also points to the gospel being rooted in the scriptures (Romans 1:1-4). Other examples: Romans 11:2-10; 15:4; 1 Corinthians 15:3-4; Galatians 3:8.

[154] These and similar texts are identified by scholars as royal sonship or enthronement passages; i.e., they envisage a king being enthroned and designated a "son of God," a notion connected with kingship throughout the Near East going back a couple of millennia before the origins of Christianity. About ten of the Psalms are considered "enthronement" or "royal" psalms.

I will tell of the decree of the Lord: He said to me, "you are my son; today I have begotten you." (Psalm 2:7, NRSV)

. . . I will raise up your offspring after you, who shall come forth from your body, and I will establish his kingdom. He shall build a house for my name, and I will establish the throne of his kingdom forever. I will be a father to him and he shall be a son to me." (2 Samuel 7:12b-14, NRSV)

These texts were combined with other biblical passages and with traditions about Jesus[155] to suggest a larger story of a divine figure carrying out God's mission to save the world, including the elevation of the chosen one to rule the world, and even to naming him "God." The following two poetic passages may have been instrumental in this process; the first is one of the "royal psalms":

The Lord says to my Lord, "Sit at my right hand until I make your enemies your footstool." (Psalm 110:1, NRSV)

Your throne, O God, endures forever and ever. . . . therefore God, your God, has anointed you with the oil of gladness beyond your companions. (Psalm 45:6a, 7b, NRSV) [156]

The understanding which emerged from combining such biblical passages is observed in capsule form in the opening of Paul's

---

[155] Jesus' use of *Abba* (Father) when addressing God (as in the Lords' Prayer—Matthew 6:9; Luke 11:2) perhaps also played a role in Jesus' being identified as Son of God. See Galatians 4:6. Much nonsense has been written about Abba meaning "Daddy" (and one continues to hear it from the pulpit!). Joachim Jeremias who admitted he once believed it, later dismissed it, partially on the grounds that Abba was used, not only by children, but also by adult sons, of their fathers. (*The Prayers of Jesus*, 1967)

[156] The Epistle to the Hebrews contains numerous passages of this sort.

letter to the churches in Rome where he introduces his gospel to churches he had not founded:

> . . . the gospel concerning his Son, who was descended from David according to the flesh and declared to be Son of God with power according to the spirit of holiness by resurrection from the dead, Jesus Christ our Lord. . . . (Romans 1:3-4, NRSV)[157]

Note that Jesus' installation as the Son of God is here associated with his resurrection. The Gospels will move that moment back into and even prior to his lifetime. Mark, followed by Matthew and Luke, identifies Jesus as the Son of God at his baptism by the voice from heaven (1:11), and again at the transfiguration (9:7), and by the Roman centurion at the crucifixion (15:39). Matthew and Luke follow this pattern, although Luke changes the words of the centurion to indicate Jesus' innocence or righteousness rather than his identity as the Son of God.. However, both Matthew and Luke's Gospels also begin with birth stories indicating that already at Jesus' birth he was God's Son. The prologue to the Fourth Gospel portrays Jesus as the incarnate Word of God; Jesus announces his own identity as the Son of God throughout this Gospel. Paul preserves for us an early version of this process and emphasizes that this title is fundamental in understanding Jesus' identity and role in the gospel. The Son of God term is in particular linked to his authoritative role in the divine plan of salvation.

Lord

"Lord" (Greek *kyrios*) had a variety of meanings attached to it. Apart from its common meaning as "owner" or "master," it was

---

[157] This is commonly regarded as an earlier confessional formulation, known, but not created, by Paul.

applied to the emperor as the lord, as well as to cultic gods (feminine form is *kyria*). In the Greco-Roman world, as Paul says, there was a multiplicity of lords:

> Indeed, even though there may be so-called gods in heaven or on earth—as in fact there are many gods and many lords—yet for us there is one God, the Father, from whom are all things and for whom we exist, and one Lord, Jesus Christ, through whom are all things and through whom we exist. (1 Corinthians 8:5-6, NRSV)

Paul recognizes that these "gods" and "lords" do exist in the sense that people worship them, thereby giving them a sort of existence. But he also believes they represent demonic powers enslaving those who worship them. Paul's antidote to belief in them is the affirmation he shares with the readers: there is one God, the Father, and one Lord, Jesus Christ. This confessional formula is a Christian modification of the Jewish prayer known as the Shema, which begins:

> Hear, O Israel: The Lord is our God, the Lord alone. (Deuteronomy 6:4, NRSV)

Confession in the one God who is the Lord (YHWH)[158] has been changed in the Christian version to create two figures: God and the Lord (Jesus). God is the Father who has given to the Lord

---

[158] These four letters (YHWH) represent the Hebrew consonants making up the name of the Hebrew God (see Exodus 3:14). Since God's name was not to be spoken, the title Adonai ("My Lord," "the Lord," or "Lord") was substituted when the biblical passages containing the divine name were read aloud. In the medieval period vowel signs were added to the Hebrew scriptures. To indicate that "Lord" was to be read instead of God's name, vowel signs for the substitute Adonai accompanied the four consonants of God's name, YHWH. Being unaware of this shorthand and its significance, Christian translators read the vowels as applicable to those particular consonants and created a new name, "Jehovah."

certain functions, including being the agent of creation as well as redemption.[159] Generally speaking, Paul no longer uses "Lord" for God except in biblical quotations or references. Jesus is now the Lord for Paul,[160] as the one to whom total loyalty and devotion are to be given since he is God's envoy to the world. Paul often states his own relationship to Christ in terms of owner (Greek *kyrios*) and slave (*doulos*) or servant (*diakonos*).[161] Paul is in the service of his master, which means his will is not his own (Galatians 2:20). This transforms the master/slave relationship into something different. The master is now embedded in the heart of the slave, reminiscent of the law written on the heart (Jeremiah 31:31).

Though not one of the titles applied to Jesus, the multifaceted Spirit is perhaps the most important term in Paul's vocabulary. His and his followers' experience of God and of Christ was mediated by the Spirit. Paul apparently saw no distinction between the Spirit of God and the Spirit of Christ. The Spirit mediated God to the community; the community was the temple in which the Spirit of God resided. Its presence was known in its gifts, not only the ecstatic kinds, but also the goodness portrayed in the lives of believers. The Spirit was the divine energy which transformed believers, remaking them into what they were intended to be: kind, non-judgmental, accepting; in a word, loving and open to the gospel of God. Paul sees the activity of the Spirit not only in his churches where divisions have been broken down, but also in scripture which foreshadows present events and gives resources for interpreting them. Spirit is the most powerful term available to Paul for integrating all the elements of his vision of an emerging new creation.

---

[159] This dual function is clearly expressed in John 1:1-14.

[160] Paul applies this title to Jesus upwards of 175 times, next only to "Christ" in frequency of usage of the four terms we are considering.

[161] See p. 257, footnote 259.

Savior

It is questionable whether the fourth term, "Savior," should even be included in this list since it is found only once in all of Paul's letters:

> But our citizenship is in heaven, and it is from there that we are expecting a savior, the Lord Jesus Christ. (Philippians 3:20, NRSV)

Since "savior" (sōtēr), "salvation" (sōtēria), and "save" (sōzō) are all derived from the same root, and Paul uses the latter two frequently to indicate the saving activity of God in Christ, it is a bit surprising not to find the first term more frequently in his letters. Paul was also surely aware that the name of Jesus was derived from a root meaning "to save" or "to help." Yet he employs "savior" only this one time, and that in reference to the return of Christ.

The term was widely used in his time: it was applied to God in the scriptures, to exceptional human beings who benefitted humankind, to the emperor, and to various divinities. Perhaps it was Paul's conception of the process of present transformation that made the term "savior" problematic to him. Perhaps he understood that the word might imply that salvation came through an external process in which nothing was required of those who are saved. Paul taught otherwise. Imitation of or identification with Christ was an essential part of the saving process. Salvation depended on a special kind of savior, whose transforming Spirit was poured into hearts, empowering recipients to bring about their own salvation (Philippians 2:12, NRSV). Those susceptible to drowning in the turbulent waters of life needed to be taught by an expert how to swim.

Finally, there is a title frequently found in the synoptic Gospels where it is placed only on the lips of Jesus, namely, "the Son of Man." While this term originally meant "humankind" or a "man," in Daniel 7:13-14 it is applied to a heavenly figure ("one like a son of man") who is given an eternal kingdom including "all peoples, nations, and languages." (NRSV) This personage, identified in Daniel as Israel (7:18, 27), is taken up by the non-canonical 1 Enoch and 4 Ezra (in the Apocrypha) as a messianic figure.[162] All four Gospels employ the term in sayings or speeches of Jesus. Otherwise, it is spoken only by Stephen who, at his martyrdom, sees "the Son of Man standing at the right hand of God." (Acts 7:56, NRSV) Somewhat surprisingly, this term has no overt place in Paul's story; he never mentions it. The Hebrew *ben Adham* and Aramaic *bar enash* (translated "son of man") are literally, "son of Adam." Adam and *anthropos* have their distinctive roles in Paul's thought which precludes them being used in another sense. If Paul had wanted to develop the child of Adam theme, he probably would have connected it to all those who live as Adam did.[163] The only Son of interest to Paul was the Son of God.

Summary

In summary, it may be helpful to distinguish three scenes in the final act of Paul's dramatic story. First, Paul's focus on the death of Jesus is evident throughout his letters, which partly explains the comparatively little attention given to Jesus' teachings. While his words are authoritative for Paul regarding specific issues, Jesus' death is effective on the grand scale by dealing with the all-encompassing human departure from obedience to God. Interpreted through Isaiah 53 in particular, Jesus' sufferings and death have an atoning effect on others. Such cleansing of the self is necessary

---

[162] One of the Dead Sea Scrolls, 4Q246, apparently refers to this heavenly figure in Daniel: "His kingdom will be an everlasting kingdom....He will judge the Earth in truth and will make peace." This manuscript, dated to the first century BCE, also calls him both Son of God and Son of the Most High.

[163] Note that Luke's genealogy of Jesus (3:23-38) goes all the way back to "Adam son of God."

for Christ's Spirit to abide there, on the model of God's earthly presence in the Jerusalem temple. Baptism and the Lord's Supper ritualize atonement for converts and their appropriation of it. They are baptized into Christ's death, and in sharing the sacred meal they announce the Lord's death (1 Corinthians 11:26).

Jesus' death is also conceived as liberation from the power of sin. The classic model is the exodus from slavery in Egypt, but Paul also draws on the contemporary practice of transferring ownership of slaves and of manumission, in which their freedom is purchased.

Finally, Christ's self-giving obedient death is the antitype of Adam's disobedience. Motivated by self-serving desire for life, Adam achieved its unintended opposite, alienation and death. The second Adam's faithfulness initiates a new start for creation.

The second scene of this act portrays what is now in process. The focus here is on the positive human response to Christ, being changed into his image, imitating him, learning and practicing the many ways in which the love he revealed is to be implemented. This can happen only in community, for that is where human relationships occur. The community is the home base where transforming love is learned and from which it ventures into the world. The death of Jesus manifests both the ultimate manifestation of God's love and the cleansing of the soul in preparation for a new creation (2 Corinthians 5:17). In this stage of development, believers are enabled to accept the suffering which follows from being out of sync with the world around them because suffering as a believer identifies them even further with Christ in his suffering.[164] As part of his body, they are in process of being infused more and more with his Spirit, and thus empowered to live accordingly. The

---

[164] "...I carry the marks [*stigmata*] of Jesus branded on my body." (Galatians 6:17, NRSV) ". . . suffering produces endurance, and endurance produces character, and character produces hope, and hope does not disappoint us, because God's love has been poured into our hearts through the Holy Spirit that has been given to us." (Romans 5:3-5, NRSV)

present scene is the time of growing enlightenment, of deepening understanding of God's plan, as well as moral regeneration.

The third scene points to the future, the arena in which hope is fulfilled. It is both an extension of the present and its perfection. Life beyond death is not an add-on for Paul, but an essential part of the whole story from the time of Adam, who lost it, to the time of Christ, who regained it for humankind. It may not be too much to claim that it is the goal which drives the story forward from beginning to end.[165] Its fundamental importance is indicated by the following quotation:

> If for this life only we have hoped in Christ, we are of all people most to be pitied. (1 Corinthians 15:19, NRSV)

The final scene thus has two parts. Beginning with the life, death, and resurrection of Jesus, it includes that which is at present the content of hope, the full manifestation of God's kingdom. While believers are in process of transformation in this life, the ultimate metamorphosis comes with their resurrection.[166] At the present time believers are in a situation of ambivalence. On the one hand, they live in the Spirit, at least partially, but they are constrained by being in a physical body and not yet in the spiritual body of the future life. Resurrection symbolizes the necessary exchange of the earthly body, the body of dust in which everyone has existed since the time of Adam, for the purified spiritual body:

---

[165] Paul sometimes uses the word "salvation" to indicate life beyond this one, but not exclusively. For example, he employs "salvation" in reference to the past (Romans 8:24—"we were saved"), the present (2 Corinthians 6:2—"now is the day of salvation"), as well as to the future (Romans 13:11—"salvation is nearer to us now than when we became believers," NRSV.)

[166] As observed earlier, Paul believed that those who were alive at Christ's coming would also be transformed. Paul can also refer to an immediate transformation on death: ". . . my desire is to depart and be with Christ . . . ." (Philippians 1:23, NRSV)

... flesh and blood cannot inherit the kingdom of God, nor does the perishable inherit the imperishable. (1 Corinthians 15:50, NRSV)

What is sown is perishable, what is raised is imperishable. . . . It is sown a physical body, it is raised a spiritual body. . . . Thus it is written, "The first man, Adam, became a living being;" the last Adam became a life-giving spirit. (1 Corinthians 15:42b, 44a, 45, NRSV)

Resurrection is not assured, as Paul's reference to the wilderness generation is intended to point out (1 Corinthians 10:1-5). Even though life with God has entered the human world, in its fullness it remains a hope, not a present possession. The focus in the present life is becoming like Christ and on not resuming the way of Adam. Life now is lived in "faith, hope, and love," a sober warning against extremism in which either faith or hope crowds out the total perspective and the centrality of love.

Thus the future dimension of the last Adam is clear, but the immediate present requires most attention. The "now" has its own form of transformation, marked not only by the gifts of and participation in the Spirit, but also by the creation of healing communities characterized by selfless caring. These communities are the one "Body of Christ" which is energized by his non-violent and compassionate Spirit. They are life-giving assemblies of people baptized into Christ's community and educated into his ways.

The concluding act pulls together the main characters and motifs about humanity gone wrong and God's movement to make it right, with the emphasis on God's action in and through the death and resurrection of Jesus. Paul's role was to tell others about this story and spell out its implications, especially for those who had not grown up Jewish.

PAUL TAKES HIS STORY ON THE ROAD

CHAPTER 8: From Arabia to Antioch

P aul's mystical experience near Damascus radically changed his convictions, priorities, and vocation. His beliefs about what God required of faithful Jews were no longer persuasive; his zeal for the traditions of his fathers had evaporated. For the first time, the angry Pharisee encountered not merely the followers of Jesus, but Jesus himself. From that experience Paul came to understand that he, not Jesus, had behaved as an enemy of God; he had actually been opposing God's chosen one sent to inaugurate the promised time of redemption. He was won over to Jesus' paradigm for living. Paul also discovered a new vocation, the proclamation of the good news by word and deed to the world beyond Israel. That mission consumed the remainder of his life.

Did Paul put it all together in a flash of enlightenment totally clarifying his past and guiding his future? Perhaps not. The revelation that came to him initiated a process continuing for the remainder of his life. True, the wording of the transformative Galatians passage we examined in Chapter 2 suggests a single, momentous event. However, everything he wrote in his letters about his conversion and its implications was from a perspective of a quarter century or more later. In any case, while Paul's life was shaped by several identifiable forces—scripture, education, his time as a Pharisee, his attempt to eradicate the Jesus movement—his mystical experience became the touchstone of his life. It motivated his actions and thought from that point on. The Christ story that we now read in his letters was an unfolding narrative which could be expressed in many different ways.

This chapter and the following three utilize the Acts of the Apostles and Paul's letters in tracing the course of his life following his encounter with the risen Christ. Because personal decisions on assumptions and details are necessary in any reconstruction of Paul's life, certainty is seldom if ever possible. Probability is often the most one can hope for, and in some cases nothing more than plausibility. Frequently, others assess the evidence differently or even make alternative judgments about what is considered evidence. For all of us, the writings themselves must be the final guides and arbiters of the story we construct of Paul's life.

The First Fourteen Years

Details of Paul's activities in the first years of his service of Christ are largely lost to us. Luke's account of Paul's time in Damascus is brief and reports only one specific event: his escape from the city by being lowered from an opening in the city wall (Acts 9:19b-25). The remainder is Luke's summary of Paul's proclamation of Jesus in the synagogues. Paul's own report of his Damascus period is also brief, touching only on his departure from and return to the city and his subsequent flight to Jerusalem:

> . . . I went away at once into Arabia, and again I returned to Damascus. Then after three years I did go up to Jerusalem to visit Peter and stayed with him fifteen days . . . . (Galatians 1:17b-18, NRSV)

> In Damascus, the governor under King Aretas guarded the city of Damascus in order to seize me, but I was let down in a basket through a window in the wall, and escaped from his hands. (2 Corinthians 11:32-33, NRSV)

The time Paul spent in Arabia is even more opaque than his Damascus sojourn. We do not know precisely where in "Arabia" Paul went and for what reason. Some commentators have speculated that he went on a retreat to the desert to contemplate his experience. Others more plausibly infer that he went to missionize in one or more of the nearby Nabatean cities to the south of Damascus. It is doubtful that he reached Petra, the desert capital of the Nabataeans, some 370 kilometers (230 miles) from Damascus. In any case, he probably aroused the suspicion and hostility of the government which led him to return to Damascus.

Relations between Nabateans and Jews were strained in those days. The Nabatean King Aretas IV[167] had been dishonored when Herod Antipas divorced the king's daughter in order to marry Herodias, and in ca. 34-35 Aretas defeated Antipas' army in battle.[168] Paul's time in Nabatea is to be placed shortly after those events. But even Damascus was soon not to be safe for Paul. Following the death of the Roman emperor, Tiberius, in 37 CE, the Nabateans gained control over Damascus and Aretas' appointed ethnarch sought to arrest Paul.

Luke's portrayal of this period omits any reference to Arabia and has Saul staying in Damascus until his forced departure. Saul does not engage in a Gentile mission in Damascus, but debates with other Jews in the local synagogues:

> For several days he was with the disciples in Damascus, and immediately he began to proclaim Jesus in the synagogues, saying, "He is the Son of God." . . . Saul became increasingly more powerful and confounded the Jews who lived in Damascus by proving that Jesus was the Messiah. (Acts 9:19b-20, 22, NRSV)

While Paul says nothing explicitly about the ethnic identity of his target audience in either Arabia or Damascus, Luke is probably correct as far as Paul's activities in Damascus are concerned—he was actively engaged in local synagogues, of which there were un-

---

[167] Aretas ruled the Nabatean kingdom 9 BCE to 40 CE.

[168] Mark 6:17-18; Josephus, *Jewish Antiquities* 18:109-115.

doubtedly many. While the prophet Ananias predicts a Gentile as well as a Jewish mission for Saul (Acts 9:15), Paul's entry into Gentile missionary activities in Acts does not occur until he and others are sent out by the church at Antioch, at least a decade after he joined the Jesus movement. That is where Luke's account of Paul's Gentile mission truly begins.

Both Acts and Paul report his flight from Damascus in remarkably similar detail, though each gives a different motive for it. True to his tendency to blame Paul's troubles on the Jews,[169] Luke writes that Paul fled Damascus to escape a Jewish plot to kill him. (Acts 9:23-25) Paul's explanation is political rather than religious—the local governor under King Aretas had given orders for Paul's arrest. (2 Corinthians 11:32-33) Paul's account of course is to be preferred. Both authors agree that his next destination was Jerusalem.

Luke is vague about the length of time Paul spent in Damascus—"After some time had passed"—while Paul specifies a three-year period before he went to "visit" Peter in Jerusalem (Galatians 1:18). But how is Paul's statement to be interpreted? Does the three-year period before his trip to Jerusalem start with his return from Arabia, or with his conversion? Does Paul follow the convention of including an initial and/or final partial year as a whole year? If so, the period to which he refers could be slightly over two years or even less. He then goes on to specify a period of fourteen years before his second visit to Jerusalem. Again, is he counting from his conversion or from his first visit? There is no scholarly consensus on the answer, but his introduction of each new stage with "then" suggests the total time from his conversion to his second trip to Jerusalem was fourteen years, not seventeen.

[169] Similar scenarios appear numerous times, e.g., at Pisidian Antioch (Acts 13:50), Jerusalem (9:29; 23:12-35), Iconium (14:2), Lystra (14:19), and Thessalonica (17:5).

Paul's time in Jerusalem as Peter's house-guest is not detailed in any of our sources.[170] We can surmise that among their topics of conversation were the implications of their respective callings for future missionary work: among the Jews for Peter and the Gentiles for Paul. Paul's later declaration to the Corinthians regarding the various appearances of the risen Christ was also probably based on first-hand accounts by Peter. The interpretation given to the death and resurrection of Jesus by the Jerusalem church would also have been part of their dialogue. But what about the teachings of Jesus which are largely absent from Paul's letters? Did Paul's encounter with the risen Christ so occupy his mind that the events of Jesus' earthly life prior to his crucifixion were pushed aside? Perhaps one motivation for creating the Gospels was to correct that omission.

After staying with Peter for a period of two weeks, Paul largely drops out of view once again, this time for over a decade. Luke's report of Paul's open preaching in Jerusalem (Acts 9:26-30) is not supported by what Paul writes in Galatians. We have to accept Paul's sworn statement ("In what I am writing to you before God, I do not lie!" Galatians 1:20, NRSV) When he went to visit Peter, he insists that he saw none of the other apostles except James, the brother of Jesus (Galatians 1:19-23). Further, he claims that had no contact with the churches in that region.

Following his visit to Peter, Paul spent the next eleven years in the north, outside the province of Judea. His identification of the area is largely consistent with Luke's account of that phase of Paul's life. The fact that Paul mentions going to the region of Cilicia suggests that Luke's depiction of his sojourn in Tarsus of Cilicia for part of that time is essentially correct. Paul was a city person; Tarsus was the main city in Cilicia, and the location of his childhood. But neither Luke nor Paul provides details about his time in

[170] The word "visit" translates the Greek verb *historeō* (from which our word "history" is derived). It does not specify the precise purpose of the visit. It could indicate that Paul visited Peter for the purpose of getting to know him, but in addition it could mean that Paul wanted to obtain information from him, to interview him.

Cilicia. Paul apparently had no occasion to refer more specifically to that period in his life, and Luke must have lacked Cilician sources, or else they were not germane to his book.

Antioch in Syria

Paul next turns up in the church in Antioch,[171] at that time the capital of the combined province of Cilicia and Syria. The congregation had its beginnings, according to Luke, when some of those who faced persecution in Jerusalem fled to this city (Acts 11:19-21).[172] There they shared their message with both Jews and Greeks. Before writing about the spread of the faith to Antioch, Luke narrated the story of Peter's conversion of the Gentile centurion Cornelius in Caesarea and his successful defense of that initiative before critics in the Jerusalem church (Acts 10:1-11:18). Luke's message is clear: the Gentile mission was inaugurated by Peter, even though Paul would soon take it over. In this way, Luke emphasizes that the spread of the Jesus movement is both under the direction of the Jerusalem apostles as well as the Spirit, and that Peter's action has established the precedent for inclusion of the Gentiles in Antioch and beyond.

According to Luke, Paul came to Antioch at the request of Barnabas who had been sent there by the Jerusalem church to work with the mixed congregation of Jewish and Gentile believers (Acts 11:19-26). Whatever the circumstances by which Paul arrived there, Antioch as a church carrying out a Gentile mission would have been a logical place for Paul to go.

---

[171] Antioch is estimated to have had a population of at least 100,000, and possibly many more in Paul's time. As a Greek-speaking commercial hub linking East and West, it prospered both in wealth and culture.

[172] Among those who fled persecution in Jerusalem was "Nicolaus, a proselyte of Antioch." (Acts 6:5, NRSV) He was one of the seven appointed by the apostles to administer the assets of the Jerusalem church.

For information about Barnabas, we are almost totally dependent on Acts. While Paul refers to him in two letters,[173] he gives
little personal information about Barnabas other than their joint
missionary work among Gentiles. On the other hand, Barnabas is
an important player in Luke's story of the early church.[174] Luke
appears to have a good deal of information about Barnabas and his
activities, most of which there seems little reason to doubt, though
verifying sources are lacking. Luke informs us that Barnabas' original name was Joseph, he was a Levite, and he was from Cyprus
(Acts 4:36). He presented the apostles who were supervising the
communal assets of the Jerusalem church with the proceeds from
some property he sold. They gave him the name Barnabas, an Aramaic term which Luke understands to mean "son of encouragement," indicating his reputation as one who powerfully proclaimed
Jesus, or perhaps pointing to his function as a charismatic prophet
(see 1 Corinthians 14:3), as Luke so identifies him in Acts 13:1.
Barnabas was held in high regard by the Jerusalem church, which
partly explains why he was sent by its leaders to assess developments in Antioch following reports of the Jesus movement's expanding to include Gentiles (11:22).[175] Barnabas was probably bi-
lingual in Aramaic and Greek, another plus for his work in Antioch.

Having become acquainted with the situation at Antioch,
Barnabas then sought out Saul to assist in strengthening the church
there. Why Saul? Luke may be correct in claiming the two were
already acquainted. Possible reasons for choosing Saul to help guide
and develop this mixed congregation include Paul's fluency in the
Greek language, his reputation as an effective evangelizer and
teacher, and his radical transformation from a persecuting Pharisee

---

[173] Galatians 2:1, 9, 13; 1 Corinthians 9:6.

[174] Barnabas' name appears 23 times in Acts.

[175] See Acts 8:14-25 where Peter and John are sent by the Jerusalem apostles to
check on missionary developments in Samaria.

to a zealous servant of Christ. Earlier in Acts, Luke had represented Barnabas as the connection between Saul and the Jerusalem
church (9:27). However, this linkage is part of the report of Saul's
activities in Jerusalem soon after his conversion, a report which
Paul denies, as we have seen. While Luke may see in Barnabas one
more link between Jerusalem and Paul, the association of Barnabas
and Paul is well documented by the latter, as is their partnership in
promoting the gospel (Galatians 2:1-10). Luke may have exaggerated its extent, but he has not created the connection between the
pair.

Barnabas and Saul were active in the church in Antioch for a
year, according to Acts 11:25-26. But Luke omits any description of
their activity in parts of Syria and Cilicia outside Antioch, even
though he is aware of it (Acts 15:41). Saul's extensive evangelistic
work in that area certainly included more than a year in the city of
Antioch followed by a trip to Cyprus and southern Asia Minor.
While Luke locates Saul only in two cities, Tarsus and Antioch,
Paul's letters never mention Tarsus and contain only one reference
to Antioch (Galatians 2:11). For both writers, Antioch is the base
for the Jesus movement in Syria and Cilicia. Barnabas and Saul
were sponsored by the church(es) there to expand the Way into
other cities and towns in those regions.

Luke next introduces a new stage in Saul's missionary work.
He writes that Barnabas and Saul were part of a five-member group
in the Antioch Christian community identified both by name and
as "prophets and teachers" (Acts 13:1). Luke does not specify which
person was a prophet and which was a teacher; perhaps some or all
were both. Teaching was a well-recognized and important activity,
common to the church and to the larger world. New converts
needed to be educated in the world view and the ethical standards
of the Jesus movement, and how the scriptures related to the new
faith. Prophets had a different function. Paul is our earliest witness
to prophecy in the early church. He holds it in high regard and

considers it a major form of revelation and source of encouragement.

The passage referring to the small group of teachers and
prophets is Luke's introduction not only to a new stage in church
development, but also to the fulfillment of Saul's calling as a missionary to the Gentiles. To this point, Luke has given no indication
that Saul has addressed Gentiles in his proclamation of the gospel.
From now on, they will be an integral part of his mission. In the
next two chapters in Acts (13-14), Saul emerges as the archetypal
missionary to Jews and Gentiles, even though Peter has preceded
him in preaching to both groups. However, Saul has much more
success among Gentiles than Jews, a theme surfacing repeatedly in
the remainder of Acts. Following his and Barnabas' foray into new
territory, they will go to Jerusalem to defend their policy of refusing to require that Gentile converts observe the Jewish Law, beginning with the initiation rite of circumcision. In this way the so-
called first missionary journey establishes the conditions leading to
the important Jerusalem conference and beyond it to Paul's future
missionary activity, beginning in Acts 15:40.

At this point we encounter numerous difficulties in tracing
Paul's movements. First, it is not easy to reconcile the sequence of
events in Acts, in which the Jerusalem conference comes between
the so-called first and second missionary journeys, with Paul's letter to the Galatians. Following his recounting of his revelation,
Paul writes:

> ...I did not confer with any human being, nor did I go up to
> Jerusalem to those who were already apostles before me, but
> I went away at once into Arabia, and afterwards I returned
> to Damascus. Then after three years I did go up to Jerusalem
> to visit Cephas....Then I went into the regions of Syria and
> Cilicia...Then after fourteen years I went up again to Jerusa-
> lem with Barnabas, taking Titus along with me. (Galatians
> 1:16b-18, 21; 2:1, NRSV)

Paul's repeated "then" signals a definite sequence of events, a memoir designed to demonstrate how little contact he had with the Jerusalem church. During the final period, he claims he was in Syria and Cilicia. However, Acts details a missionary excursion into Cyprus, Pamphylia, Phrygia and Lycaonia, all in the southern part of the province of Galatia. Paul never alludes to such a trip. It is difficult to believe that Luke has concocted it. So where does it fit into a Pauline chronology?

If Paul's statement concerning his whereabouts during this period is taken at face value, then he had not yet founded the Galatian churches.[176] It would have been to Paul's advantage to mention having been in Galatia since doing so would further demonstrate his lack of contact with the Jerusalem church leaders. If the Galatian churches did not yet exist, their founding cannot be correlated with the account in Acts of the first missionary journey to southern Galatia.

The alternative would be to accept Paul's brief account of where he spent the years between his two visits to Jerusalem as only a partial summary, not a complete itinerary of his location(s) during that period. He does not indicate that he never left Syria and Cilicia. But this explanation seems forced and does not take into account Paul's detailed sequence of his travels. Paul obviously could not omit exceptions to be thrown back in his face by his opponents who had come to Galatia.

Both positions have their defenders, but the weight of the evidence favors that the Galatian churches had not been founded during the eleven-year period mentioned by Paul. Their origin cannot be fitted into the time-frame of Luke's account of the so-called first

---

[176] See Martyn, *Galatians*, 183-184. Likewise, the letter of James of Jerusalem detailing a compromise to settle the dispute at Antioch following Paul's return from the so-called first missionary journey also omits any reference to Galatia, being addressed only to the believers in Syria and Cilicia. (Acts 15:23)

missionary journey which came prior to the Jerusalem conference. Paul enables us to give an approximate dating to that conference, fourteen years after his conversion, i.e., ca. 48-49 CE. The founding of the Galatian churches must belong not to Luke's first missionary journey, but to the second. However, in what follows we shall accept the order of Luke's narrative without assuming that he is describing the birth of the churches to which Paul's letter to the Galatians was written.

The First Missionary Journey:
Cyprus, Pamphylia, South Galatia

It has become customary in modern times to name the account in Acts 13-14 of the expedition of Barnabas, Paul, and John Mark to Cyprus and southern Asia Minor the "first missionary journey." Neither Luke nor Paul uses that term, and it is not entirely appropriate. The concept of Paul's three missionary journeys is derived from the mistaken assumption that Antioch continued to be his home base from which he "journeyed" to found new churches or strengthen existing ones.[177] While that may have been Paul's pattern in his earlier days in Syria and Cilicia, the reality is that he was on the move much of his life from this point on, spending only as much time at any one location as necessary to initiate and solidify his work there. There was no home base.

Further, there is no evidence that the Christians in Antioch sponsored any of Paul's missionary endeavors after the trip described in Acts 13:4-14:26. Paul never mentions Antioch again after his dispute there with Peter (Galatians 2:11-14). Acts reports one further contact of Paul with the church there (18:22-23), but without details. Nevertheless, the nomenclature of three missionary

---

[177] Luke mentions three departures of Paul from Antioch—Acts 13:3; 15:36-41; 18:22-23.

journeys is now embedded in discussions of Acts, and will be utilized in what follows.

According to Acts, it was an act of prophecy that led to the first missionary expedition from Antioch (Acts 13:2-3). The spokesperson for the Holy Spirit is an unspecified prophet. In addition to Paul's inaugural visionary/prophetic revelation, Luke indicates that Paul's life as an advocate of Christ continued to be under divine guidance.[178] His first missionary journey from Antioch illustrates that theme. Perhaps it would be more accurate to say Barnabas' missionary journey since Luke makes it appear that Barnabas was in charge, at least at the outset. Barnabas's name precedes Saul's whenever the two are mentioned together: in taking aid to the Judean brethren (11:30), in returning to Antioch from Jerusalem (12:25), in the list of prophets and teachers at Antioch (13:1), and in their joint mission up to the time of their audience before Sergius Paulus, proconsul of Cyprus.

However, at the very point at which Luke exchanges the name Saul for Paul, Paul becomes the prime representative of Christ in the mission. When the group, which includes Barnabas' nephew John, also known as Mark, leaves Cyprus, Luke calls them "Paul and his companions." (13:13) At their next evangelizing stop, Antioch of Pisidia, it is Paul who proclaims the gospel (Acts 13:14-41). As the main speaker, it is he who is identified by the Gentiles in Lystra as the god Hermes (14:12).[179] Further, it is not Barnabas but Paul who is stoned (14:19), presumably because he was perceived to be the leader. Luke is telling us that on this mission Paul came into his own as the chief missionary of Christ to the Gentiles.

However, this initial missionary expedition does not start off as directed to the Gentiles. The "work" to which Barnabas and Saul are called, as becomes evident later, is to proclaim Jesus in the syn-

---

[178] Acts 16:6-7, 9-10; 19:21; see also 21:10-14.

[179] Hermes was a Greek god with many functions, including that of carrying messages between the gods and humans.

agogues, primarily to the Jews and secondarily to "God fearing" Gentiles who are listening in to what is essentially a Jewish conversation. Paul's special designation as one sent to the Gentiles develops out of his experience in which Jewish opposition turns him more and more to the Gentiles. Thus Luke is able not only to blame the Jews for their own refusal of the gospel but paradoxically also to credit them for Paul's intensified mission to the Gentiles. Here we see another expression of the interplay between divine intention and human opposition that is found first in the story of Jesus. In Luke's time Jewish rejection of the Jesus movement and the primarily Gentile identity of the church were becoming so obvious that he connected the two as cause and effect, while at the same time maintaining divine direction of the movement.

Cyprus

Cyprus may have been included in the mission's itinerary because Barnabas had come from there (Acts 4:36). Luke also reports that some of those fleeing persecution in Jerusalem following the death of Stephen went to Cyprus, as well as to Phoenicia and Antioch. Further, Cypriots were among those who proclaimed Jesus to Greeks in Antioch (Acts 11:19-20). On his final trip to Jerusalem, Paul and his entourage will stay in Caesarea at the home of Mnason of Cyprus, who, like Barnabas, is identified as an early disciple. Luke thus attests in several ways to connections of the early church with Cyprus. The faith had apparently already reached the island before the missionary team from Antioch arrived, but that plays no part in Luke's story.

Landing at the eastern port city, Salamis,[180] Barnabas and Saul go to the local synagogues and engage those in attendance:

---

[180] Salamis was an ancient city, but highly Hellenized and Romanized by the first century CE. Among the ruins are the usual Roman amenities—amphitheater, baths, temples, gymnasium, agora or forum, and aqueduct.

"For in every city, for generations past, Moses has had those who proclaim him, for has been read aloud every Sabbath in the synagogues." (Acts 15:21, NRSV)

This quotation from James' speech summarizes how widespread Judaism was in the Gentile world. "Moses" here is shorthand for the entire body of Jewish teaching, but especially the Torah. Synagogues both in the homeland but especially beyond served as gathering places for educational and cultural purposes, as well as religious. They were the Jewish counterpart of common assemblies of various voluntary associations in the Hellenistic/Roman world of that time. Synagogues also shared an important characteristic with the philosophic schools inasmuch as their adherents could be construed as disciples of a teacher, in this case Moses. Jews gathered to learn, discuss, and follow Moses' teachings. Some Gentiles likely considered Judaism as another philosophic tradition, akin to Epicureanism[181] or Cynicism[182] or Stoicism. In any case, they were welcome to hear expositions of the teachings of Moses. This meant that the early Christian evangelists could address both Jews and Gentiles in a single venue.

Acts contains no report of converts resulting from evangelizing in the synagogues of Salamis. The mission appears to have been a failure, though apparently Luke has no information about what actually occurred there. The party next travels down the length of the island (ca. 160 kilometers, or 100 miles) to Paphos, the provincial capital. Here they make their sole convert on Cyprus, Sergius Paulus, the proconsul (Acts 13:12). Much speculation has been ex-

---

[181] Named after Epicurus (341-270 BCE), who taught that the highest good was human happiness, defined largely as an absence of pain and the presence of pleasure.

[182] The name is derived from the Greek word for dog, *kuōn*, and describes the Cynics' shameless disregard for social conventions. Highly critical of social values and practices, they taught that only living the "natural" life led to happiness.

pended on the question of why in his narrative of Saul's first contact with a Roman governor, Luke introduces Saul's Roman name "Paul" (Acts 13:9) and employs it from that point on, with the exceptions of Paul's recitations of his conversion. It may be a matter of different sources, or simply changing to the familiar name by which Paul was known when Acts was being written. It is not likely that the name of the governor had any bearing on the matter.

Luke is fond of stories of conversions of influential Romans who favored the Christian cause and of Paul's wonder-working. The two are combined in this case. Elymas, probably a court magician close to Sergius Paulus, tries to dissuade the governor from accepting Paul's gospel. However, Paul's superior wonder-working power, plus his "teaching about the Lord," impressed the governor enough that he became a believer. Paul and his companions (Barnabas and John Mark) now leave for the mainland of Asia Minor.

Perga in Pamphylia

The missionaries sail north to Pamphylia, a district which was currently jurisdictionally linked to Lycia but had previously been joined respectively to the provinces of Cilicia, Asia, and Galatia. Luke does not specify which of the two possible routes they took from the coast to their destination, Perga, which is several miles inland. Founded originally by the Hittites, then populated mostly by Greeks following the Trojan War, and dominated by the Romans in the second century BCE, in Paul's time Perga, like Salamis, was a wealthy and cultured city in the Hellenistic/Roman style.[183]

While Acts makes no mention of a synagogue in Perga, Jews from Pamphylia are included in the list of nations present at Pente-

---

[183] Excavations of the city continue. Its remains include monumental city gates, stadium, aqueducts, baths, public fountain, gymnasium, temples and statuary. W. Ward Gasque, "*Perga*," *ABD* 5:228.

cost (Acts 2:10). Luke apparently lacked a source giving details of Paul's visit to the city; he gives no report of preaching at Perga until the return trip (Acts 14:25), and then only briefly with no mention of converts. However, Luke does associate one internal issue between members of the missionary party with this city. While there, for some unexplained reason, John Mark leaves to return to Jerusalem. It may be that the missionaries' original plans were to evangelize Pamphylia and did not include leaving the coastal plain for the interior. John Mark may not have agreed with the changed itinerary and abandoned the mission.

In his letter to the Galatians, Paul reveals that they originally heard the gospel from him because of his "physical infirmity," literally, his "weakness of the flesh" (Galatians 4:13, NRSV). Unfortunately, he does not specify what that illness was. Some scholars have speculated that Paul may have suffered from malaria and left the coastal plain for the higher and drier interior where there was also opportunity to proclaim the gospel. Further, his "thorn in the flesh" and "a messenger of Satan to torment me" (2 Corinthians 12:7, NRSV) may indicate recurring bouts of malaria which plagued him the rest of his life. The reference in Galatians may be to one of those chronic attacks. Whether it occurred at this or another time is unknown. The issue is complicated further by the fact that we cannot be certain of the geographical location of the Galatian churches to which Paul wrote.

Pisidian Antioch, Iconium, Lystra, and Derbe

Having left Perga, the two missionaries cross the Taurus mountains to the interior, a journey of about 240 kilometers (150 miles) which involved ascending from sea level to about 4,000 feet (over 1,200 meters). They go to four cities not far from each other in the southern part of the Roman province of

Galatia:[184] Antioch near Pisidia, Iconium, Lystra, and Derbe. One of numerous cities in the eastern empire bearing that name,[185] Antioch was strategically designated a Roman colony in 25 BCE by the emperor Augustus. Army veterans were settled in such colonies to aid in stabilizing the surrounding area. Lucius Sergius Paulus, the governor of Cyprus recently converted by Paul, apparently had family and property connections with Antioch; perhaps he suggested to Paul a mission in Antioch.[186]

According to Luke, the missionary strategy of Paul and Barnabas was to go first to the local synagogue in whatever city they were in (Acts 13:14; 14:1). This is an ongoing theme in Acts, but it also was probably their practice. The missionaries utilized an existing social structure to which they as Jews had ready access and which potentially could supply converts. Whether held in a home or in a dedicated building, the weekly synagogue meeting was open to Jews, proselytes (Gentiles who had converted to Judaism), and God-fearers (interested Gentiles who had not converted). Thus the missionaries did not have to gather an audience; it was already in place when they arrived. As visiting learned Jews with a variant perspective on the scriptures, the missionaries convinced the officials of the synagogues to allow them to present their message during the regular Sabbath meeting.

Paul gives his first extended missionary sermon in the synagogue, successfully persuading both fellow Jews and proselytes to believe his message. But, quite understandably, this led to a schism between those who accepted the new teaching and those who didn't. In response to the latter, Paul feels justified in announcing

---

[184] Luke uses city and territorial names here, not the provincial title of Galatia.

[185] Antioch in Syria was founded ca. 300 BCE by one of Alexander's generals, Seleucus, and named after the latter's father. Ten of the descendants of Seleucus who ruled the Seleucid kingdom from the third to the first century BCE bore the name of Antiochus. Antioch near Pisidia was founded in the third century BCE by one of those kings.

[186] Stephen Mitchell, "Antioch of Pisidia," *ABD* 1:264-265.

that his mission from then on will not include the Jews, but only Gentiles, in keeping with Isaiah's prophecy (Isaiah 49:6). An important element of Luke's conception of the origins of Pauline Christianity, this motif finds its initial expression in Pisidian Antioch (Acts 13:46). It is restated again in Corinth (Acts 18:6), and finally in Rome (Acts 28:28). In all three cases Paul gives up on his mission to the Jews and turns exclusively to the Gentiles.

This theme in Acts should not be confused with Paul's own views. For Paul, "to the Jews first" was largely a historical statement inasmuch as Jesus addressed his message to Jews, and his disciples continued that practice following his death. The Gentile mission in which Paul was engaged came later; he was an apostle "untimely born" (1 Corinthians 15:8, NRSV). While the Paul of Acts repeatedly gives up on a Jewish mission; not so the Paul of the letters, as Romans demonstrates (see especially 11:25-27). However, despite the proclamation to cease preaching to Jews, Luke is not consistent: in the next city Paul and Barnabas once again open their mission by preaching in the synagogue.

According to Acts, members of the Jewish community who opposed Paul's teaching had influence in high places, especially with local officials who forced the missionaries to vacate the city. Leaving Antioch, they travel some 150 kilometers (90 miles) southeast to Iconium (modern Konya, Turkey), a city with three millennia of history situated on the interface between the Phrygian mountains to the west and the Lycaonian plain to the east. Over the previous three centuries it had become Hellenized and now was a large and prosperous city on the highway linking Syria and Ephesus. Luke writes that the missionaries' experience there duplicated what had happened in Antioch—many conversions of both Jews and Greeks followed by Jewish and Gentile opposition. Luke does not explain how Paul and Barnabas, in contrast to their time in Antioch, were able to remain in Iconium for a "long time," only terminated when they heard of impending violence against them (Acts 14:5-6).

Fleeing from Iconium, the missionaries move on to Lystra, about 30 kilometers (some 20 miles) to the south-west in the district of Lycaonia. Ethnically distinct from the citizens of Iconium, though also Hellenized, they could still speak their native language (Acts 14:11). Under Augustus, the city had been made a small Roman colony in 6 CE. Here Luke incorporates the story of a different kind of pagan response to the missionaries. After Paul heals a man "crippled from birth," the observers infer that the missionaries must be high gods, Zeus and Hermes, worthy of receiving sacrifices. With great difficulty, Barnabas and Paul restrain them, employing traditional Jewish missionary teaching to persuade the Gentiles to abandon their idolatry and worship the living God. But opposing Jews from Antioch and Iconium arrive, and this time, the missionaries do not escape. Paul is stoned and left for dead outside the city, but disciples give him aid and take him back into the city. The next day he and Barnabas proceed to the final city on their journey, Derbe. Paul must have made a remarkably speedy recovery!

Derbe is another Lycaonian city about 100 kilometers (60 miles) southeast from Lystra on the road leading through the Cilician Gates to Tarsus. Luke reports numerous conversions in Derbe, but has no stories as such. Later he mentions that a Gaius of Derbe was part of Paul's entourage of seven when he undertook his final journey to Jerusalem (Acts 20:4). The missionaries now retrace their steps, presumably somewhat surreptitiously, visiting the newly-founded congregations in Lystra, Iconium, and Antioch, and then travelling down to the Pamphylian coast from which they return to their home base in Antioch in Syria.

Thus the first missionary journey is completed. The focal point is the mission in southern Galatia. That is where Paul's archetypal sermon is preached, where mixed congregations are formed, where Jewish opposition leads to the expulsion of the missionaries, and where they revisit the congregations to "strengthen their souls." None of this occurs in Cyprus or in Pamphylia, which seem to be stepping stones toward their real goal in the southern interior of Asia Minor. Their only convert before arriving at Antioch near Pisidia is Sergius Paulus.

This account of a missionary expedition sponsored by the church at Antioch in Syria illustrates what may have happened on numerous occasions during Paul's association with Antioch. Whether it is based on an actual itinerary as are some later parts of Acts has been questioned. Doubts about its accuracy are raised by the very fact that Paul makes no reference to any of the churches named, unless it be assumed that his letter to the Galatians was written to churches founded on that journey, as many scholars maintain. In any case, this journey is the only missionary activity in Acts, outside Antioch, where Paul and Barnabas are together.

Negotiations at Jerusalem

Paul writes in Galatians that his second trip to Jerusalem occurred "after fourteen years," probably counting from the time of his conversion.[187] He and Barnabas were sent as an official delegation from the Antioch church to arrive at a resolution of the differences which had arisen within the Jesus movement, especially involving, on the one hand, the "circumcision party," and on the other, those who accepted Gentiles without circumcising them. The Gentiles in question were probably members of the Antioch church and other congregations founded under its auspices.[188]

---

[187] General agreement has not been reached on the historical date of the conference. Jewett, for example, following John Knox and others, holds that Paul's trip to Jerusalem in Acts 18:22 was actually related to the occasion of the apostolic conference. Jewett goes on to date the conference in October, 51 CE following the founding of the Corinthian church (*A Chronology of Paul's Life*, 78-87). Martyn gives a date of ca. 48 CE, prior to Paul's mission to north Galatia and Macedonia (*Galatians,* 182-183, note 237). The whole issue is complicated and involves an overall dating scheme correlating numerous other events in Acts and Paul's letters.

[188] Martyn, *Galatians,* 208-209.

Luke had earlier written about a division between the "Hebrews" and the "Hellenists" in Jerusalem, the latter being persecuted and forced to leave the city, some of whom fled to Antioch where they formed the core of a more liberal form of the Jesus movement. This could have created some of the conditions leading to the present conflict between Antioch and the Jerusalem Christian leaders.

Acts reports the same official trip mentioned by Paul, but counts it as Paul's third visit to Jerusalem. According to Acts 11:27-30, Paul and Barnabas had earlier gone to the "elders" in Judea (read, Jerusalem) with material aid for the churches affected by the famine predicted by the prophet Agabus. This famine may have been the one mentioned by Josephus, which can be dated ca. 46-47 CE, during the reign of the emperor Claudius (41-54 CE), as indicated in Acts.[189] It apparently affected primarily Judea, despite Luke's phrase "all the world." (Acts 11:28, NRSV).[190] Since the Christians in Antioch were able to send assistance to Judea, they were not rendered destitute by the famine, the cause of which is not identified. Josephus relates that Helena of Adiabene, in Jerusalem at the time, financed shipments of dried figs from Cyprus and grain from Egypt to aid the needy in Jerusalem.[191]

In the account in Acts, the so-called famine visit of Barnabas and Paul to Jerusalem occurs prior to the mission to Cyprus and southern Asia Minor. Paul however, indicates that his second visit to Jerusalem was for the purpose of clearing the air regarding the gospel he (and Barnabas) had been proclaiming (Galatians 2:1-10). He does not mention a famine visit. Its existence or at least its tim-

---

[189] Luke writes that the famine happened about the time of the execution of James, the brother of John, by order of Herod (Agrippa I). Since Agrippa died in 44 CE, Luke's dating of the famine must be fairly accurate.

[190] Luke uses the same phrase regarding Caesar Augustus' order for a tax enrolment (which likewise would have been limited to Judea) following the removal of Herod's son, Archelaus, as its administrative head. (Luke 2:1).

[191] *Jewish Antiquities* 20:51-52.

ing is called into question by Paul's insistence that he had not gone to Jerusalem between his visit to Peter and the conference visit. There have been attempts to consider the famine visit, the Jerusalem conference, and even the visit of Acts 18:22 as duplicates or triplicates of a single event in order to account for the five trips to Jerusalem in Acts versus Paul's three. The identity and timing of the famine visit of Acts remain a puzzle.

The accounts of the two authors concerning the Jerusalem conference do seem to refer to the same event. The narratives contain a number of points on which they agree.[192] First, the motivation is identical in both cases:

> Then certain individuals came down from Judea and were teaching the brothers, "Unless you are circumcised according to the custom of Moses, you cannot be saved." And after Paul and Barnabas had no small dissension and debate with them, Paul and Barnabas and some of the others were appointed to go up to Jerusalem to discuss this question with the apostles and the elders." (Acts 15:1-2, NRSV)

> Then I laid before them (though only in a private meeting with the acknowledged leaders) the gospel that I proclaim among the Gentiles, in order to make sure that I was not running, or had not run, in vain. But even Titus, who was with me, was not compelled to be circumcised, though he was a Greek. (Galatians 2:2b-3, NRSV)

Paul's Law-free gospel to the Gentiles was an affront to the conservative Jewish Christians who maintained the continuing validity of the entire Jewish Law, including the circumcision of Gentile converts. The conflict was not to be resolved by argument or

---

[192] For more on this, see Betz, *Galatians,* 81-83.

appeal to scripture, but only by a face-to-face meeting between the two parties. Without a resolution, both Paul's Gentile mission and the unity of the early church were in jeopardy. The earlier positive assessment of Paul's preaching spread among the Judean churches, "The one who formerly was persecuting us is now proclaiming the faith he once tried to destroy." (Galatians 1:23, NRSV), needed to be reaffirmed.

Second, Paul and Barnabas travel from Syrian Antioch, where the issue had come to a head, to Jerusalem. Paul says he went there because of a revelation (Galatians 2:2), implying that he was not responding to a summons by the leaders in Jerusalem. Yet, the team that goes to Jerusalem looks very much like an official delegation (Acts 15:2-3). In any case, the gospel which God had called Paul to preach had to be defended against those who denied its truth.

Third, both Luke and Paul agree that there were three parties present for at least part of this meeting: (1) Paul and Barnabas who defend their gospel and practice of not circumcising Gentiles; (2) their critics and opponents, named by Paul as "false brothers" and identified by Luke as (Christian) Pharisees, who maintain the traditional Jewish position that Gentiles had to be circumcised in order to be incorporated into the people of Israel; (3) the Jerusalem leaders, James the brother of Jesus, Cephas (Peter), and John, the latter two both Jesus' disciples, and members of the twelve. Paul identifies James, Cephas, and John as "acknowledged pillars" (Galatians 2:9).

In regard to the "false brothers" who spied on them (Galatians 2:4), Paul refers back to earlier occasions when they appeared in one or more of his communities to gather evidence against Paul and Barnabas. These same people were then in a position to accuse Paul and Barnabas and bear witness against them before the Jerusalem pillars at the conference.

For Paul the matter went to the very heart of the gospel, especially his belief that the good news implied freedom from the

Law as a vehicle of salvation for Gentiles. The Law was part of Israel's history; it was never intended for the Gentiles. Further, even for the Jews it played a temporary role, preliminary to the coming of the Messiah. Now that Christ had come, faith in him as God's Son and his teaching of love as the fulfillment of the Law rendered the Law superfluous. Jewish Christians could continue to observe it if they desired, but it no longer had a major role in God's plan of salvation. Christ could not be subsumed under the Law, but was God's agent of salvation alike for Jew and Gentile.

The presence of his accusers provided Paul the opportunity to confront them directly and present his own position before authorities recognized by his critics, authorities who decided in favor of Paul and Barnabas (Galatians 2:3-9).

The grammar of this portion of Galatians leaves much to be desired. Sentences are begun but not completed as Paul's mind and emotions outrun his words. His point, however, seems clear enough: the gospel of freedom from the Law which he and Barnabas defended was accepted by the Jerusalem pillars. An important demonstration of that fact was that they had not required circumcision of Titus, Paul's Greek companion.[193] From Paul's point of view Titus provided the definitive test case.

The "truth of the gospel" is recognized in the core agreement which Paul is about to state—Gentile believers did not have to be circumcised and consequently were not subject to observing the other commandments of the Jewish Law. Their salvation came not through the Law but exclusively by the act of God in Christ to be received in faith. To claim otherwise would be tantamount to nullifying the gospel.

The result of the meeting was the assurance that the gospel preached by Paul and Barnabas among the Gentiles was admitted to be legitimate by James, Cephas, and John, "acknowledged pillars."

---

[193] Titus is not mentioned anywhere in Acts, but only in Paul's letters, both undisputed (2 Corinthians: 2:13; 7:6, 13, 14; 8:6, 16, 23; 12:18; Galatians 2:1, 3) and disputed (2 Timothy 4:10; Titus 1:4).

The agreement reached included only two stipulations which Paul readily accepted, that his Gentile churches would contribute to the relief of the "poor in Jerusalem,[194] and that Peter was recognized as the apostle to the Jews while Paul and Barnabas would go to the Gentiles.[195]

While Acts agrees in some of the essentials with Galatians, it presents a quite different scenario. First, Peter is an ardent ally and defender of Paul's position. He retells the story of his own earlier conversion to the Gentile mission (Acts 10:1-28). Indeed, the apex of Peter's speech could as easily have been delivered by Paul. Luke even represents Peter as saying that Jews as well as Gentiles are saved by grace (Acts 15:11). Peter needs no convincing of the legitimacy of a circumcision-free gospel. He stands with Paul in opposition to those Christians who had brought their Pharisaic beliefs into the new faith and wanted to impose them on others (15:5).

Second, while Paul understands leadership to be distributed more or less equally among the pillars of the Jerusalem church, Luke concentrates decision-making power in James. Having heard presentations from all sides, including Peter, Paul, and Barnabas, as well as from Paul's opponents, James renders his decision—a compromise (15:19-20). On the one hand, the inclusion of Gentiles in God's plan is recognized and supported by reference to Amos 9:11-12. On the other, while circumcision is not required, certain obligations are expected of Gentile converts.

---

[194] There is no evidence that this remembrance of the poor is related to the story in Acts of the relief brought by Paul's and Barnabas to Judea because of the prophecy of Agabus (11:27-30). Martyn sees the responsibility regarding the poor directed at the church at Antioch rather than at Paul as an individual (*Galatians*, 206-208).

[195] No mention is made that Paul was recognized as an apostle, presumably because the Jerusalem leaders refused to consider him an apostle in the same sense that Peter was. Paul could be regarded as an emissary of the Antioch church, while Peter was called and sent by Christ.

214

Third, these requirements are then detailed in a letter to be delivered to the Gentiles in the churches of Syria and Cilicia, beginning with Antioch:

> For it has seemed good to the Holy Spirit and to us to impose on you no further burden than these essentials: that you abstain from what has been sacrificed to idols and from blood and from what is strangled and from fornication. If you keep yourself from these, you will do well. (Acts 15:28-29, NRSV)[196]

Three of the four prohibitions are derived directly from the Torah. First, eating food sacrificed to an idol would constitute an act of idolatry, the most egregious sin from which all others flow.[197] Second, the consumption of meat which has not been thoroughly drained of blood breaks a commandment frequently stated in the scriptures.[198] Third, fornication (sexual immorality, Greek *porneia*), closely associated with idolatry, refers in general to sexual malpractice but also includes prohibited degrees of marriage.[199] The other restriction which disallows eating meat from an animal that has died by strangulation would seem to be unnecessary in view of the prohibition against blood. Possibly it was meant as representative of a group of forbidden ways of slaughtering animals in

---

[196] The same elements are listed in James' original decision (Acts 15:20) but in different order. A third list, found in 21:25, agrees with the order in 15:29.

[197] Exodus 20:3-5; Deuteronomy 5:7-9. In 1 Corinthians Paul applies the prohibition to meat purchased in the public market as well as to food consumed in a pagan cultic meal (8; 10:14-33).

[198] Genesis 9:4; Leviticus 3:17, 7:26; 17:10-14; 19:26a; Deuteronomy 12:16, 23; 15:23; 1 Samuel 14:34. Some have interpreted "blood" in the passage in Acts as a reference to murder—as if murder were a common practice among Gentiles, and murderers would be acceptable to Jewish Christians as long as they agreed not to continue killing people! Different readings of Acts 15:20 in ancient MSS make a definitive interpretation difficult.

[199] See Leviticus 18:6-23.

which the blood would not drain from the animal's body when it dies.[200]

This letter was to be delivered to Antioch by two representatives of the Jerusalem church, Judas and Silas. Both are identified as prophets who later "encourage and strengthen the believers" in Antioch (Acts 15:32, NRSV). After Paul leaves Antioch he and Silas will deliver James' decision as they visit the churches founded on the first missionary journey (Acts 16:4), even though James' letter is addressed only to the churches of Syria and Cilicia.

Paul never mentions James' letter, and on the principle that a primary source (Paul) takes precedence over a secondary source (Acts), scholars generally conclude that the letter was not part of the agreement.[201] Some doubt its existence, suggesting that its origin is due to Luke's own creativity, just as are the speeches of the participants in the conference.[202] However, other scholars believe that Luke possessed a copy of the letter.

As for the letter's contents, Paul himself would not necessarily disagree with parts of it. For example, he himself expresses outrage over an improper marriage and explicitly deals with patronage of prostitutes in the Corinthian church (1 Corinthians 5, 6). In the same writing, he deals at length with food sacrificed to idols, but his treatment of the issue is ambiguous, both supporting the avoidance of such food (1 Corinthians 10:14-22) and allowing it for those who genuinely believe pagan gods do not exist (1 Corinthians 8, 10:23-11:1). In neither the issue of sexual immorality nor food sacrificed to idols, however, is there any mention of the letter from Jerusalem. If Paul was aware of it, he chose to ignore it.[203]

---

[200] Strangulation of animals is never mentioned in the Jewish scriptures.

[201] While Paul had occasion to refer to the letter, to do so would have recognized Jerusalem's authority over himself, which he was not likely to do.

[202] E.g., Haenchen, *Acts*, 468.

[203] Meier, as well as others, makes a convincing case that the letter was a compromise offered by James to the church at Antioch so that Jewish and Gentile Christians could eat together. It was formulated and implemented after Paul left

216

We shall return to the contents of the "apostolic letter" later. For now, we note its importance in Luke's overall agenda. It serves to support his presentation of Paul's mission by providing a constant link to the parent church at Jerusalem. Luke is aware that two forms of authority are present in the Jesus movement: charismatic and traditional, the spiritual and the apostolic. Whereas all authority originates with the divine Spirit, human checks and balances are provided by the authoritative disciples of Jesus whom Luke identifies as "the apostles and the elders" of the Jerusalem church. In Luke's view, Paul's authority is strictly charismatic; he and his gospel must be validated by the divinely appointed authoritative leaders in Jerusalem. This dual schema of authority is necessary to bring unity to the church. The apostolic letter is an important element in that larger picture. It demonstrates that what Paul preaches as a result of his independent revelatory experience is acceptable— with certain reservations—to those who knew Jesus in the flesh.

The Jerusalem conference also plays a central and indispensable role in the structure of Acts. Its literary location is more important for Luke than its actual historical date, of which he may not have been aware.[204] The conference settles the question of circumcision of Gentile converts, thereby making possible Paul's continued mission to the Gentiles. Luke has now set the stage for the expansion of the church into Europe.

Thus Acts and Paul agree on the pivotal issue resolved at the Jerusalem conference—circumcision is not to be required of Gentile converts, an important victory for Paul and Barnabas. However, while this resolution may have seemed at the time reasonable, it might be taken to imply that there were two gospels, one for the Jews (Peter's) and one for the Gentiles (Paul's). Likewise, it did not

---

Antioch on his second missionary journey. Brown and Meier, *Antioch and Rome*, 42-43.

[204] Luke does not attempt to date the conference by correlating it with other publicly known events or political figures, a procedure he often follows elsewhere.

bring about a definitive settlement of the relationship of Christ and the Law for Jewish believers; on the assumption that no one can serve two masters, which of the two was to be the master?[205] Elsewhere, Paul seems ambivalent about Jewish Christian observance of the Law; did he himself as a Jew observe it or not?

> To the Jews I became as a Jew, in order to win Jews. To those under the law I became as one under the law (though I myself am not under the law) so that I might win those under the law. To those outside the law I became as one outside the law (though I am not free from God's law but am under Christ's law) so that I might win those outside the law. To the weak I became weak, so that I might win the weak. I have become all things to all people, that I might by all means save some. (1 Corinthians 9:20-22, NRSV)

What appears as waffling to fit the company being kept would probably be defended by Paul as an example of the freedom given with his apostolic commission to preach the gospel. As a Jewish Christian, Paul was free to observe Jewish commandments, but he was not required to do so. Their former importance was now replaced by life in Christ with its single commandment, to love the neighbor, thereby fulfilling all the commandments. On the other hand, the Gentile Christian should not start obeying the Law, and especially he should not seek circumcision (1 Corinthians 7:18) since that would imply that the Law was still a requisite of salvation.

The question whether it was necessary for Gentile converts to be circumcised was not limited to the early Christians. Josephus relates the relatively recent case of a Gentile king of a small territo-

---

[205] The Gospel According to Matthew presents one position: nothing in the Law is to be dismissed. Those believers who teach otherwise (such as Paul?) are not to be highly regarded (5:19). The concept of the Law's eternal validity is opposed by Paul.

ry in upper Mesopotamia (modern northern Iraq) who received contradictory instruction from two Jews about circumcision. Izates of Adiabene (reigned 31-51 CE), a contemporary of both Philo and Paul, learned about Judaism from a merchant named Ananias. When Izates discovered that his mother, Helena, had already "been brought over to their laws," he desired to do the same and decided to be circumcised. Fearing negative reaction from the people, both Helena and Ananias tried to dissuade Izates. According to Josephus, Ananias told Izates that he could "worship God even without being circumcised . . . for it was this that counted more than circumcision."[206] However, the king is then persuaded by one Eleazar from Galilee, known for his strictness in keeping the Law, that circumcision was necessary for a Gentile to convert to Judaism. Despite the risk to his position, his life, and the lives of others, Izates was convinced and was circumcised. The issue was not merely theoretical, but very real for Izates and others of his family and people interested in the Jewish faith, as well as for Paul and Gentiles contemplating conversion.

While Luke gives the conference a central position in Acts because of the role it plays in his literary outline, in fact the conference also had a key position historically in the course of Paul's mission. Without the agreement regarding his gospel, Paul's mission would have been compromised and indeed subverted by his opponents who would have claimed support for their position by the Jerusalem church (which happened anyway). Paul was keenly aware of what was at stake when he went to Jerusalem to lay out precisely what he and Barnabas had been preaching among the Gentiles. Paul was undoubtedly initially pleased with the results of the conference, but that would soon change.

---

[206] Josephus, *Jewish Antiquities* 20:41.

Conflict over Purity Observance in Antioch

The Jerusalem conference completed, Paul and his companions returned to Antioch, confident that a crisis had been averted and the way was open for inclusion of the Gentiles without further challenge. Sometime later, Cephas (Peter) also came to Antioch, where his ambivalent behavior led Paul to conclude that he had reneged on the previous agreement:

> But when Peter came to Antioch, I opposed him to his face, because he stood self-condemned; for until certain people came from James, he used to eat with the Gentiles. But after they came, he drew back and kept himself separate for fear of the circumcision faction. And the other Jews joined him in this hypocrisy, so that even Barnabas was led astray by their hypocrisy. But when I saw that they were not acting consistently with the truth of the gospel, I said to Cephas before them all, "If you, though a Jew, live like a Gentile and not like a Jew, how can you compel the Gentiles to live like Jews?" (Galatians 2:11-14, NRSV)

Although this event took place in a different city in another province, what Paul here describes was continuous with the Jerusalem conference. After the Antioch deputation left to return home, the "circumcision faction" whose objections to Antioch's non-circumcision of Gentile converts had made the conference necessary and who had tried to influence its outcome, continued their attack. Unsuccessful in achieving their first goal, they now pursued a different path by focusing on dietary regulations. Paul's letter to the Galatians allows us to reconstruct the course of events. The following stages may be discerned:

1. Cephas came to Antioch. His motive is not stated. Perhaps he came to participate in a continuing mission to Jews in Antioch and environs, or perhaps to make certain that the outcome of the Jerusalem conference was represented by other than Paul and Barnabas. In any case, while there he regularly shared in meals with Gentile members of the church.[207] Paul describes this as "living like a Gentile."

2. Some representatives of James arrive, following which Cephas refuses to eat with Gentiles. Paul attributes Cephas' change of behavior to fear of the "men of the circumcision."

3. Cephas' example sets off a chain reaction among all the other Jewish Christians who now also refrain from eating with Gentile Christians. Paul brands this attitude as "hypocrisy," behavior "inconsistent with the truth of the gospel."

The field of conflict has now shifted from circumcision to food laws, a matter which had not surfaced previously except in James' letter, the conditions of which Paul does not admit to be part of the Jerusalem agreement. It should be recognized that asking Jewish Christians to contravene their purity regulations as a matter of policy was not to be taken lightly. Eating with Gentiles in a context where the Jewish believers did not control the source of food and its preparation would not be possible if they took food purity seriously. Years later we see Paul more sympathetically dealing with Jewish Christian consciences regarding this matter (e.g., Romans 14), but at this time he is unbending. For Gentile and Jewish believers to be prohibited from eating together unless the former observed Jewish food laws was a denial of the unitary fellowship which was an essential part of the "truth of the gospel." Both Baptism and the Lord's Supper in which "there is no longer Jew or Greek" (Galatians 3:28, NRSV) would be evacuated of their meaning.

---

[207] The Greek verb tense indicates this was not a one-time occurrence but happened over a period of time: "he used to eat."

In Paul's thinking, purification by Christ's self-sacrifice implied that former purity rules were to be left in the past. Either Christ was the reconciling and unifying factor between humans and God, and between Jew and Gentile, or else "Christ died for nothing." (Galatians 2:21, NRSV) His purifying death replaced all purifying commandments and rituals. For Paul, there was no compromise on such a fundamental matter. Before meeting Jesus, Paul's own purity practices were part of his self-definition as a Separatist, a Pharisee. Afterward, those practices were part of the "garbage" he discarded. Christ and separatism were incompatible.

But Paul was the odd man out. The entire Jewish Christian segment of the Antioch church, including even his colleague Barnabas, sided with Cephas. In exasperation, Paul denounces Cephas publicly. How could he who had lived like a Gentile now require Gentiles to live like Jews? Peter's reply is not recorded.

How did this situation come about? The pivotal event was obviously the arrival in Antioch of representatives of James. They had brought with them something that addressed the practice of Jewish and Gentile believers eating together. What was that something? We know of only one candidate, the apostolic letter described in Acts 15.

The contents of James' letter qualify the formerly unqualified acceptance of Paul's policy regarding Gentile entrance into the Jesus movement. It would require Gentiles to follow at least some Jewish practices of food selection and preparation. Gentile believers would no longer be able to eat with family and friends who did not also observe food purity according to the Jewish way, or to accept meat customarily handed out to the public at festivals by public officials. Kosher meat markets would have to be patronized, if they were locally available. These were huge impositions and, from Paul's perspective, to what end? He had given up the idea that some foods were clean and others unclean. That was part of the Judaism he now considered irrelevant to the kingdom of God. Worse, the very notion cut at the heart of his gospel of pure grace, of the unqualified and equitable love of God for all humanity revealed in Christ.

Luke's representation of the letter from James is consistent with the conditions surrounding the conflict over purity at Antioch, but he wrongly gives it a place in the Jerusalem agreement. Paul's letter to the Galatians rules out any direct connection between James' letter and the conference. He insists that at the conference the Jerusalem leaders "contributed nothing to me" (Galatians 2:6). But now that was precisely what was happening at Antioch. At Jerusalem it had been agreed that he and Barnabas would go to the Gentiles; now, James would burden Paul's gospel of Gentile freedom from the Law with a selection of purity regulations from the Law. James' subsequent unilateral "addition" to his gospel was contrary to the Jerusalem agreement, one more attempt to "enslave" the Gentiles. There was a principle at stake on which Paul would not bend. The compromise offered by James would allow Gentiles and Jews to eat together. But to Paul, its acceptance implied an imposition of the Jewish Law on Gentiles, which was out of the question. Paul insisted on both retaining his Law-free gospel and the practice of unrestricted eating together.

Luke's placing of James' letter within the Jerusalem agreement appears to be the position taken by Paul's opponents in Galatia. Paul counters with his own recollection of the sequence of events; he tries to set the record straight, even swearing an oath to strengthen his case. But the subsequent account in Acts became the definitive description. It smoothed over the disagreements in which Paul was engaged in order to present a unified picture of the early church. Perhaps Luke's insistence on unity was one reason that he does not utilize Paul's letters.

The result of the blowup in Antioch was alienation between Paul and Peter, Paul and Barnabas, and Paul and the other Jewish Christians at Antioch. According to Acts, both Paul and Barnabas continue missionary work, but each with a new companion. Luke minimizes the seriousness of the separation of Paul and Barnabas, explaining that it was due to a disagreement over whether to take John Mark on their next trip. There is no reference in Acts to the schism which arose over purity issues in Antioch of which Paul writes. Peter's presence in Antioch, the representatives of James arriving in Antioch, and a conflict between Peter and Paul are not mentioned in Acts. Their absence points to Luke's desire to promote both the appearance of past unity and the actualization of future unity. Paul reveals the real issue because it is related to the Galatian situation facing him, even though it meant acknowledging that he lost the debate there over observance of purity laws. The church at Antioch followed its own conscience, or at least the conscience of the Jewish Christians. Paul followed his convictions and with a new companion left Antioch for a new mission field.

Summary

The first fourteen years of Paul's life after his call to take the story of Christ to the Gentiles were spent in the East, primarily in Syria and Cilicia. Initially, he had gone into Arabia, probably for a short time, and then returned to Damascus. Three years after his revelation he went to Tarsus and then to Antioch, having stopped in Jerusalem to spend a couple of weeks with Peter, Jesus' most famous follower. In Antioch he teamed up with a senior evangelist, Barnabas. Various missions by the two in Syria and Cilicia were sponsored by the congregations of Antioch. Their missionary strategy is well represented in Luke's story of the first journey. Under Barnabas' direction, he and Paul address both Jews and God-fearers in local synagogues, create mixed congregations of believers, and move on to repeat that procedure. They return later to provide further support to these churches.

Luke's account of an actual foray into Cyprus, Phrygia, and Lycaonia (the last two in southern Galatia) is difficult to harmonize with Paul's letter to the Galatians. Whether or not that journey is based on reliable sources, it certainly can be taken as a model representing Luke's view of what Barnabas and Paul were doing over an extended period of time.

In any case, the missionaries' policy of not following the traditional practice of incorporating male converts into Israel through circumcision came under fire from the "circumcision party" based in Jerusalem. Consequently, the church at Antioch sent Paul and Barnabas to confer with the authorities in the Jerusalem church. It was a church-to-church meeting through their key leaders. The result was an agreement with three elements. First, circumcision would not be required of Gentiles. Second, Barnabas and Paul would confine their mission to the Gentiles, while Peter would be the apostle to the Jews. Third, the Antioch church would financially contribute to supporting the "poor" in the Jerusalem church.[208]

Following the conference, a second conflict arose when James sent a delegation to Antioch with an additional set of requirements. The circumcision issue was settled, but Jewish Christians who still followed the dietary laws were placed in a difficult situation when eating with Gentile Christians. James' letter provided a solution, namely, for the Gentiles to follow some basic purity regulations. If they did not accept that proposal, then Christians of Jewish background should not eat with Gentile believers. This policy was embraced by the Jewish Christians at Antioch, but not by Paul who saw it as a disregard of the "truth of the gospel." Inasmuch as it was another imposition of the Law on Gentiles, it denied the primacy of God's grace and acceptance of a new era in God's plan to heal humanity.

Paul and the other Jewish Christians at Antioch were at such cross-purposes that he could no longer be associated with their missions. Leaving with a new companion, he turned to the West. No longer connected to a base congregation, he was virtually on his own as he entered a new phase of his life as an envoy of Christ.

---

[208] One suspects that the "relief visit" of Acts 11:27-30 must have had some connection to Antioch's agreement to support the poor in Jerusalem. However, if there was a connection, precisely what it was continues to elude scholars.

CHAPTER 9: From Antioch to Corinth

L uke has carefully prepared the reader for Paul's "second" missionary journey. Barnabas has been replaced with a new colleague, Silas. Considerable information about Silas has already been supplied which the reader is expected to remember.[209] It is significant that Paul's new partner, like Barnabas, is also closely connected to Jerusalem. Despite the troubles caused by the conservative Jewish Christians there, the Paul of Acts does not cut off relations with the Jerusalem church. Continued linkage between Paul and Jerusalem is essential. Paul's authority as a missionary is derived not only from his divine calling, but also from the foundational Jerusalem church. Paul and Silas will be together for an extended but undetermined period, presumably throughout the second missionary journey. Both Luke and Paul make their final references to him in connection with Paul's initial activity in Corinth, ca. 50 CE (Acts 18:5; 2 Corinthians 1:19). Assuming that Silas in fact did join Paul when he left Antioch, we can also assume that Silas had a change of heart and now agreed with Paul's negative response to the apostolic missive from Jerusalem, despite Luke's account.[210]

---

[209] Silas is mentioned 12 times in Acts, and twice in Paul's letters where he uses the Latin version of his name, Silvanus (1 Thessalonians 1:1; 2 Corinthians 1:19). According to Acts 16:37, Silas was a Roman citizen.

[210] Is it believable that one of James' representatives entrusted to deliver the missive requiring Gentile believers to observe purity laws was the same person chosen by Paul as his future evangelistic companion when he left Antioch? If so, he must have undergone a radical change of mind. Another possibility is that the Silas of Acts and the Silvanus of Paul's letters are two different persons. Luke may have known of a companion of Paul by the same name, and assumed that he was the Jerusalem Silas. Such an identification would provide additional continuity between Paul and the leaders in Jerusalem.

Leaving Antioch, the two missionaries travel overland through Syria and Cilicia, revisiting Christian communities founded earlier (Acts 15:41). Luke had previously not mentioned churches in Syria and Cilicia other than at Antioch. Their appearance here comes as a surprise, though Paul writes that he was in that area during the time between his two visits to Jerusalem (Galatians 1:21). Although he gives no information about founding churches there, we would expect them to have been created and sustained during that period of his life.

Luke then traces the journey of Paul and Silas into southern Galatia, where they visit the congregations at Derbe and Lystra, formed during Paul's first missionary trip. In the latter city Timothy, highly regarded by the Christians in Lystra and Iconium, joins the missionary team at Paul's invitation. Despite the agreement in Jerusalem, the letter from James to the church in Antioch, and Paul's own policy regarding Gentiles, Paul requires Timothy to be circumcised. How is that to be explained, when Paul so vigorously opposed those who require circumcision of Gentiles at the Jerusalem conference? The answer is that Timothy's father was a Greek while his mother was Jewish (and Christian). Technically, therefore, Timothy was a Jew, even though he hadn't been circumcised.[211] At a later time, Paul states the policy which may explain his decision to have Timothy circumcised:

> So whether you eat or drink, or whatever you do, do everything for the glory of God. Give no offence to Jews or to Greeks or to the church of God, just as I try to please everyone in everything I do, not seeking my own advantage, but that of many, so that they may be saved. Be imitators of me, as I am of Christ. (1 Corinthians 10:31-11:1, NRSV)

---

[211] While this is a possible, even probable, explanation, historical evidence for the definition of a Jew as one born of a Jewish mother is lacking for the first century.

Luke's explanation is consistent with Paul's policy: it was "because of the Jews who were in those places, for they all knew that his father was a Greek." (Acts 16:3, NRSV) Paul was not opposed to circumcision of Jews, only of Gentiles. He needed to demonstrate that policy. Circumcision had not been required of Titus at the Jerusalem conference even though he was a Greek. Paul's policy was affirmed. Likewise in the present case. Timothy, an uncircumcised Jew, was being circumcised for a particular practical reason, namely, to avoid unnecessarily offending other Jews and perhaps other Jewish Christians. That action was intended to facilitate Paul's proclamation of the gospel. Paul had more than enough opposition from his Jewish compatriots without courting more.

We gather from no fewer than eleven references to Timothy in Paul's authentic letters[212] (and four in the disputed letters[213]) that Timothy became an important and highly esteemed player in Paul's missionary endeavors.[214] His Greek name, "he who gives God honor," was fitting, according to Paul's glowing reports of him. Mentioned as the co-sender of four of Paul's letters[215] (and probably the secretary who wrote them at Paul's dictation), Timothy is described as brother, co-worker, and Paul's "child," i.e., his convert.[216] He becomes the trusted representative of Paul, who will

---

[212] 1 Thessalonians 1:1; 3:2, 6; 1 Corinthians 4:17; 16:10; 2 Corinthians 1:1, 19; Philippians 1:1; 2:19; Philemon 1; Romans 16:21.

[213] Colossians 1:1; 2 Thessalonians 1:1; 1 Timothy 1:2; 2Timothy 1:2. Timothy is also mentioned in Hebrews 13:23, and in Acts 16:1; 17:14-15; 18:5; 19:22; 20:4.

[214] Luke calls Timothy a "disciple," one of his two favorite terms for Christians, found nearly thirty times in Acts ("brother" or "brethren" appears nearly forty times; "believer" is used only three times, though English translations often use it to translate the Greek word for brother, *adelphos*). Although Luke mentions the disciples first being called Christians in Antioch (Acts 11:26), he never again employs that designation.

[215] 2 Corinthians, Philippians, 1 Thessalonians, and Philemon.

[216] This imagery points to the classification of Christian assemblies as "fictive families." While Paul often refers to other believers as "brothers" or "sisters," he

later send him to congregations earlier formed to encourage and build them up. Paul may even include Timothy (and Silvanus) in his reference to "apostles of Christ" in 1 Thessalonians 2:7. None of Paul's team receives greater praise from him than Timothy.

Luke next describes in the briefest fashion a lengthy and arduous trip up through the territories of Phrygia and Galatia and nearly to the southern border of Bithynia (Acts 16:6-8). Forbidden by the Spirit to undertake either of two planned initiatives, first into the province of Asia to the west and then into Bithynia in the north, the missionary party proceeds to Troas on the Aegean coast.[217]

The Galatian Churches

Before following Paul's journey further, we pause to consider the issue of the location of the churches addressed in his letter to the Galatians. Many scholars believe their origin is suggested in Acts 16:6-8 where Luke describes the path taken by Paul and his companions. He refers first to Phrygia and then Galatia, apparently suggesting that Paul traveled through the traditional area of the Celts. Although the account in Acts has the team then turning westward, it is speculated that before then they had gone to one or more of the cities of Pessinus, Gordium, and Ancyra (modern Ankara, Turkey), where they founded the churches addressed

---

sometimes alludes to becoming the "father" of his converts: "my child, Onēsimus, whose father I have become" (Philemon 10, NRSV); "my beloved children" (1 Corinthians 4:14, NRSV). In passing, we note that the author of the Gospel According to Matthew insisted on applying "father" to God alone: "Call no one your father on earth, for you have one Father—the one in heaven." (Matthew 23:9, NRSV) Likewise, he disallowed the titles "rabbi" and "teacher" ("instructor" in NRSV) to be applied to anyone except Jesus (23:10).

[217] Was the reason he did not go into Bithynia that churches had already been established there? "Thus I make it my ambition to proclaim the good news, not where Christ has already been named, so that I do not build on another's foundation. . . ." (Romans 15:20, NRSV)

in Paul's letter to the Galatians (the North Galatia Hypothesis). Other scholars hold that the Galatian churches are those named in Acts, which Paul founded during his "first" missionary journey in the cities of Pisidian Antioch, Iconium, Lystra, and Derbe (the South Galatian Hypothesis).

The casual reader of Acts would naturally assume that the churches addressed in Paul's letter to the Galatians must have been those named in Acts 13-14, in the southern part of Galatia. However, residents of that part of the province were not actually Galatians in the ethnic sense. The real Galatians were descendants of migrating Celts (Gauls) who had settled in northern Asia Minor in the early third century, BCE. In ca. 25 BCE, the emperor Augustus annexed their territory and combined it with other ethnic territories to create the province of Galatia cutting down through the center of Asia Minor from northeast to southwest. Thus by Paul's time "Galatia" could signify either the territory of the Celts in the north or the whole province which incorporated a number of territories.

In the body of his letter, Paul scolds his audience as "foolish Galatians." (3:1) It seems strange that Paul would address people who belonged to diverse ethnic groups as Galatians. Therefore, it is argued, the letter must have been written to churches in the territory where the ethnic Galatians lived.

What can be gleaned from the reference in Acts 16:6 to the sequence in the "region of Phrygia and Galatia?" Like the title "Galatia," this dual reference is ambiguous. It could be taken as a reference to two different territories, first the Phrygian and then the more northerly Galatian. The implication would be that Paul successively went through Phrygia into Galatia where he founded the Galatian churches. However, the phrase could also refer to the area in which Antioch was located, where the Phrygian territory and the province of Galatia coincided. That view is supported by Luke's use of the same names, but in reverse order, in 18:23 which reads "the Galatian region and Phrygian." (NRSV) In this case,

Paul was on his way to Ephesus, ruling out a route into northern Galatia. Luke's employment of this territorial combination is clearly too ambiguous to serve as evidence either way.

A more relevant piece of evidence is that Paul's letter assumes the readers are Gentiles. He warns them against being circumcised (5:2-3; 6:12), hardly appropriate for Jewish Christians. Their exclusively Gentile background is directly stated:

> Formerly, when you did not know God, you were enslaved to beings that by nature are not gods. (Galatians 4:8, NRSV)

Acts indicates that mixed congregations resulted from the apostolic proclamation in Pisidian Antioch and Iconium. The content of Galatians would not be appropriate for them, but quite relevant to churches in the north where no evidence of first-century Jewish settlement has turned up.

Further, in his letter tracing his relative lack of direct contact with the Jerusalem church, Paul omits any reference to spending time in Galatia prior to the Jerusalem conference. If the Galatian churches had been founded before his second trip to Jerusalem, he surely would have mentioned it as it would add to his evidence for his independence of Jerusalem.

On the other hand, there are questions raised by the North Galatia Hypothesis. Barnabas is repeatedly mentioned in Acts as Paul's partner during their mission to the four cities in the south. Likewise, in his letter to the Galatians, Paul refers to Barnabas as if the readers know him. On his second missionary trip up through Asia Minor into ethnic Galatian territory, Barnabas was no longer with Paul, at least according to Acts. However, he is obviously known to the Corinthian believers as Paul' companion (1 Corinthians 9:6).

Further, Luke knows of no churches in the northern part of Galatia, but he does have knowledge of those in its southern area. In particular he is able to provide details about Timothy's family in

Lystra and his reputation there and in Iconium. If Paul founded churches in north central Galatia, why is Luke unaware of them? If he did know about them, what reason would he have for excluding them from his account?

In regard to the opening address in his letter to the Galatians, is it likely that Paul would employ "Galatians" in the ethnic sense? In contrast to Luke, Paul normally uses provincial rather than territorial names.[218] When he addresses his letter to "the churches of Galatia" (Galatians 1:2), he is almost certainly employing the word "Galatia" in the provincial sense. The same phrase is used in 1 Corinthians 16:1, and it is reasonable to assume it has the same meaning in both places.[219] That Paul who declared that in Christ former ethnic divisions no longer existed would use an ethnic designation in the address of one of his letters seems unlikely. Further, most cities of that period were a mixture of various ethnic groups. To take literally Paul's phrase "foolish Galatians" would imply that their churches were composed exclusively with descendants of the Gauls.

Another relevant issue is Paul's missionary strategy after he severed connections with the church in Antioch. We must beware of allowing Acts to determine our picture. While Paul may have continued to address where possible both Jews and God-fearers who attended the synagogues, that was not necessarily always his procedure, or even his primary one. He had not planned to evangelize in Galatia, as he tells us:

---

[218] Paul's geographical nomenclature includes both cities and provinces. For the cities: Jerusalem, Cenchreae, Corinth, Athens, Ephesus, Troas, Damascus, Antioch (in Syria), Philippi, Thessalonica, and Rome. For the provinces: Judea, Illyricum, Spain, Macedonia, Achaia, Galatia, Syria and Cilicia. He also mentions Arabia, which was not yet a Roman province in his time. The provincial status and geographical limits of Cilicia were fluid under Roman rule. It was administered by the governor of Syria from early in Augustus' reign.

[219] Parallels are found in Paul's references to the believers or churches of Macedonia (2 Corinthians 8:1; 11:9; 1 Thessalonians 1:7, 8; 4:10) and of Achaia (Romans 15:26; 1 Corinthians 16:15; 2 Corinthians 1:1; 9:2; 11:10; 1 Thessalonians 1:7, 8).

You know that it was because of a physical infirmity that I first announced the gospel to you; though my condition put you to the test, you did not scorn or despise me, but welcomed me as an angel of God, as Christ Jesus. (Galatians 4:13-14, NRSV)

If there were no Jews in this area in Paul's time, how did he make contacts in order to evangelize? Did he hire someone to care for his health needs and convert that person, and then contact others through her or him? After recovering from his illness, did he then find employment in a workshop and proclaim his message to other workers and customers? There are various possibilities, but no hard evidence to guide us. However, the fact that most of Paul's churches to whom he wrote letters were predominantly Gentile in composition suggests that he did find ways to proclaim the gospel apart from synagogues.[220]

Although there are enough unanswered questions involved with both hypotheses to caution against certainty, the North Galatia Hypothesis has slightly more to recommend it and will be assumed from this point on. The Gentile make-up of the congregations addressed in Paul's letter to the Galatians and the fact that they had not yet come into existence when the Jerusalem conference was held are not otherwise sufficiently explained.

The uncertain location of the Galatian churches has been raised not only to inform the reader of the issues, but also because it is a reminder of the difficulties in attempting to reconstruct Paul's activities as a founder and nurturer of congregations. In addition, it serves as an example of looking to scholarly proposals rather than uncritically accepting the account in Acts as "gospel truth."

---

[220] E.g., in the "lecture hall of Tyrannus" in Ephesus. (Acts 19:9, NRSV)

Philippi

At Troas the missionary party is persuaded by a night vision of Paul's, not mentioned in his letters but only in Acts 16:9-10, to cross the Aegean to Macedonia. In the vision or dream Paul sees a Macedonian requesting help, which the missionaries interpret as a divine directive. Once again, Luke's story reaches a turning point at which God shows the way forward through a revelatory vision.

At this point, a new source is introduced by Luke. It has the character of a travel itinerary and has been variously called the "we-source," the "we-passages," or the "Travel Document." Though unlikely, it is not impossible that the author of Acts is also the author of these sections. There is nothing to distinguish them literarily from the rest of Acts apart from their use of the first person plural, their greater detail, and the fact that they deal mostly with sea voyages. Many scholars have accepted these four passages as parts of an actual travel diary. Tradition has it that the diarist was Luke the physician, the author of Luke-Acts, who must have joined Paul's entourage at Troas. Alternatively, some see here the hand of Timothy. But why would so much of Timothy's journal be missing when he had been with Paul since they were at Lystra and would be present much of the time from this point on? Likewise, the notion that the writer was Silas who had presumably accompanied Paul since leaving Antioch in Syria is subject to the same criticism. That the author of Acts has created the appearance of a travel diary in the interests of verisimilitude is also not convincing.

In any case, the missionary party, taking advantage of favorable winds for sailing northwest, now embarks on a two-day boat trip to Neapolis, the port city for Philippi to which they subsequently proceed. Philippi was located on the Via Egnatia, the main east-west Roman highway between the Adriatic Sea and the city of Byzantium on the Sea of Marmara. Philippi was a Roman colony originally established for military veterans. Here the missionaries attend a Jewish "place of prayer"[221] outside the city walls. Their first convert is the wealthy Gentile "God-worshiper" Lydia, a trader from Thyatira in the province of Asia.[222] She offers to host the missionaries, and her house becomes their base of operations and the meeting place for converts (Acts 16:15, 40), in other words, a house-church.[223] In Roman social terms, she becomes their patron, i.e., she performs generous services to Paul and his entourage, who in turn become her clients. In another sense, the missionaries are the patrons and she is the client since her salvation has been gained through them, and she repays the favor by hosting them and providing a meeting place for converts.[224] In either case, each benefits from the transaction.

Luke goes on to narrate a second string of related events, beginning with Paul's exorcism of the spirit[225] possessing a fortune-telling slave girl. Having now lost the income she brought her owners, they bring charges of disturbing the peace against Paul and Silas. The Roman authorities have them beaten with rods and jailed. During the night an earthquake loosens the prisoners' chains and the jailer is converted by Paul. The next day Paul and Silas are released and leave the city.

---

[221] This phrase usually refers to a synagogue, but synagogues were normally located within cities, not outside them.

[222] It is possible that by the term "worshiper of God" Luke only means that she was a pious woman, but more likely that she was a Gentile adherent of Judaism. "Lydia" is also the name of the territory in which Thyatira was located.

[223] Paul refers to "the church in your house" (Philemon 2), and "the church in their house" (1 Corinthians 16:19; Romans 16:5). The earliest congregations met in houses of wealthy Christian patrons. Dedicated church buildings came much later.

[224] Seeking wealthy patrons as early converts in a new area was likely part of Paul's strategy. A meeting place where a community of believers could be developed and which provided a base for converting others was essential.

[225] Identified by Luke as a "Pythonic spirit," i.e., the spirit of divination associated with the Delphic Oracle inspired by the god Apollo who had killed the resident dragon Python.

All this information is found primarily in Acts. Paul's letter to the Philippian church does not mention Lydia or the church in her house. Likewise, the stories about the overnight imprisonment of Paul and Silas, a consequence of Paul's exorcism of the slave girl (Acts 16:16-18), the earthquake, and the conversion of the jailer and his household have no parallel in Paul's letter.[226]

However, Paul does write that "we had already suffered and been shamefully mistreated at Philippi. . . ." (1 Thessalonians 2:2, NRSV), a statement consistent with their arrest and having been illegally beaten and jailed, even though they were Roman citizens. Also, in 2 Corinthians 11:25 he refers to having been beaten with rods three times, one of which could have been this event. Further, in Philippians 1:30 Paul compares the difficulties he faced and still faces in Philippi with those experienced by his readers in Philippi. The word here translated "struggle" (Greek *agōn*) is drawn from the athletic arena; it can refer to the contest itself, the concentrated effort of the athlete to win, or the pain involved in competing. Paul thinks here of his ministry as a contest and of himself—and other Christians—as athletes in a race (Philippians 2:16; 3:13-14). Racing imagery contains numerous dimensions which can be exploited as metaphors of the Christian life—the necessary discipline to complete the course, the pain of long-distance running, perseverance, keeping one's thoughts on the prize and the honor it brings.[227] Paul assumes that suffering is involved in this race; Christ himself set the example.

Neither Paul nor Luke indicates the length of time Paul and his company spent in Philippi. The account in Acts is sketchy; Luke is more interested here as elsewhere in Paul's itinerary and

---

[226] While the story of the slave girl is assigned by Luke to the Travel Document, the accounts of the earthquake and the miraculous release of Paul and Silas from their chains are not. With the exorcism, the first we-passage in Acts ends.

[227] The racing metaphor is employed primarily by Paul; outside his letters (1 Corinthians 9:24, 26; Galatians 2:2, 5:7; Philippians 2:16) it is found only in 2 Timothy 4:7 and Hebrews 12:1.

deliverances from danger than in the make-up and character of churches he founded. Acts gives the impression that Paul and his companions were in Philippi for a very short time, being forced out of the city by the local Roman authorities soon after their arrival. Paul's letter suggests a more extended stay, long enough to establish a thriving congregation and forge long-lasting bonds with its members.

In contrast to most of the cities visited by the missionaries, there was apparently no synagogue in Philippi; neither author mentions a Jewish presence beyond the "place of prayer" where some women were gathering (Acts 16:13, 16). [228] The charge brought against Paul and Silas identifies them as Jews advocating anti-Roman customs (Acts 16:20-21) in this Roman colony. The crowd also demonstrates an anti-Jewish attitude, supporting the conclusion that the city was not friendly to Jews. Opposition to the missionaries came strictly from Gentiles. When Paul later writes about facing "danger from Gentiles," (2 Corinthians 11:26) his thoughts may have included his experience in Philippi. As in Galatians, nothing in Philippians points to a mixed congregation.

Thessalonica

When Paul and his missionary team left Philippi, they traveled west on the Via Egnatia, to Amphipolis, about 50 kilometers (30 miles) from Philippi. Apollonia was yet another day's travel west.[229] Acts merely indicates that the missionaries "passed through" these cities, with no elaboration. Neither city is mentioned in Paul's letters. The party then pushed fur-

---

[228] Excavations in the ancient city have turned up no evidence of a synagogue.

[229] Apollonia was in the news in 2000 when a solid gold wreath of the 4th century BCE was discovered in a farmer's field in the immediate area of the city. The city walls were subsequently located and it was determined that the city could have had a population of about 10,000, approximately the size of Athens at that time.

ther west to Thessalonica, the capital of the province, where the proconsul resided.

Luke reports that there was a synagogue in Thessalonica, and of course, Paul went there to proclaim Jesus as the Messiah. Over a period of three Sabbaths he persuaded some Jews, many pious Greeks, and "not a few of the leading women," that the Messiah had to suffer and die (Acts 17:2-4). Such a novel idea did not mesh with traditional Jewish beliefs, as Peter demonstrated in the Gospels (Mark 8:31-33 and parallels). As in Antioch of Pisidia, Iconium, and Lystra, Jewish opposition arose and Paul was forced to leave. Such opposition is understandable; after all, from their point of view, these strangers were not only peddling unbelievable ideas, they were also attempting to make inroads into their membership and adherents who supported the local Jewish community. While Jewish opposition to the Jesus movement is an ongoing theme throughout Acts, that does not mean that Luke has made it up. It is inherently realistic and probable. Paul himself testifies to it in his letters.

Luke's literary pattern which molds his information about Paul's missionary work in specific cities is fairly consistent. Paul arrives at a certain city, goes to the synagogue where he preaches Jesus as the Messiah, provokes opposition, usually from Jews but occasionally from Gentiles, and is forced to flee to the next city in which the process is repeated. Where Paul's letters to specific churches exist, they are the main sources of information about those congregations. Where such letters do not exist, the life of these congregations is largely a blank.

Acts reports that some of the Jews in Thessalonica were persuaded by Paul and Silas, but that it was mostly Gentiles who were converted. Paul's letter to the Thessalonians suggests the believers there were exclusively Gentiles:

> . . . you turned to God from idols, to serve a living and true God. . . . (1 Thessalonians 1:9, NRSV)

Such a statement would be far off the mark if addressed to Jewish Christians. Yet, Luke reports a specific set of events involving a person who likely was a Jewish Christian. Luke writes that the Jews provoked a mob which, unable to locate the missionaries themselves, attacked the house of Jason. His role is not identified, but we can assume it was similar to Lydia's in Philippi. That is, Jason was the host of the local assembly of believers. Jason is a fairly common Greek name given to Jews whose Hebrew name was Joshua (Aramaic Yeshua). Paul later mentions a Jason present with him in Corinth (Romans 16:21), identified as his "relative" or perhaps a fellow Jew (Greek *syngeneis*). They may be the same person, but the name is too common to be certain. In any case, the probability is that Jason in Thessalonica was a Jewish Christian, which backs up Luke's claim that some Jews were persuaded by the missionaries. However, Jason's Jewish identity is not necessarily inconsistent with the Gentile character of the church addressed by Paul.

Jason and other believers were brought before the city authorities and accused of hosting trouble-makers who were teaching that there was another king beside Caesar. This is a serious charge, similar to the one brought against Jesus, and explains why Paul and his companions are spirited out of the city that night.

Paul's letter to the Thessalonians draws a parallel between its Gentile recipients and the churches in Judea:

> For you, brothers and sisters, became imitators of the churches of God in Christ Jesus that are in Judea, for you suffered the same things from your own compatriots as they did from the Jews, who killed both the Lord Jesus and the prophets, and drove us out; they displease God and oppose everyone by hindering us from speaking to the Gentiles so that they may be saved. Thus they have constantly been fill-

ing up the measure of their sins; but God's wrath has over-taken them at last. (1 Thessalonians 2:14-16, NRSV)[230]

Some scholars have suggested that this passage is an interpolation. However, the evidence for its authenticity is overwhelming. Perhaps Paul was still stinging from the Jewish attack on the missionaries at Thessalonica reported by Luke, those who were acting to prevent them from speaking to the Gentiles. In any case, Paul cannot be absolved from writing this passage.

Taken at face value, this passage is shocking in its attack on Jews—by another Jew! Yet, when examined more closely within the context of the point Paul is making, it becomes less reprehensible and more comprehensible. This passage concludes a series of statements beginning in 1:6, focusing on something the missionaries and the believers in Thessalonica have in common: persecution. Two instances of "imitation" stand out: First, in being persecuted the readers became imitators of Paul and his fellow missionaries—and of Jesus himself (1:6); i.e., all three parties shared ill-treatment from those who oppose their commitment to the gospel and their new way of life.

Second, the readers imitated the Judean churches in the sense that both were persecuted by their own people, Jews in Judea and Gentiles in Thessalonica. What Paul writes is not an indictment of Jews per se, but of those, especially in Judea, who violently opposed the gospel—as he himself had originally done! In particular, he targets those who would prevent the Gentile mission in which he was engaged. This was a time of profound conflict in the Jewish communities between those Jews like Paul who were introducing a new way of being Jewish and other Jews who defended traditional Judaism, its Law and its temple. The conflict would continue until

---

[230] This passage is the larger part of what has been called a "second thanksgiving," beginning with 2:13.

240

the Jesus movement shifted its sights primarily, even exclusively, to the Gentiles and took on a new, non-Jewish identity.

Having expressed his gratitude that the Thessalonians were persevering in their faith despite persecution, Paul turns to some areas where further growth was needed. Initiation into Paul's communities began with baptism during which confession of faith was made by the convert. As far as is known, baptism had been practiced by all the Christian groups from the time of Jesus' disciples on.[231] They had taken over the practice from John the Baptist. He baptized other repentant Jews as ritual purification, removal of their sins so that they could face the coming Day of Judgment with confidence. Christian baptism went a step further—it was also associated with the giving of the Spirit to the believer. (See Acts 19:1-7)

Paul develops his own meanings for baptism, all closely related to faith. Baptism symbolizes a transition from the old to the new. It encapsulates the act of turning away from the Adam in oneself and the entry of Christ's transforming Spirit. As Christ died on the cross, so the convert dies to all that alienates him/her from God. Being buried with Christ in the waters of baptism leads to being raised with him into newness of life (Romans 6:3-4).[232] The issue thus is life and death.

Paul was not much interested in conducting the baptismal ceremony itself. He indicates that he himself did not baptize many people at Corinth—he can remember only a few (1 Corinthians 1:14-16). The reason is that:

"Christ did not send me to baptize but to proclaim the gospel . . . ." (1 Corinthians 1:17, NRSV)

---

[231] Only John's Gospel mentions that Jesus' disciples were baptizing during his lifetime. (John 4:1-2)

[232] Note that Paul avoids implying that believers are resurrected in being baptized. Resurrection is future, not present.

Proclaiming the gospel, however, was not concluded when converts were made. Paul's letters exist because of his continuing relationship with the communities being formed. The time following baptism may be considered as the continuation of "sanctification" (1 Thessalonians 4:3-8) which began with baptism. This term "sanctification" (Greek *hagiasmos*) expresses an important concept in Paul's writings, as well as in early Christianity in general.[233] Paul knew that high on the Jewish priority list was the sanctification of all aspects of life, to become a holy people set apart for God's purposes. He imports this idea into his work with Gentiles. He addresses his converts as "saints" (*hagioi*),[234] not because he believes they have achieved a "saintly" life in the mediaeval or modern senses of the term, but because they have been liberated from sin, have joined Christ's body, have been made holy by Christ's sacrifice, and are called to act in holy ways in imitation of Christ.[235] One of the most obvious areas where Gentiles needed to pay special attention was in their sexual ethics, to avoid the whole range of sexual immorality included in *porneia*. Thus Paul cautions his readers to exercise self-control and good judgment and not cross into forbidden territory:

> For God did not call us to impurity but in holiness. (1 Thessalonians 4:7, NRSV)

---

[233] For example, in its verbal form in the Lord's Prayer (Matthew 6:9; Luke 11:2), this term points to actively honoring God's name, which perhaps interprets the requirement of the Third Commandment of not misusing the name of God (Exodus 20:7a).

[234] Three fourths of all uses of "saint" in the NT are found in the writings of the Pauline tradition, including the disputed epistles. Most examples are in the undisputed letters.

[235] "Already" and "not yet" are sometimes called the indicative ("you have been made holy") and the imperative ("now act like it").

Warnings regarding sexual practices will surface again in Paul's letters to the Corinthian "saints" and to the Romans.[236] Sexual improprieties must have been an ongoing concern to Paul and their correction a normal part of his instruction to the Gentiles in all his churches.

A second topic arising from Timothy's report to Paul (1 Thessalonians 3:1-2, 6), or perhaps from a letter Timothy brought from the Thessalonians, concerns "brotherly love" (*philadelphia*). Paul highly praises his readers: they have already been taught by God and their love extends even beyond their own city, so they do not need further instruction from Paul. He is content to urge them to continue what they are doing, "more and more." Involved in that brotherly love is:

> . . . to aspire to live quietly, to mind your own affairs, and to work with your hands, as we directed you, so that you may behave properly towards outsiders and be dependent on no one. (1 Thessalonians 4:11-12, NRSV)

Paul's mention of manual labor may indicate that his converts in Thessalonica were primarily artisans, among whom he had been employed because of his leatherworking skills. His advice not to depend on anyone may warn against receiving compromising patronage from an outside source; perhaps Paul wants the Christian communities to be as self-reliant as possible in order to be free from pressures to live according to worldly values.

Paul's letter to the Thessalonian believers was written within a few months after he left their city, probably in late 49 or early 50 CE. As happened so frequently, his missionary team had been forced to leave town (Acts 17:10), probably long before they would have preferred. Life as a Christian missionary was uncertain in the

---

[236] 1 Corinthians 5:1; 6:13, 18; 7:2; 2 Corinthians 12:21; Romans 2:14-17 (see Chapter 12 below).

extreme; plans often had to be modified. Luke suggests a very short stay in Thessalonica by his mention of three Sabbaths (17:2). Paul's letter does not necessarily contradict Acts on this point; indeed, it expresses his intense anxiety for the continuity of the church there, pointing perhaps to his feeling that he had not finished the job before leaving. It also expresses profound affection for them and relief over learning that his anxiety about the depth of their faith was unfounded.

Beroea

Once again, Paul takes advantage of darkness to leave a city where his evangelistic activity has provoked serious opposition. According to Acts, he and Silas flee to Beroea, some 100 kilometers (60 miles) distant and to the south of the Via Egnatia on which they had been traveling. Like Thessalonica, Beroea had a synagogue. Unlike Thessalonica, the missionaries had substantial success among the Jews as well as the Greeks. No Pauline letter to this congregation has survived, if indeed he ever wrote to them. None of his extant letters even mentions the city. Our only evidence of his activity there comes from Acts 17:10-14 and 20:4, where Luke mentions that Sopater from Beroea is among Paul's travel companions on his final trip to Jerusalem.

When Jews from Thessalonica arrive to oppose the missionaries, Paul leaves Beroea. For some unexplained reason, Silas and Timothy were able to remain there (Timothy had not been mentioned since joining Paul's company in Lystra until now), while Paul is accompanied by some of his new converts to the coast and on to Athens, probably by ship to the port of Piraeus. When his guides/body-guards left him in Athens to return home, Paul instructed them to urge Silas and Timothy to join him soon (Acts 17:15). We shall see later that this separation of Paul from both of the other two members of his team does not match what Paul himself writes.

Athens

As the initial stop on Paul's itinerary for the province of Achaia, Athens proved to be a special challenge. Acts focuses not only on the local synagogue(s), where Paul attempts to persuade both Jews and interested Gentiles of the validity of his teaching, but also reports that he engaged in proclaiming the gospel daily in the market place. There he encountered and debated with representatives of two of the leading philosophical schools, Epicureanism and Stoicism. Invited to the Areopagus[237] to expound further on his teachings, Paul delivers his famous sermon, which of course was composed by Luke. (Acts 17:22-31)[238] Paul persuades a few Athenians,[239] but does not succeed in forming a Christian community in Athens.

No Jewish opposition is mentioned in Acts, despite Paul's debates in the synagogue; this alone suggests Paul's lack of success there. Paul's single reference to Athens is in 1 Thessalonians 3:1 which only mentions the city as the location from which Timothy was sent back to Thessalonica to follow up on the missionaries' earlier work there. Paul has nothing to say about opposition or success in Athens, nor even proclaiming the gospel there. Apart from this one reference, Paul's letters would not suggest that Athens had even been on his itinerary.

---

[237] The very identity of the "Areopagus" is in dispute. Does Luke mean Mars (Ares) Hill, the rocky hill below the Acropolis, or the court or council (the Areopagites) which had traditionally met on the hill?

[238] Note the differences in the two analyses of Gentile religiosity found here and in Romans 1. In Acts 17, Gentiles recognize and worship a god they have not succeeded in naming. In Romans, Paul is much more unforgiving of Gentile waywardness; idolatry is idolatry, and ignorance is no excuse!

[239] Luke names two converts in Athens: Dionysius and Damaris, a male and a female. By naming specific people, Luke is probably indicating they were people of note. We know nothing of Damaris except her uncommon name. Dionysius, on the other hand, is said to be a member of the Council of the Areopagus.

According to Acts 18:5, Silas and Timothy were reunited with Paul not in Athens but later in Corinth. Luke coordinates their reunion with Paul's instructions to the Beroeans to have his two co-missionaries come to him as soon as possible (Acts 17:15). Luke appears not to be aware that in fact the three had been together in Athens, as 1 Thessalonians reveals, and that Timothy was sent back to Thessalonica from there.[240] 1 Thessalonians, which was written from Corinth after Timothy had rejoined the team following his mission to Thessalonica (1 Thessalonians 3:1-2, 6), names as its senders all three of the missionaries: Paul, Silvanus, and Timothy.

Corinth

Corinth was the missionaries' next stop after leaving Athens; Acts and Paul agree on that. Although the two cities were both in southern Achaia, they were very different. Athens was a comparatively small city; its claim to fame was its long history, democratic traditions, and educational achievements and opportunities. Corinth was a relatively young and prosperous city situated on a major sea trade route. Destroyed by the Romans in 146 BCE, it had been rebuilt as a Roman colony a century later by Julius Caesar. Its designation as the capital of the province of Achaia by Augustus plus its favorable location with access to two ports greatly aided its rapid development as a commercial center. When Paul and his companions arrived there in ca. 49-50 CE, Corinth was the leading city in the province of Achaia.[241]

---

[240] This error calls into question Luke's account of Paul's flight from Beroea, according to which Silas and Timothy were left behind.

[241] First century Corinth is sometimes wrongly accused of being an exceptionally "loose" city because of the geographer Strabo's story of its temple of Aphrodite offering a thousand female prostitutes. His account was about the former Greek city which was destroyed in 146 BCE, not about the rebuilt Roman Corinth of Paul's time (Strabo died before Paul began his ministry).

Luke's first report of Paul's stay in Corinth connects him to a married couple of Christian Jews, Aquila and Priscilla.[242] They had been deported from Rome along with other Jews by the emperor Claudius, probably in 49 CE, because of rioting led by "Chrestus."[243] Presumably, this expulsion of Jews was prompted by ongoing discord among them arising from the preaching of Christ in Roman synagogues.

Paul's initial contact with Aquila and Prisca, however, may have come about not only because they were a source of news about the state of the Jesus movement in Rome, but also because he was seeking employment in their leather-working business.[244] The couple provided Paul with both employment and lodging. Paul later testifies to their continued friendship and participation in the Jesus movement after they and Paul had moved to Ephesus (1 Corinthians 16:19; Acts 18:18) and finally after the couple had returned to Rome (Romans 16:3-5a).

Repeating one of his common motifs, Luke has Paul initially proclaiming Jesus in the synagogue during the Sabbath services, but after meeting strong opposition, turning to the Gentiles. But here Luke gives us conflicting information. On the one hand, he presents a picture of a frustrated Paul giving up on the Jews and turning exclusively to the Gentiles (Acts 18:6-7). On the other hand, he then refers to the chief of the synagogue, Crispus,[245] and his household becoming believers, thereby encouraging "many of the Corinthians" to convert (18:8). Luke's agenda sometimes clouds his presentation. In any case, the picture is of a mixed congregation,

---

[242] Paul calls her Prisca. Priscilla is the diminutive of Prisca.

[243] Suetonius, *Life of Claudius* 25:4. Suetonius was an early second century Roman historian.

[244] Acts 18:3 is our major source for the nature of Paul's trade. While Paul's letters refer to his working with his hands, they never specify his trade.

[245] Crispus is named as one of the few believers personally baptized by Paul in Corinth (1 Corinthians 1:14).

which is indeed what we encounter in Paul's correspondence with the Corinthian church.

After the arrival of Timothy from Macedonia,[246] Paul undergoes some major changes in his activities. He leaves his job, finds new living quarters with one of the devoted Gentile God-fearers, Titius Justus, and evangelizes full-time. How could he afford to do that? He must have received financial assistance from some source. Paul later writes regarding his work among the Corinthians:

> I robbed other churches by accepting support from them in order to serve you. And when I was with you and was in need, I did not burden anyone, for my needs were supplied by the friends who came from Macedonia. (2 Corinthians 11:8-9a, NRSV)

Perhaps it was not only the church in Philippi that sent him gifts, but also other Macedonian churches.[247] Paul is now able to expand his labors in the gospel rather than in the leather-working shop.

According to Acts, Paul spent eighteen months in Corinth, exceeded in length only by his subsequent stay of up to three years in Ephesus. He specifies a few people he baptized in Corinth: Crispus, Gaius, and the household of Stephanas (1 Corinthians 1:14, 16). The latter are mentioned elsewhere as the first converts (literally, "first fruits") in Achaia (1 Corinthians 16:15).[248]

---

[246] Paul mentions that Timothy had recently arrived to join "us." (1 Thessalonians 3:6). The "us" indicates that Silvanus/Silas was already with Paul when Timothy arrived.

[247] One is tempted to assume that when Timothy came to Paul in Corinth, he brought those gifts with him. But Paul refers to believers from Macedonia. Perhaps they accompanied Timothy. When carrying a substantial amount of money, it was advisable to travel with trusted others.

[248] Paul's words raise doubts about Luke's claim regarding the prior conversion of Dionysius and Damaris in Athens (Acts 17:34).

248

At some point during his stay in Corinth, Paul was brought before the proconsul by Jews with the accusation:

> "This man is persuading people to worship God in ways that are contrary to the law." (Acts 18:13, NRSV)

The proconsul, Gallio, rightly perceived that the charge was a Jewish matter concerning their Law and irrelevant as far as Roman law was concerned. He refused to hear the case and referred it back to the accusers, reminding them that they had autonomy in enforcing their own Law.

The mention of Gallio has long provided an extra-biblical anchor point for dating Paul's time in Corinth. Unfortunately, Luke does not inform the reader in what part of Gallio's tenure or of Paul's stay in Corinth this event occurred. However, it must have been in either 51 or 52 CE. [249]

Luke next makes the surprising announcement that Paul was leaving Corinth for Syria, accompanied by Priscilla and Aquila as far as Ephesus. Before proceeding from Ephesus, he visited the local synagogue where he refused their invitation to stay longer, but promised to return. Landing next at Caesarea, he went up to Jerusalem and greeted the church there, then went down to Antioch. Thus ended his "second" missionary journey.

Luke provides no explanation for Paul's return to Antioch, nor gives any details. If Luke's account is accurate, this visit to Jerusalem would be Paul's fourth, but his third according to Paul's account in Galatians. The lack of details regarding this visit to Jerusalem and Antioch makes it impossible to know to what extent Luke's account is correct. At any rate, it provides a dividing point between Paul's "second" and "third" missionary journey.

---

[249] Inscriptional evidence indicates that Gallio was proconsul of Achaia for a year starting in May, 51 CE.

Summary

When Paul and Silas left Antioch following Paul's disagreement with the Jewish Christians there as well as with Peter, Barnabas, and the representatives of James, their eyes were set on regions beyond Syria and Cilicia. The missionary pair became a trio when Timothy joined Paul and Silas. Blocked from traveling into the more populous western parts of the province of Asia and into Bithynia in the north, they went into northern Galatia where at least two churches were founded. Then they traveled to Troas on the coast and crossed to Macedonia. From Philippi in eastern Macedonia to Corinth in Achaia they founded more churches, though not without opposition from both Jews and Gentiles.

Luke's narrative provides a chronological framework for this "journey" from Antioch, but as we have seen, parts of his chronology are suspect. Once the Travel Document begins in 16:10, there is reason to believe that Luke's order of events is more reliable, at least in those parts of Acts incorporating the diary, than in the previous chapters. While he inserts some stories and legends relating to Paul's work in various cities, Luke is throughout more concerned with Paul's itinerary and the extent of his mission than with the character and life of the congregations he founded. For the latter and for insights into Paul's character, thought, and relationships with his congregations, we must rely on Paul's letters.

CHAPTER 10: In Ephesus Part 1

The Account in Acts

One of the larger gaps in our knowledge of Paul's activities relates to the period between his first visit to Ephesus in the company of Aquila and Priscilla and his return to Ephesus. We have no information from Paul's letters concerning this time and very little from Acts. In three brief verses (Acts 18:22-23; 19:1) Luke covers Paul's long sea voyage to Caesarea, up to Jerusalem and down to Antioch. From there Paul begins his "third" missionary journey, retracing his path of the previous journey through the regions of Galatia and Phrygia. Departing from his earlier route to the north, he turns west into the province of Asia and down the highway to Ephesus. No companion is mentioned and there are no stories regarding contacts en route, only that "he went from place to place...strengthening all the disciples" (Acts 18:23, NRSV) in Galatia and Phrygia. Luke obviously has in mind here the churches founded during the "first missionary journey."

Paul's choice of Ephesus as a mission field was well considered. It was a large city with an estimated population of a quarter million making it among the largest in the empire. As a seaport at the western terminus of the road leading across southern Asia Minor to Antioch in Syria, it controlled major trade routes, which meant a constant traffic with potential for the spread of the new faith. Like Thessalonica for Macedonia and Corinth for Achaia, it was the seat of Roman government for the province of Asia. Finally, it had a large Jewish community through which Paul could make initial contact with Gentiles who had some knowledge of Israel's God and the scriptures.

With his arrival back in Ephesus, we would expect Paul to team up once more with Prisca and Aquila. Although their names are never mentioned again in Acts after Paul's arrival, we know they were still in Ephesus when Paul wrote 1 Corinthians while in that city during the mid-50s. Greetings from the couple to the Corinthian Christians are included in that letter along with the information that they were hosting a congregation of believers in Ephesus (1 Corinthians 16:19). Following the death of the emperor Claudius in October 54 CE and the revoking of his edict to have Jews removed from Rome, the couple must have returned to Rome sometime in the next two years since they are greeted in Paul's letter to the Romans (16:3-4), written in the winter of 56-57 CE.

Luke has collected several stories about Paul in his Ephesian period.[250] One seems unrelated to Paul's Gentile mission, but may have been included in order to illustrate an unusual albeit minor source of converts. Paul discovered a group of "disciples" who were not part of the Spirit-led tradition which Luke is describing (Acts 19:1-7). They had received the baptism of repentance proclaimed by John the Baptist. This raises the question whether they were John's disciples or some combination of the Baptist and the Jesus movements. There is no doubt that some Jews had believed John to be the Messiah, as is recognized in Luke's Gospel:[251]

> . . . all were questioning in their hearts concerning John, whether he might be the Messiah, John answered. . . , "I baptize you with water; but one who is more powerful than

---

[250] No authentic letter to the church in Ephesus has been preserved, if indeed Paul ever wrote to them. The NT letter to the Ephesians is one of the six disputed epistles attributed to Paul. While many scholars maintain its authenticity, many others, myself included, regard it as written by a follower of Paul to address a later situation. Despite its title, the writing does not address issues specific to any one church as do Paul's authentic letters. Further, the words "in Ephesus" in 1:1 are missing in some ancient manuscripts.

[251] See also the repeated denials that John the Baptist was the Messiah in the first chapter of the Fourth Gospel. That strongly suggests that some people claimed that he was the expected Messiah.

I is coming . . . He will baptize you with the Holy Spirit and fire." (Luke 3:15-16, NRSV)

Spirit baptism distinguishes the new stage of salvation history following Jesus' resurrection:

"This," he said, "is what you have heard from me; for John baptized with water, but you will be baptized with the Holy Spirit not many days from now." (Acts 1:4c-5, NRSV; see 11:16)

It is unlikely that the "disciples" in Ephesus considered John the Baptist to be the Messiah.[252] By referring to this group as disciples and believers (Acts 19:1-2), Luke indicates that they are followers of Jesus, but were unfamiliar with baptism by the Spirit. Jesus himself had been baptized by John with his baptism of repentance. But following Jesus' resurrection baptism became associated with reception of the Spirit among his followers, and was administered in the name of Jesus. The Spirit comes only with Jesus, not with John.[253] When Paul encountered the disciples in Ephesus, he baptized them into the charismatic movement he and the apostles represented.

Another of Luke's stories has similar elements. Before Paul's arrival in Ephesus, Apollos of Alexandria has been introduced. Characterized as "eloquent" (or learned), powerful in the scriptures, and "enthusiastic," he "had been instructed in the Way of the Lord" and "taught accurately the things concerning Jesus." (Acts 18:24-28, NRSV) Nevertheless he needed further education in the "Way of God" since he, like the group Paul met, knew only the

---

[252] Of the 28 appearances of the term "disciple" in Acts, all others clearly point to followers of Jesus.

[253] Luke 3:16, 22; 4:1, 14, 18; Acts 1:5, 8; 2:4, 38; 4:8. Luke was aware that during John's lifetime he had disciples (Luke 7:18-24; 11:1).

baptism of John the Baptist. This account is even more difficult to understand than Luke's story about the Ephesian disciples. If Apollos possessed an accurate knowledge about Jesus, why had he not been baptized as a Christian? And what kind of missionary work did he carry on in the synagogue?

Luke had good reason to bring Apollos into the Ephesian portion of his narrative. Along with Priscilla, Aquila, and Paul, Apollos was part of the early history of the Christian movement in both Ephesus and Corinth.[254] Having been instructed more fully by Paul's co-workers, he became associated with the Pauline mission from then on.

Luke's next story is about Paul's initial activity in the synagogue in Ephesus (19:8-20). After some success, he moves his disciples and his venue to the "lecture hall[255] of Tyrannus" where he continues teaching for two years (19:9-10).

Luke now turns to a topic he had mentioned only three times before, namely, Paul's power to work miracles: once regarding Bar-Jesus, also known as Elymas, in the court of Sergius Paulus (13:6-11) on Cyprus, once in Lystra where Paul enabled a man crippled from birth to walk (14:8-10), and finally in Philippi where he exorcised the slave girl (16:16-18). Luke now tells of pieces of cloth acquiring healing power after they had touched Paul. He also passes on an account of some Jewish exorcists attempting exorcisms in the name of "the Jesus whom Paul proclaims." (19:13) Finally, Luke relates that some converts publicly burned their books on magic.[256] None of these stories has a parallel in Paul's letters.

---

[254] 1 Corinthians 1:12-4:6; 16:12.

[255] Greek *scholē* literally means "the place where teachers and students get together." Since it is identified with a particular name, it probably refers to an actual building. More on Paul's use of this lecture hall in Chapter 13.

[256] Magical formulations are well attested among the papyri found in Egypt.

Two further items related by Luke bring us into closer contact with Paul's correspondence with the churches of Corinth and Rome. First, his travel plans:

> Now after these things had been accomplished, Paul resolved in the Spirit to go through Macedonia and Achaia, and then to go on to Jerusalem. He said, "After I have gone there, I must also see Rome." (Acts 19:21, NRSV)

> Now concerning the collection for the saints . . . . I will visit you after passing through Macedonia . . . . (1 Corinthians 16:1a, 5a, NRSV)

> I desire, as I have for many years, to come to you when I go to Spain. . . . At present, however, I am going to Jerusalem in a ministry to the saints . . . . (Romans 15:23b-24a, 25, NRSV)

As we shall see later in greater detail, the remainder of Paul's life was organized around his envisaged trips to Jerusalem, Rome, and Spain. He did get to Jerusalem and Rome, but the latter under conditions not of his choosing, while Spain remained an unrealized dream.

Finally, immediately prior to Paul's final departure from Ephesus, Luke relates a near-riot in the city. Paul does not specifically mention this event, but he does allude to something which had greatly frightened him, probably an imprisonment pending trial on a charge that carried the death penalty. Second Corinthians and perhaps Philippians are sources relating to that event. They will be considered in the next chapter.

The Corinthian Letters

During his time in Ephesus Paul began an extensive correspondence with the Corinthian church. As a consequence, we know more about that Christian community than any of his other churches, or for that matter, of any other first century church. We not only learn about the difficulties the Corinthians caused Paul, we observe Paul in action, not as an evangelist but as a teacher, debater, and counselor. We watch him creating arguments intended to persuade his readers to see things differently—his way—and to change their behavior. We read new things about his past. We learn how he interprets the rites of Baptism and the Lord's Supper. We see him defending his apostleship and putting it into a larger perspective. We discover portions of his letters that are out of place and some that are forgeries intended to undercut some of his radical teachings concerning the leadership of women. After reading his Corinthian letters we have a new level of understanding and appreciation of his rhetorical and theological skills. In short, these two letters are a treasure for anyone interested in this man's teaching and mission.

His subsequent letter to the Romans envisions a future visit to that city, but he had not yet been in Rome and had played no role in the founding of the churches there. The letters to the congregations in Thessalonica and Philippi express Paul's concern and gratitude for their continued viability, but provide few specifics of their congregational lives. His letter to the Galatian churches is a snapshot of Paul's consternation over unfolding events that he fears indicate some in the churches there are substituting "another gospel" for the one he taught them. The Letter to Philemon addresses one specific issue. But in none of these cases do we learn what happened next.

The Corinthian correspondence, on the other hand, covers a substantial period of time. According to Acts, Paul spent eighteen months in Corinth (ca. 50-52) exceeded in length only by his subsequent stay in Ephesus, during which time he was in close communication with the Corinthian church.

Paul's work as an apostle was not confined to making converts. He was a community developer, not a travelling evangelist who left town after a brief campaign to save souls. Otherwise, his letters would not have been written. Conversion was only the beginning of a process of guidance, counseling, encouragement, and reeducation into a new life-style. While Paul initiated that process, his time with the new believers was often limited, sometimes by outside forces which necessitated his early departure from that city. Other believers, whether members of Paul's missionary team or locals, had to carry on where he left off. For example, knowing the opposition to himself in Thessalonica, Paul had sent Timothy back there to continue what had been started (1 Thessalonians 3:1-3). Leaders within the church were also expected to do their part:

> But we appeal to you, brothers and sisters, to respect those who labor among you, and have charge of you in the Lord and admonish you; esteem them very highly in love because of their work. (1 Thessalonians 5:12-13a, NRSV)

Of course, Paul hopes that every member of his congregations will take on this role of supporting others, of building each other and the whole church up. Such a commitment demonstrates that they have internalized Christ, have taken seriously Paul's urging to imitate himself, just as he imitates Christ.

Paul's letters played an important role in his pastoral activities. He communicated frequently with the church at Corinth, writing perhaps as many as eight letters of which we have knowledge. At least one preceded 1 Corinthians; scholars have posited that five or six letters were combined to form 2 Corinthians. All these were written over a period of two years or so. This continuing correspondence allows us to identify and follow certain issues which had arisen within the Corinthian church and between the believers there and Paul.

1 Corinthians

The writing known to us as 1 Corinthians was partially a response to a letter from the church in Corinth, and partially to what Paul had heard about them. The letter reveals strains within the community itself and between some of its members and Paul. Before discussing the questions contained in their letter to him, he gives his attention (in six chapters) to three matters not mentioned in their letter.[257] Paul had received oral reports about these issues which he considers too serious to ignore or even postpone until later in the letter.

Internal Conflict at Corinth

The first disquieting report to Paul involved discord within the congregation, arising from loyalties to different figures—Paul, Apollos, Cephas (Peter), and Christ, especially the first two.[258] Over a period of four chapters, Paul responds in a variety of ways focused on the implications he sees inherent in the lack of unity in the Corinthian church. His solution: return to basics, i.e., the source of unity, the self-giving Christ at the center of Paul's story.

---

[257] Although Paul writes that "those of Chloe" reported quarreling in the Corinthian church, they probably reported the other two problems also. "Those of Chloe" could mean those in her household, but also her business representatives, who, as well as she, were believers. It is uncertain whether they belonged to the church(es) in Corinth or in Ephesus.

[258] It is not certain that Peter had been in Corinth. Paul's reference to him may be rhetorical, not historical. Christ is also mentioned, perhaps indicating those who had risen above the bickering that characterized the first three parties and held a position similar to Paul's as he develops it in this letter.

258

Paul faces a particularly sensitive issue here since he is one of the principals involved. His situation is made even more difficult because Apollos, who is present as he writes (16:12), is the other principal. Each has had a role in the development of the church in Corinth, and each had his admirers there. It is now Paul's task as the apostolic founder of the church to bring about an amicable resolution of the divisions which his and Apollos' work has unintentionally produced. His strategy is twofold.

First, Paul argues that the Corinthians' quarrels based on elevating one leader above another are inappropriate for people committed to the new spiritual standards of egalitarianism:

For as long as there is jealousy and quarreling among you, are you not of the flesh, and behaving according to human inclinations? For when one says, "I belong to Paul," and another, "I belong to Apollos," are you not merely human? (1 Corinthians 3:3b-4, NRSV)

Second, Paul reminds them that apostles and teachers are only servants of the one who sent them:

What then is Apollos? What is Paul? Servants through whom you came to believe, as the Lord assigned to each. I planted, Apollos watered, but God gave the growth. So neither the one who plants nor the one who waters is anything, but only God who gives the growth. . . . For we are God's servants, working together; you are God's field, God's building. (1 Corinthians 3:5-7, 9, NRSV)

The servant figure is one of Paul's favorite terms for characterizing the role of the apostle or missionary of Christ.[259] The

[259] "Servant" translates both *diakonos* and *doulos* and sometimes *pais*. *Doulos* designates a slave. In Roman society of Paul's time, slaves were not only dominated but owned by their master. An ideal slave was fully attuned to and carried out,

servant's defining mark is trustworthiness, i.e., accurately representing the master's interests. In calling Apollos a servant like himself, Paul was being exceedingly generous. Apollos was not one of his team, nor was Paul privy to Apollos' decision to missionize in Corinth. Paul could easily have considered Apollos an outsider who had interfered in his work, a late-comer building on the foundation laid by Paul. Although identified as a Jew in Acts, he is never designated by Paul as a fellow-Jew, nor as a co-worker. However, Paul put Apollos and himself on the same level as servants. Perhaps Apollos was treated in this graceful manner because the problem did not reside in Apollos but in those who regarded him and Paul as competitors to the point of quarreling over their respective merits.

Later in this letter, Paul will devote a substantial section (chapter 13) to unpacking more fully what is at stake: individualistic egotism versus concern for the well-being of others. In the present section, Paul concludes with an ironic, almost sarcastic passage, contrasting the Corinthians' self-assessment with that of apostles (Apollos is not included as an apostle) who live by a different standard:

> We are fools for the sake of Christ, but you are wise in Christ. We are weak, but you are strong. You are held in honor, but we in disrepute. To the present hour we are hungry and thirsty, we are poorly clothed and beaten and homeless, and we grow weary from the work of our own hands. When reviled, we bless; when persecuted, we endure; when slandered, we speak kindly. . . . I am not writing this to make you ashamed, but to admonish you as my beloved

---

even anticipating, the wishes of the master. A *diakonos* (used in this passage) is distinguished from a slave largely by not being property. Services rendered by both slave and servant may be the same. *Pais* is literally a child, but as a term used of a servant it emphasized an inferior social position, similar to the English word "boy" in some modern contexts. See Harrill, "Slavery," *NIB* 5:298-308.

children. . . . I appeal to you, then, be imitators of me." (1 Corinthians 4:10-13a, 14, 16, NRSV)

As an apostle, Paul has not only brought them the gospel and laid the foundation for a new kind of community, he also models what is expected of them—new life in Christ. Here as elsewhere he exhorts his readers to imitate him—as he does Christ.[260] Paul is not referring to specific deeds but to an all-encompassing attitude guided and characterized by regard for neighbor.

We now learn that Timothy has already been sent or is being sent to Corinth[261] to remind them of his practices, as he taught in all his congregations (1 Corinthians 4:17). Paul's practices which they are to imitate are Christ's ways: the exchange of worldly status and power for a new honor system; alignment with God's will rather than with the standards of the world; building up the community of believers rather than seeking personal advantage.

Immorality in the Congregation

The second item in his informants' oral report, but understandably absent from the Corinthians' letter, involves a serious moral matter: a member of the congregation is "living with his father's wife," who is therefore technically the man's step-mother (5:1, NRSV). This, Paul admonishes, was not even a pagan practice. Both Roman and Jewish law forbade marriage be-

---

[260] See 1 Corinthians 11:1; Philippians 3:17. Behind this advice is the common experience of children learning by imitating their parents. Josephus also refers to children's imitation: The Law "orders that they [children] shall be taught to read, and shall learn both the laws and the deeds of their forefathers, in order that they may imitate the latter. . . ." (Josephus, *Against Apion* 2:204; see Deuteronomy 6:7, 11:19)

[261] It is possible to read the Greek either as "I have sent Timothy" or "I am sending Timothy." Either corresponds with 16:10-11. Timothy is not included in the opening of the letter which indicates he was not present when it was written.

tween step-son and step-mother, if indeed these two in Corinth were married, which is doubtful. Paul is also appealing to the common Jewish characterization of Gentiles as immoral people.[262] *Porneia*, or sexual immorality, was specifically prohibited in the apostolic letter to Gentile believers (Acts 15:20).[263]

In a previous letter to the Corinthians, now lost, Paul had warned them against associating "with sexually immoral persons" (5:9).[264] He now explains that he had been referring to immoral people <u>within</u> the congregation, not to those in the larger society. His demand is that they assemble the church and deliver the (male) offender (the woman is apparently not a member of the congregation and therefore not mentioned) over to Satan," i.e., to the realm from which all Gentiles had come, "for the destruction of the flesh." Exactly what Paul meant is a matter of controversy among scholars; some think he was actually talking about the death of the individual. Others believe, as is my view, that he had in mind a ritual of excommunication. Just as there was a ritual of inclusion, so also there was one of exclusion. The character of the social entity identified as "those in Christ" had to be consistent with the gospel of Christ. Therefore, the holiness of the congregation was not to be corrupted by the unholy:

> But now I am writing to you not to associate with anyone who bears the name of brother or sister who is sexually immoral or greedy, or is an idolater, reviler, drunkard, or

---

[262] Paul frequently employs the argument known as "from the lesser to the greater." In this case, if even the Gentiles do not engage in this kind of behavior, how much more should the believing Corinthians avoid it?

[263] *Porneia* is a general term covering a wide range of sexual immorality, including forbidden degrees of marriage.

[264] Sometimes 2 Corinthians 6:14-7:1 is claimed to be part of that letter. As will be argued later, this passage deals with a different issue from the one addressed in 1 Corinthians 5:9.

robber. Do not even eat with such a one. (1 Corinthians 5:11, NRSV)

The "flesh" to be destroyed was not the physical body of the offender, but his "fleshly" attitudes. In that sense, the "flesh" was to be delivered back where it came from, i.e., to the realm of Satan. The purpose of the ritual was to face up to the reality of the situation and take action to save the individual (as well as the congregation), i.e., to bring him to his senses so that he may repent and be saved on the coming day of judgment. It is not to be confused with the medieval practice of condemning heretics to death in order to save their souls.

Post-baptismal sin (Paul does not call it that) was to become an important issue in the future. It appears that Paul already had faced this problem and had devised a way to deal with it. It should be recognized that Paul's command was not limited to this particular situation, but included all instances of immoral behavior as such, starting with idolatry, the source of all immorality.

Lawsuits, Judging, and Admonishing

Paul moves on to address a third divisive issue, lawsuits of one member of the congregation against another (1 Corinthians 6:1-8). His directions are simple: settle the conflict yourselves. If one believer must take another believer to court, the regular courts should not be used since the judges would be unbelievers and therefore would be using standards inconsistent with those of the believers. Rather, the conflict should be adjudicated in-house, with a member of the congregation appointed as the judge.[265] Better yet, learn to forgive one another and avoid adversarial acts.

---

[265] Paul's model is the Jewish community which had the right to apply Jewish law in internal matters.

In dealing with each of the three matters in the oral report Paul has received about the congregation at Corinth, the word "judge" has come up. First, regarding their positioning of one missionary or teacher over another, Paul writes:

> But with me it is a very small thing that I should be judged by you or by any human court. I do not even judge myself. I am not aware of anything against myself, but I am not thereby acquitted. It is the Lord who judges me. Therefore, do not pronounce judgment before the time, before the Lord comes . . . . (1 Corinthians 4:3-5a, NRSV)

Regarding the one who was living with his father's wife he writes:

> For though absent in body, I am present in spirit; and as if present I have already pronounced judgment in the name of the Lord Jesus on the man who has done such a thing. . . . For what have I to do with judging those outside? Is it not those who are inside that you are to judge? God will judge those outside. (1 Corinthians 5:3-4a, 12-13a, NRSV)

Finally, concerning lawsuits between members of the congregation:

> Do you not know that the saints will judge the world? And if the world is to be judged by you, are you incompetent to try trivial cases? Do you not know that we are to judge angels—to say nothing of ordinary matters? . . . Can it be that there is no one among you wise enough to decide between one believer and another . . . ? (1 Corinthians 6:2-3, 5a, NRSV)

Taken as a whole, parts of these statements appear to be self-contradictory. On the one hand, the Corinthians are told "not to pronounce judgment before the time," and on the other Paul has "already pronounced judgment in the name of the Lord Jesus" on the offender. When one takes into account also the issue of lawsuits where they are told to find a judge from among themselves to decide internal disputes, it is apparent that clarification is required.

The first thing to note is that in all these cases the stage is set in relation to the final judgment when Christ judges everyone, with those "in Christ" also taking part.[266] But what differentiates present judging from the final judgment, leading Paul to write "do not pronounce judgment before the time?"

Obviously, making judgments is part of living. Every moment requires choosing this or that. Not judging in that sense is not an option. The command not to judge, therefore, cannot be taken literally to mean avoiding making judgments about others. So what does it mean? The issue is also posed in Matthew's Sermon on the Mount:

> "Do not judge, so that you may not be judged. For with the judgment you make you will be judged, and the measure you give will be the measure you get. Why do you see the speck in your neighbor's eye, but do not notice the log in your own eye? Or how can you say to your neighbor, 'Let me take the speck out of your eye,' while the log is in your own eye? You hypocrite, first take the log out of your own eye, and then you will see clearly to take the speck out of your neighbor's eye." (Matthew 7:1-5, NRSV)

---

[266] A variant of this motif is found in the Sayings Source (Q) utilized by Matthew and Luke. See Matthew 19:28 and Luke 22:30. In those cases, however, the judges of the new age are the twelve disciples, not all those in Christ, and those to be judged are the twelve tribes of Israel, not the world.

As Betz has pointed out,[267] this passage belongs to the genre of ethical teaching. First, it deals with a well-known and universal phenomenon, our human proclivity to notice the imperfections of others while being oblivious to our own. While the initial statement is a generalized prohibition, the issue turns out to be the proper procedure for making judgments. It begins with a warning—if you are going to make judgments about others, be prepared for others, including God, to make judgments about you. Further, the same standards by which you judge others apply to yourself. You cannot get away with judging others by their deeds and yourself by your intentions.

Second, the passage recognizes that others do sometimes need to be corrected. However, before embarking on that risky enterprise, self-examination and self-correction are necessary. The hyperbole of the speck of dust and the log or plank recognizes the necessity of correction, its dangers, and how to proceed.

Paul practices this same caution against judging, which likely goes back to Jesus.[268] While in one sense not judging others is basic to the love ethic, in another sense judgments leading to what Betz terms "fraternal correction" are indispensable in any community. Paul's letters are replete with such corrections of his converts, and he advises others to take up that task, and his churches to be subject to people who are qualified to perform that role.[269] The members of a congregation are, after all, a family, with Paul playing the

[267] Betz, *The Sermon on the Mount*, 486-493.

[268] The Jesus Seminar rated verses 3-5 as probably coming from Jesus but with reservations. (Funk, et al., *The Five Gospels,* 153)

[269] "My friends, if anyone is detected in a transgression, you who have received the Spirit should restore such a one in a spirit of gentleness." (Galatians 6:1, NRSV) See also Matthew 18:15-17 where directions are given for dealing with conflict between believers. Similar to Paul's sentence of excommunication, the unrepentant offender is to be treated "as a Gentile and a tax collector." Luke's Gospel gives brief and straightforward directions: ". . . if another disciple sins, you must rebuke the offender, and if there is repentance, you must forgive." (17:3, NRSV) Cases where repentance is not forthcoming are not mentioned.

part of the monitoring father. There is no evidence that Paul is familiar with the formulation of Matthew 7:1, but some of his writings are reminiscent of its content:

> Therefore you have no excuse, whoever you are, when you judge others; for in passing judgment on another you condemn yourself, because you the judge, are doing the very same things. (Romans 2:1, NRSV)

Legitimate judging and correcting are urged:

> Can it be that there is no one among you wise enough to decide between one believer and another . . . ? (1 Corinthians 6:5b, NRSV)

Paul's caution not to pronounce judgment and his directive for his readers to judge their own lawsuits are not as inconsistent as they initially seem. Both are part of the ethical reeducation of those who have responded to his summons and are now members of his congregations. Admonishment is necessary, but it should not become an excuse for engaging in gossip, judgmentalism, and other expressions of the human inclination to dishonor others.

Concerning Those Who Have Sex with Prostitutes

Paul now returns to the issue of *porneia* which was interrupted by his discussion of lawsuits. Included in the oral report he has received is the topic of prostitution, or rather, to employ a modern term, "johns" who patronize prostitutes. He introduces his response with a generalized list of disqualifications for entering the kingdom of God (1 Corinthians 6:9-11). Of the ten items on it, four involve sexual improprieties, including prostitution. Paul reminds some of the Corinthians about their own past, both before and after becoming believers. Through baptism they have been initiated into a new life in which their former activities are no longer acceptable. Paul then quotes the first of several slogans they are employing to justify their behavior and proceeds to examine them from a different angle:

"All things are lawful for me . . . ." "Food is meant for the stomach and the stomach for food . . . ." (1 Corinthians 6:12- 13, NRSV; see also 10:23)

Ironically, the Corinthians may have derived their first slogan from Paul's own teaching about freedom. If they are free, then everything is lawful or permitted. Paul agrees, but with provisos: everything may be permitted the free person, but not everything is for the best. Individualistic freedom which ignores the health of the community is self-defeating, for it is the community that makes possible that freedom. What superficially appears to be freedom is actually a new slavery. As for food and the stomach (euphemisms for sexual appetite), they belong to this age, not to the kingdom of God. Paul will later expand on the ideas stated here. His immediate concern is that *porneia* is not only being practiced but rationalized:

Do you not know that your bodies are members of Christ? Should I therefore take the members of Christ and make them members of a prostitute? Never! Do you not know that whoever is united to a prostitute becomes one body with her? For it is said, "The two shall become one flesh." (I Corinthians 6:15-16, NRSV)

With a barrage of arguments Paul aims to demolish acceptance of prostitution as permissible for believers. New life in Christ is a repudiation of all that is contrary to it. He concludes by urging them to "glorify God in your body," i.e., to behave in a way consistent with their new life.

Paul's Response to their Letter

Paul next begins to address the issues raised in the Corinthians' letter to him (1 Corinthians 7:1). They had touched on several topics: male-female relationships in a variety of circumstances (chapter 7); food sacrificed to idols (chapter 8); Paul's policy of not accepting payment for his apostolic work (chapter 9); idol-worship (chapter 10); spiritual gifts (chapters 12-14); resurrection of the dead (chapter 15); and the collection for the saints in Jerusalem (16:1-4).[270] In addition, he admonishes the Corinthians for something else reported to him: their eating of the Lord's Supper inappropriately (11:17-34). Some of the material in chapters 7-16 seems out of place, two portions appear inauthentic.

Male-Female Relationships

Chapter 7 illustrates Paul's way of dealing with subjects which may have been especially delicate for him as a single male who, as far as is known, had never been married. He covers a variety of relationships between men and women, from celibacy to remarriage to mixed marriages.

He begins with what is generally considered to be a quotation from their letter which seems to mean, "Are we allowed to have sex at all, even within marriage?" (7:1b) Paul's own preference is that his converts be celibate, so that they have more time to devote to serving Christ. However, he considers celibacy to be a "gift" from God, and recognizes that not everyone shares it. The negative side of celibacy is vulnerability to sexual immorality. Jews did not need to visit Herculaneum or Pompeii to see evidence of its pres-

---

[270] However, it has been argued that the phrase introducing each of the subsequent topics may only indicate that Paul is moving on to a new topic, not that the Corinthians had raised these matters in their letter. Margaret M. Mitchell, *Paul and the Rhetoric of Reconciliation*. HUT 27. Tuebingen, 1991. Cited in Betz and Mitchell, "Corinthians, First Epistle to the," *ABD 1: 1144*.

ence among Gentiles. Despite his personal preference, Paul's realism leads him to encourage marriage as a general principle, in order to avoid temptation. Within the marital relationship neither partner should refuse the other's desire for sexual intercourse. However, if they mutually agree, they could cease such activity for a specific period of time in order to concentrate on prayer (7:5). Since temptation could overpower good intention, that period of time should be limited.

Having laid out general principles for everyone, especially married couples, Paul turns next to the *agamoi* (unmarried) and the *chērai* (widows), i.e., those whose marriage has been terminated, probably by death of their spouses, and who may be contemplating remarriage (7:8). It is uncertain precisely what Paul means by the Greek term *agamos*, which is simply the negative of "married." However, in view of its being paired with widows he probably was thinking of widowers. Should widows and widowers remarry or not? Self-control was the deciding factor. Once again, Paul states his preference that they remain as he did, unmarried. However, if they were not proficient in keeping their passions under control, then they should remarry.

The next topic is divorce (7:10-11). Here Paul cites the prohibition of Jesus against divorce (see Mark 10:2-12 and parallels, also Matthew 5:32). Neither partner should separate from the other. In Mark's Gospel, a partner who divorces and remarries breaks the commandment to avoid adultery, since they became one when they were married. Paul seems to allude to this dictum in his direction for a wife who has divorced her husband to remain single or be reconciled with her husband. No second marriage for her. Paul surprisingly does not apply the same rule to the husband. He assumes that both partners are believers.

Paul now turns to "the rest," i.e., mixed marriages where one partner is a believer and one is not (7:12-16). This situation would arise when either the wife or the husband became a convert, but not the other. We learn now that Paul assumes Jesus' commandment against divorce applies only when both partners are believers. Jesus gave no ruling concerning mixed marriages, so Paul gives his own. Interestingly, the decision whether or not to stay together is given to the unbeliever. If he or she agrees to continue the marriage, the believer must not initiate separation. Paul then makes a strange (to us) statement:

> For the unbelieving husband is made holy through his wife, and the unbelieving wife is made holy through her husband. Otherwise, your children would be unclean, but as it is, they are holy. (1 Corinthians 7:14, NRSV)

Can holiness be transferred from one who is a believer to another who is not? Paul is thoroughly familiar with the idea that uncleanness is contagious, but here the purity of believers can be passed on to others. Converts have become holy through believing the gospel and being baptized into Christ. How could others become holy without going through that process? The problem is compounded by reference to the children also being sanctified. One believing spouse makes the other spouse holy, and together they sanctify their children. Paul may have in mind the passage from Leviticus dealing with the sin offering; "Whatever touches its flesh shall become holy. . . ." (6:27, NRSV) Could Paul be reflecting here on the Eucharist (Jesus as the atoning sacrifice) and applying it to the children of those who eat it?

The situation of mixed marriages is reminiscent of the one faced by Ezra when, upon his return from Babylon, he discovered many Jews had married outside the faith. His resolution was straightforward—mixed marriages were to be annulled (Ezra 9-10). There is no evidence that the Corinthians contemplated such action, but it is not beyond possibility that the thought had occurred to some of them.

Paul's logic is odd to us and not easy to follow, but what he is getting at seems to be this: the believing spouse need not fear contamination by contact—including sexual contact—with the unbelieving spouse. On the contrary, the holiness of the believer is a positive—and stronger—influence on the other; the spouse is "sanctified" by the believer. Because both parents are now holy, their children also are holy. This is an extraordinary development, even reversal, of our normal understanding of the clean/unclean categories so important to the Judaism in which Paul was raised. We might say it is overly optimistic to hope that holiness or spiritual health is contagious, but perhaps Paul was onto something.

However, if the unbelieving spouse does not want to continue the marriage, divorce is acceptable. Living in a hostile marriage where the two partners no longer share basic values is not required. Separation which enables peace is preferable. The conversion of one spouse and not the other was probably not uncommon.[271]

Paul now interrupts his orderly treatment of various situations regarding male and female relations to bring up one of his principles for guidance in a variety of circumstances, including these:

> . . . . let each of you lead the life that the Lord has assigned, to which God called you. This is my rule in all the churches. Was anyone at the time of his call already circumcised? Let him not seek to remove the marks of circumcision. Was anyone at the time of his call uncircumcised? Let him not seek circumcision. Circumcision is nothing, and uncircumcision is nothing; but obeying the commandments of God is everything. Let each of you remain in the condition in which you were called. (1 Corinthians 7:17-20, NRSV)

---

[271] The Gospel According to Luke also points to conflict within families, presumably over differing responses to Jesus (12:51-53). See also the shorter version in Matthew 10:34-36 which is part of the charges to the mission of the disciples. Family harmony is not to be valued over discipleship. See also Mark 3:33.

Paul then repeats the principle with an illustration from slavery. The reason, as he will soon explain, for his rule is that the transition from this age to the new age with the return of the Lord is imminent. Changing the conditions of one's present existence is an unnecessary complication.

His rule prepares the reader for his treatment of the next category ("virgins," both male and female) who are contemplating or planning marriage (7:25-38). Once again, he has no command of the Lord, so his readers must be satisfied with Paul's "opinion," which is that people should remain as they are. In Paul's view, this world's time is passing and believers are to be oriented toward the coming world (7:31b). His considered judgment applies not only to single people, but also to those who are already married (7:27) and those who are engaged to be married. Paul reiterates that marriage is not a sin, but for practical purposes and undivided devotion to Christ, the single state is preferable (7:38). It should go without saying that he is referring only to believers.

Finally, Paul once again addresses wives whose husbands have died (7:39-40). In his earlier discussion, he had not cautioned them to avoid marriage to unbelievers. He now corrects that omission, reiterating his general rule. However, if the widow wishes to remarry, she may—but only "in the Lord," i.e., to another believer.

Before moving on, we take note of a passage in 2 Corinthians which, I believe, also addresses the general issue of marriage of believers. 2 Corinthians 6:14-7:1 has long been recognized as an insertion which breaks into Paul's thought development; the following verse (7:2) picks up where the previous one (6:13) leaves off. The intervening material has nothing to do with what precedes and what follows. Some scholars have questioned whether Paul actually wrote the intrusive material; its highly dualistic language seems at home in some of the Dead Sea Scrolls.[272] Others defend its Pauline

---

[272] This is hardly a valid argument for the non-Pauline origin of the interpolation. Dualistic language, we have already seen, is characteristic of Paul.

authorship, but speculate that it came from one of his letters now lost, perhaps the one mentioned in 1 Corinthians 5:9 which cautions against associating with immoral people.

However, while obviously out of place in 2 Corinthians, the passage is consistent with Paul's treatment of male-female relationships in 1 Corinthians 7. It can be seen as an interpretation of a biblical passage justifying Paul's policy regarding marriage of a believer. The key to its meaning is in the opening sentence:

> Do not be mismatched with unbelievers. (2 Corinthians 6:14, NRSV)

The Greek term for "mismatched' is *heterozugountes*. *Zugos* is a yoke, often meant metaphorically as a burden. *Hetero* means "other;" thus the word literally means "yoked with another (or different) kind." Paul could have in mind one of two commandments:

> You shall not plow with an ox and a donkey yoked together. (Deuteronomy 22:10, NRSV)

While the two animals would certainly be "mismatched," the actual term used by Paul is absent from the passage. The other possibility is found in Leviticus immediately following Paul's favorite commandment, "You shall love your neighbor as yourself."

> You shall not let your animals breed with a different kind . . . . (Leviticus 19:19, NRSV)

The Greek version of this passage is of special interest as it does include a word with the root *heterozug-*. In fact, Leviticus 19:19 and 2 Corinthians 6:14 contain the only examples of that word in the Septuagint and NT. Paul has almost certainly derived his declaration, "Do not be mismatched with unbelievers," from this passage in Leviticus. As in the case of a believing widow who wishes to remarry (1 Corinthians 7:39), Paul's rule against believers being mismatched with unbelievers refers to mixed marriages contracted following one potential spouse becoming a Christian. The believer has a radically different orientation from the unbeliever, and Paul proceeds to drive home his point with five rhetorical questions illustrating his main point:

> Do not be mismatched with unbelievers. For what partnership is there between righteousness and lawlessness? Or what fellowship is there between light and darkness? What agreement does Christ have with Belial? Or what does a believer share with an unbeliever? What agreement has the temple of God with idols? (2 Corinthians 6:14-16a, NRSV)

The five contrasts characterize the world of those who imitate Christ (righteousness, light, Christ, believers, God's temple) versus the world of paganism (lawlessness, darkness, Belial, unbelief, idols). The two worlds are too far apart to be integrated, even in marriage.

The final pair of contrasts brings Paul to a second chain of images drawn from several biblical texts,[273] which continues the theme of incompatibility between believers and unbelievers. He concludes by urging the readers to live a pure (holy) life uncontaminated by any impurity derived from being "mismatched." (7:1)

Separated as it is from an explanatory context such as 1 Corinthians 7, this passage might erroneously be taken as encouraging believers to divorce their unbelieving spouses. That step is specifically prohibited in 1 Corinthians 7:12-13. But when viewed in the light of 1 Corinthians 7, this text clearly establishes the biblical foundation for Paul's policy of forbidding the contracting of mixed marriages. It may originally have been part of his discussion in 1

---

[273] Leviticus 26:12; Ezekiel 36:28; Isaiah 52:11; 2 Samuel 7:14.

Corinthians 7 with which it certainly has more affinity than with anything in 2 Corinthians. How or why it became detached from the earlier letter and inserted into the collection that became 2 Corinthians is impossible to determine, but that seems a possibility. Or it may have been part of a letter now lost which dealt with the same topic as 1 Corinthians 7:39. Possibly it was originally part of the letter to which Paul refers in 1 Corinthians 5:9.

Re: Food Sacrificed to Idols

Chapter 8 deals with the second issue raised in the Corinthians' letter to Paul, food sacrificed to idols. He responds by first quoting three more of their slogans they used to support their freedom to satisfy their appetites, not only in regard to sex but also food (and drink). Once again, Paul agrees with their partial truths, but adds some necessary qualifications:

> . . . we know that "all of us possess knowledge." . . . we know that "no idol in the world really exists," and that "there is no God but one." (1 Corinthians 8:1, 4, NRSV)

Paul cautions that knowledge is a two-edged sword; a truth grasped may lead to arrogance on the part of the knower. Knowledge can be used to injure others. Here we see Paul characteristically assessing actions or attitudes in terms of their impact on others in the community, the body of Christ. Knowledge, as used here, is a possession of the individual; love is communal, aimed at the good of others. Further, while one's knowledge that there is only one God allows one freedom to eat meat sacrificed in connection with a pagan temple, restraint is necessary if the conscience of another believer would be damaged by eating that meat. Love always must rule over personal insistence on being right or pushing an opinion or attitude onto others. Paul will return to this topic later in the letter.

Interlude: Chapters 9-11

Following his discussion of whether one should eat food sacrificed to idols, Paul writes three more chapters before he next introduces a topic with the formula used in 7:1 and 8:1, "Now concerning."

Chapter 9 deals with a defense of Paul's apostleship and the reason he has refrained from claiming any compensation for his service to the Corinthians. It relates more to the first four chapters than to its present place in the midst of a discussion concerning food sacrificed to idols and worship of idols. Any connection with its context seems tenuous at best.

Chapter 10 picks up not only the issue of eating meat sacrificed to idols earlier discussed in chapter 8, but also once again the topic of sexual immorality (chapters 5 and 6). The two matters (idolatry and *porneia*) are closely related. The Corinthian's maxim that "all things are lawful for me" (6:12, NRSV) is repeated along with Paul's rebuttal, "but not all things are beneficial." (10:23, NRSV) Two different scenarios involving sacrificial meat are then advanced. But first, Paul makes it clear that a believer must avoid idolatry as well as *porneia* (10:7-8). Sexual immorality and being "in Christ" cannot coexist; likewise, one cannot partake both of the table of the Lord and the table of demons (10:21). Sexual immorality is a consequence of idolatry.

As in chapter 8, the basic principle Paul follows is the consideration of the conscience of others. Meat purchased in the market is acceptable for the believer, as long as no questions are asked. Further, when dining at the invitation of a non-believer, one can eat whatever is offered. But if someone informs the believer that the food has been offered in sacrifice, then it should be refused because the conscience of the other would be compromised (10:28-29). This may be difficult for moderns to comprehend; perhaps Paul means that when one knowingly eats sacrificial meat in the company of others, they infer that one is taking part in a ritual activity of paganism, not of the Christian faith. That would lead them to question their companion's integrity and thereby to dishonor Christ. Paul's final counsel sums up the entire chapter and more:

> So, whether you eat or drink, or whatever you do, do everything for the glory of God. Give no offense to Jews or to Greeks or to the church of God . . . . (1 Corinthians 10:31-32, NRSV)

11:2-16—Interpolation?

Chapter 11 contains one of the most perplexing portions of 1 Corinthians, verses 2-16. Internally, it is less than consistent, and some of it approaches the nonsensical. It cannot be reconciled with Paul's even-handed treatment of men and women in chapter 7, targeting as it does women to be regulated in an assembly for worship, especially concerning such seeming trivialities as their hair style and head covering. As such it is reminiscent of a portion of the second century writing, 1 Timothy 2:9-10. The latter, however, goes on to exclude women from teaching and other positions of authority over men; they are to be silent learners (2:11-12). The Corinthian passage assumes that women are able to pray and prophesy (teaching is not mentioned)—but only with their head properly covered (11:5).

The imagery employed in this section differs from anything found elsewhere in Paul's undisputed letters, particularly the hierarchical way in which the word "head" is used:[274]

---

[274] Apart from 1 Corinthians 11, Paul uses the word "head" only twice—in a quotation in Romans 12:20 from Proverbs and 1 Corinthians 12:21. Neither is comparable to its use in 1 Corinthians 11.

But I want you to understand that Christ is the head of every man, and the husband is the head of his wife, and God is the head of Christ. (1 Corinthians 11:3, NRSV)

In this formulation a woman has no direct relationship to Christ, but only through a man, presumably her husband. Both the image and the way it is used are quite inconsistent with Paul's characteristic way of relating believers with Christ—they are "in Christ" or members of his body (the church), or Christ is "in them." Paul employs the image of the body itself to demonstrate the unity and equal value of its various parts, not its hierarchical structure, which is contrary to his gospel. The members of the congregation are all equally in Christ; they all have equal access to him; they are all children of God. The four-fold structure which moves from God to Christ to man to woman is a paradigm foreign to Paul. It is clearly designed to promote male dominance, the very thing Paul opposes as belonging to the old age now replaced by Christ (Galatians 3:27-28).

There is nothing elsewhere in Paul's letters similar to the employment of "head" as it is used in 11:3. The closest parallel is found in another post-Pauline writing:

Wives, be subject to your husbands as you are to the Lord. For the husband is the head of the wife just as Christ is the head of the church, the body of which he is the Savior. Just as the church is subject to Christ, so also wives ought to be, in everything, to their husbands. (Ephesians 5:22-24, NRSV; see also Colossians 3:18)

This text has both similarities to and differences from 1 Corinthians 11:3. While the subjugation of women to men is the same in both cases, Ephesians does not refer to God as the head of Christ; indeed, God is left out of the series. And Christ is the head of the church instead of being the head of every man. The notion that Christ is the head of men is strange indeed.

The idea that a man is the "image and reflection" of God, while a woman is the reflection of man, is another construction unparalleled elsewhere in Paul's authentic writings. Limiting the image of God to one gender might have arisen as a distorted interpretation of Genesis 1:27 and 2:7, by taking the generic word for humankind (Adam) as meaning only a male, and omitting the second part of 1:27 where both genders are created in the image of God. Or it could possibly arise by ignoring that passage in favor of the second creation story in which the man is created first. In any event, Paul emphasizes the unity of humankind rather than its divisions. For Paul, Christ overcomes divisions, but the author of 1 Corinthians 11:2-16 has a different agenda.

Finally, this portion of chapter 11 bears no relationship to its context. Some scholars have questioned its authenticity, rightly in my opinion. It is not the only portion of 1 Corinthians whose Pauline authorship should be questioned, as we shall see below. In my view, this passage has been interpolated into 1 Corinthians in order to justify a later movement away from Paul's own treatment of men and women as equally qualified for leadership roles, a movement observable in Ephesians and 1Timothy and in another interpolated passage in 1 Corinthians.

An interpolation must be suspected when the content of a passage is extraneous to its context, and especially when the previous and following sentences flow seamlessly, as in this case. An equally or even stronger argument is found when the passage contains statements which contradict an important position of the larger document. I Corinthians 11:2-16 meets both of these criteria. To argue otherwise is to accuse Paul of abandoning his gospel.

The Lord's Supper

The second part of chapter 11, verses 17 through 34, is undoubtedly Paul's. It concerns another report from his informants about behavior in the church at Corinth, in this instance the way in which they partake of the Lord's Supper. Some members are impatient and begin the meal before others arrive. This demonstrates to Paul that they do not understand that the Lord's Supper is a ritual meal which symbolizes communal solidarity, not a collection of private dinner parties which can proceed at their own pace. To humiliate the latecomers is not an act of love.

Paul responds by reciting the tradition of the Lord's Supper[275] as the proper foundation of the communal meal, a tradition which he has received and which he passes on, ultimately coming from "the Lord Jesus" himself during his final meal (11:23-25). Paul urges "discernment" of the essential connection between the meal and its meaning; otherwise, the meal is corrupted and becomes destructive rather than beneficial. His final words on this topic:

> So then, my brothers and sisters, when you come together to eat, wait for one another. If you are hungry, eat at home, so that when you come together, it will not be for your condemnation. (1 Corinthians 11:33-34a, NRSV)

The principle behind Paul's critique is the unity and faithfulness of those who belong to the body of Christ. Whatever threatens to divide or dishonor believers is unacceptable and demonstrates that the significance of Paul's story has not been fully grasped. Otherwise, believers would not act in ways injurious to fellow believers—and to themselves. The common meal is not to

---

[275] Paul's tradition about the Lord's Supper is the earliest testimony to it. From whom did he receive the tradition? Peter is the most likely candidate (Galatians 1:18).

satisfy physical hunger—that can be done anywhere—but to celebrate God's love revealed in Christ's death.

Re: Spiritual Gifts

At this point, Paul once again employs his formula for moving on to another topic, "Now concerning." (12:1) He had touched on the subject of spiritual gifts[276] in the introduction to the letter (1:7). In general terms, spiritual gifts seem to be those new abilities which have become part of the believer's character and which reinforce the new standard of mutual care. Paul here begins an extensive treatment of those abilities which comprises the next three chapters. He starts, logically enough, with the source of spiritual gifts, the Spirit of God. This Spirit enables one to confess "Jesus is Lord," to become a believer and maintain that status. The opposite acclamation, "Let Jesus be cursed," even if spoken in an ecstatic state, cannot come from God. Paul may be alluding here to their former ecstatic experiences as pagans, and providing a criterion for distinguishing the Holy Spirit from other, perhaps demonic, spirits.[277]

Paul then emphasizes the variety of gifts[278] proceeding from the one Spirit. Interestingly, he also adds to such gifts "services" (*diakoniai*)[279] coming from the one Lord and "activities" or "opera-

---

[276] The Greek word is the plural *pneumatika*, literally, "spiritual(s)." Derived from *pneuma* (spirit), it could refer either to spiritual people or spiritual gifts. The context here indicates that gifts are meant.

[277] One of the spiritual gifts is the ability to discriminate between spirits (1 Corinthians 12:10).

[278] Here the term is the plural of *charisma*. A charisma is a gift, or a favor. The plural emphasizes multiple expressions of the Spirit, in contrast to a narrow range of more apparent "spiritual" (ecstatic?) manifestations.

[279] *Diakonia* has a range of meanings, from waiting on tables to proclaiming the gospel. It covers anything done in service of another. Here the one served is God.

tions" (*energēmata*) from the one God.[280] By bringing in these further manifestations of spiritual gifts, Paul puts them into a larger context which has the effect of correcting over-emphasis on the more spectacular ecstatic experiences. Gifts of the Spirit are spread throughout the congregation; no one is excluded.

Preceding his list of gifts from the one Spirit is Paul's all-important focus: from the one Spirit each believer receives gifts to be used for the common good (1 Corinthians 12:7-11). The repetition of "Spirit" in the passage emphasizes its importance in Paul's thinking and practice. His churches are intended to be spiritual communities, inspired and guided not only by spiritual values but by the very Spirit of God present and manifested in every aspect of their lives as the body of Christ. These include the ecstatic spiritual gifts so dearly prized in the church at Corinth, but also many others which are not so obviously spiritual manifestations. The point is that such gifts are not intended for individual bragging rights but for "edification" ("construction") of the one body composed of many members and enlivened by the one Spirit. Individuals are a part of the body; they do not exist independently inasmuch as they all belong to Christ. Paul assumes that each person possesses his or her own gift(s) to contribute to the upbuilding of the community.

The discussion of spiritual gifts will continue in chapter 14, but first Paul presents "a more excellent way" in the well-known chapter 13. He places spiritual gifts in a new light which outshines all others. Several well-recognized and universal values in the church are relativized in comparison to love: speaking in tongues is so much noise unless the speaker also embodies love. Prophetic powers, knowledge of divine secrets, even the deepest levels of faith leading to the surrender of all wealth and one's own life cannot

---

[280] Note the tripartite terminology—Spirit, Lord, God—an early precursor of the later Trinitarian formulation, but with a very different meaning.

compare with love. The characteristics of love[281] are then personified:

> Love is patient; love is kind; love is not envious or boastful or arrogant or rude. It does not insist on its own way; it is not irritable or resentful; it does not rejoice in wrongdoing, but rejoices in the truth. It bears all things, believes all things, hopes all things, endures all things. (1 Corinthians 13:4-7)

The final section of the chapter contrasts the permanency and completeness of love with the transiency and partiality of other spiritual gifts, such as prophecy and knowledge. Even among the great triad of faith, hope, and love, love retains its primary place.[282]

Whether Paul created this chapter on the spur of the moment or inserted an earlier composition into his letter is uncertain, but the care with which it has been constructed may suggest the latter. However, its content is consistent with his other responses to the situation in Corinth. "Rude" readily connects with his earlier assessment of their attitude toward latecomers at the Lord's Supper. "Boastful" and "arrogant" characterize those who see their ability to speak in tongues as a mark of their spiritual superiority.

---

[281] It is an understatement to say that the English noun "love" and verb "to love" are inadequate translations of the Greek noun *agapē* and verb *agapaō*. The English "love" has to cover a wide range of meanings: the romantic (erotic); family affection; friendship; and selfless acts on behalf of others. Most NT writers prefer the *agapē* word group to indicate what we would call unconditional and selfless love, but the author of the Fourth Gospel also uses the verb *phileō* (to love affectionately, as in friendship) with much the same meaning. When referring especially to God's love of humanity expressed in Christ and believers' love for each other, Paul usually turns to the *agapē* word group, but he does occasionally employ words expressing mutual affection from the *phil-* group (1 Corinthians 16:22; Romans 12:10; 1Thessalonians 4:9). The Greek *erōs* (erotic or passionate love) is not found in the NT.

[282] See below, Chapter 13.

"Wrongdoing" brings to mind the issues of sexual immorality and idol worship. The primacy of love is apparent elsewhere in this letter and others: "Let all that you do be done in love." (16:14, NRSV) All the commandments are summarized in the commandment to love the neighbor (Romans 13:9-10). When Paul advises his audience to imitate himself, just as he imitates Christ (1 Corinthians 11:1), he is pointing to his own observance of the commandment to love the neighbor. Christ is the ultimate model or manifestation of love. Those who live in Christ live in love, serving others rather than self.

Following his panegyric on love, Paul returns to his treatment of spiritual gifts. While excelled by love, they are still worth pursuing. In particular he promotes the gift of prophecy because it encourages, consoles, and builds up others in the church (i.e., it is a direct manifestation of love). On the other hand, speaking in tongues is a conversation between the individual and God, with no benefit to others—unless someone translates or explains. Its attachment to love is tenuous and conditional. Paul's bottom line:

. . . since you are eager for spiritual gifts, strive to excel in them for building up the church. (1 Corinthians 14:12, NRSV)

Paul does not denigrate the ecstatic forms of spiritual gifts; he points out that he himself speaks in tongues. In the assembly, however,

. . . I would rather speak five words with my mind, in order to instruct others also, than ten thousand words in a tongue. (1 Corinthians 14:19, NRSV)

Paul quotes Isaiah 28:11-12 as an indicator of a cautionary approach to speaking in tongues—the phenomenon is a sign for unbelievers or outsiders. The sign, however, is negative, revealing that those speaking in tongues are manic, crazy. Their unintelligible speech leads outsiders to think that they are "out of their minds." In contrast, prophecy has a profound effect on unbelievers by "unmasking" them, disclosing the secrets of their hearts (14:25) and leading to their conversion. Perhaps Paul is speaking from personal experience, remembering his contact with the prophet Ananias.

Guidelines follow for ordering the activities of the assembled community (1 Corinthians 14:26b-33a), providing us a rare glimpse into this aspect of early church life. Music, teaching, poetry, ecstatic speech and prophecy were contributed by the members. Clearly, these were charismatic assemblies in which each person had opportunity to participate. Paul's instructions for collecting money for the Jerusalem church specify doing so on the first day of the week (according to the Jewish calendar), i.e., Sunday (1 Corinthians 16:2). Where and when the practice of meeting on the day of Jesus' resurrection began is unknown, but it was apparently the standard in Paul's congregations.

Finally, Paul was constrained to urge a balance between openness to individual contributions and communal order so as to protect the values inherent in spiritual gifts and respect for one another.

14:33b-36—Definitely an Interpolation

The remainder of the section on spiritual gifts is found in 14:37-40 where Paul's comments on prophets and prophecy are summarized. Between 14:33a and 14:37, however, there is a section which has nothing to do with spiritual gifts. It is an obvious and widely recognized interpolation,[283] once again intended to subvert Paul's teaching of equality of the sexes and, in this case, to exclude women from participating in discussions during the assembly:

---

[283] The interpolation is indicated in the NRSV by being enclosed in parentheses. Verses 34-35 are found in some Greek manuscripts after verse 40.

As in all the churches of the saints, women should be silent in the churches. For they are not permitted to speak, but should be subordinate, as the law also says. If there is anything they desire to know, let them ask their husbands at home. For it is shameful for a woman to speak in church. Or did the word of God originate with you? Or are you the only ones it has reached? (1 Corinthians 14:33b-37, NRSV)

Taking his cue from Paul's directions that speakers in tongues should be silent in church unless there is an interpreter present (14:28), an editor or later copyist has inserted 14:33b-36. The motive is clear: to silence women in the Christian assemblies. The fact that the previous interpolation in 11:2-16 assumes that women do speak in church, at least ecstatically and perhaps also rationally (11:5), is not acknowledged. The two insertions obviously came from different hands, but with similar motives.

Most Pauline scholars who do not seek biblical support for male dominance at the present time recognize this section in chapter 14 as an insertion. Once more, the closest parallel is in 1 Timothy:

Let a woman learn in silence with full submission. I permit no woman to teach or to have authority over a man; she is to keep silent. For Adam was formed first, then Eve; and Adam was not deceived, but the woman was deceived and became a transgressor. (1 Timothy 2:11-14, NRSV)[284]

This passage gives two reasons derived from the Law to support the subordination and silencing of women: the priority of Adam over Eve in the second creation story in Genesis 2, and Eve's deception by the serpent in Genesis 3. We saw earlier (Chapter 3) that in his

---

[284] The submission motif is also found in Titus 2:5.

one reference to Eve (2 Corinthians 11:3) Paul does not blame Eve for the human condition. Rather, it is Adam who is the figurehead in Paul's thought for the predicament of humankind, not as a cause but as an archetype of all who in their alienation from God are enslaved to sin. The author of the interpolation seems to have in mind the same interpretation of the Adam and Eve story that is found in 1 Timothy 2:11-14 where it is written, "as the law also says." Both refuse to recognize or accept Paul's position that male dominance belongs to the old age, now replaced with equality in Christ in which gender divisions are replaced by unity(Galatians 3:28).

The two passages (1 Corinthians 14:33b-36 and 1 Timothy 2:11-14) stand in sharp contrast to 1 Corinthians 7 in which equality of men and women in Christ is assumed. They are also inconsistent with Paul's mention of women in leadership positions in Romans 16: Prisca the wife of Aquila, Phoebe a *diakonos* of the church at Cenchreae, and Junia who was Paul's fellow prisoner, "prominent among the apostles" and a believer before Paul was. He refers to other women in Romans 16, but we lack information about their roles. Paul also names two female church leaders in Philippi, Syntyche and Euodia, who worked with Paul in furthering the gospel (Philippians 4:2).

The conclusion to which all this evidence points is that 1 Corinthians 14:33b-36 is a forgery inserted into Paul's letter to subvert Paul's own teaching regarding the equality of men and women in the communities of Christ. It was one thing to accept his arguments and practices regarding breaking down the wall between Jews and Gentiles.[285] Allowing women the same privileges as men was another matter. The same was true regarding slave and free, as we shall see later.

---

[285] See Ephesians 2:11-22.

Re: Resurrection

Chapter 15 deals with a topic not mentioned so far in this letter—resurrection of believers who had died. It is occasioned by a report that some in the church at Corinth do not believe in resurrection (15:12). In his usual fashion, Paul addresses the matter by starting with the foundational statement of the gospel—the death and resurrection of Christ:

> For I handed on to you as of first importance what I in turn had received: that Christ died for our sins in accordance with the scriptures, and that he was buried, and that he was raised on the third day in accordance with the scriptures, and that he appeared to Cephas, then to the twelve. Then he appeared to more than five hundred brothers and sisters at one time, most of whom are still alive, though some have died. Then he appeared to James, then to all the apostles. Last of all, as to one untimely born, he appeared also to me. (1 Corinthians 15:3-8, NRSV)

The last sentence is obviously Paul's own addition to what he had received. A literary analysis suggests that the earliest part of the passage concluded with Jesus' appearance to the twelve, the rest being information Paul had gleaned from other contacts. There is no other NT reference to an appearance to 500 believers or to an appearance to James the brother of Jesus. Paul's point here is that the proclamation of Jesus' resurrection is validated by a variety of first-hand human testimony, including his own.

Paul does not reveal the source of the appearances tradition as he had the tradition of the Lord's Supper. It was no doubt common property among the churches at that time. When 1 Corinthians was written, the tradition of the appearances had taken on the features of an early creed, with established wording. Since Paul had spent 15 days with Peter three years after Paul's conversion, it is not unreasonable to assume that he was then privy to an early stage of the appearances tradition involving Peter and the twelve.

The position Paul is arguing against is not stated until after he has recited the testimony to Christ's resurrection. The issue is not the resurrection of Christ, which the Corinthians accepted, but that of believers, and perhaps of unbelievers also to face judgment. Christ's own resurrection is presented as evidence of resurrection, per se (1 Corinthians 15:12).

A concern about resurrection had arisen earlier among the believers at Thessalonica. The expectation of the early return of Jesus led to the assumption that they would all be alive at that time. But some had died. Paul had assured them that believers who had died were not excluded from the kingdom of God; they would be raised to participate with the living in the full manifestation of the new age (1 Thessalonians 4:13-18).

In 1 Corinthians Paul addresses a different matter: the concept of resurrection as such, with no reference to a time-frame. Logic dictated that if those who do not believe in resurrection are right, then Christ himself was not raised and therefore the faith of believers is futile, a pitiful prospect. The salvation of all believers is at stake because belief in the raising of Jesus was the basis of new life in Christ and of hope of sharing his life in the new world. Paul then reaffirms the proclamation of Christ's resurrection and states its significance for believers:

For since death came through a human being, the resurrection of the dead has also come through a human being; for as all die in Adam, so all will be made alive in Christ. (1 Corinthians 15:21-22, NRSV)

Here Paul introduces the connection he has drawn between Adam and Christ, the first man and the last, two antithetical figures incorporating all those who correspond to them. Prior to the Messiah, all human beings were "in Adam" but now those who identify with God's Messiah are "in Christ." Thus there are now two forms of humanity. Both types are still subject to physical death, but the latter has hope of life after death.

Paul now moves on to present a scenario of the events of the end time, just as he had done in 1 Thessalonians 4:13-18. Though the two accounts differ in some details as well as in the motivations which led to their inclusion in their respective letters, they agree on the main point: Christ is the source of the believer's life, after death as well as before.

Paul continues with another supporting argument. He calls attention to some Corinthians who practice vicarious baptism. If the dead are not raised, what is the reason for that practice? It appears that ritual baptisms on behalf of dead relatives or friends were performed so that they also could participate in the coming resurrection of believers. Paul neither praises nor criticizes the practice; he only calls attention to the logical contradiction of the practice if the dead are not raised.

He now adds his own life experience to his appeal—if the dead were not raised, there would be no explaining his daily exposing himself to danger:

> If with merely human hopes I fought with wild animals at Ephesus, what would I have gained by it? If the dead are not raised, "Let us eat and drink, for tomorrow we die." (1 Corinthians 15:32, NRSV)[286]

Next, a new but related issue is posed; it is not clear whether it was a real question raised at Corinth, or merely an aspect of Paul's rhetorical style in which he anticipated and answered an objection. In either case, he answers the question with his well-known botanical analogy: a new plant is different from the seed

---

[286] The quotation is from Isaiah 22:13. Paul does not mean that he literally fought with wild animals in the arena at Ephesus. Those thrown to the predatory animals didn't survive. The saying is a metaphor of vigorous and dangerous conflict.

from which it grew. Likewise, though a physical body is sown, a spiritual body is raised. Both continuity and transformation characterize the plant and the human body. In the human case, the change applies to both the living and the dead; therefore, it is of no consequence whether believers are alive or dead when Christ returns and effects the transformation of "flesh and blood" into a spiritual form appropriate for the kingdom of God (1 Corinthians 15:50.

The Concluding Chapter

The final chapter is a collection of largely unrelated items. Paul gives directions for the collection of money he plans to take to Jerusalem (16:1-4). Next, he details his impending travel plans which include staying in Ephesus until Pentecost, then traveling through Macedonia to Corinth and perhaps residing there during the winter when travel by sea was too dangerous (16:5-9).[287] Some of his co-workers are mentioned: Timothy and Apollos,[288] both of whom had previously been in Corinth, and unnamed "other brothers," perhaps including the Erastus mentioned in Acts 19:22.[289] Also named are three believers from Achaia, Stephanas (who had delivered the letter from the Corinthians) and his household, plus Fortunatus and Achaicus. Greetings are sent from Paul's co-workers in Corinth who had moved to Ephesus, Aquila and his wife Prisca, and from all the Asian congregations. The letter con-

---

[287] We learn more about his upcoming visit to Corinth in 2 Corinthians and Acts 20:1-3.

[288] Timothy has already been dispatched to precede Paul, perhaps to prepare the collection (previously mentioned in 4:17; see also 2 Corinthians 8 and 9; Acts 19:21-22) in Macedonia and Achaia. Apollos had decided not to go to Corinth at this time.

[289] In Romans 16:23 Paul mentions an Erastus who was a city official in Corinth. These are probably two different persons. For a fuller discussion, see Meeks, *The First Urban Christians,* 58-59.

cludes with Paul's personal greeting in his own hand and a blessing, as well as a reminder that those who do not love the Lord stand under a curse!

Thus ends the letter we know as 1 Corinthians. It provides an introduction to the stormy relationship between Paul and the Corinthian church which developed while he was in Ephesus. But his following letters to Corinth, some written in Ephesus and some subsequently, contain the sequel.

CHAPTER 11: In Ephesus: Part 2

During his stay in Ephesus,[290] from ca. 53 to 55 or 56 CE, Paul was laboring on a number of fronts. On the one hand, he was actively involved in missionary work in Ephesus itself (1Corinthians 16:8-9), and perhaps also served as advisor to evangelists working in areas outside the city.[291] At the same time, he was in contact with churches founded earlier in Galatia, Macedonia, and Achaia and engaged in nurturing and guiding them. That activity resulted in a spontaneous sea trip to Corinth and numerous letters going back and forth to certain of his congregations. Indeed, most of his extant letters were probably written during this time: 1 Corinthians, Galatians, Philippians, Philemon, and a substantial portion of 2 Corinthians. Communications from his churches have understandably not survived, and we are aware of two of his letters that have been lost.[292]

We know that Paul was in Ephesus when word came regarding troublesome developments in Corinth, which led to the flurry of letters preserved in 1 and part of 2 Corinthians. He may have been in Ephesus when he learned of the possible defection of his churches in Galatia. And it was likely in Ephesus that Epaphroditus, the messenger from Philippi, and Onesimus, the slave of Phi-

---

[290] Acts 19:8-10 indicates Paul was in Ephesus for two years and three months. In the speech to the Ephesian elders (20:31), Paul says he was there for three years. Both may be correct since sometimes part of another year was counted as a whole year.

[291] Paul includes greetings from "the churches of Asia" in 1 Corinthians 16:19. This may suggest the existence of congregations outside Ephesus itself.

[292] Paul refers to a prior letter to the Corinthians in 1 Corinthians 5:9. In 16:1 he writes about instructions given to the Galatian churches regarding the collection of money for the poor in Jerusalem. These instructions are not found in his letter to the Galatians.

lemon, found Paul. All together, they put a heavy emotional burden on him, and his resulting lament is perfectly understandable (2 Corinthians 11:28-29).

Wishing to direct his energy primarily toward creating new outposts of the kingdom of God, Paul found much of his time was being expended instead in maintaining his existing communities. But that effort proved to be more beneficial to us because it resulted in our first-hand access to his story.

Paul's Letter to the Galatians

In his surviving letter to the Galatians, Paul develops further certain themes inherent in his story from the beginning: the figure of Abraham as the first believer and the blessing of his offspring; the transitory nature of the Law and its role as a child-monitor; and the Spirit versus flesh as relevant categories regarding ethical guidelines. He also refers to himself, perhaps for the first time in a letter, as an apostle of Christ.[293] He makes it clear that in using that term he is to be distinguished from those who were sent out as missionaries by a sponsoring congregation.[294] He is also claiming the same role as the Jerusalem apostles.[295]

We tentatively concluded earlier that the Galatian churches were located in the central northern part of the province of Galatia rather than in the south. Paul traveled to that territory after termi-

---

[293] In 1 Thessalonians 1:1 Paul gives himself no special designation to distinguish him from Sylvanus and Timothy; in Philippians 1:1 Paul and Timothy are both identified as "servants of Christ Jesus;" in Philemon Paul calls himself a "prisoner of Christ Jesus;" The other four undisputed letters all identify him as an apostle (Galatians 1:1; 1 Corinthians 1:1: 2 Corinthians 1:11: and Romans 1:1).

[294] "As for our brothers, they are messengers of the churches . . . ." (2 Corinthians 8:23, NRSV) "Messengers" translates Greek apostoloi, which could also be rendered as "ambassadors" or "delegates."

[295] "Do we not have the right to be accompanied by a believing wife as do the other apostles and the brothers of the Lord and Cephas?" (1 Corinthians 9:5, NRSV)

nating his role as an apostle/evangelist/teacher on behalf of the church in Syrian Antioch and setting out on his own as an itinerant missionary. Because of an undisclosed illness en route, he departed from his planned schedule, which may have had Bithynia rather than Galatia as his immediate destination. Having spent enough time in northern Galatia to establish two or more congregations, perhaps in different cities, he traveled on to the Aegean coast and crossed to Macedonia and Achaia, where churches were created in Philippi, Thessalonica, Beroea, and Corinth. Then, for some unknown reason, after a brief visit to Ephesus, Paul returned to Jerusalem and Antioch. Following that visit, he returned to Ephesus via the overland route, according to Acts. Whether he detoured to visit the churches in Galatia is in dispute, but the evidence for that happening is meager (Acts 18:23; Galatians 4:13).

During his two to three years in Ephesus, disturbing news came to Paul regarding the Galatian churches. Outsiders had come there and were teaching them that Paul's teaching was fundamentally flawed. They said that he had falsely claimed that Gentiles did not need to observe the Jewish commandments, and that they were not required to be incorporated into Israel through circumcision. He was accused of corrupting the gospel of the mother church in Jerusalem in order to attract converts.[296] The newcomers had come to Galatia to teach Paul's converts the truth on which their salvation depended.

Paul's response includes several arguments in defense of the gospel he had proclaimed in Galatia. First, his gospel was derived from a revelation from God (1:11-2:1), not learned from any human source. It was certainly not a corruption of the Jerusalem gospel since he had no contact with Jerusalem for three years after he started evangelizing. Further, after a brief visit with Peter he had no further contact with Jerusalem for another eleven years. To-

---

[296] Those who had come to the Galatian churches were out of step with the decision announced both by Paul (Galatians 2:7-9) and Luke (Acts 15:19); i.e., circumcision of Gentiles would not be required.

ward the end of that fourteen year period, the Jerusalem leaders had accepted the legitimacy of his gospel, which was identical to that proclaimed by Barnabas (2:2-10).

Second, even though he and the churches in Jerusalem and Antioch had a falling out after the conference, their differences were not over circumcision of Gentiles, but ritual purity laws that James wanted to impose on Gentiles (2:11-21). Paul saw such new regulations as a back door intended to force the Law on Gentiles. He had resisted them in order to preserve the truth of the gospel for the very people to whom he was writing!

Third, his critics had appealed to the scriptural passages regarding Abraham as the father of the chosen people into whom Gentile believers needed to be inducted through circumcision (3:15-18.). Abraham himself had been circumcised as a seal of the covenant God was establishing with him and his descendants. Therefore, believing Gentiles must also be circumcised.

Paul champions a different interpretation. As we saw above in Chapter 5, when God accounted Abraham's faith as righteousness (Genesis 15:6), the latter was still a Gentile. The promise regarding his descendants preceded Abraham's circumcision. Therefore, Abraham was the father of believing Gentiles without their being circumcised as well as the father of those who were circumcised. Righteousness comes by faith, regardless of whether the faithful are circumcised or not. Christ, not the Law which requires circumcision, is the one who heals. To turn to the Law is to nullify the effects of Christ's death on behalf of humanity. The cross, not circumcision, is the ultimate symbol of God's love.[297] The Spirit of Christ, not the Law, is the source of the miracles happening in the

---

[297] Two millennia of exposure to the symbolism of the cross have blunted its original significance for Paul. For him it is the point at which the way of God and the way of the world most clearly intersected. The world's most emphatic "no" to Jesus is spoken through its use of the cross to kill him. God's emphatic "yes" is heard through "the word of the cross" (1 Corinthians 1:18) and seen in the resurrection appearances.

believers' midst. God's promise to Abraham to bless the nations is not changed by the introduction of the Law through Moses centuries later. The Law itself was not the promised blessing, but only a temporary custodian of Israel until the new covenant of faith in Christ was revealed. The Law now belongs to the past, but Christ to the present and future.

Fourth, Paul appeals to his audience's charismatic experience, in particular to their ability to address God as "Abba! Father!" which demonstrates their status as adopted children of God (4:1-10). They have been redeemed from slavery to the "elements of the cosmos." This phrase normally designates the elements out of which the cosmos was made, e.g., earth, air, fire, and water. The elements were sometimes regarded as existing in opposing pairs, such as air and fire, earth and water. Martyn makes a case that Paul extends such oppositions to Jews and Gentiles.[298] The opposites in his present concern are circumcision and non-circumcision, or Law and not-Law, the dividing line between Jews and Gentiles. The cosmos which separated Jew and Gentile is the old cosmos which Paul has left behind. The cross of Christ marks the end of the world in which such divisions determined existence and the beginning of a new creation (Galatians 6:14-15).

Paul points back to the revelation which was also the occasion of his conversion. His world of Judaism had been destroyed, crucified to him and he to it. Likewise, by implication, the world of his audience, the pagan counterpart of the Law, should have been crucified to them and they to it. The death of the Son of God was the beginning of a new world.

Fifth, Paul's allegorical interpretation of the two wives of Abraham and their sons is intended to enlighten his audience regarding their own situation (4:21-5:1). Children of the slave woman (Hagar) are slaves (to the flesh—including circumcision), while children of the free woman (Sarah) are free (having been liberated

---

[298] Martyn, *Galatians*, 401-406.

by the Spirit). The women themselves represent the two covenants, one encompassing the Law, the other the new covenant of Christ. Paul's point is transparent: the Galatians who seek circumcision are still living in the dying cosmos, living in slavery to it rather than in the freedom of the new creation introduced by Christ.

Paul's assumptions and logic lead him to state plainly the stark alternatives facing the Galatians:

> Listen! I, Paul, am telling you that if you let yourselves be circumcised, Christ will be of no benefit to you. (Galatians 5:2, NRSV)

He could have written something similar if the addressees were Jewish Christians who were considering renouncing their Judaism by removing the marks of their circumcision (1 Corinthians 7:17-20). To believe that ethnic and religious identity are relevant is to miss the whole point of Paul's story, namely, that Jesus is the cornerstone of a new creation which is now replacing the first creation. One either lived according to the corrupted standards of the old world or according to the principles of the new world. No compromise between the two is possible.

We do not know the reception this letter received in the Galatian churches. The fact that Paul sent a second letter to them giving instructions for raising a fund to be delivered to the Jerusalem church suggests a favorable outcome (1 Corinthians 16:1). On the other hand, when he later wrote to the Romans and mentioned the churches participating in the collection, the Galatians are not included (Romans 15:25-26). We can be sure, however, that the contents of his letter to the Galatians were shared with the Jerusalem church by his opponents. Paul's sharply critical comments about those who claimed the backing of the Jerusalem leaders would not rebuild the bridge between Jerusalem and Paul which he demolished at Antioch. Paul had good reason to fear that the Jerusalem leaders were predisposed to refuse his offering. His anxiety is evident when he asks the Roman churches to pray that his mission be safe and successful (Romans 15:30-32).

Philippians

P aul's letter to the Philippians is certainly authentic, but whether it was originally a single letter, or two, or even three, continues to be debated. It contains certain elements which raise questions about its unity. For example, there are two "finales" in the letter. The first (3:1) suggests the letter is drawing to a close after the first two chapters; it also appears to refer to a previous letter. The second is near the end of the letter (4:8). In addition, there is a marked change in tone and subject matter between what precedes 3:1 and what follows, from urging the audience to "rejoice in the Lord" to Paul's invective against the "dogs" and "evil workers," epithets apparently alluding to the circumcision party. These and other considerations have led to numerous hypotheses regarding the literary composition of the letter, the sequence of the various sub-letters, where and when each was written, and for what purpose. The partition approach might be convincing if there were more agreement among its proponents regarding what belongs to each letter. Many scholars continue to maintain the unity of the letter, claiming that most if not all of the problematic features of the letter can be explained by careful examination of the letter's rhetorical features. For our purposes, the solution of these issues is not necessary, and in what follows the integrity of Philippians will be assumed.

The primary occasion of the letter was a response to the most recent gift to Paul from the church at Philippi. From the beginning, this church had given financial support to Paul's missionary endeavors (Philippians 4:15-16).

Paul's policy, probably derived ultimately from Barnabas, his earlier mentor, was not to accept money from those currently being evangelized (1 Corinthians 9:6). Their subsequent support of further missionary work was a different matter, as we see in Paul's comment to the Corinthian church:

> I robbed other churches by accepting support from them in order to serve you. (2 Corinthians 11:8, NRSV)

He could have been more specific: "I robbed the church at Philippi in order to serve you Corinthians." Financial backing for his mission from a community which was not wealthy made a lasting impression on Paul. The most current expression of its generosity was conveyed to him while he was in prison.[299] It was brought by a member of the Philippian church:

> . . . Epaphroditus—my brother and co-worker and fellow soldier, your messenger and minister to my need. . . . I rejoice in the Lord greatly that now at last you have revived your concern for me; indeed, you were concerned for me, but had no opportunity to show it. . . . I have received from Epaphroditus the gifts you sent. . . . (Philippians 2:25; 4:10,18b, NRSV)

It is not difficult to see why the Philippian Christians came to have a special place in Paul's affection. His letter to them reveals no strained relations between them and himself as does his correspondence with the Corinthians and Galatians. He repeatedly expresses his gratitude for their support of himself in his work and in his imprisonment. In addition to their messenger Epaphraditus, Paul mentions by name two women who apparently had had an unfortunate falling out, Euodia and Syntyche (Philippians 4:2-3). While not given a specific title, they were obviously part of the leadership of the church at Philippi. While Paul was still there they

---

[299] It is possible that this letter was written after Paul arrived in Rome as a prisoner. However, the weight of evidence, to my mind at least, points to Paul's Ephesian imprisonment.

had "struggled" along with him and others to promote the "work of the gospel." Their present disagreement over some undisclosed matter was of sufficient concern to Paul to mention it in a letter to the whole congregation. He urges them to follow Christ's behavior pattern laid out earlier in the hymn (2:6-11). As co-workers with Paul, they are expected to embody the master story. The identity of the "loyal companion" is unknown.

More than any other of Paul's letters, with the possible exception of 1 Thessalonians, Philippians may accurately be described as a "friendship" letter, revealing the endearing relationship between Paul and his converts at Philippi.[300] Their continuing financial commitment to Paul and his work led him to write of their relationship as a partnership (*koinōnia*) in the gospel (1:5). The hardship accepted by Epaphroditus in delivering their gift and perhaps staying on to serve Paul during his imprisonment also touched him deeply.

The only evidence of Paul's direct contact with the Philippians following his first departure from that city is the mention of the multiple gifts he received from them. As in the case of Epaphroditus, those gifts would have been delivered by one or more of their own. That practice began very soon after Paul left Philippi. While he was in the next city, Thessalonica, they sent gifts to him at least twice (Philippians 4:15-16). Nowhere does he mention earlier letters from or to them, though such probably accompanied their gifts and it is likely that Paul would have responded upon their reception, as in this case. It is possible that numerous of Paul's letters, for whatever reason, did not survive to be included in the later collection of his letters.

We know of at least one and probably two subsequent visits of Paul to Philippi after he wrote this letter. While on his way by land from Ephesus to Corinth before taking the collection to Jerusalem, he would have passed through Philippi. Perhaps that was

[300] Fitzgerald, "Philippians," *ABD*: 5, 320.

where Titus and Paul were reunited while the former was returning from Corinth (2 Corinthians 7:6-7; 8:6).[301] A few months later Paul went through Philippi again while en route to Jerusalem (Acts 20:3-6; Romans 15:25).

Philemon

This short communication is exceptional among Paul's letters. The other six undisputed epistles are all addressed to communities. This one is written primarily to an individual, Philemon, but also mentioned in the address are two other persons and the "church in your house."[302] Apphia is probably Philemon's wife, and Archippus may be their son. After greeting the others, Paul turns exclusively to Philemon.

Paul writes this letter to make a "request" concerning a slave named Onesimus, who has come to Paul while he is imprisoned.[303] We are uncertain how Onesimus found Paul. Probably, Onesimus was a runaway slave who had wronged his owner in some way, perhaps by stealing something from him (Philemon 18-19a). After fleeing, Onesimus then sought out a friend of his owner to intervene on his behalf, a well-known scenario from the Roman world.

Another possibility is that Philemon had dispatched Onesimus to serve Paul while he was in prison, as the Philippians had done by the hand of Epaphroditus. Onesimus may have been de-

---

[301] Titus accompanied Paul and Barnabas to Jerusalem for the apostolic conference (Galatians 2:1, 3 where we learn Titus is a Gentile, perhaps from the church at Antioch). He next appears in Ephesus and Corinth as Paul's agent in finalizing the collection in Corinth. He is not mentioned as part of Paul's team (comprised of Paul, Silvanus, and Timothy) during Paul's original evangelization efforts in Corinth (2 Corinthians 1:19).

[302] "Your" is singular, signifying that Philemon's house is a meeting place for a congregation.

[303] As in the case of Philippians, the letter to Philemon was likely written while Paul was imprisoned in Ephesus, rather than in Rome.

layed in returning to his master. In either case, Onesimus feared reprisal and Paul intervened on his behalf.

Paul's request of Philemon may be more complex that initially appears. First, he wants Philemon to accept Onesimus warmly, just as he would welcome Paul himself. Second, Paul would like to have Philemon send Onesimus sent back to him so that he could be of service to Paul while he was in prison, thus demonstrating his "usefulness"[304] to both Philemon and Paul. Third, Paul may have been making a special appeal in view of the changed relationship between owner and slave.

During his time with Paul, Onesimus was converted. That development introduced a new factor into the relationship of Philemon and Onesimus—they are now "brothers," i.e., both are members of the one body of Christ. While it was permissible for believers to own slaves, Paul may have seen a contradiction in a believer owning a Christian slave. In embracing Christ, converts entered into a new relationship with one another in which the unity of believers was a defining characteristic. Since Christ is one ("many members, yet one body," 1 Corinthians 12:20, NRSV), members of his body are also one.

The basis of Paul's position may be seen in the same baptismal creed which we earlier saw proclaims solidarity between men and women, Jews and Greeks, slave and free (Galatians 3:27-28). This creed had been developed, no doubt by Paul himself, as part of an entry ritual into his communities. It articulates in a few well-chosen words Paul's conviction that the fundamental unity of redeemed humanity overrides all divisions. The cosmic oneness sought by all mystics revealed itself to Paul when he perceived that Jesus was the forerunner of a new world order governed by love rather than hatred, peace rather than fear, equality rather than hierarchical relationships, mutual respect and compassion rather than indifference. Those who believe in this new order—the kingdom of

---

[304] The Greek name Onēsimus means "useful," a name commonly given to slaves.

God rather than the kingdoms of this world's Caesars—are required to reject existing social, national, and religious divisions and the cultural ideologies maintaining them. By naming three major divisions in that world—ethnic, class, and gender—this creed sets the pattern of a new life ethic at all levels of individual and social existence. The community of Christ is to be the present earthly expression of the realm of God in Paul's communities.

We see in his letter to Philemon an example of the implementation of Paul's policies for his churches—the old relationship between slaves and their owners had to be changed.[305] This is Paul's "Emancipation Proclamation." Paul was not on a campaign to release all slaves (neither was anyone else in that world), which in any case was not in his power. His jurisdiction was limited to the believing communities he had established.

It might appear that asking for the manumission of Onesimus contradicts Paul's principle that Christian slaves should not seek freedom. (1 Corinthians 7:21-24). But the situation regarding Onesimus is similar to that of Paul having Timothy circumcised (Acts 16:3; see above, pp. 231-232). In both cases, Paul's actions seem to contradict his general rule. In both, however, the rule does not take into account the particular circumstances. Timothy had a Jewish mother and was known to be Jewish. Paul could hardly expose himself to the charge that he was encouraging Jewish men not to be circumcised. In the present case, it was not the slave but Paul who was requesting his freedom. Paul's "rules" were not necessarily absolute. Context had to be taking into account. The same was true regarding his "rule" relating to marriage in 1 Corinthians 7.

Though Paul apparently would have preferred to keep Onesimus with him to serve him (verses 11, 13), he is returning him and placing his future back into the hands of Philemon, a

---

[305] For more on this topic, see Borg and Crossan, *The First Paul*, 31-45.

somewhat risky venture for Onesimus, but necessary since he was still owned by Philemon.

Was Paul's request to grant Onesimus his freedom successful? Possibly. In his letter to the church at Ephesus, traditionally dated ca. 110 CE, Ignatius of Antioch identifies the bishop of Ephesus as a person named Onesimus.[306] Church tradition goes further and declares that bishop Onesimus of Ephesus (or Byzantium) was the same person named by Paul in his letter.[307] It is an intriguing possibility.

Where were Philemon and the church in his house located? If the letter to the Colossians were regarded as authentic, an answer would be apparent—since Colossae was in the Lycus valley east of Ephesus, Philemon must have lived in or near that town, possibly in Laodicea, about five kilometers (three miles) from Colossae. The two letters have in common seven names: Onesimus, Archippus, Aristarchus, Epaphras, Mark, Demas, and Luke. Onesimus is explicitly identified as "one of you" (Colossians 4:9). But since Colossians is excluded from the list of Paul's undisputed letters, that solution is not viable. Yet the two common lists may have some as yet unknown connection.

The close of Paul's letter contains an important clue regarding Philemon's location:

One thing more—prepare a guest room for me, for I am hoping through your prayers to be restored to you. (Philemon 22, NRSV).

Two inferences arise from this sentence. First, in several ways Paul has been putting pressure on Philemon to accede to his re-

---

[306] Ignatius, *Ephesians* 1:3; 6:2. This Onēsimus was one of a delegation of four from Ephesus who traveled to Smyrna to visit and encourage Ignatius when he was being transported as a prisoner from Syrian Antioch to Rome.

[307] Bishop *Onēsimus* is given a place in the calendars of the Roman Catholic and Orthodox churches, and is included among their martyrs.

quest for the release of Onesimus, and possibly also to have him sent back to Paul. Now, by suggesting that if things go well, he will make a personal visit to Philemon, Paul is letting him know that it would be prudent to respond promptly and positively to Paul's request. Second, it sounds like Philemon's home was not a great distance from the prison in which Paul is writing this letter. While it possible that Philemon lived in one of the cities on Paul's planned route from Ephesus to Corinth, it is also possible that he lived near or even in the very city in which Paul was imprisoned, i.e., Ephesus. If so, then we would have in this brief communication an unrecognized letter of Paul to an Ephesian, or at least an Asian, convert and the church in his house.

More Letters to Corinth

During Paul's two-to-three year stay in Ephesus he composed all of 1 Corinthians and most of 2 Corinthians. The remainder of the latter was written in Macedonia, probably in Philippi or Thessalonica, while Paul was en route to Corinth for his final sojourn there in the winter of 56-57.

There is good reason to believe that 2 Corinthians is a compilation of several letters. A number of considerations point to different stages in a developing situation being addressed. As many as six portions of 2 Corinthians have been identified as all or parts of originally independent letters. Taking into account an otherwise unknown letter mentioned by Paul, plus 1 Corinthians, his letters to the Corinthians add up to eight. It may be helpful to describe what to many scholars is a reasonable sequence of events in which Paul was involved, and to identify the letter related to each.[308]

---

[308]See Betz, "Corinthians, Second Epistle to the," *ABD* 1:1148-1154; Georgi, "Corinthians, Second Letter to the," *IDB*, Supplementary Volume, 183-186. See also Towner, "Corinthians, Second Letter To", *NIB* 1:744-751.

Admittedly, not all students of Paul agree with this scenario. Some continue to maintain the integrity of 2 Corinthians. However, others believe that the sudden shifts in tone and content found at several points in the letter point to numerous compositions over a period of time.

First letter: Lost

Paul's reference in 1 Corinthians 5:9 to an earlier and otherwise unknown letter is our only indication of this letter's existence. One topic of that letter was the avoidance of any "brother" who engages in immoral behavior, an issue that Paul addresses more fully in 1 Corinthians 5 and 6. He goes on to explain that he was not referring to general society or "the world," but specifically to the congregation of believers. Paul mentions the earlier letter because he believes the Corinthian church had misunderstood his meaning regarding breaking off contact with immoral persons and consequently was tolerating an internal situation which they need to deal with.

Second letter: 1 Corinthians

The writing we know as 1 Corinthians contains Paul's responses to a set of questions from the church at Corinth and to oral communications from "Chloe's people."[309] (1:11) Written from Ephesus prior to Pentecost (16:8; May or June) in 54 or 55 CE, it contains one definite (14:33b-36) and another probable (11:2-16) non-Pauline interpolation, as we have seen. The remainder is Paul's.

---

[309] The phrase, "those of Chloe," refers either to Chloe's employees or slaves. She was apparently in business in Ephesus and her people had returned from Corinth and reported to Paul disturbing things about the church there.

The next five letters have been assembled by an editor into a single document, the so-called 2 Corinthians. In addition, 2 Corinthians 6:14-7:1, which is not related to the developments involving the rest of 2 Corinthians and which we considered earlier as possibly originally part of 1 Corinthians or another letter, was included in the compilation.

Third letter: 2 Corinthians 2:14-6:13; 7:2-4

This is the earliest portion of 2 Corinthians. It is sometimes dubbed "the first apology."[310] It was composed after Timothy had returned to Paul from Corinth following his mission to deliver and interpret 1 Corinthians (1 Corinthians 4:17; 16:10-11). Likewise, Titus, who had been sent there to begin the collection for the Jerusalem church, had returned to Ephesus. Both representatives were in a position to inform Paul of developments in Corinth following the reception of 1 Corinthians.

Given the escalating verbal attacks against Paul, this letter is a remarkably controlled and calm defense of his apostleship and integrity (in contrast to his anger expressed in Galatians). There had been charges brought against him (and perhaps against Timothy and Titus also), originating with recently-arrived missionaries who carried letters of recommendation[311] (2 Corinthians 3:1). They pointed out that Paul lacked such recommendations, implying that he had been engaged in self-promotion which rendered his claim to be an apostle problematic. Further, Paul's gospel had no positive

---

[310] "Apology" is here meant not as an expression of regret for an offence committed, but in the classical sense of a defense, including an explanation of one's action that has been criticized or judged. The "second apology" is 2 Corinthians 10:1-13:10, the fourth letter.

[311] Those letters may have come from the Jerusalem church and identified their bearers as its apostles. Paul's comparison of Moses' fading glory with Christ's abiding glory suggests these apostles emphasized the importance of obedience of the Law by Gentile converts.

role for the tradition of his own people. Moses had delivered God's Torah, but Paul at best ignored Moses and at worst attacked him and the Law. Paul's story treated the Law as temporary, whereas in fact it was eternal.

Paul's defense is that his converts are the only letter of recommendation that is required. His missionary approach has been to appeal to the inner person rather than relying on externals like letters from some third party. As for the Mosaic covenant, it was written on tablets of stone. We are now living in a new era where the Spirit writes on human hearts, under a new covenant (2 Corinthians 3:6).[312] Moses' glory had faded, and he veiled his face to keep the people from noticing. The veil remains for those who fail to see the fulfillment of prophecy in Jesus, and the coming of the age of "the Lord, the Spirit" who writes on human hearts, bringing freedom from the old dispensation (2 Corinthians 3:18).

Further, the difficulties and sufferings he and his co-workers have faced testify to their integrity and commitment. They do not depend on personal qualities and qualifications, but proclaim the gospel of Jesus Christ in spite of their sufferings and their failings according to human standards. In fact, their weaknesses highlight the power of God's Spirit. An ego-driven gospel is an oxymoron. Authentic apostles are called to be servants, not masters:

> For we do not proclaim ourselves; we proclaim Jesus Christ as Lord and ourselves as your slaves for Jesus' sake. . . . But we have this treasure in clay jars, so that it may be made clear that this extraordinary power belongs to God and does not come from us. (2 Corinthians 4:5, 7, NRSV)

Paul can hardly be considered a proponent of the modern "prosperity gospel!" Here he defends the actions of himself and his

---

[312] Jeremiah 31:33; Ezekiel 11:19. Note also the words of institution of the Lord's Supper in 1 Corinthians 11:25—"This cup is the new covenant in my blood." (NRSV) That is, in Jesus' death.

missionary party who, in solidarity with Christ, exhibit weakness and poverty. He goes on to point out the basic error of his opponents who focus on outward appearances rather than on the heart, on which the Spirit is writing (2 Corinthians 5:12).

By clarifying the reasons why he and his co-workers do what they do, and explaining their approach to ministry, Paul is supplying his readers with arguments to answer his critics. They are in the middle of the conflict and the ones who are most affected. It is up to them to judge who is right and act accordingly.

Following this letter, Paul's escalating anxiety over the Corinthian situation got the better of his judgment. On an impulse he made an impromptu sea voyage from Ephesus to Corinth in order to confront his critics face to face. It turned out to be a bad idea. Rather than resolving the conflict, the unannounced confrontation made it worse. Humiliated in front of the church he had founded, Paul returned to Ephesus and wrote a scathing letter.

Fourth letter: 2 Corinthians 10:1-13:10

Paul's final communication to Corinth while he was in Ephesus is this intense and pointed letter. Sometimes called "the letter of tears," as Paul himself later characterizes it (2:4), it is another but more heated defense of his apostleship and his person. Paul may have wondered if he was reliving the conflict with the churches in Galatia. Even though the issues were different, the very foundation of his work was once again being attacked. This letter supplies further information about his critics and more details about their criticism. We also now learn that his detractors included not only the recently arrived missionaries, but also a member of the Corinthian congregation. The letter opens with Paul's repetition of a negative characterization of himself which must have arisen in his hasty visit to Corinth:

> I myself, Paul, appeal to you by the meekness and gentleness of Christ—I who am humble when face to face with you, but bold toward you when I am away! . . . For they say, "His letters are weighty and strong, but his bodily presence is weak, and his speech contemptible." (2 Corinthians 10:1, 10, NRSV)

The criticism alluded to here may be part of the summary of a report on charges brought against Paul prepared by a delegation in the Corinthian church, or it may be only what one individual was saying, to which others had not objected. In any case, it was an extremely hurtful thing to say about Paul and he had no choice but to defend himself against such a personal attack. Obviously, his previous calmer letter had failed to persuade his readers of his innocence and integrity.

Paul now goes on the offensive: his critics should remind themselves that they are not alone in belonging to Christ: ". . . so also do we." (10:7) In comparing Paul with other missionaries they reveal their lack of understanding. It appears the Corinthians have not absorbed the lesson contained in Paul's earlier lengthy response to their own practice of playing the game of favorite missionaries and dragging himself and Apollos into their foolishness. Instead of confronting the new arrivals, the Corinthians seem to be returning to their old competitive paradigm.

Consequently, Paul lays out his own qualifications to be compared to those of his critics. He and his companions were the first to bring the gospel to the Corinthians. Further, Paul's team does not boast about churches they did not establish as his critics are doing (10:15-16; see Romans 15:20). Indeed, boasting or praising should only be about the Lord; self-commendation is worse than worthless. At this point Paul makes a daring leap into irony and sarcasm; it was risky because the recipients might take him literally. Nevertheless, his strategy leads him to play the part of the fool, one who does not display good sense and he now engages in the very thing he has just condemned—boasting [313] or self-commendation, but for a different purpose. If no one in Corinth will take his part, then he must do it himself. But rather than defend himself directly, he puts on a clever performance as a fool for the next chapter and a half (11:1-12:11; see also 1 Corinthians 1:20-28; 4:10). He has accused his critics of lacking understanding or not exhibiting good sense (10:12); now he will join them in foolish verbalization.[314] The following is the most extensive piece of irony and sarcasm in any of his letters. Paul intends to demonstrate that if his detractors want to play "qualifications," he can beat them at their own game:

> Did I commit a sin by humbling myself so that you might be exalted, because I proclaimed God's good news to you free of charge? I robbed other churches by accepting support from them in order to serve you. And when I was with you and in need, I did not burden anyone, for my needs were supplied by the friends who came from Macedonia. So I refrained and will continue to refrain from burdening you in any way. (2 Corinthians 11:7-9, NRSV)

Paul argues that refusal to accept remuneration from the Corinthians was not an indication that he was not a genuine apostle of Christ or that the Corinthians were being duped. True, Jesus had

---

[313] The reader may wonder about Paul's frequent use of "boast" or "boasting" (some 20 times) in the Corinthian correspondence. Boasting or self-praise is an expression of hubris, inordinate over-estimation of self-worth. For Paul, boasting or praise is to be directed exclusively to Christ and his achievements in bring salvation to the world. Paul considers his greatest strength to be his ability to recognize that in his weaknesses (in worldly terms) the power of his story is best conveyed. He is not using the story to advance himself, but those to whom he tells it.

[314] Foolishness of course is to be understood as the direct opposite of wisdom. 1 Corinthians 3:18 and Romans 1:22 use a different word than this passage does, but the meaning is similar: stupid, unintelligent, senseless, lacking understanding and contact with reality. Paul especially associates bragging with foolishness.

decreed that those who proclaimed the gospel had the right to be paid for their work, but he, Paul, had refrained from taking advantage of that right. The reason for his non-remuneration policy at Corinth was to deliver the gospel free of charge, both to lessen the burden on the Corinthians and perhaps also to assuage suspicions that he was just one more itinerant huckster of ideas.

Why does Paul find it necessary to defend his practice of non-compensation for his labors? It had obviously become an issue at Corinth. One would think that by not asking for financial support his motives would not be questioned. His missionary competitors have probably suggested that Paul had planned it that way. He had craftily refused support in order to lay the groundwork for a much larger scam, namely, the collection of cash he was in process of assembling. Paul was planning to abscond with the money he claimed to be raising for charity. Such an attack on Paul's integrity would explain his defense of his practice of not accepting money for his evangelistic services at Corinth.

Paul then goes on the attack against his accusers, even to the point of calling them names, a common rhetorical strategy:

> And what I do I will also continue to do, in order to deny an opportunity to those who want an opportunity to be recognized as our equals in what they boast about. For such boasters are false apostles, deceitful workers, disguising themselves as apostles of Christ. And no wonder! Even Satan disguises himself as an angel of light. So it is not strange if his ministers also disguise themselves as ministers of righteousness. Their end will match their deeds. (2 Corinthians 11:12-15, NRSV)

Paul earlier had reminded his readers that he as well as they belonged to Christ. He is not so generous concerning the newcomers who questioned his integrity.

In the midst of his "foolish" monologue, Paul pauses to differentiate between his true self in Christ and the role he is playing. He also makes it clear that he is acting like a fool on his own initiative, not under command of the Lord. He has temporarily foolishly exchanged his spiritual perspective for the worldly standards according to which they seem to be operating. Then he returns to his sarcasm, pointing out how willingly his "wise" readers tolerate the "fools" who were making "slaves" of them (2 Corinthians 11:19-21). But the main targets of his rhetoric are the super-duper-apostles who challenge Paul's authority:

> Are they Hebrews? So am I. Are they Israelites? So am I. Are they descendants of Abraham? So am I. Are they ministers of Christ? I am talking like a madman—I am a better one: with far greater labors, far more imprisonments, with countless floggings, and often near death. Five times I have received from the Jews the forty lashes minus one. Three times I was beaten with rods. Once I received a stoning. Three times I was shipwrecked; for a night and a day I was adrift at sea; on frequent journeys, in danger from rivers, danger from bandits, danger from my own people, danger from Gentiles, danger in the city, danger in the wilderness, danger at sea, danger from false brothers and sisters; in toil and hardship, through many a sleepless night, hungry and thirsty, often without food, cold and naked. And, besides other things, I am under daily pressure because of my anxiety for all the churches. Who is weak, and I am not weak? Who is made to stumble, and I am not indignant? (2 Corinthians 11:22-29, NRSV)

This extensive list of life-threatening and stress-producing difficulties Paul had encountered up to that time could have been substantially expanded if it were composed after he had arrived at Rome under arrest. But even as is, it is an impressive recitation of the hardships he had undergone in the previous twenty or so years as a missionary to the Gentiles. No doubt his confidence that his opponents could not match it was justified. The list ironically leads up to Paul's most powerful card, and indeed illustrates it—his weaknesses. None of the preceding adds to his worldly honor; on the contrary, it demonstrates he lacks the things that bring honor since he was poor, without a home of his own, sometimes reduced to depending on others, a laborer, often imprisoned, beaten by both Jewish and Roman authorities—all this in addition to not having an impressive body and being a poor speaker.

He now adds to the list of his weaknesses two more items. He had been a fugitive from justice when he fled the attempt of King Aretas in Damascus to arrest him. More seriously, he failed in his prayer for God to heal his malady (2 Corinthians 11:30, 32-33, 12:1b, 7b-10). Both were demonstrations not of strength but of weakness, which paradoxically proved to be the strength he relied on.

Here we see a restatement of Paul's reversal of cultural values: the power and wisdom of God versus the power and wisdom of the world, and the foolishness of God in contrast to the foolishness of the world. Paul's gospel of loving the neighbor stands against the world's values; it is not part of the ladder to worldly success. The emerging new and healthy creation stands in stark opposition to the old sick world of competition and hostility between individuals and collectives.

Paul's emphasis on weakness is itself seemingly weakened by his introduction of one of his mystical experiences in which he was "caught up into Paradise and heard things that are not to be told . . . ." (12:4, NRSV) His ability to have such extraordinary access to the world of the divine is hardly an example of weakness. How does Paul's revelatory or visionary experience cohere with his weaknesses?

First, Paul is not certain how to identify the person taken up into heaven; maybe it was himself, maybe not. Further, he doesn't know if that person was "in the body or out of the body." (12:2, NRSV) Lacking that knowledge, he leaves the matter unresolved.

Second, even if his readers perceive that he is writing about himself, he dissociates himself from the mystic being described (2 Corinthians 12:5-6).

Third, Paul was not allowed to tell others the details of this experience, thereby denying him one more possibility of boasting about it.

Fourth, the event is not related for its own sake; rather, it is an introduction to his failed prayer to have his "thorn in the flesh" removed. He was given the affliction to keep him "from being too elated" with his revelations (12:7, NRSV), i.e., to remind him that even revelations are not to be bragged about. As a finale to his "foolish" speech, Paul chides his readers again:

> I have been a fool! You forced me to it, for I ought to have been commended by you. For I am not at all inferior to these super-apostles, even though I am nothing. The signs of a true apostle were performed among you with utmost patience, signs and wonders and mighty works. How have you been worse off than the other churches, except that I myself did not burden you? Forgive me this wrong! (2 Corinthians 12:11-13, NRSV)

Leaving his foolish tirade behind, Paul informs his readers of his travel plans. His next trip to Corinth is impending. When he arrives, if necessary he will exercise his power of tough love, not to tear them down but to build them up (13:10). There is also still to be resolved the matter of sexual immorality and other issues mentioned in 12:21.

The concluding chapter (13), apart from the final three verses, is a summary and an appeal to his readers to do the right thing. Verses 11-13, concluding with a three-fold benediction that would become a standard element of Christian liturgies, probably originally belonged to the next letter but is placed here as a fitting conclusion to the whole collection of letters now comprising 2 Corinthians.

This letter was taken to Corinth by Paul's representative and mediator, Titus. After sending Titus on his mission, Paul intended to remain, at least temporarily, in Ephesus to continue with his missionary work there. However, an unexpected situation arose. According to Acts 19:23-41, Paul became the target of an attempt by Demetrius the silversmith to turn the Ephesian public against him. Paul was seen as a threat to the silversmith business in Ephesus, reliant as it was on the continued prosperity of the temple of Artemis. However, thanks to the calming influence of the town clerk, a riot was averted and Paul escaped without being physically harmed. After a last meeting with the believers in Ephesus, Paul departed from the city.

Paul never mentions this incident, but he does report the emotional state he and some companions were in regarding a potentially fatal situation:

We do not want you to be unaware, brothers and sisters, of the affliction we experienced in Asia; for we were so utterly, unbearably crushed that we despaired of life itself. Indeed, we felt that we had received the sentence of death . . . . (2 Corinthians 1:8-9a, NRSV)

Unfortunately, true to his habitual style, Paul does not provide the necessary details for us to know what had happened. While he refers to Asia as the location of the calamity, the site of the event was almost certainly Ephesus.[315] It is possible that his "affliction"[316] was the silversmith's attack on Paul and his colleagues as

[315] Luke also uses Asia and Ephesus interchangeably (Acts 20:16).

[316] The NT term *thlipsis* (tribulation, affliction) is a general term indicating an oppressive condition proceeding from an external source, with either or both physical and mental/emotional consequences.

stated in Acts. However, Paul's choice of words strongly suggests an imprisonment. The Greek term *apokrima*, which the NRSV translates as "sentence," normally refers to an official decision or report. It is not likely that Paul uses it as a metaphor. Rather, he and some of his team had been jailed to await the decision of a judge on a charge which could lead to their execution. As it turned out, they were relieved at the outcome.

Philippians yields a similar snapshot, but taken while Paul was still in prison awaiting trial.[317] While this account packs less emotional weight than 2 Corinthians 1:8-11, the possibility of death is present in both. Philippians adds further information. First, mention of the praetorium points to Paul's imprisonment in the local governor's headquarters. However, it is not evidence of any specific city or province. Second, his present imprisonment post-dates the confinements mentioned in 2 Corinthians 11:23. Third, the charges against him have something to do with his proclamation of the gospel, which was undoubtedly the case in most if not all his imprisonments. But rather than hindering his evangelical work, his imprisonment has actually furthered it. The whole praetorium has heard about the gospel as a result, and other believers have gained courage to proclaim it (Philippians 1:12-18).

Before relating the Demetrius episode, Luke informs the reader of Paul's plans to leave Asia, travel first to Macedonia and Achaia, then to Jerusalem, and finally to Rome (Acts 19:21-22). Two of his assistants, Timothy and Erastus were sent ahead to Macedonia.[318] Mention of Timothy is reminiscent of Paul's instructions in 1 Corinthians 16:10-11 for his readers to treat Timothy hospitably when he arrives in Corinth. However, the two texts

---

[317] Philippians 1:12-26.

[318] An Erastus is also named by Paul as the *oikonomos* of the city of Corinth (Romans 16:23). An *oikonomos* is a manager placed in charge of some operation, private or public. Here it may designate either a city official of high status, perhaps the treasurer of Corinth, or a person lower down in the financial administration of the city, perhaps a slave with training in finance.

do not refer to the same event. In his letter Paul was expecting Timothy to return to him in Ephesus, while Luke envisages Timothy preceding Paul on his trip through Macedonia to Corinth. Further, Timothy was with Paul in Macedonia when 2 Corinthians 1:1 was written. His instructions regarding Timothy while Paul was still in Ephesus precede the other references to Timothy by several months at least. Finally, Acts has Timothy and Erastus being sent to Macedonia, not to Corinth. Luke seems ignorant both that Titus was dispatched to Corinth at this time and of Paul's correspondence with the church there.

When Paul left Ephesus this time, he was never to return. Luke's account of Paul's final journey to Jerusalem portrays him bypassing Ephesus but stopping in Miletus, about 80 kilometers (50 miles) distant. From there he sent word to the elders of the church in Ephesus to come to him (Acts 20:17). Such a tactic meant a delay in Paul's journey, so there must have been a good reason for it. His most recent experience there had convinced him that it was too dangerous to be seen ever again in Ephesus.

Summary

P aul's two to three years in Ephesus were spent creating and nourishing a Christian presence there while maintaining previously formed congregations in Corinth, and probably also in Galatia and Philippi. In the absence of any authentic correspondence with Ephesian congregations, we know very little about them.

On the other hand, Paul's Ephesian period leaves us with substantial information about churches in other cities. His letters to them tell us not only about life in the churches addressed, but also about Paul's experiences and the Jesus movement in general. We learn that peace and harmony did not reign; there was far too much variety among Jesus' followers in their views of his identity, his relationship to the Torah and God, his mission, his achievements, his death and resurrection and their meaning, the interpretation of his teachings, and the authority of various apostles. Luke attempts to smooth things out as much as possible. Paul's writings, arising as they did out of the give and take of the moment, more realistically reveal the differences and the resulting conflicts between missionaries with varying outlooks as well as tensions within congregations. We shall learn more about those conflicts and tensions regarding the Corinthian church in the next chapter.

CHAPTER 12: From Ephesus to Rome

When Paul departed from Ephesus in 55 or 56 CE, he was on his way to Corinth for the third and final time. His last visit had been a human-relations disaster to which he had responded with his angry fourth letter to the Corinthians. Titus was both the courier of the letter and Paul's envoy with a mandate to attempt a salvage operation. Following his time in Corinth, the length of which would depend on circumstances, Titus was to travel north and east through Macedonia. He would meet Paul en route traveling in the opposite direction, perhaps in Troas if the Corinthian assignment was completed in sufficient time.[319]

But Titus was not to be found in Troas. Acts is silent about this leg of the apostle's trip, while Paul supplies only a few details. An opportunity to proclaim the gospel in Troas emerged, and he could barely resist the temptation to stay longer. Only the absence of Titus led Paul to press on to Macedonia where he would be stopping in city after city to supervise the collection for Jerusalem. Somewhere in that province, probably either in Philippi or Thessalonica, Titus and Paul finally met. Titus brought good news; the Corinthians had accepted Paul's defense of his actions and had already taken significant steps toward reconciliation. A relieved and grateful Paul responded with yet another letter to be delivered prior to his arrival in Corinth.

---

[319] There was likely already a Christian presence in Troas, but neither Luke nor Paul gives any information about its beginnings. The Travel Document in Acts reports the existence of a church there the following year (Acts 20:5-12). Paul mentions Troas only in 2 Corinthians 2:12. He and his team may have established the foundation of a congregation in Troas before their first crossing to Macedonia.

Fifth letter: 2 Corinthians 1:1-2:13; 7:5-16; 13:11-13

Paul's most recent (fourth) letter to the Corinthians (2 Corinthians 10:1-13:10), supported by the presence of Titus, had finally achieved the desired effect. The church was now persuaded of Paul's integrity and his authority as an authentic emissary of Christ. This welcome news called for a gracious response. The opening and closing of the fifth letter later provided the framework into which the other letters now comprising 2 Corinthians were inserted by the collector/editor.[320] The fifth letter is often called "the letter of reconciliation" for reasons its contents make apparent.

It opens with a blessing which substitutes for Paul's usual thanksgiving (2 Corinthians 1:3-6a). This short composition on affliction and consolation has a dual purpose. It extends to the Corinthians the hand of fellowship, calling attention to their joint participation in suffering and consolation. It also expresses Paul's reflection on his recent experiences, his "affliction" in Asia, and his relief at escaping the near-death situation mentioned earlier, capped by finally meeting Titus on his return from Corinth.

Like the thanksgivings of other letters, the affliction/consolation blessing leads into the main topic of the letter: the most recent developments in his relationship to the Corinthians. He continues with an explanation of the contents and motivation of his "letter of tears" and the reason he hadn't visited his readers as promised: he wanted to avoid another "painful visit" (2 Corinthians 2:1-4).

Paul then briefly recounts his frustrated desire to evangelize further in Troas, while waiting for Titus to return from Corinth. Finally, he grew impatient and went on to Macedonia. His "affliction" followed him: "disputes without and fears within." (7:5,

---

[320] Betz, "Corinthians, Second Epistle to the," *ABD*, 1:1149.

NRSV) With the coming of Titus, Paul received a double dose of comfort—the presence of Titus and the news he brought of reconciliation with Corinth.

The Corinthian crisis was past. Titus' good news complemented the consolation begun in his escape from Ephesus. Affliction and consolation were the ongoing counterpart of the cross and resurrection of Jesus. Both were to be expected by those who identified with Christ.

Paul had more to communicate to the Corinthians, but it would require a separate letter. His collection for the needy among the Jerusalem Christians was still in process, and he expected the reconciled Corinthian congregation(s) to resume their commitment to it.

Curiously, while Luke mentions Paul's intention to go to Jerusalem following his journey through Macedonia and Achaia, he provides the reader with no motive for the trip. Without Paul's letters, we would be unaware that the collection had become a major driving force during this period of his life. Paul now turned his attention to the administrative details involved in completing the collection and having representatives of the various churches appointed to accompany him as guards and monitors on the trip to Jerusalem.

During his lengthy semi-circular journey to Corinth, Paul continued his correspondence with his converts there. In the absence of a public postal system,[321] Paul had created his own postal network that included primarily his companions, some of whom he could send as his personal representatives to read and explain his letters to the assembled believers. Both Timothy and Titus served in that capacity. Highly trusted members of his churches were also potential letter carriers as they traveled to this or that city; for example, Phoebe from Cenchreae was very likely the courier of

---

[321] The official postal system, sort of a "pony express," was limited to administrative and military business. Blumell, "Travel and Communication in the NT," *NIB*: 5:652-656.

Paul's letter to the Romans (Romans 16:1-2). Long distance communication was slow, expensive, and required patience—all characteristics difficult for us today to appreciate fully.

Sixth and Seventh Letters: 2 Corinthians 8 and 9

Paul had agreed at the Jerusalem gathering to "remember the poor" in Jerusalem, i.e., to raise funds (not just once, but continually) from the Gentile churches to assist the poor among the Jerusalem Christians. At that time Paul had been working as part of a missionary team sponsored by the church at Antioch in Syria. The agreement in Jerusalem was binding on the church represented by Paul and Barnabas. In his letter to the Galatians, Paul writes that he had been "eager" to perform this service. It would not only bring material relief to the poor in Jerusalem, but also demonstrate solidarity between Gentile and Jewish churches.

However, as Martyn points out, it appears that Paul only now, years after the conference and no longer officially connected with the Antioch church, decides that he himself would personally engineer a collection for the destitute among the Jerusalem Christians.[322] Why now and not earlier? After he had broken with Antioch, Paul no longer felt obliged to honor the church-to-church agreement between Antioch and Jerusalem. But his present strained relations with both Antioch and Jerusalem led Paul to reconsider; his own personal effort to assist the church in Jerusalem might demonstrate his goodwill toward its leaders and his desire to be reconciled with them.

From the earliest days, creating a movement which included both Jews and Gentiles on equal footing had proved problematic. Paul's solution was expressed in his baptismal formula, in which the singularity of Christ overrides the division between Jew and

---

[322] Martyn, *Galatians*, 206-207, 222-228.

Greek (Galatians 3:28). But other Jewish Christians considered themselves bound not to eat with uncircumcised Gentiles, at least if the latter supplied some of the food. Whose position would win the day? [323]

Paul hoped that a generous act of the Gentile churches would both demonstrate their solidarity with their Jewish Christian brethren and counter some of their suspicions about Paul and his teaching. It was an opportunity for the Gentile churches under Paul's direction to contribute to the unity of the Jesus movement. In addition, Paul may have hoped to gain Jerusalem support for his planned mission to Spain. He may also have thought that better relations with the Jerusalem church would result in a decrease in attacks on his gospel. All in all, Paul believed so strongly in the potential of the collection that he postponed his mission to Spain and placed his own life in great danger in order to implement it.

Paul mentions the collection for the impoverished believers in Jerusalem in five letters, two of which were written during the period he was in Ephesus (1 Corinthians 16:1-2) and during his final sojourn in Corinth (Romans 15:25-26). The third letter is the lost one written to the Galatians mentioned in 1 Corinthians 16:1. Paul's most extensive treatment of the collection, however, is found in the two short letters found in 2 Corinthians 8 and 9.[324] They contain detailed instructions for two different recipients, the Corinthian congregation (chapter 8) and the other churches of

---

[323] Mark 7:19 reflects Paul's position regarding food purity--all food is pure. The parallel in Matthew 15:17 omits this sentence, suggesting that Matthew's church continued to observe Jewish food regulations as required by the Torah (Leviticus 11). Matthew does retain Mark's statement regarding what defiles, i.e., that which proceeds from the heart, not what goes into the mouth or eating with un-washed hands (15:18-20). Washing of course was a religious ritual, not a hygienic requirement. Pharisaic extensions of other priestly requirements (see Exodus 13:17-21) to the laity were not binding for Matthew's community, in contrast to the commandments regarding clean and unclean foods which continued to be observed.

[324] The following discussion is indebted to Betz, *2 Corinthians 8 and 9*.

Achaia (chapter 9).[325] Notably, the fifth letter treated above was addressed both to Corinth and to the other churches in Achaia (2 Corinthians 1:1), a unique form of address among Paul's letters.

The current letter to the Christians in Corinth begins with Paul's commendation of the generosity of the believers in Macedonia. Despite their own poverty, the Macedonians eagerly volunteered to contribute to the fund for the Jerusalem poor. With their example in mind (and mentioned to the Corinthians), Paul was appointing Titus to return to Corinth to complete the collection which he had begun the previous year. Along with Titus Paul is sending two "messengers of the churches" (8:23, NRSV).[326] One "is famous among all the churches for his proclaiming the good news. . . ." (8:18, NRSV) He had been appointed by the Macedonian churches to aid in supervising the delivery of the collection. The other, also unnamed, Paul finds reason to recommend but says nothing further about him. However, Titus is identified as Paul's official representative, the leader of the delegation. He is Paul's "partner and co-worker" in this matter and no doubt the bearer of this letter authorizing his appointment as chief fund-raiser (8:6, 23). The other two representatives provide assurance of propriety so that nobody can accuse Titus and Paul of fraud or embezzlement. Their presence with Titus would also augment security.

Paul is careful to indicate that the collection is voluntary and that the Corinthians' own financial well-being should not be jeopardized by donating to the fund. All gifts should be according to means.

---

[325] Apart from Athens and Corinth, Acts names no Achaian cities where Paul was active. Paul mentions Achaia seven times in four of his letters: 1 Thessalonians 1:7-8; 1 Corinthians 16:15; 2 Corinthians 1:1; 9:2; 11:10; Romans 15:26. Paul names three cities in Achaia as locations of house churches: Athens, Corinth, and Cenchreae, one of the two ports controlled by Corinth.

[326] The Greek word translated "messengers" is *apostoloi*, i.e., "apostles." For this meaning of apostle, see also Philippians 2:25; Acts 14:4, 14.

This letter, Paul's sixth to Corinth of which we have knowledge, probably accompanied the fifth, the letter of reconciliation. The two letters address different needs, the one responding to the recent changes for the better in the Corinthian church, the other informing the Corinthians on procedures now being put in place to complete the collection, and validating Titus' central role in that process.

The fund-raising letter to the churches of Achaia (chapter 9) begins with reference to the name of the collection, which the NRSV renders as "the ministry to the saints" (9:1) and Betz translates as "the charitable collection for the saints."[327] The same wording is found in the letter documenting Titus' appointment (8:4). The readers had been occupied earlier in raising the requested funds under Titus' leadership (2 Corinthians 8:6, 10); presumably that preparation included both the Corinthian and other congregations in Achaia. Paul has even boasted to the Macedonians that the Achaian churches have been ready since the previous year. However, he now gives the Achaeans advance notice that their readiness is about to be tested. Sending his deputation to them is a precautionary move against the possibility of an embarrassing situation when he arrives, perhaps in the company of some Macedonians.

As in the fund-raising letter to Corinth, Paul encourages the Achaians to be generous in their voluntary giving, reminding them of the divine generosity shown in Christ and that their own generosity demonstrates their love and glorifies God. His final words highlight the basis of the life they now live, and are obviously intended to motivate their participation in the collection: "Thanks be to God for his indescribable gift!" (2 Corinthians 9:15, NRSV)

This completes our cursory examination of the different letters comprising the document we know as 2 Corinthians. There are those who continue to regard all of them as parts of a single letter. However, many scholars find the arguments for the above analysis

---

[327] Betz, *2 Corinthians 8 and 9*, 90.

and identification of separate letters persuasive. The perspective adopted here coheres with the rapidly changing situation in Corinth and with Paul's growing preoccupation with the gift for the Jerusalem Christians.

Winter in Corinth

Other than the brief summary statement in Acts, Luke provides no information about the period following the dispatch of Titus and his two companions before Paul arrived in Corinth, where he was to stay for three months. Likewise, apart from a reference to Illyricum (Romans 15:19), Paul gives no details about the remainder of his trip through Macedonia to Corinth. It is not clear whether he had actually missionized in the province of Illyricum, or had only gone as far as the Macedonian territory adjacent to the southern border of that province. In any case, he fulfilled his intention of visiting the Corinthians and spending the winter with them (1 Corinthians 16:5-6). When he left Ephesus, he had not yet decided whether to accompany the delegation taking the collection to Jerusalem. After arriving in Corinth, he indicated in his letter to the Romans that he had made that decision, a fatal one as it turned out.

Paul's Letter to the Romans

During his three months in Corinth, Paul wrote his longest and most carefully considered letter. It differs from all his other letters inasmuch as it was the only one written to a group of congregations[328] which he had neither founded nor visited. It was composed when Paul was planning to enter a new mission field, having completed his work in the East:

---

[328] Jewett argues that there were numerous congregations in Rome when Paul wrote, even more than the five to seven often estimated (*Romans,* 62).

. . . from Jerusalem and as far around as Illyricum I have fully proclaimed the good news of Christ. (Romans 15:19b, NRSV).

Why does he write that he began in Jerusalem if in fact he had not been engaged in missionizing there? Why not Damascus or Antioch? Perhaps he was thinking of a scenario similar to the one in Acts: Jerusalem was the center of the Jewish world and the home base of the Jesus movement.[329] In a sense, Paul could claim he had preached the gospel in Jerusalem inasmuch as he had successfully defended his Gentile gospel at the conference a few years earlier. The phrase "as far around as Illyricum" suggests a conception of the Mediterranean Sea as an elongated ellipse with human habitations on its borders.[330] Paul's missionary travels had taken him from Jerusalem around the eastern end of the Mediterranean through Asia Minor, Macedonia, and Achaia to Illyricum, the Roman province across the Adriatic from Italy. That he had "fully proclaimed" the gospel may indicate that Paul considers that wherever he went he had told the complete and genuine story of Christ and its implications for the Gentiles. Possibly he also means that he has completed his mission in that particular geographical area. His policy had been to break new ground, to plant churches in key cities from which the movement would be spread by his followers.[331]

Paul's choice of Spain as his next mission field is perhaps to be explained by the prophetic mandate (Isaiah 49:6) which launched his Gentile mission and sent him to "the nations" and to the "end of the earth."

---

[329] Acts 1:8 (see also 2:5-11) gives a précis of the spread of the faith from Jerusalem to Rome.

[330] Such as is found in the Peutinger map (Google it for further information).

[331] To support this policy Paul quotes but substantially modifies Isaiah 52:15 (Romans 15:21).

From a Mediterranean perspective, the "ends of the earth" (Acts 1:8), if taken literally, might be identified with the Iberian peninsula, the western limit of the inhabited world as imagined in Paul's time. In any case, Paul believed that no missionaries of Christ had yet arrived in that area. A practical factor in his decision to go there may have been that Spain was devoid of Jewish settlement. He could count on performing his evangelistic work without Jewish opposition. If conservative Jewish Christian missionaries had not yet arrived in Spain, his proclamation of his Law-free gospel to Gentiles would be unhindered by them. On the other hand, there would be no God-fearers in Spain whose knowledge of the scriptures would expedite their understanding of Paul's story. However, Paul had already faced and overcome that hurdle in Galatia, Philippi, and Thessalonica.

Spain posed a problem which Paul had not yet encountered. Up to that point, his world had consisted of Jews and Gentiles, all or mostly Greek-speaking. His calling had been to the latter, which he referred to as the *ethnoi*, i.e., non-Jews, or *Hellēnes*, i.e., Greeks. In his earlier writings, he regards Gentiles as a single entity. But there is a shift in Romans, where Paul extends his mission field beyond Jews and Greeks to "barbarians" (Romans 1:13-15). This passage introduces a new categorization of Gentiles: they consist of those who speak Greek and participate in Greek culture, i.e., are "civilized," and of those who are "barbarians."[332] "Barbarians" here refers to the indigenous Spanish people who do not belong to Greco-Roman culture, and were therefore considered inferior by "civilized" people. The introduction of barbarians into Paul's understanding of his Gentile mission is significant. First, it points to a

---

[332] The Greek word *"barbaros"* refers primarily to language which is not understood. In the only other usage of this word in his letters, Paul compares speaking in tongues to using "barbaric" language, i.e., language which is not comprehended by the hearers, or so much babble to them. In Acts 28:2, 4 the NRSV translates *barbaroi* as "natives," i.e., those whose language is not understandable to those who are shipwrecked.

radical departure from his previous missionary work. His next mission would involve not only a change in geography, but more importantly in language and culture. Second, it would require marshaling support on a much larger scale than in the past. His plan must have caused some of his missionary companions to shake their heads in disbelief.

The intimate connection between Paul's intent to conduct a mission in Spain and the content of Romans has been traced in detail by Robert Jewett in his massive commentary.[333] The logistics of such a mission would have been formidable. On the whole, Spain had not participated in the Hellenization of the central and eastern Mediterranean countries. The Greek that Paul spoke would have been of no direct use in the Spanish provinces where Latin was the administrative language of the rulers and various tribal languages or dialects were spoken by the ruled. An evangelist would require translation services, first into the Latin of the Roman administrators and then into the local language. Jewett makes a case that Paul was asking the Roman churches, some members of which might have connections in Spain, to assist him in setting up the infrastructure for his proposed mission. Phoebe of Cenchreae, who had been a patroness to Paul and others, is serving as his personal representative to the Roman churches in this matter as well as supporting his proposed mission financially (Romans 16:1-2).

Given his intention to secure the backing of the churches in Rome for his mission to Spain, certain features of Paul's letter to the Romans become clearer. For example, the final chapter of this letter contains a long list of individuals (26) plus some groups in Rome to be greeted, numerically far exceeding those to whom Paul usually sends greetings.[334] They range from former missionary col-

---

[333] Jewett, *Romans*.

[334] The sheer number of names mentioned in Romans 16 was taken by earlier interpreters as evidence that it did not belong to Paul's original letter to Rome, since he would not have known so many persons in Rome. Rather, chapter 16 must have been part of a letter to Ephesus where Paul had lived and worked for

leagues, such as Prisca and Aquila, to other missionaries such as Urbanus, Tryphaena, Tryphosa, and Persis, and to his former fellow prisoners Andronicus and Junia. He includes some persons about whom he had only heard, including a group with a connection to the imperial household, "the family of Narcissus," and another related to the Herodian family. By citing not only their names, but also making favorable comments about them, Paul clearly aims to establish good relations with the Roman congregations.

The content of Romans is complex and invites detailed study. For our purposes, it is sufficient to note only three matters of importance to Paul for obtaining his audience's support for his mission to Spain.

First, he needed to clear the air regarding his teachings. Paul had become a controversial figure and he wanted his audience to hear his side of the controversy. Consequently, he laid out in unparalleled detail the story he told among the Gentiles so that his audience could judge for themselves its legitimacy (Romans 1-8). We have already traced the elements of that story in regard to Adam, Abraham, Moses, and Jesus.

Second, there were rumors circulating that Paul was an apostate and taught Jews to abandon the Law.[335] It was important that he set the record straight. He considered himself a faithful Jew; he did not believe that God had abandoned his traditional people. He envisaged that Gentile believers are not a replacement for Israel, but are becoming incorporated into Israel.[336] His numerous quotes

---

an extended period. There is widespread agreement today that Romans 16 only makes sense in a Roman context.

[335] See James' conversation with Paul in Acts 21:20b-21 where Paul is informed that he is rumored to be teaching Jews to give up circumcising their children, observing other Jewish customs, even ignoring Moses.

[336] Paul makes a distinction between a "spiritual" and a "fleshly" (short for "flesh and blood") Israel. He considers the former to be the true Israel along with the "spiritual" Gentiles. See Romans 2:28-29. Attempts to limit "Israel" to Israelites are not convincing.

from the Jewish scriptures demonstrated his familiarity with and high regard for them. He included portions of Jewish Christian creeds in his arguments, thereby honoring their formulations. But the pièce de résistance was the extended discussion regarding the disappointingly minor response of the Jewish people to the gospel of Jesus (Romans 9-11). While some Israelites had joined the Jesus movement, most had not. Paul appeals to the biblical image of the remnant to explain that development. But even those who do not at present belong to the remnant have not been rejected by God, as some Gentile believers might be tempted to conclude. The refusal of the majority of Israel to accept the gospel is only temporary; when they realize that the Gentiles are obtaining the salvation that Israel seeks, they will join the Gentiles in acknowledging Christ. All this is according to the plan of God who desires the healing of all the nations, Israel as well as the Gentiles.

Third, Paul was aware of a worrisome division in the Roman congregations which could jeopardize their participation in his Spanish mission. The fundamental problem was a familiar one to Paul. It was inherent in the Jesus movement which brought together people of different ethnic identities, including Jews. Many Jewish Christians continued to distinguish between clean and unclean foods, and to observe the Sabbath and other holy days. Those of Gentile background rejected such distinctions. Paul knew from experience that each group tended to judge and look down on the other. That situation was dividing the Roman congregations. It needed to be addressed in order to make possible united support of his mission to Spain (part of chapter 12 and 14:1-15:13).

Paul had earlier dealt with such inner- and inter-church issues at Antioch and again at Corinth. However, the division at Antioch was not the same as those addressed in Corinth and Rome. The issue at Antioch, from Paul's point of view, was the attempt by James to impose the Law, albeit a minimal version, on Gentiles. Requiring Gentiles to observe any part of the Law other than the commandment to love one another, identical to the law of Christ,

334

denied the supreme role of Jesus in God's plan. There were not two ways in God's plan to heal humanity, but only one.

At Corinth, there had been no attempt to impose purity regulations on Gentiles. The issue there was not even a matter of Jewish/Gentile relations, but of insensitivity to the consciences of other believers. The specific issue involved Gentiles with two different convictions regarding idols. After their conversion some became convinced, emotionally as well as intellectually (as was Paul), that since idols had no reality, believers were free to eat meat which had been sacrificed in a pagan temple. Other converted Gentiles had not yet achieved that emotional freedom. Paul cautions the enlightened ones to consider the conscience of those who still think of food as offered to idols (1 Corinthians 8:1, 4, 7-9; see also 10:23-11:1). Newly acquired knowledge does not immediately create a new conscience in everyone. Reeducation of the conscience may take time. Consequently, Paul counsels those whose knowledge was accompanied by a clear ("strong") conscience to be considerate of those whose consciences were still weak. Insistence on being right or having one's own way regardless of its effect on others contravenes the love ethic (1 Corinthians 13:4-5a).

Paul's letter to the Romans shows the same concern for sensitivity to the needs of others. The faithful community includes those who are troubled by the idea of eating unclean food and those who are not. The second group is identified as the "strong" (in faith or conscience), the first as the "weak":[337]

> I know and am persuaded in the Lord Jesus that nothing is unclean in itself; but it is unclean for anyone who thinks it unclean. If your brother or sister is being injured by what you eat, you are no longer walking in love. . . . Everything is indeed clean, but it is wrong for you to make others fall

[337] This use of comparative terminology was probably initiated by those who considered their faith to be strong and the faith of the others weak.

by what you eat; it is good not to eat meat or drink wine or do anything that makes your brother or sister stumble. (Romans 14:14-15a; 20b-21, NRSV)[338]

The Roman situation addressed by Paul has features of both the Antiochian and the Corinthian situations. As at Antioch, a distinction is made between Jewish and Gentile believers, in Romans by the use of the term "unclean." However, Roman Gentiles are not being forced or even encouraged to obey any part of the Law. Rather, as at Corinth, the issue is lack of care for others who are not yet totally free of their pre-Christian convictions. In contrast to Antioch, the Gentile believers in the Roman churches hold the upper hand. As those who are stronger in faith, they are urged by Paul to be considerate of those who hold different opinions. Food and drink are not important in and of themselves, but their potential for conflict requires them, like every other aspect of life, to be subject to the basic criterion of love of neighbor. Likewise, those who still insist on observing laws concerning food, drink, and holy days should not judge those who consider them unimportant. In both cases, believers are to keep in view the wellbeing of others and act accordingly.

Although not as significant as the above three matters, Paul also reveals some anxiety about his audience's relationship with the ruling powers. His Spanish mission will require cordial relations with government officials. Whether Paul actually knows of any problems in that area, or whether he is simply being proactive, is unclear. In either case, the principle to which he appeals is the same as found in Mark 12:17—be respectful of authority, pay the required taxes, and give what is due to God (Romans 13:7). If any

---

[338] Paul has softened the approach he earlier took in Syrian Antioch (Galatians 2:11-21) where he accused Peter of hypocrisy for changing his mind about eating with Gentiles. Now he counsels understanding of those who differ over the food issue. He implies that the issue is not of great importance and people should not make it a deal-breaker for mutual acceptance.

Roman believers acted illegally, not only would they create problems for themselves and the Christian community, but Paul's plans would also be severely jeopardized.

Finally, Paul informs his audience that he himself was engaged in healing the division between himself and the Jerusalem church. The relief fund for the Jerusalem Christian community being raised under his direction was aimed not only at improving conditions for the poor at Jerusalem, but also at demonstrating the healing care of the Gentile churches for the Jewish Christian members of God's family. Cross-border compassion was basic to Paul's gospel.

Back to Jerusalem

Paul was fully aware of the dangers in returning to Jerusalem (Romans 15:30-31). Even if he were not subjected to hostile actions by the Judean unbelievers, the charitable fund might be rejected by the saints there. Nevertheless, the stakes were so high that he was determined to accompany those who were to deliver the collection, being convinced that his personal presence at Jerusalem was essential to the success of his plan.

We are dependent on information found almost exclusively in Acts for the remainder of Paul's career. After spending three months in Greece, his plan to go by sea to Syria was interrupted by discovery of a Jewish plot on his life. As a result, he and his entourage abandoned their intention of a sea voyage and took the land route from Corinth through Macedonia (Acts 20:3) for the first leg of their journey.

Acts lists the names of seven men who accompanied Paul and identifies the provinces (a city in one case) from which they came (Acts 20:4). Two of those men (Sopater and Timothy) send greetings in Romans 16:21. Luke's list of church delegates covers three of the provinces in which Paul had evangelized: three representatives from Macedonia, two from Asia, and one from Galatia (assuming that Timothy is not regarded as a representative of the Galatian churches).[339] Surprisingly, Luke does not mention delegates from Achaia. This is particularly puzzling since Paul specifically wrote that he would send letters with those approved by the Corinthians to take their gift to Jerusalem (1 Corinthians 16:3). Perhaps they now trusted him and his companions enough to consider them their representatives.

The inconsistency between the account in Acts and Paul's own statements is apparent. Luke gives no explanation of why these particular people assembled to go with Paul to Jerusalem. He includes representatives from Asia, whom Paul does not mention as participating in the collection, and omits mention of those from Achaia, to whom Paul does refer. It is not certain that they all accompanied Paul from his starting point, or whether some of them joined him at Troas (Acts 20:5). It would make little sense for the Asians, for example, to travel from Ephesus to Corinth only to reverse their path later, unless they were needed for guard duty. Likewise, Gaius from Derbe in south Galatia would undertake a very long trip west before returning east (unless he was already in Corinth). Timothy was with Paul at that time, and the presence of the three Macedonians is explained by their earlier expectation of embarking from Corinth.

Luke's account contains nothing about the party retracing their journey across Macedonia until it incorporates once again the Travel Document (Acts 20:5), absent since Paul left Philippi on the "second missionary journey." It is the only testimony to Paul's journey from Philippi to Troas and on around the coast of Asia Minor and finally, after some stops, to Caesarea and Jerusalem.

---

[339] It is curious that in his letter to the Romans, Paul mentions only Macedonia and Achaia as participants in the offering. In 1 Corinthians 16:1 he writes that they should follow the same directions that Paul had given to the Galatian churches. Since their participation is not mentioned in Romans, we can assume that the churches in Galatia declined Paul's request (Martyn, *Galatians*, 222-228).

Into this source, however, Luke has made some insertions. For example, Paul's final speech to the Ephesian elders at Miletus (Acts 20:17-35) is almost certainly Luke's own composition. In contrast to the contemporary perspective of the Travel Document, it looks back upon Paul as an apostle of orthodoxy and a model Christian leader to be emulated by subsequent clergy, similar to the viewpoint of the Pastoral Epistles.[340] It is Paul's farewell speech to his churches in the province of Asia, anticipating his death as a martyr. The prophecy of Agabus at Caesarea (Acts 21:10-14) also strikes the note of martyrdom.

Jerusalem and Caesarea

The following long narrative (Acts 21:17-26:32), covering the period from the time the party arrived in Jerusalem up to Paul's departure from Caesarea as a prisoner, cannot be assigned to the Travel Document, even though it is introduced with a "we." That Luke incorporates information from sources in this section is not in question, but his editorial hand is evident everywhere. He is a master at weaving information into a gripping story, but the result is not history in the modern sense, nor is this whole section to be taken as eye-witness testimony. Favorite Lucan themes are evident throughout: Paul is saved by Roman justice from Jewish plots against his life; Roman army officers and procurators always act properly and find nothing illegal in Paul's actions; Paul is consistently represented as a loyal and observant Jew and in harmony with church leaders in Jerusalem.

Paul's mission to deliver the collection requires meeting with the leaders of the Jerusalem church, including James. Since Luke still refuses to identify the collection as such,[341] it is not clear in

---

[340] Haenchen, *Acts*, 596-597.

[341] Luke has Paul say: "Now after some years I came to bring alms to my nation and to offer sacrifices." (Acts 24:17, NRSV) Clearly Luke knows about the collec-

Acts what the purpose of the meeting was. Luke's avoidance of the actual reason for Paul's trip to Jerusalem is probably to be explained by its inconsistency with his purposes in writing Acts. Perhaps he knows more than he wants to say about the reception Paul received from the Jerusalem leaders, that in fact they refused the collection. Such an embarrassing conclusion to Paul's heroic efforts to unify the church would not have been acceptable to Luke. However, thanks to Paul's letter to the Romans, we can surmise the purpose of the meeting—to negotiate the conditions under which the collection would be accepted.

Members of the Jesus movement who held very different points of view attended that meeting: on the one hand, the Jewish Christian leaders of the Jerusalem church, and on the other, Paul, the champion of Gentile Christianity, and his companions. Paul's proclamation of Christ as the one sent by God for the salvation of all people implied that the Torah did not fulfill that role. His scathing critique of the Jerusalem leaders in his letter to the Galatians had no doubt been reported to them. They still observed the commandments and worshiped in the temple. For them, Jesus had not abrogated their heritage. They were also aware of rumors that Paul was advising Jews not to circumcise their children.

Once again James came up with a proposal, this time to test publicly whether Paul in fact was a loyal, observant Jew. Four men in the Jerusalem church had undertaken a Nazirite vow,[342] but they lacked the finances for the concluding temple sacrifices. Paul agreed

---

tion, but is not prepared to recognize its significance as Paul's attempt to heal a fractured Jesus movement.

[342] Nazirite vows could be made for almost any purpose and for any length of time from 20 days up to a lifetime. The key elements were the final offering to be made in the Temple and the cutting of the hair at that time. It was not inexpensive; the financing of four sets of sacrifices was a substantial undertaking. See Numbers 6:13-21 for the scriptural laws regarding the sacrifices.

to subsidize their costs, an act commonly regarded as pious and laudatory.[343]

However, before the final day when the redemption of the vows would occur, some Jews from Asia recognize Paul in the temple. They identify him as ". . . the man who is teaching everyone everywhere against our people, our law and this place." (Acts 21:28, NRSV) Paul is publicly accused of bringing one of his Gentile companions, Trophimus of Ephesus, into the parts of the temple reserved for Jews,[344] thereby sparking a riot. Paul and no doubt Trophimus were saved from certain death by the Roman security forces stationed near the temple in the Antonia,[345] a fortress built for security purposes on a high promontory just outside the northwest corner of the temple complex overlooking the city and the temple area.

Arrested and taken to the Antonia, Paul requests permission to address his accusers and delivers a speech of defense, the first of several designed by Luke for the prisoner Paul. These speeches provide opportunities for Luke to highlight the key elements of Paul's life story and his proclamation of Jesus. Paul's speech to the people is drowned out by the crowd when he begins to speak of his

---

[343] Where did Paul get the money to pay for the sacrifices? Was it taken from the collection for the poor?

[344] Gentiles were allowed onto the Temple mount only in the so-called court of the Gentiles. Beyond that area, the Temple precinct was reserved for Jewish use. It was divided into four areas of increasing sanctity—the court of the Israelite Women, the court of the Israelite Men, the court of the Priests, and the Most Holy Place. The latter was reserved for the High Priest to enter once a year on the Day of Atonement. Between the court of the Gentiles and the court of the Women was a low wall with stone slabs placed at intervals, some inscribed in Latin, some in Greek, warning that non-Jews who crossed that boundary were responsible for their own death, which would follow. One of those slabs was discovered in the 19th century.

[345] The Antonia was constructed soon after King Herod captured Jerusalem in 37 BCE and named after his friend and benefactor, Marc Antony. It was destroyed in 70 CE by the Roman army under Titus.

Gentile mission. Upon learning that Paul is a Roman citizen, the tribune refrains from torturing him to gain information and holds him overnight. The next morning he places Paul before the official Jewish court, the Sanhedrin, to see what charges they bring against him. Paul manipulates the court into a divisive argument over resurrection, in which the Pharisees, but not the Sadducees, believe. The Pharisees find nothing wrong with one of their own. To avoid violence, the tribune takes Paul back into custody. That night Jesus reveals to Paul that as he had borne testimony in Jerusalem, so he must also in Rome (Acts 23:11).

Paul's nephew gets wind of a Jewish plot to kill Paul and informs the tribune, Claudius Lysias, who sends Paul under heavy guard to the procurator Felix in Caesarea along with an explanatory letter. Thus Paul leaves Jerusalem for the final time.

Paul is imprisoned in Caesarea for more than two years. During that time he has an audience with the procurator Felix and his Jewish wife Drusilla. Felix delays a decision, hoping to receive a bribe from Paul. Then Felix is replaced by a new procurator, Porcius Festus. In order to avoid a trial by his enemies in Jerusalem, Paul plays his last remaining card, a legal appeal to be tried in Rome by Caesar. Before being taken from Caesarea, Paul appears also before the Jewish king Agrippa II and his sister Bernice.

Romeward Bound

After its absence since Acts 21:18, the Travel Document picks up again when Paul is turned over to Julius the centurion who has the responsibility of delivering Paul and other prisoners to Rome.[346] This source continues until they arrive in Rome (Acts 27:1-28:16). Their journey is traced as the merchant ship works its way around Cyprus to Myra in Lycia where they

---

[346] At least two of Paul's friends accompanied him: Aristarchus of Thessalonica (Acts 27:2; see also 19:29, 20:4, and Philemon 24 where Aristarchus is with Paul in prison), and the author of the Travel Document.

transfer to another ship. It is too late in the year for safe sailing and their ship carrying grain from Alexandria to Rome is blown off course.[347] Finally, they are shipwrecked on Malta—Paul's fourth experience of a shipwreck (see 2 Corinthians 11:25).

Although the Travel Document covers this journey, much of the narrative betrays Luke's literary hand and his eulogistic treatment of Paul.[348] For example, rather than being a helpless prisoner, Paul is in control much of the time, giving both advice and orders. He foresees the looming disaster at sea and is instrumental in saving all on board. His miraculous powers enable him to survive the bite of a snake on Malta, and as had happened at Lystra (14:11), the observers declare him a god. Like an orator before an audience, he continues delivering speeches (27:21-26), even during a raging tempest when hope of being saved is slight. Through an angel, Paul is told that he "must stand before the emperor." (27:24) Yet, it is not always easy to discern in detail the sutures between the Travel Document, other sources, and Luke's own compositions. The final product often retains the impression of the report of a first-hand observer/participant, and at the same time serves the interests of the author of Acts who wishes to glorify Paul. What is missing in this whole section, however, is any depiction of Paul the evangelist. Not until he addresses the Jewish leaders in Rome does he even mention the name of Jesus.

After spending three months hosted by the islanders, those who had been on the wrecked ship (276 persons; Acts 27:37) boarded another Alexandrian ship that had wintered in Malta. The

---

[347] Sailing in the eastern Mediterranean became increasingly dangerous after the middle of September, and normally ceased during a four month period starting November 11 (Haenchen, *Acts*, 700). The Fast mentioned in Acts 27:9, which was already past when the ship reached Fair Havens on Crete, is Yom Kippur, which comes on the tenth day of the Jewish month of Tishri (late September or early October).

[348] We cannot assume that every time Luke uses "we" that what follows belongs to the Travel Document, especially when it is not part of the actual itinerary.

favorable March winds brought them progressively to Sicily, Rhegium on the mainland, and finally to Puteoli where Paul and his companions were allowed to stay for a week with some Christians, no doubt in the presence of a guard.

Rome

The travel itinerary which had begun when Paul first left Asia and was given guidance for entering Europe ends with his entry into Rome (Acts 28:16). From that point on, Acts gives the impression that Paul has no further contact with the churches in Rome, but turns rather to attempt once again to convert Jews. They dedicate a full day to hearing Paul's arguments from the scriptures regarding the kingdom of God and Jesus. As elsewhere, some Jews are convinced and others are not. For the third and final time, Paul reiterates that due to Jewish unbelief, salvation is being given over to the Gentiles who are receptive. Acts concludes with Paul's living in Rome and for the next two years proclaiming the gospel to all who came to him.

Two things are noteworthy here: First, while Luke obviously knows that Paul died in Rome, but not necessarily when or how, he does not describe the event or even mention it. One of Luke's purposes in writing Acts is to trace the progress of the gospel from Jerusalem to Rome. The Jerusalem church no longer existed. The center of Christianity had shifted to the capital of the empire, at least in Luke's eyes. He gives Paul the primary role in bringing the faith to Rome. During his final two years there Paul proclaimed Jesus and the kingdom of God to Gentiles in Rome. Having completed his story of the origins and spread of the Jesus movement from Galilee and Judea to Rome, and of its transition from a Jewish sect to a Gentile religion worthy of legitimation by the Roman government, Luke had no need to go further. Paul's death lay outside Luke's purpose; besides, his contemporaries already knew of it but, like Luke, not necessarily the details. Alternatively, Luke and others in fact did know that Paul had died either by execution or in the fire that razed much of Rome in 64 CE. Silence about how Paul died was more advantageous for Luke's story than blaming any Roman official for it.

Second, and related to the first point, while Acts refers to believers both in Puteoli and in Rome, the latter even traveling about 65 kilometers (about 40 miles) to meet Paul at Three Taverns, Luke then drops them from the following narrative. It is as if they no longer existed. Paul's letter to the Romans written only a few years earlier from Corinth should leave no doubt about the bond Paul felt and wished to strengthen with the Roman churches. Did they abandon Paul when he needed them most? Clearly Luke's picture of Paul's time in Rome is partial in the extreme, perhaps primarily due to his need for Paul only to complete his career in Rome. An earlier and vibrant Christian presence there would not be consistent with Paul's evangelizing in Rome and having a significant role in founding the Roman churches.

There have been many attempts to demonstrate that Paul survived a first Roman sojourn, went to Spain, and then returned to Rome where he was martyred after a second imprisonment. Appeal is made primarily to two sources. One is the letter from Clement, traditionally regarded as the third bishop of the church in Rome, addressing the Corinthian church, and dated near the close of the first century:

> By reason of rivalry and envy the greatest and most righteous pillars were persecuted, and battled to the death. Let us set before our eyes the noble apostles: Peter, who by reason of wicked jealousy, not only once or twice but frequently endured suffering and thus, bearing his witness, went to the glorious place which he merited. By reason of rivalry and contention Paul showed how to win the prize for patient endurance. Seven times he was in chains; he was exiled, stoned, became a herald [of the gospel] in East and West, and won the noble renown which his faith merited. To the

whole world he taught righteousness, and reaching the limits of the West, he bore his witness before rulers. And so, released from this world, he was taken up into the holy place and became the greatest example of patient endurance. (1 Clement 5:1b-7)[349]

The ambiguity of Clement's words makes it difficult to ascertain his meaning regarding the "limits of the West." On the one hand, from the perspective of the city of Rome, that term might be taken to mean Spain, the western limit of Europe bordering on the Mediterranean. On the other hand, Clement implies that the "limits of the West" is where Paul "bore his witness before rulers" and was "released from this world." That Paul died in Rome rather than Spain is the undisputed testimony of tradition. His earliest biographer, the author of Acts, implies that conclusion, if only by his silence about any other place of Paul's demise. Speculation about a release from a Roman prison, a further ministry in Spain, a return to Rome, and another imprisonment terminated by Paul's execution in Rome is not convincing, in my opinion. Clement's vague reference to Paul's last days strongly suggests that he was not privy to any more information about Paul's death than was Luke. Further, the phrase "limits of the West" may not have any geographical significance at all, but like the "end of the earth" (Acts 1:8), is only a common verbal expression. Or Clement may only mean that Paul reached his own limit as he missionized in his western direction when he reached Rome.

The second source supposedly testifying to Paul's release, followed by another period of evangelizing, a second arrest, trial, and execution, is comprised of the three Pastoral Epistles. In this interpretation, they are regarded as genuine letters written by Paul during a hypothetical period between his acquittal and his final demise. These writings in fact present a picture of an orthodox church bat-

---

[349] Richardson, *Early Christian Fathers*, 45-46.

tling heresy, in particular of the Gnostic persuasion.[350] It seems likely that their authors knew Acts and made use of it in creating the scenarios in the Pastorals. Most telling, the Pastoral Epistles, like 1 Clement, do not refer to more than one imprisonment.[351] They draw on what was known of Paul to give verisimilitude to their purpose of combating doctrinal aberrations of a time later than Paul's. They are pseudepigraphic writings, i.e., written under the name of a famous person of the past to gain credibility for their teachings.

All this is to say that we have no reliable information about Paul after he reached Rome other than that given in Acts. Our best guess is that he either died along with many other Christians in Rome when Nero unleashed his insanity on them in 64 CE, or that he was executed prior to that persecution.[352] The most complete documentation of Nero's attack on the Roman Christians is given by an early second century Roman historian (who was unsympathetic to Christians and Jews), writing about the fire that destroyed much of Rome in 64 CE:

> But all human efforts, all the lavish gifts of the emperor, and the propitiations of the gods, did not banish the sinister belief that the conflagration was the result of an order. Consequently, to get rid of the report, Nero fastened the guilt and inflicted the most exquisite tortures on a class hated for their

[350] Gnosticism as understood here is a form of Christianity which developed in the 2nd century CE. It features Jesus as the savior sent to earth by the unseen God (who was not the creator of this evil world) to bring the saving knowledge of the way things really are. Jesus' death, if it truly happened, was of no significance, and certainly did not "save" people from their sins. Sin itself was problematic; the human problem was not sin but ignorance. Attaining true knowledge was the solution of the human predicament. Several later New Testament writings show awareness of and opposition to this competing interpretation of Jesus.

[351] Dibelius and Conzelmann, *The Pastoral Epistles*, 3.

[352] Artistic representations of Paul normally contain a sword, indicating his execution by beheading.

abominations, called Christians by the populace. Christus, from whom the name had its origin, suffered the extreme penalty during the reign of Tiberius at the hands of one of our procurators, Pontius Pilatus, and a most mischievous superstition, thus checked for the moment, again broke out not only in Judea, the first source of the evil, but even in Rome, where all things hideous and shameful from every part of the world find their center and become popular. Accordingly, an arrest was first made of all who pleaded guilty; then, upon their information, an immense multitude was convicted, not so much of the crime of firing the city, as of hatred against mankind. Mockery of every sort was added to their deaths. Covered with the skins of beasts, they were torn by dogs and perished, or were nailed to crosses, or were doomed to the flames and burnt, to serve as a nightly illumination when daylight had expired.

Nero offered his gardens for the spectacle, and was exhibiting a show in the circus, while he mingled with the people in the dress of a charioteer or stood aloft on a car. Hence, even for criminals who deserved extreme and exemplary punishment, there arose a feeling of compassion; for it was not, as it seemed, for the public good, but to glut one man's cruelty, that they were being destroyed.[353]

Prior to this event, individual Christians had occasionally faced hostility from Roman officials, as Paul testifies. Jewish Christians had been expelled from Rome along with other Jews fifteen years earlier, but there is no evidence of lives being lost. When Paul wrote to the Romans in the winter of 56-57 CE, he could still consider Roman government, including Nero's behaviour as emperor, reasonable and legitimate. Therefore he advises his readers to obey those who represent the government (Romans 13:1-7).

---

[353] Church and Brodribb, *The Annals of Tacitus* 15:44.

That advice was appropriate in the early years of Nero's reign. He had acted to reform the administration of justice; he had not shown special antipathy toward either the Jews or the Christians. The conflict that broke out in Judea and which led to the Jewish war was still in the future. Paul had no reason to suspect that in a few years Nero would carry out a pogrom aimed at Roman Christians. Paul continued to assume that government would be a stabilizing, rational, and responsible force in society. He did not anticipate what happens when government acts in an arbitrary and irrational manner and seeks scapegoats to blame for its own mistakes and to perpetuate its own power.[354] After the Nazi holocaust we wonder how Paul could have been so naïve. As a general statement about obeying the laws of society, his position is understandable. As an absolute dictum about all governments in all times, it is of course unacceptable. But Paul was writing about conditions of his time, not ours.

Paul already knew from first-hand experience that advocating a controversial cause could lead to personal suffering. If he was among those tortured and killed on Nero's order, he personally experienced the depths to which governing authorities can descend. We can only assume that he continued to affirm the victory over death he had been proclaiming for three decades.

Summary

Geographically, Paul's missionary career is not well described according to the traditional three-journeys pattern. The sources themselves suggest that it went through five phases. Each involved breaking new ground, and each led him into danger. During the first stage Paul confined himself to the East, be-

---

[354] In stark contrast to Romans 13 is Revelation 13, written ca. forty years after Paul's letter to the Romans. In traditional apocalyptic imagery, the Roman Empire is portrayed there not as the servant of God but as the Christians' worst enemy.

ginning with Arabia and Damascus. We have very little information concerning these initial three years. Whether he evangelized solo or with others is not known.

The second stage encompassed his close relationship with the Christians in Antioch in northern Syria. There he worked with Barnabas during missionary expeditions sponsored by the Antioch congregations. Luke portrays one such mission to Cyprus and southern Asia Minor resulting in the creation of Christian communities in four cities in South Galatia, and in growing Jewish awareness of and opposition to the Christian evangelists in the Diaspora. During his time as a missionary of the Antioch churches, increasingly vocal opposition arose from others within the Jesus movement, especially from former Pharisees in Jerusalem who did not accept Paul's policy of not requiring the circumcision of his Gentile converts. Following a decision favorable to Paul and Barnabas, a second dispute over purity matters in the church at Antioch led Paul to break with Barnabas and the other Jewish Christians in the mixed congregation there.

The third stage began when Paul chose a new partner, Silas (Silvanus), and severed his missionary relationship with the church in Antioch. The pair travelled overland through Syria and Cilicia with the intention of evangelizing in the province of Asia. Timothy joined the team in Lystra. Unable at this time to fulfill their goal of a mission in the province of Asia, they turned north. After founding churches in north Galatia, they proceeded to Macedonia. Congregations were established in major cities with the expectation that the faith would spread to surrounding regions. They continued this policy upon arriving in Achaia, turning first to Athens. However, the Athenians proved more resistant to (or uninterested in) the gospel than expected, so they moved on to Corinth where their message was well received and house churches were formed. After a year and a half there, Paul returned to Jerusalem and Antioch via Ephesus. This trip is not documented by Paul.

The fourth stage of his career opened with his overland journey from Antioch back to Ephesus, where he hoped to fulfill a dream of several years duration. During his time in Ephesus he engaged in an extensive correspondence with several of his churches, those in Corinth, Galatia, and Philippi, plus writing his brief note to Philemon. The last two letters were written while Paul was in prison. Unlike several of his other churches, his work in Ephesus is not documented by a letter to a congregation there.[355]

The fifth and final stage of Paul's life as a missionary began with his flight from Ephesus. Still in doubt about the loyalty of the churches in Corinth, he traveled to Macedonia where he visited churches founded earlier. Receiving news from Titus that the Corinthian believers had reaffirmed their confidence in him, he could now give his attention to completing the collection of money for the poor among the Jerusalem Christians. Moving on to Corinth, he spent the winter of 56-57 there waiting for favorable sailing conditions in the spring to embark for Judea. During that time he wrote his letter to the Romans, delicately requesting their support of his intended mission to Spain and informing them of his travel plans. He would go to Jerusalem with the relief fund and then make a stop in Rome on his way to Spain. But events in Jerusalem did not unfold as planned. The offering of the Gentile churches apparently was not accepted. Further, Paul was arrested in a riot and eventually transported to Rome where he died at an unknown time and in undetermined circumstances.

Fully a quarter of Acts is devoted to this last phase of Paul's life. Like Jesus, Paul was on the way to martyrdom. Jesus traveled to Jerusalem, Paul to Rome. Each was betrayed by his own people, and subjected to a trial before a Roman tribunal. However, Luke does not pursue the parallel to its logical and actual conclusion. The reason that Paul's death is not acknowledged is likely that he

---

[355] Paul makes only two references to Ephesus (1 Corinthians15:32; 19:9-10). The adversaries in the second passage may be the same people as the "wild animals" of the first passage.

died anonymously along with many other Christians in Nero's persecution in 64 CE. Luke leaves that whole event out of his account in order to avoid stirring up more governmental attacks on the church. It was enough that Paul confronted and testified before the seat of power in Rome, just as Jesus had done in Jerusalem. Though left unexpressed, in Luke's mind, as it undoubtedly was in Paul's, Paul's life ends as it was lived, in imitation of Jesus.

CHAPTER 13: 12 Reasons for Paul's Success

Students of religion commonly ask three questions of those who participate in new religious movements: why they joined, why they remained, and in the case of those who leave the movement, why they left. Since there is no direct access to Paul's converts, with only his letters and to a lesser degree Acts as indirect sources, our conclusions will not have the level of certainty we might desire. Yet, they are worth pursuing inasmuch as they are an important part of the larger picture of the biography of Paul. Some of the following reasons for joining Paul's groups are fairly obvious; others are more speculative, but all are interrelated.

What were the needs which people felt that Paul met? What were the benefits they hoped to achieve? How did he persuade them to join a group which was so far outside the main cultural stream as to be considered foolish by some, subversive and potentially dangerous by others, and the object of hostility by many? Why did they remain, and what might have led them to withdraw?

Reasons for joining one of Paul's communities were no doubt diverse, depending on the particular circumstances of the individual. Paul's initial converts in each city may have had different reasons for taking him seriously than those who later joined a functioning community. Jews brought a different perspective to their hearing of Paul's message than Gentiles. Gentiles themselves were differentiated according to their station in life, as well as their experience of and attitudes toward the Jewish tradition. The God-worshipers among the Gentiles were of particular interest to Paul; they had already gained some knowledge of Jewish practices, moral codes, scriptures, history, and ideas. Paul's terminology would be much more comprehensible to them than to other Gentiles.

The fact of Paul's success is found in the survival of the Pauline tradition, as witnessed both in the communities he founded and in the letters he wrote. But how do we determine <u>why</u> he succeeded in his mission? It will take some imagination on our part, but I suggest the following: Paul's first biographer mentions various venues in which Paul could proclaim his message, from synagogues to patrons' homes to workshops to governors' courts to the steps of the Antonia to prison to ships to the house he lived in at Rome, etc. One particular example is especially intriguing. During his stay in Ephesus, Paul took his disciples from the synagogue in which he had been making converts, and moved to a new venue, the "lecture hall of Tyrannus" where he gave daily teachings for two years so that, as Luke claims, all the Asians heard about Jesus (Acts 19:10). While Luke certainly exaggerates the size of Paul's audience, he may be correct in calling the reader's attention to the fact that this was a departure in Paul's strategy. Leaving the synagogue for a neutral space meant that Paul now had a venue which was under his control. He was also possibly free from working for a living, thanks to financial support from some unknown source, so that he could concentrate on proclaiming and fine-tuning his message and managing his churches.

We have observed that most of Paul's letters were probably written during his time in Ephesus: Galatians, 1 Corinthians, Philippians, Philemon, and a large portion of 2 Corinthians. Indeed, it is probable that only the first and last of his letters, 1 Thessalonians and Romans, were not penned during that period. We saw earlier the sharp contrast between Paul's congenial relationship with the church at Philippi and his difficulties with the Galatian and Corinthian churches. Paul had reason to fear that the Galatians were actually going to cut ties with him, and even the Corinthians were waffling in their allegiance to his leadership. All this came at the same time that Paul was carrying out an extensive mission in Ephesus, perhaps even supervising missionary outreach to other Asian cities.

It would be interesting to know the interplay between his lectures and debates in Tyrannus' hall and the letters he dictated at that time. His letters and his debates must have enriched each other. Unfortunately, we do not have his lecture notes, but we do have his letters. In any case, it was a period of maturation in Paul's thinking as he faced conflicts on numerous fronts.

In 1 Corinthians, in the midst of a discussion on not allowing spiritual gifts to drive wedges between members of the community, Paul inserts his famous poem on love. He frames it as the concluding and most important element of a triad:

> And I will show you a still more excellent way. . . . And now faith, hope, and love abide, these three; and the greatest of these is love. (1 Corinthians 12:31; 13:13, NRSV)

These three kinds of experience had already been mentioned in Paul's letter to the Thessalonians (1:3), but here they are made central to the believers' experience of being "in Christ." It appears that Paul's presentation is becoming more explicitly organized and universalized. Faith, hope, and love are fundamental personal realities in which any thoughtful person would be interested. They relate to our past, our future, and our present. The simplicity, applicability, and precision of this terminology entice us to examine these terms more closely.

1. Faith

Faith (Greek *pistis*) is the key term Paul uses to designate positive response to the proclamation of Jesus as the appointed one of God who leads the way to reconciliation and harmony between God and humanity. While the term can also be used as a designation of "The Faith,"[356] for Paul, faith was not a religious system but a personal experience of trusting the gospel as true. Faith and Christ are inextricably linked; i.e., Paul does not consider the possibility of faith in anything else than in the gospel of Christ.

In contrast to its grammatical form in the English language, faith is not only a noun but also a verb in Greek. The verb is usually translated as "to believe." This may introduce confusion for the reader since "belief" can mean either to believe something, like a fact, a statement, or a proposition; or it can mean to believe in something or someone, like believing in exercise, in science, or in a leader. Paul's usage is of the second type, to believe in. To believe in God or Christ or the Spirit or the Christ story means to embrace them, to love and serve them, to be devoted to them.[357]

However, in contrast to Paul's limiting the concept of faith to a Christian perspective, in fact faith is a broadly human phenomenon, similar to what we call a worldview. It is an all-encompassing way of looking at the world, which identifies certain components as the center around which everything else is organized. Faith is directed toward our core stories, whether expressed or implied, which enable us to cope with the reality of our experience. In that broad sense, faith is not an option. Without faith in whatever it is that we trust to be reliable and worth giving ourselves to, neither individuals nor societies could rise above chaos.

Therefore, the important question for every person and society is, what is worth having faith in? Does the object of faith enhance or demean life? Does it bring joy or misery? Is the only legit-

---

[356] For example, 1 Timothy 1:2; 2 Timothy 4:7. The word "faith" is seldom used in this sense by Paul, though see Galatians 1:23. He can also write about faith as an abstract concept, but by far the majority of the occurrences of the noun (about 70) in his letters regard faith as personal belief or commitment. The verb based on the same root is found about 30 times, nearly all of which are about believing in or having faith in Christ.

[357] Borg, *Speaking Christian*, Chapter 10.

imate object of faith that which is scientifically provable or is there also room for what is beyond that form of proof? Proof is part of a preexisting faith stance which itself is not subject to being proved true or false. In a sense, faith always involves taking a risk; its "truth" or "falsity" is known by engagement.

The faith of which Paul speaks and writes is not a magical formula for achieving unredeemed desires. It is the decision to embrace and live the story in which Christ is the primary model of being human; it is an attitude and a perspective in which love is the all-important reality at the center of one's worldview.

While faith in a worldview is not amenable to proof, it is intimately connected to experience. The basic conviction that governed Paul's life proceeded from his own experience, both mystical and otherwise. His transformation from persecutor to participant in the Jesus movement was a demonstration for him of the power, love, and grace of God. His subsequent experience as an apostle of Christ validated his faith. Faith was the door for entry into and participation in the community of Christ. Faith was commitment to the new worldview in which Jesus was "Son of God," the exemplar of ideal humanity whose life, death, and resurrection also revealed the Spirit of God acting for the good of human beings.

In his teaching Paul did not offer a set of doctrines to be believed, but something for people to believe in. He taught by word and example a new worldview by which joyful and meaningful life could be found. That is an intriguing possibility, but it could only be tested by daring to try it.

Yet, as important as faith was for Paul, it was not the most important aspect of life in Christ. He draws on a saying known to us from the Synoptic Gospels to demonstrate this point:[358]

. . . if I have all faith so as to remove mountains, but do not have love, I am nothing. (1 Corinthians 13:2, NRSV)

---

[358] Mark 11:23; see also Matthew 21:21 and Luke 17:6.

Paul's triad is not a list of three discrete elements of the new life, but intimately related aspects of life for those maturing according to the new paradigm. Yet it is clear where he places his emphasis: "...the greatest of these is love."

2. Hope

Hope stands in relation not only to faith and love, but also to its opposite, the "wrath of God." The "good news" is to be understood as the alternative to the "bad news." When Paul uses the word "hope," he is thinking of participation in "eternal life," or in the divine life, a matter of widespread concern in the first century. The Jewish apocalyptic version of life after death which informed Paul's perspective envisaged a final judgment encompassing the living and the deceased (Romans 2:6-8). Paul argues that while the "day of judgment" is in the future, there is in full view a present judgment on sin which should be recognized as a clue to or foretaste of the coming final judgment. Sin, the rejection of God, has its origin in idolatry, typified in Adam's primal act of ignoring God's commandment. Paul illustrates some of the results generated by idolatry, starting with the sexual but covering just about every form of unrighteous human action, including covetousness, envy, murder, deception, gossip, slander, boastfulness, hard-heartedness and ruthlessness. Sin does not go unnoticed by God; it provokes his "wrath" [359] and will undergo judgment in God's law court.

---

[359] The Greek word is *orgē*, which is normally translated as "anger." It is used in the NT exclusively of God's response to sin and primarily indicates the action God takes rather than his emotion. God's "wrath" is found three times in 1 Thessalonians and 11 times in Romans. The primary meaning of divine wrath in the OT arises from human refusal to recognize the authority of God (as in the case of idolatry and injustice), and is intended to bring about repentance.

Paul argues that God allows people to determine their own fate, both in this life and in the hereafter.[360] By choosing idolatry rather than the living God, people are given up to the consequences of their actions, which create further disruption of their created nature in this life. The end result of this course is subjection to God's wrath on the "day of judgment," the coming time when all people, living and dead, are called to account for the way they conducted their lives.

The concept of God's wrath or judgment on sin is deeply embedded in biblical writings, both in the OT and NT. It was emphasized in the preaching of John the Baptist who castigated the Sadducees and Pharisees as they came to be baptized (Matthew 3:7) and continued by Jesus in his own teaching (Matthew 12:36-37). The author of Hebrews reminds his readers whom he fears may give up their faith in Christ that they will face severe consequences:

> For we know the one who said, "Vengeance is mine, I will repay." And again, "The Lord will judge his people." It is a fearful thing to fall into the hands of the living God. (Hebrews 10:30-31, NRSV)[361]

Paul is content with pointing to the reality of the coming judgment as such; he does not fill in the details. The Jewish word Gehenna[362] (usually translated as "hell" in English Bibles), the Greek Tartarus[363] and Hades[364] are never found in Paul's letters. He

---

[360] However, Paul also retains his Pharisaic belief in predestination (Romans 9:17-18). Paul regards his own calling as the result of God's prior decision (Galatians 1:15-16).

[361] The quotation is from Deuteronomy 32:35. Paul employs the same quotation in Romans 12:19. He also has it in mind when writing 1 Corinthians 4:4-5.

[362] The term is found primarily in sayings of Jesus in the synoptic Gospels, indicating a place of lasting punishment after death.

[363] Found only in 2 Peter 2:4 where it is translated as "hell."

[364] Found only in Matthew, Luke-Acts, and Revelation.

seems disinterested in places or characteristics of punishment. Rather, his concern is with God's judgment as such against those who sin. The assurance of God's wrath and a day of judgment carries a somber message about the importance of cleaning up or rectifying one's life.

Having delivered the bad news, or at least a warning, about the wrath of God, Paul turns to the good news. Instead of a life trajectory leading to death, a joyous life both now and in the hereafter is possible. The death and resurrection of Christ form not only the foundation of his divine/human story and his ethical exhortations, but also are the pathway to life. If one dies with Christ to the image of Adam, one is enabled to live by bearing the image of Christ. Spiritual maturity requires the implantation of God's Spirit, prefigured in Christ's resurrection.

Paul presents the resurrected Christ as the "first fruits"[365] of eternal life. Christ initiated a pattern of human living which prepared people for admission into eternal life, in which they participate both during their lifetime and afterward. Paul keeps the two in tension, emphasizing their common relationship to the kingdom of God. In his Christ story the path to life passes through death, i.e., the death of Christ, in three senses. First, Jesus' death reveals the love of God for humanity, Jesus' own faithfulness to his mission, and prepares for the infusion of the Spirit into believers. Second, in identifying with Christ's death one dies to the old alienated way of life, and thereby makes space for a transformed life. Dying with Christ to the way of the world is part of the discipline in the race to the goal of life. (See 1 Corinthians 9:24-27) Third, the death of

---

[365] In Jewish agricultural practice, the first fruits were the earliest produce of the field and flocks; they were to be set aside and dedicated to God by offering them to the priests. This act released the rest of the harvest for human consumption. In 1 Corinthians 15:20, the resurrection of Jesus is said to be "the first fruits of those who have died." (NRSV) Paul is here arguing against the skepticism about resurrection held by some in the Corinthian church. His point is that the resurrection of Christ is an indication that the main harvest is yet to come.

Christ was the necessary preliminary to his being raised. Death and resurrection are two sides of the same coin of salvation. The resurrection of Jesus cements hope for the believer.[366]

Hope is not an ironclad guarantee but an assurance[367] based on present experience. A taste of God's love now gives one hope. Further, expectation of eternal life is provisional since it depends on God's knowledge, wisdom and justice, of which we have only a glimmering (1 Corinthians 13:12). Like the other spiritual benefactions, eternal life is a gift from the divine (Romans 6:23). Rather than proof, believers have hope.

Hope is an essential part of life in the present. Paul's observation of a series running from endurance to character to hope (Romans 5:4) reveals his perspective. Perseverance in faith develops the self and that in turn makes one hopeful regarding eternal life.

Without hope for the future, life loses one of its pillars. Paul's message offered an expectation of life in communion with the eternal God. Present experience of the divine presence, especially as evidenced in the transforming power of love, gives confidence that hope is not misplaced (Romans 5:5). The activity of the Spirit enables hope just as it makes faith possible. Both proceed from the heart rejuvenated by love. Obtaining guidance for moving away from the wrath of God and toward eternal life with God and Christ was perhaps an important reason for joining one of Paul's communities.

---

[366]See Paul's reflection on his own uncertain future while in prison (Philippians 1:19-26).

[367] Paul's statement in 2 Corinthians 5:5 where he characterizes the Spirit as a "guarantee" should not be misconstrued. The Greek word here means a down payment or a pledge, or an advance payment in a transaction. It creates an expectation that the contract will be fulfilled. The present experience of the Spirit gives the believer confidence that there is more to come.

3. Love

Paul's love poem in 1 Corinthians summarizes his experience of the divine, whether named as God, Jesus, or the Spirit. Even if the theological connection were removed, the poem still reveals his profound awareness that the most basic of all human needs is to be loved and to love.

It might surprise the reader to learn that in his approximately sixty uses of the term "love," Paul's references to loving God are very few.[368] He never quotes the First Commandment as Jesus does in the first three Gospels.[369] Neither is Paul's teaching based on exhorting people to love God. His experience has informed him that love first proceeds in the opposite direction. The common factor found in all the elements of Paul's "good news," including his interpretation of Jesus' death, his ethical principles, and the motivation behind his own mission to the Gentiles, is God's love, often expressed as grace (*charis*), i.e., a gift of God.

Next to God's love one might assume that Paul would place love of neighbor since that commandment is basic to his teaching. However, loving the neighbor (and God) is possible only when God's Spirit is active in the person. The presence of God is experienced not only as the knowledge that the very nature of God is love, but primarily in participating in that love.

The second stage then leads to the third, which is indeed the love of neighbor. Although Jesus declared that this commandment from Leviticus 19:18 was in second place, Paul elevates it to the blue ribbon position:

---

[368] Romans 8:28; 1 Corinthians 2:9, 8:3.

[369] Mark 12:30, 33; Matthew 22:37; Luke 10:27. Like Paul, the Fourth Gospel never mentions the Great Commandment; instead, it introduces a "New Commandment." (13:34) The author of this Gospel also joins Paul in emphasizing God's love (the most famous example is in 3:16) and Christ's love (13:1; 14:21; 15:9, 12). The Fourth Gospel never mentions human love of God, except the lack of it (5:42). Loving Jesus appears several times (8:42; 14:15, 21, 23, 24, 28; 21:15-17).

"The commandments . . . are summed up in this word, 'Love your neighbor as yourself.'" (Romans 13:9, NRSV; see also Galatians 5:14)

The question posed to Jesus regarding the identity of neighbor (Luke 10:25-37) is not asked in any of Paul's writings. Yet he gives an answer, starting from the ones closest to his readers. Like the Fourth Gospel, Paul emphasizes the love that members of his communities should give to each other:[370]

". . . love one another with mutual affection; outdo one another in showing honor." (Romans 12:10, NRSV; see also 13:8 and 1 Thessalonians 4:9-10)

Yet Paul goes beyond the Fourth Gospel and joins the Synoptics in extending love beyond the community:

"So then, wherever we have an opportunity, let us work for the good of all, and especially for those of the family of faith." (Galatians 6:10, NRSV)[371]

The two reaches of love—immediate and extended—are part of a continuum. The congregation is the primary arena in which love is experienced and practiced. The church is the new family, an idea found not only in Paul's letters but in other NT writings also.[372]

---

[370] In John, loving one another is represented as a new commandment, delivered by Jesus (13:34).

[371] This sentence is a summary of the last two chapters of Galatians. It points back especially to the "fruit of the Spirit" (5:22-23), which is "love, joy, peace, patience, kindness, generosity, faithfulness, gentleness, and self-control." (NRSV) Working for the good of all removes any limitation to the identity of the neighbor: "...the Christian is expected to do good to all mankind." (Betz, *Galatians*, 311)

[372] For example, see Mark 3:35, Matthew 12:50 and Luke 8:21.

The face-to-face community is the base in which love is taught, formed, and nurtured. From that training ground, Paul expects that love will be extended to those who are not members of the community. His urging of the believers in Corinth to express love in every act (1 Corinthians 16:14) is a call to exercise love as the fundamental life principle, the fulfilment of the primary commandment, regardless of the recipients. The ultimate test of love's depth is located in the believer's response to the "enemies" outside the faith community. Paul writes that he and his companions practice and counsel the behavior taught by Jesus:

> "When reviled, we bless; when persecuted we endure; when slandered we speak kindly." (1 Corinthians 4:12b-13a, NRSV)

> "Bless those who persecute you; bless and do not curse them. . . . Do not repay anyone evil for evil . . . . No, if your enemies are hungry, feed them; if they are thirsty, give them something to drink; for by doing this you will heap coals of fire on their heads. Do not be overcome by evil, but overcome evil with good."[373] (Romans 12:14, 17, 20, NRSV)

---

[373] This passage incorporates most of Proverbs 25:21-22. Paul could hardly mean that "coals of fire" is a symbol of revenge, since that obviously is antithetical to the kind treatment of enemies. In 2 Esdras 16:53 (in the Apocrypha), there is a similar image: "...God will burn coals of fire on the head of everyone who says, 'I have not sinned before God and his glory.'" (NRSV) This certainly points to vengeance, as does the image of burning coals in Psalm 140:10. But the immediate context of Paul's use of the image counsels kindness and denounces vengeance. In another context, Paul suggests a different reason for practicing kindness, "Or do you despise the riches of his kindness and forbearance and patience? Do you not realize that God's kindness is meant to lead you to repentance?" (Romans 2:4, NRSV) Following that line of thought, the meaning of "heaping coals of fire on his head" suggests that kind treatment may open the enemies' eyes and set them on the path to repentance and salvation. Further, Paul reminds the recipients of the letter in a quote from Deuteronomy 32:35 that judgment and sentencing of the enemies are not in the recipients' hands, but God's. As Paul wrote earlier in this letter (1:18-32), God allows people to choose their own path and the consequenc-

The literary masterpiece of 1 Corinthians 13 is not merely a beautiful poem on the subject of love, but a call for deep reflection on what it means to be a loving person, and on the final and supreme location of love in the scheme of things.

Paul's identification of these three fundamental and essential areas of human experience—faith, hope, and love—must have attracted attention. It should be noted that the first two are primarily individual experiences, with no inherent immediate connection to other people. The third, however, is both individual and communal. Love involves relationship, even if its motive force is rooted in one or other of the parties involved. Love may anticipate that the relationship become reciprocal, but it transcends that outcome.

The question then becomes, how is love to become the dominant force in one's life? Paul's answer is to be found in the communities he established. They were intended to give concrete substance to his vision of the new way of life in Christ.

4. Paul's Communities

A fundamental requirement for personal and social growth is belonging to a caring and nurturing community. Community is the matrix of human development, not only for children but also for adults. The basic unit of human connections is of course the family, but families are not always healthy environments for their members; nor are the substitutes to which people often gravitate.

Paul understood the importance of community in which lives could be changed for the better. His experience of the synagogue was no doubt significant in his upbringing, but his model had become the kingdom of God as taught by Jesus and made evident in his life, death, and resurrection. Paul's congregations were con-

---

es to which it leads. What Paul means by the "wrath" of God are the negative consequences set in motion by alienation from God. (See Jewett, *Romans*, 776-777) ceived as training centers for transforming character and relationships in preparation for the fullness of the kingdom of God now approaching. His congregations were also therapy clinics where addictions to destructive patterns of living could be identified and healed.

Paul drew upon several images to symbolize the special nature of the kind of community he was creating, all of which illustrate its organic unity. Ordinary family terminology pointed to the close relationship of the members: they were brothers and sisters,[374] Paul was metaphorically their father. He also employs other metaphors. For example, in one passage (1 Corinthians 3:6-17), Paul used three images in succession to characterize the community: they were God's field, with the missionaries as God's agricultural workers; God's building, with Paul laying the foundation and Apollos building on it; and God's temple in which God's Spirit dwells.

One of Paul's most memorable metaphors for the congregation is the human body, considered as both a complete and functioning organism and composed of many parts.[375] Each part contributes to the whole and benefits from it. Applied to the community of Christ, each member contributes to the collective and each is nourished by it. The image serves to break down unhealthy hierarchies in favor of equality under a common "Lord" (the Spirit) and to replace the notion of "us and them" with unity.

Another reminder of oneness and equality is Paul's inclusive use of the term "children of God." God makes no distinction, so why should the members of God's community?

If we take the believing community in Corinth as representative of Paul's churches in general, we can make a few observations

---

[374] "Brothers" is found in every letter of Paul's. Although masculine in form, it includes both genders. "Sister" is used when a particular woman is indicated. Modern translations add "sisters" to "brothers" in most cases in order to clarify that Paul's intent was inclusive.

[375] I Corinthians 12:12-30; Romans 12:4-8.

of their common activities. They apparently assembled[376] weekly on Sundays (1 Corinthians 16:2). The purpose of coming together was to provide opportunity for members to solidify and enhance their identity as participants in Christ. They joined regularly, probably weekly also, in the Lord's Supper, the common meal which celebrated their unity in Christ. These were both charismatic gatherings which encouraged openness to the Spirit, and educational. Paul gives us a glimpse into the meetings:

> When you come together, each one has a hymn, a lesson, a revelation, a tongue, or an interpretation. Let all things be done for building up. (1 Corinthians 14:26b, NRSV)

Paul applauded the Corinthians' gifts of tongues and prophecies, but he insisted upon order and the primacy of rational speech for building up the community.

If a community had recently received a letter from Paul, it would be read to the assembly and no doubt discussed at length. The reader was probably Paul's representative who had delivered the letter. That person also was responsible for explaining Paul's meaning if that was in question. No doubt his letters were periodically retrieved from the churches' archives and read to the gathering.

Regular assembly to attend to the affairs of the *ekklēsia* was all the more necessary because its members spent most of their time living and working in a world out of sync with their new lifestyle. Continual affirmation of their identity as members of Christ and care of each other was necessary for survival.

Paul taught not only that the community of believers was the body of Christ, giving it a sacred identity, but also that each believer was entering into a communion, even union, with Christ and

---

[376] Paul's usual term to designate the community was *ekklēsia,* the Greek common word "assembly," regardless of the purpose for coming together. This word is usually rendered as "church" in English translations of the Bible.

God through the Spirit. Full union or communion with God is the goal of the mystic, and Paul proclaimed a gospel which offered the mystical experience. Christ had opened up this possibility and now his followers were walking the path, growing into the likeness of the redeemer. Retreat from society was not required, only an exchange of the norms of this age for life in Christ:

> Do not be conformed to this world, but be transformed by the renewing of your minds, so that you may discern what is the will of God—what is good and acceptable and perfect. (Romans 12:2, NRSV)

Those who yearned for a caring, welcoming, and supportive community which offered opportunity for personal growth, interaction, and a vision of a new era would find Paul's congregations worth exploring. But old cultural patterns are not easily changed. Paul's expectations of his converts challenged them. He had a special interest in addressing two marginalized groups: slaves and women. They were no longer to be regarded as inferior to their counterparts, i.e., the free citizens and males, whose superior status was enshrined in cultural attitudes and in law. A third division of concern was located in the social and legal structures which separated Jews and Gentiles.

In Paul's teaching and in the communities he founded, as we have seen (Galatians 3:28-29; see also 1 Corinthians 12:13), these three sets of divisions were directly tackled in his baptismal liturgy which signaled what converts were getting into. We turn now to the significance of Paul's baptismal liturgy for the specific groups named.

5. Slaves

The egalitarian character of the communities Paul founded must have been attractive to those who were low in the class structure of Roman society, especially slaves. Although some slaves rose to high positions and substantial wealth, the vast majority were at the bottom of the socioeconomic pyramid. Paul's reordering of the honor system in his communities gave status to those who were neither wise by worldly standards, nor powerful, nor of the noble class (1 Corinthians 1:26). However, we should not suppose that Paul pitted the poor against the wealthy or that the Jesus movement attracted only the lower classes, neither of which is supported by his letters. His vision of communities in Christ has a place for everyone, even the financial manager of the city of Corinth (Romans 16:23),[377] business owners (Phoebe, Lydia, and perhaps Chloe), and those well enough off to host the gatherings of an expanding group of believers. Paul's attitude toward his own wealth (or lack thereof) is succinctly expressed in his declaration that he had learned to be content with whatever he had (Philippians 4:11-13). Participation in a community in which class structures are regarded as irrelevant must have been welcome to many, giving hope especially to those normally excluded from such relationships.

6. Women

Paul's insistence that women as well as men are full members of Christ's body would certainly have been good news to many women. In contrast to the later movement apparent in

---

[377] All three synoptic Gospels include the saying about how hard it is for the rich to enter the kingdom of God (Mark 10:23-27; Matthew 19:23-26; Luke 18:24-27). Despite the woes pronounced on the privileged in Luke 6:24-25, only this Gospel relates the story of the wealthy Zacchaeus (19:1-10) who repents. Acts contains several accounts of the rich and powerful who respond positively to Paul's proclamation.

the Pastoral Epistles to deny women leadership roles, in Paul's congregations gender was irrelevant. The evidence is plentiful. Numerous women exercising leadership are mentioned by Paul, e.g., Phoebe of Cenchreae (Romans 16:1-2), who is described as a *diakonos* in the church there and who has "been a benefactor of many and of myself as well." Luke refers to Lydia of Thyatira living in Philippi, "a dealer in purple cloth," a valued luxury good (Acts 16:14). She hosted the developing congregation of Philippian believers in her home (Acts 16:15, 40). Paul identifies by name two other women in Philippi, leaders in the church there (Philippians 4:2-3). Luke also writes that the church at Thessalonica contained "not a few of the leading women" of that city (Acts 17:4). Romans 16 mentions nine women: among others Prisca who along with her husband Aquila had been a co-worker of Paul in Corinth; Mary "who has worked very hard among you;" Junia, who was "prominent among the apostles;" and Rufus' mother, "a mother to me also." We can assume that these were not the only women of note in Paul's churches.

The fact that the rituals for entering and celebrating participation in this new community were the same for both women and men is another signal of gender equality in Paul's version of the Jesus movement. Paul's baptismal formula (Galatians 3:27-28) makes explicit the radical character of the gender relationship in his congregations. Becoming part of a community where equal treatment with men was assured by its leader must have been a strong attractant to women who had that choice.

7. Jews

While Paul's revision of the story of Israel was abhorrent to some Jews, it obviously was attractive to others. Locating the purpose of the entire Law in the love commandment as Jesus had done may have had a certain appeal, especially as it was being not only preached and taught, but also embodied in Paul's communities. If they, like the Hellenists of Acts 6-7 were dissatisfied with temple ideology, they would appreciate the reconfiguration of Israelite history and religion which spelled the end of animal sacrifice in religious practice. Daring to believe that the Messiah had actually come, they may have found the signs of his spiritual presence in Paul's assemblies of believers convincing. Living in the cosmopolitan world of the eastern Roman Empire, they may have also been attracted to Paul's approach to a Jewish mission to the Gentiles unencumbered by the traditional legal barriers between the two. Despite the exclusivistic ritual and ideological structure promoted by Pharisaism, Judaism retained a universalistic core based on one God who was the creator of all people. Paul drew on and emphasized this prophetic core.

While Paul had agreed at the Jerusalem conference that he and Barnabas would go to the Gentiles and Peter to the Jews, in practice that was not feasible even if he attempted to abide by it, which he apparently didn't. His gospel was for everyone, and at least some of his congregations contained a mixture of Gentiles and Jews. Those Jews who retained the ancient dream of Israel as a light to the nations may have been especially attracted to Paul's version of that mission.

8. Gentiles

All proponents of the Jesus movement were faced with the question of the terms under which Gentiles were to be incorporated into it. Circumcision was the mark which had always set Jews apart from other nations since the time of Abraham (Genesis 17:9-10). Circumcision was the outward sign of the covenant between God and Abraham. It seemed logical to the earliest Christians that since salvation was for Abraham's descendants, converts to Christ needed also to be circumcised.

Paul disagreed, for several reasons. First, circumcision symbolized the division between Jews and Gentiles. His gospel was about uniting, not dividing people. Second, circumcision perpetuated not only the division between males and females, it also implied that only males were significant converts. Females were not included in the debates over proselytes. Further, the rift between the genders originating in Eden which left women under the control of men[378] had now been healed in Christ. Third, there was the practical matter that circumcision was painful and potentially dangerous in an age prior to antiseptic medical practices and antibiotics. There can be little doubt that it was a deterrent that discouraged Gentiles from converting. Why else would special names (God-fearers, God-worshipers) be applied to those Gentiles who attended synagogues but didn't convert? Anything which hindered Gentiles coming to Christ was to be resisted.

Paul felt a special responsibility to resolve this issue of circumcision of Gentiles. After all, he was the divinely appointed apostle to the Gentiles (Galatians 1:1). The gospel that had come to him in a revelation introduced a new era, a new covenant for all people, not just the Jews. New wine required new wineskins. The terms under which Gentile converts would enter the *ekklēsia*, the assembly of God's people, had to be redefined to conform to the gospel which offered equal acceptance to all, regardless of their ethnic, class, or gender distinctions. Those who entered Paul's communities might come from different directions, but they would all come in by the same door.

Paul had only two requirements for entering the communities of Christ: declaration of faith and baptism. Nothing further was required. These two items were open to anyone regardless of gender, class, or ethnic identity.

It should not be overlooked that Paul accepted those whose moral record was not unblemished. Following his quotation of what was probably a traditional list of those who engage in various forms of bad behavior, who, he assured his readers, would not in-

---

[378] Genesis 3:16; see above, Chapter 4.

herit the kingdom of God (1 Corinthians 6:9-10), Paul reminds his readers: "And such were some of you."

A fresh start on a new path in an accepting community is not something to be scorned. The message that Gentiles are accepted unconditionally into the body of Christ through a process open to all must have been a major factor for those facing the question of whether to join one of Paul's communities.

9. Paul's Personality

Despite Paul's physical appearance and his unsophisticated speech,[379] his personal presence must have played an important role in the success of the movement he championed. On the one hand, he embodied certain qualities and achievements which were admired in the world of his time. He was intellectually sharp, well educated in the traditions of his people, knowledgeable and adept in the interpretation of its scriptures, exhibiting some written skill in rhetoric and debate, and able to formulate compelling arguments.

Yet, he eschewed many of his past achievements, claiming they were worthless. In telling about his past, he explained that he had actually persecuted those who believed as he now did. But when a divine intervention led him to see the light, he underwent a radical transformation into the person he now was. This was a testament to the transforming power of God, not to himself.

On the other hand, the teaching he now promoted was not in tune with the world his listeners inhabited. He warned them that

---

[379] "His letters are weighty and strong, but his bodily presence is weak, and his speech contemptible." (2 Corinthians 10:10, NRSV) "You know that it was because of a physical infirmity that I first announced the gospel to you; though my condition put you to the test, you did not scorn or despise me, but welcomed me as an angel of God, as Christ Jesus." (Galatians 4:13-14, NRSV) ". . . whenever I am weak, then I am strong." (2 Corinthians 12:10, NRSV)

those who accepted his teaching could not expect the approval of their neighbors. He was asking his hearers to go through a radical change and to be part of a new community that marched to a different drummer. They must be prepared to face rejection and hostility.

Few would take that step unless Paul exhibited in his own person something very appealing. His teaching, no matter how convincing, had to be accompanied by actions and character. He preached kindness, egalitarianism, compassion, peace, joy, righteousness, and love. Unless he practiced what he preached, who would take him seriously? A story of a loving God would lack conviction unless supported by persuasive evidence. It would be greatly strengthened, however, if the proclaimer demonstrated that he/she was a living example of what was proclaimed, in this case, a genuinely loving person. Narratives about worldviews and ethical living need models.

Paul's letters contain many examples of his awareness of the necessity of and commitment to modelling the gospel. On the one hand, his constant focus on love in his letters demonstrates the core of his message. On the other, his letters also reveal how keen he was to prove that his actions matched his words. Modelling of the gospel had to begin with the one who proclaimed it; otherwise, he would not be able to say:[380]

I appeal to you then, be imitators of me. (1 Corinthians 4:16, NRSV)

---

[380] The concept of imitation is related to that of the father/son relationship, a critical part of the familial image. Paul considers his converts to be his children (1 Corinthians 4:15; 1 Thessalonians 2:11; Philippians 2:22), and fathers are responsible for their children's development into good people. Likewise, children have a duty to honor their father (and mother—Exodus 20:12).

What looks like shameless arrogance could only be persuasive if his message and his character were integrated. A second passage extends the imitation motif to other believers:

> Brothers and sisters, join in imitating me, and observe those who live according to the example you have in us. (Philippians 3:17, NRSV)

Paul is not the only one to be imitated; his missionary companions and certain members of the congregation are also worthy of imitation.[381] But the origin and foundation of the imitation motif emerges in this quote:

> Be imitators of me, as I am of Christ. (1 Corinthians 11:1, NRSV)

The imitation of Christ permeates Paul's message, directives, behavior, and rituals. It is imbedded in his baptismal liturgy. It guides his responses to conflicts and crises that emerge in his communities. It is inherent in the identification of the community as the body of Christ. Christ is the model for all who follow him; he is both the revelation of God's love and the epitome of the new human being for everyone in their search for the good life and their new identity (Galatians 2:20).

Paul's mystical image of identification with Christ differs from that of discipleship in the Gospels and Acts. We noted earlier that Paul's writings do not contain the word "disciple." Why would he reject or at least ignore such a key term which other Christian leaders were using? Perhaps it was because he, who had been a disciple of the Pharisaic school, had too many bad memories of that period in his life, especially that it had resulted in his perse-

---

[381] See also Hebrews 13:7, NRSV—"Remember your leaders...and imitate their faith."

cution of the followers of Jesus (and therefore of Christ himself, according to Acts 9:5). Perhaps Paul avoided the discipleship concept because, not being one of Jesus' original disciples, he lacked the first-hand knowledge of Jesus and his teaching which they had. Paul's conversion had not happened through listening to any of Jesus' followers; his enlightenment had come via a different route, not from the Galilean Jesus, but from the resurrected Christ. Or perhaps Paul ignored the image of discipleship because he wanted no one to think he was just another Hellenistic philosopher seeking paying disciples. His understanding of the gospel led him in a different direction.

Christian discipleship simply was not part of Paul's experience. His transformation had come unmediated by others, but directly from God who had revealed to him the gift of divine love. Mysticism emphasizes personal experience, and Paul was no exception. Following his vision of the Son of God, he gave up the "traditions of my ancestors." His world now included ecstatic prophecy and other Spirit-inspired phenomena, as well as a radical inner transformation including a new worldview. Accordingly, his focus is not primarily on teaching about love, but on its actual emergence in human lives as a result of the gift of the Spirit.

The bestowal of the Spirit of God, Paul believed, Jesus had made possible, and the process he initiated continues to happen. The community as the body of Christ enlightened and empowered by the Spirit of Christ continues the transforming work of Christ who was infused with the Spirit.

Participation in the Christ figure bears tangible fruit on both the individual and communal levels. Discernible change in attitude and behavior which brings inner peace and joy and positive relations with others can be very persuasive. For Paul, the imitation of Christ is a very different reality from profession of belief or being a member of a group, even a "Christian" one. Imitation of Christ is participation in his Spirit and being empowered by it. Love then is no longer confined to the circle to which one belongs but universalized.[382]

Paul's personality as an effective leader, counselor, and teacher must have been an important factor not only in the creation but also in the survival of his communities. The evidence is amply demonstrated in his letters. He replies thoughtfully to his followers' concerns and questions; he encourages, he gives guidance and consolation; he expresses not only his arguments, but also his feelings openly; and he provides them with extensive and imaginative reflections relative to their personal and collective existence. He aims to keep his communities united by persuasion rather than authoritarian pronouncements. He addresses them with respect, affection, and honesty. His appeal for them to imitate him requires that he himself continues to imitate the one who is at the center of their faith.

New ideas, especially about the basics of life, compelling as they may be on the rational level, must have an emotional component to bring about individual and communal transformation. The combination of reason and feeling evident in Paul's letters gives an authority to his own person which surely was one more reason why people were drawn to his version of the Jesus movement—and did not abandon it under outside pressure.

10. Moral Teachings

Paul's teaching struck a workable balance between a high morality and personal freedom. One reason for Gentile interest in Judaism was its moral code, but Judaism's many rules and its social barriers between Jews and Gentiles must have been constraining factors discouraging full conversion. Paul's gospel re-

---

[382] Using familial terms rather than imitative, Matthew makes a similar point: "Love your enemies . . . so that you may be children of your Father in heaven . . . . Be perfect, therefore, as your heavenly Father is perfect." (Matthew 5:44, 45,48, NRSV) Paul uses both familial and imitative imagery.

placed the Law with freedom in Christ, with only one commandment covering all moral issues. His proclamation was founded on love rather than a law code. It is striking that Paul never appeals authoritatively in his letters to the Ten Commandments when giving guidance about behavior.[383] He does quote from lists of good and bad actions and attitudes, but only as illustrations of what one should or should not do as an expression of love,[384] rather than as rules.

However, love does not come with an indexed set of directions for every occasion. Members of Paul's communities brought particular issues to him for guidance. We saw in Chapter 10 how Paul's answers to the divorce question included two directives, one from Jesus regarding the prohibition of divorce of two believers, and one of his own concerning the permissibility of divorce in a mixed marriage. Both answers were based on principles inherent to the new reality in which love provides the foundation of morality, but loving action has to be intelligently determined according to the situation.

Personal behavior was to be founded on principles of fairness, respect, mercy, and compassion. It was never to proceed from anger, resentment, or urges arising from self-seeking. That which was genuinely good for the other or the common good was the motivating consideration. Behavior was loving and "righteous" when it was based on the core teaching of Paul's gospel, the loving acts of God.

The simplicity of such an approach to attitudes and behaviour of course could be misunderstood as allowing moral anarchy, as apparently happened to some degree in Corinth and probably

---

[383] His reference in Romans 13:9 to four of the commandments is for the purpose of showing that the love commandment of Leviticus 19:18 covers them all.

[384] For lists of negative qualities, see Romans 1:29-31; ("works of the flesh") and Galatians 5:19-21. For their positive counterparts ("fruit of the Spirit"), see Galatians 5:22-23.

elsewhere also.[385] Paul's antidote to libertinism was the reminder that believers were not independent individuals but a community dedicated to obeying the one commandment, which meant they were to care for each other. It was up to individuals living in community to align their own lives with that commandment, and to call each other to account when they failed.

Love involves the development of a self capable of responding morally, that is, making loving choices, when faced with the perplexities of life. The possibility of growing into such a person must have made its impact on some of Paul's audience, both before and after joining one of his communities.

11. Power, Signs and Wonders

We have seen how Paul's inclusive and egalitarian gospel addressed particular demographics of his time and place. In addition, the importance of his own personality, the role he placed in community development, his moral guidance, and his Christ story all contributed to the success of his mission. We turn now to a subject which is more difficult for moderns to appreciate, yet which Paul himself saw as very important. It is likely that others did also.

What was the impact on prospective converts and members of his congregations of what Paul refers to as "signs and wonders and mighty works?" And to what did those three terms actually refer? It is true that extraordinary powers were expected of and often assigned to those who claimed to represent a transcendent reality. Such special powers certainly contributed to their reputation and acceptance of their teachings. There can be little doubt that as time went on, stories of their wonder-working powers accumulated, as they certainly did later in Paul's case. However, that Paul himself

---

[385] See Galatians 5:13—"For you were called to freedom, brothers and sisters; only do not use your freedom as an opportunity for self-indulgence, but through love become slaves to one another." (NRSV)

believed that his ministry was being accomplished by more than his own words and deeds is amply illustrated in numerous places in his letters:

> . . . our message of the gospel came to you not in word only, but also in power and in the Holy Spirit and with full conviction. . . . you received the word with joy inspired by the Holy Spirit . . . . (1 Thessalonians 1:5a, 6b, NRSV) [386]

> Well then, does God supply you with the Spirit and work miracles among you by your doing the works of the law, or by your believing what you heard? (Galatians 3:5, NRSV)

> My speech and my proclamation were not with plausible words of wisdom, but with a demonstration of the Spirit and of power, so that your faith might rest not on human wisdom but on the power of God. (1 Corinthians 2:4-5, NRSV)

> And God has appointed in the church first apostles, second prophets, third teachers; then deeds of power, then gifts of healing, forms of assistance, forms of leadership, various kinds of tongues. Are all apostles? Are all prophets? Are all teachers? Do all work miracles? Do all possess gifts of healing? Do all speak in tongues? Do all interpret? (1 Corinthians 12:28-30, NRSV)

---

[386] "Power" translates the Greek *dynamis*. Its basic meaning is the ability to produce a desired result. This word is used exclusively in the NT of supernatural power, primarily divine but also demonic. It is sometimes also translated as "miracle" (Galatians 3:5). A second term is closely related to *dynamis,* namely, *energeia* (energy), and is commonly used in its verbal form. Energy is the activity performed by the release of power and is the term often employed to indicate the working of the Spirit in believers.

The signs of a true apostle were performed among you with utmost patience, signs and wonders and mighty works. (2 Corinthians 12:12, NRSV)

For I will not venture to speak of anything except what Christ has accomplished through me to win obedience from the Gentiles, by word and deed, by the power of signs and wonders, by the power of the Spirit of God . . . . (Romans 15:18-19a, NRSV)

Paul insists that he—and other missionaries—are only the human agents of Christ or God; they are "ambassadors for Christ" (2 Corinthians 5:20). In and of themselves, they do not possess extraordinary power. By referring to the "power(s)" of the Spirit and "signs and wonders,"[387] Paul suggests an association with the "signs and wonders" mentioned in the scriptures,[388] thereby claiming continuity with the history of Israel.[389] But he is also pointing to actual phenomena experienced by believers in his churches, which he identifies as healing, prophecy, speaking in tongues and their interpretation. Paul no doubt agreed with others in the Jesus movement who considered such extraordinary phenomena to be one form of the testimony of the Holy Spirit, which must have added another layer of persuasion for accepting the gospel. These manifestations of the Spirit were matched by others which could also be considered to be signs and wonders, such as the redirection and reeducation of converts. The experiences of reconciliation, joy, and peace might also have been understood as miraculous.

---

[387] The Greek word for wonder is *teras*. In the NT it is only found in the plural in conjunction with "signs" (Greek singular *sēmeion*). A wonder is that which is awe-inspiring or makes one stop to consider, "What is really going on here and what does it mean for me?"

[388] Especially in reference to the Exodus (e.g., Exodus 7:3; Deuteronomy 4:34; 34:11-12) but also regarding powers of prophets (Deuteronomy 13:1-2).

[389] Jewett, *Romans*, 910-911.

Interestingly, in contrast to the external evidence of power, Paul places his own weaknesses, his lack of observable power, and especially his sufferings, as the point at which God's power was manifested in his life. For Paul, the power of God comes in paradoxical ways, all of which were signs of the workings of the Spirit.

The vocabulary available to Paul to point to the transcendent in human experience was of course already set by contemporary usage and the Bible. It is not possible at this distance to precisely identify all the phenomena that Paul has in mind, or how in today's English we might describe them. But wonder, awe, and surprise are part of our experience also. Sometimes, we are amazed at events—and left wondering. Perhaps most amazing are the changes for good that can come over people and situations. Note also that the above quotations include such things as joy, belief (faith), Paul's own speech, proclamation, and patience as manifestations of God's Spirit. Paul believed that human transformation can become a sign pointing to the active presence of the Spirit of God. Perhaps prospective converts did too.

There is also the importance of belonging to something greater than self and one's immediate environment. Paul offered that possibility in his Christ story.

12. Paul's Christ-Story

Paul's version of the Christ story, which he called *hē euangelion*, "the good message," exhibits two important features of story-telling. First, it is about a subject of prime interest to the audience, in this case life and death. It explains why humanity, individually and collectively, now exists in a fractured condition, and how transcendent forces are now in operation to bring about its recovery.

The narrative develops in stages, as we saw earlier in the section, "Healing of the Nations." Three biblical males and two females play the major roles. Primal man and woman are persuaded by a disruptive figure to distrust their Creator, thereby losing access to the tree of life. A second man and his wife begin the process toward reconciliation by discovering the power of faith in God. Moses is given a double role as liberator from foreign control of the people and as lawgiver. The Law he mediates defines God's requirements for life, but it does not empower people to resist the sin which alienates from God.

The main character is now introduced. His true home is (at least metaphorically) in heaven, which he leaves in order to enlighten and save human beings from their addiction to sin. This figure, also known as the Son of God, is the model of selflessness. He has no self-centered ego to serve and protect, but is motivated by his love for the world created by his Father. Having faithfully completed his mission, he returns to heaven where he is declared ruler of the universe. His entire career is encapsulated in what has become known as the Philippians hymn:

Who, though he was in the form of God, did not count equality with God as something to be exploited, but emptied himself, taking the form of a slave, being born in human form, he humbled himself and became obedient to the point of death—even death on a cross. Therefore God also highly exalted him and gave him the name that is above every name so that at the name of Jesus every knee should bend, in heaven and on earth and under the earth, and every tongue should confess that Jesus Christ is Lord, to the glory of God the Father. (Philippians 2:6-11, NRSV)

Whether Paul composed this hymn himself or quoted it is uncertain. In either case it provides a précis of the dénouement of his gospel. Paul presents it as a model of the selflessness he was proclaiming.[390]

---

[390] The hymn is introduced with the directive for the readers to incorporate the mind of Christ (Philippians 2:5).

Stories of selfless sacrifice for others inherently appeal to the imagination. They can also be models for shaping behaviour. The popular 20th century American western books, comics, and movies followed a pattern in which locals incapable of saving themselves from the bullies are rescued by a heroic figure. In that case, however, the hero is transcendent to the situation only in the sense that he rides into town from somewhere else and after his saving acts leaves town. His reliance on violence to save others works solely because he is better at using the tools of violence than are his enemies.[391] He performs heroically, taking risks on behalf of others to "save" them. But as a model, he encourages violence which perpetuates itself. His method is inconsistent with his goal. Further, he is an individualist with no inherent relationship to the community.

Paul's story is quite different. His hero (a word not found in the NT) is non-violent, self-giving, righteous, innocent, and he gives his life for all, including his enemies. He teaches loving the neighbor, which requires consistency between method and goal. It's a very different story.

However, there is a second dimension of Paul's presentation of the Christ story that is equally as important as its plot. The listener is included in the story and has an active role to play. At every point Paul's narrative involves the audience—he is actually talking about them. Their similarity to Adam and Eve is evident. Like Abraham they are summoned to have faith in God. They know the demand to observe external rules, and the temptation to disobey. The believer's life story was to be re-written in the light of Christ's. Personal participation is an essential part of the story. Hearing is accompanied by doing; i.e., the goal of the action of Christ is the transformation of the hearer into a child of God. Paul's story was to be lived by the believer; indeed, its power depended on his/her

---

[391] See Robert Jewett's numerous books on popular American mythic stories of salvation.

internalizing it. Perhaps the most moving lines in his story are found here:

> For while we were still weak, at the right time Christ died for the ungodly. Indeed, rarely will anyone die for a right-eous person—though perhaps for a good person someone might actually dare to die. But God proves his love for us in that while we still were sinners Christ died for us. (Romans 5:6-8, NRSV)

Paul's drama was focused on love. On the first level, it was about the love of God for human beings, then about human love for God, next about mutual love among believers, and finally about love for those whose love is not returned. Such a well-composed story about love with its many dimensions can be very moving.

FINAL COMMENTS

The Paul who emerges from a careful examination of his own authentic writings is vastly different, even unrecognizably so, from the popular image of a grumpy, woman-hating au-thoritarian who is best ignored. In fact, Paul was a pioneer in his time and his legacy, though often unfairly tarnished, continues into our time.

Paul was determined to make widely known that a new world was on the horizon, and that it was intimately related to the life, death, and resurrection of Jesus. His vision of a social and cul-tural, even cosmic, transformation included a key role for himself. God was calling him to be an instrument of human make-over on a massive scale.

Such a vocation necessitated an appropriate reformulation of the Christ story to make it more applicable to Gentiles. Traditional messianic terminology like "son of David" or even "Messiah" itself in its former meaning lacked resonance for those who were not

Jews. Likewise, the Law of Moses was ethnic specific and largely irrelevant for Gentiles, especially regarding those commandments which required separation between Jews and Gentiles. Paul found in the Adam figure a character symbolizing both the dark side of humanity and prefiguring the Christ who brought unity, light, and life. These two figures representing two worlds, one passing away, the other emerging, and two ways of living formed the beginning and end points of Paul's story.

This basic narrative framework was filled out with other universal motifs. Paul saw in the Christ story an invitation to everyone regardless of gender, ethnicity, and social class to join in a world-embracing transformation. The story of Adam was their old story to be discarded in favor of their new participation in the Christ narrative. The law of Christ, love, was now the one commandment of God for all, the transforming power of God being shared with all humanity.

Love is a sturdy foundation for a community. To build a world on it is perhaps an impossible dream. Achievable or not, that was Paul's vision. Who has a better one?

THE PRIMARY SOURCES

CHAPTER 14: Paul's Letters

When I was a young boy, we lived in a farmhouse down a dirt road. With each trip over that road during the rainy season, it became increasingly difficult to keep the car out of the deepening ruts and even more so to steer out of them once the wheels had dropped in. I remember hearing a story, probably apocryphal, of a similar road with a sign, "Choose your ruts carefully; you're going to be in them a long time!"

Deciding what sources are to be used for the story of Paul is crucial, for the outcome is greatly influenced by the choice exercised at the outset. Fortunately, we are the heirs of a cloud of witnesses who have gone before us in the critical analysis of the relevant sources. More than two centuries of historical, linguistic, and literary research in the letters of Paul and Acts have clarified the issues and offered solutions to many of the problems facing Paul's biographers. However, there remain numerous unresolved issues which require decisions based on the best judgment one can muster. Lacking clear objective evidence, scholars can either keep silent or speculate on these uncertainties. Consequently, the portrait of Paul they create will differ. One can safely say that a definitive biography of Paul is not yet on the horizon and perhaps never will be. This is due not only to varying judgments about the sources employed, but also to the different perspectives brought to bear on those sources.

It is generally agreed that the story of Paul's life must be based primarily on his letters and secondarily on the Acts of the Apostles, plus whatever other sources are deemed helpful. Paul's name is not to be found in any Roman or Jewish writing of his era. That is hardly surprising; even Jesus is not mentioned in any Roman source of the first century, and only briefly in one Jewish writing published late in the first century.[392] Prior to the sixties the followers of Jesus were of little interest to the Roman government unless they were involved in public disturbances. Indeed, the Romans seem not to have distinguished sharply between the Jesus movement and the general Jewish populace until 64 CE when Nero blamed the Christians for the fire that destroyed much of Rome and unleashed the first persecution of Christians by the Roman government.

Likewise, we should not expect to find Paul's name in Jewish writings of that period. Before his conversion, he was too young and inexperienced to gain attention either as a teacher or for other reasons. Following his joining the Jesus movement, he would have been considered an apostate. While that might have been a qualification for at least a negative recognition, apparently it was not.

Consequently, we are limited to Christian sources. Paul was something of a legend in his own time among his fellow members of the Jesus movement, though a controversial one. Then, as now,

---

[392] "About this time there lived Jesus, a wise man, if indeed one ought to call him a man. For he was one who wrought surprising feats, and was a teacher of such people as accept the truth gladly. He won over many Jews and many of the Greeks. He was the Messiah. When Pilate, upon hearing him accused by men of the highest standing amongst us, had condemned him to be crucified, those who had in the first place come to love him did not give up their affection for him. On the third day he appeared to them restored to life, for the prophets of God had prophesied these and countless other marvelous things about him. And the tribe of the Christians, so called after him, has still to this day not disappeared." (Josephus, *Jewish Antiquities* 18:63-64) As it now stands, this passage has obviously been redacted or even totally composed from a Christian point of view. Its claims that "Jesus was the Messiah" and that he appeared on the third day to those who loved him could only have been written by a Christian. It has been argued that behind the interpolation there was an original reference to Jesus that did not make faith claims. A second passage which mentions Jesus is generally considered to be authentic: "Ananus [the high priest] . . . convened the judges of the Sanhedrin and brought before them a man named James, the brother of Jesus who was called the Christ, and certain others. He accused them of having transgressed the law and delivered them up to be stoned." (Josephus, *Jewish Antiquities* 20:200)

some revered him, and some despised him. However, due largely to his new and radical version of the Jewish tradition and his success in bringing Gentiles into the Jesus movement, no one could ignore him. When the Acts of the Apostles was composed, Paul's fame was such and his communities notable enough that over half of that writing was devoted to him and his activities. The only other NT writing which mentions Paul is 2 Peter, which demonstrates knowledge of his collected letters but not of Paul himself. The author recognizes that Paul's letters contain not only wisdom but also difficulties and opportunities for misinterpretation (2 Peter 3:14-16).

As we saw earlier, Paul is also mentioned in 1 Clement, a letter from a representative of the Roman Christians to those living in Corinth.[393] However, it adds no information to what can be known about him from Paul's own letters and Acts.

A substantial number of other Christian writings of the first two centuries of this era have survived which demonstrate some knowledge of Paul, or are ostensibly about him, or claim to have been written by him. For example, when Ignatius of Antioch was being taken in chains to Rome to face wild animals in the arena, he wrote ahead to the Christians in Rome. In this letter he makes an even briefer reference to Paul than we find in 1 Clement:

> Pray Christ for me that by these means I may become God's sacrifice. I do not give you orders like Peter and Paul. They were apostles: I am a convict. They were at liberty: I am still a slave. But if I suffer, I shall be emancipated by Jesus Christ; and united to him, I shall rise to freedom. (Ignatius, *To the Romans* 4:3)[394]

---

[393] 1 Clement 5:5-7; 47. The occasion for Clement's letter was a resurgence of strife within the congregation(s) at Corinth, reminiscent of Paul's time.

[394] Richardson, *Early Christian Fathers*, 104.

Ignatius obviously knew the tradition that Peter and Paul were both considered to have exercised apostolic authority in Rome. No doubt he was familiar with Paul's letter to the Romans. For the notion that Paul was at liberty in Rome, he may be relying on Acts 28:16, 30. In any case, he adds nothing of substance about Paul.

Other later sources take the reader even further into a different world from Paul's time, and while perhaps interesting in and of themselves and even valuable as sources for a later era, contribute nothing reliable to the study of Paul himself. That leaves Paul's letters and Acts as the basic material from which to glean the story of Paul's life.

The Pauline Letter Collection

Contemporary Bibles contain 13 letters attributed to Paul. Earlier editions such as the King James Bible assigned to him a 14th letter, the Epistle to the Hebrews. Interestingly, the earliest substantial manuscript of Paul's letters, known as P46 (a papyrus codex), dated to the early 3rd century, contains Hebrews, which is located between Romans and 1 Corinthians, according to the criterion of length.[395] A bit earlier, Clement of Alexandria (late 2nd century CE) also testified to the conviction that Paul was the author of Hebrews. However, about the same time that P46 was published, the Alexandrian scholar Origen registered a dissenting view, stating that the diction of Hebrews was more elevated than Paul's less sophisticated language, but its ideas were worthy of Paul. Origen proposed that one of the apostle's followers was the actual author of Hebrews. In the 16th century, Martin Luther and others set the stage for the modern view that Paul could not have written Hebrews. Indeed, Paul's name is not found in the writing, nor does

---

[395] Actually, Hebrews is slightly longer than 2 Corinthians, but to avoid separating the two Corinthian letters it was placed before them.

it follow the form of Paul's letters. Modern Bibles place Hebrews after the 13 Pauline letters, and without Paul's name at the heading. No one any longer defends the Pauline authorship of Hebrews.

The other 13 letters all claim Paul as their author, but many scholars argue that three of them, the so-called Pastoral Epistles, did not come from Paul himself, and were composed at least 40 years after his death. They reflect a new historical situation which was deemed to require adjustments to some of Paul's teachings, especially his acceptance of female leadership in his congregations. They exhibit significant terminological differences from Paul's undisputed letters. Their primary purpose is to establish regulations and doctrine for congregations to follow. Any study of Paul that includes these three letters as source material is unacceptable to this group of scholars.

There is less agreement on three other letters: Colossians, Ephesians, and 2 Thessalonians. The vocabulary and the issues treated in Colossians raise serious doubts about its authenticity. Ephesians in part seems to be a reworking of Colossians and exhibits a literary style not characteristic of Paul's undisputed letters. It addresses not one or even several of his congregations, but the wider church. Though much of it is couched in Paul's characteristic terminology, its concern is primarily the promotion of theological doctrines for the church universal. As such, it lacks the concrete grounding in specific situations characteristic of the undisputed letters. While some scholars regard either or both Colossians and Ephesians to be genuine Pauline letters, since there is not widespread agreement over their authenticity it is best to exclude them from our primary data base.

Second Thessalonians closely follows 1 Thessalonians in structure and content, but contains elements which seem to contradict the earlier letter. In the first letter the day of the Lord comes without any warning sign (1 Thessalonians 5:1-4). The second letter contains information about prior signs, the "rebellion" and the revelation of "the lawless one," about which Paul says he has personally told them (2 Thessalonians 2:1-5). This writing also testifies that it was written at a time when letters falsely attributed to Paul were circulating (2:2), a situation not very likely during his lifetime. For these and other reasons, many scholars reject 2 Thessalonians as an authentic letter of Paul's.

That leaves seven letters for our primary source base: Romans, 1 and 2 Corinthians, Galatians, Philippians, 1 Thessalonians, and Philemon. After two centuries of scholarly investigation of the thirteen letters assigned to Paul in the NT, agreement has been achieved that these seven are definitely genuine. Varying degrees of disagreement remain regarding the other six. [396]

The Character of Paul's Letters

The notion that his letters would become part of the scripture of a world religion would have been incomprehensible to Paul. He expected, at least in the early years, that the form of this world would not extend beyond his own lifetime. Even when faced with the possibility of imminent death he was still confident that the day of the Lord was not far away. Further, he had no intention to write anything approximating any of the literary works of his time. His letters do employ sophisticated rhetorical features; [397] after all, they were created primarily to convince, persuade and inspire. In addition, he expected them to be read to the entire church or group of house churches to whom he was writing, some members of which were probably illiterate. Even the letter to Philemon was more than a private letter, being addressed also to the church which met in his house.

---

[396] Borg and Crossan point out that each of these three groups of writings represents Paul differently: while the Paul of the authentic letters is "radical," the Paul of the Pastorals is "reactionary," and the Paul of Ephesians, Colossians, and 2 Thessalonians is "conservative." (*The First Paul*, 14-15.)

[397] This is especially true of the Letter to the Galatians, as Betz has demonstrated in detail. (*Galatians*)

But Paul's letters were not treatises on the eternal verities or theological doctrines. They addressed in a timely manner particular situations as they arose. They are written from an "I" or "we" to a "you" or "you-all." They were composed in a conversational mode utilizing the common non-literary language of the time known as Koine Greek, the language of the market place and other everyday activities, including letter-writing.

Some of the contents of his letters appear disjointed as if Paul had dictated what he wanted to say on that subject, left it only to return to it at a later time. Sometimes he sets off onto a new topic and doesn't come back to the earlier one. Even his most carefully constructed writing, the Epistle to the Romans, does not approach the literary quality of Hebrews, 1 Peter, or Luke-Acts. Rather, Paul's letters should be regarded as necessary substitutes for his preferred personal presence with the recipients.

Nevertheless, what Paul lacks in elevated literary style, he makes up in content and passion. Much of the content of his writings is argumentative, staking out and defending a position. A few portions soar poetically, e.g., the well-known love-chapter (1 Corinthians 13). No other author whose writing made it into the NT so reveals his own personality or pours out his feelings, both positive and negative. Once the reader pays his or her dues in becoming acquainted with Paul's vocabulary and style, it becomes apparent why his letters were collected and published for wider use in the early church.[398]

As mentioned above, Paul's letters do contain discontinuities in subject matter and argumentation. Some of these may be due to other causes than his intensity and fast-paced thinking. There are reasons to believe that in at least one case the collector or an editor of his writings has combined more than one letter intended for the same destination into a single entity. As we saw earlier, 2 Corinthi-

---

[398] Paul's collected letters constituted the first stage of what became the New Testament. The collection itself probably went through several stages.

ans is widely believed to be a compilation of several letters written over a relatively brief period. As a single letter written at one particular point in this sequence of events, it poses difficult problems. Likewise, many scholars are convinced that Philippians is composed of two or three letters sent at different times to the church at Philippi. That hypothesis would explain the location of what looks like a closing in the middle of the letter, followed by a completely new topic and mood.

Finally, lack of continuity within a letter, combined with other considerations, sometimes points to later interpolations into the original writing. Two examples in 1 Corinthians were examined in chapter 10.

All seven of the undisputed letters are Paul's communications to specific persons and groups about concrete matters. Letters of the type that Paul wrote should not be confused with the more general letter or epistle, intended for wider distribution. A number of these are found in the NT; examples are the writings attributed to James, John, Jude, and Peter, traditionally known as the "Catholic [General] Epistles."

The Writing of Paul's Letters

Paul normally dictated the contents of his letters to a secretary who did the actual writing, even though a scribe is specifically mentioned only in Romans 16:22. It is very unlikely that Paul would ever have hired one of the local professional scribes, but always used one of his close companions or at least a trusted believer for that role. It is also probable that it was Paul's practice to include in the opening of his letters the name of the person taking dictation, along with his own name. In that case, Timothy ("our brother") would have served as scribe for at least three and possibly four of the undisputed letters. His name appears along with Paul's at the beginning of 2 Corinthians, Philippians, I Thessalonians (which includes also Silvanus), and Philemon.

When 1 Corinthians was written, Timothy was not present with Paul, but somewhere on the road between Ephesus and Corinth (1 Corinthians 16:10). Consequently, another person served as the secretary for this letter, namely, Sosthenes (1 Corinthians 1:1).

The writing materials used by Paul's secretaries were those which had been in use for millennia: papyrus, stylus, and ink. Papyrus, from which we get our modern word "paper," came both in single sheets and in rolls which consisted of sheets glued together. It was manufactured in large quantities from the pith of the papyrus plant which grew in marshes along the Nile River in Egypt. Thousands of short documents and fragments of documents written on sheets of papyrus, such as invoices, receipts, school children's practice notes, magical texts, and private letters, have been recovered since the late 19th century from ancient trash heaps buried in the sands of Egypt. The short letter of Philemon would have required only a sheet or two like many of those papyri. Paul's longest letters, such as Romans and his correspondence with the Corinthians, may have been written on rolls. In any case, whether on rolls or single sheets, none of Paul's original letters has survived.

Paul depended on scribes to write his letters, not because he himself was unable to read and write; any student of the Torah learned those skills at an early age. However, developing the neat and rapid writing facility of the trained scribes, some of whom knew a form of shorthand, was a different matter. Paul's reference to the large letters he formed when writing Galatians 6:11 suggests it would normally have taken him too long to do the actual writing of a letter. However, sometimes he takes the pen and writes a short final greeting at the end of a letter (1 Corinthians 16:21).[399] Though not always specified, this was likely his usual practice, as it was with other letter writers of the period. No secretary is mentioned in Galatians; it is possible, but not probable, that Paul wrote the

---

[399] In Philemon 19 Paul takes the stylus and pretends to write an IOU.

entire letter himself. His reference to his large letters in 6:11 is not part of a concluding greeting, in contrast to 1 Corinthians 16:21.

Both Colossians 4:18 and 2 Thessalonians 3:17 employ the same expression as found in 1 Corinthians 16:1: "I, Paul, write this greeting with my own hand." (NRSV) On the assumption that these writings post-date Paul, the copying of this feature may be seen as an attempt to validate their Pauline authorship. 2 Thessalonians 3:17b adds a further attempt to claim authenticity, "This is the mark in every letter of mine; it is the way I write." (NRSV) That is a bit of an exaggeration since some of his letters lack that personal touch.

The form in which we know Paul's letters is vastly different from the original manuscripts. When his scribes took dictation, they did not divide what they wrote into chapters and verses for easy reference. That development happened many centuries later, concluding with the numbering of verses in the sixteenth century following the invention of printing. Indeed, the originals were not even divided into words; rather, the scribe produced a continuous string of letters with neither word separation nor punctuation. While our contemporary Bibles indicate by means of punctuation marks where Paul quotes from another source, e.g., from the Greek translation of the Hebrew scripture or from an earlier letter from the party addressed, his first readers lacked that assistance.

The written letter was primarily an aid for converting its contents back into oral speech, which was the basic form of interchange. Our modern reliance on the written word is largely a result of the cultural shift that occurred in the West following the invention of the printing press in the 15th century. It is interesting that the cell phone has now undergone a similar shift from being an oral tool of communication to its current predominant use for "texting," no doubt soon to be replaced with voice-activated technology. In order to fully appreciate Paul's letters, it is necessary to realize that he lived in an oral culture, and made use of the written letter not to produce "literature" but to facilitate speaking and hearing, as if he were present with the recipients.

Structure of a Pauline Letter

The titles of Paul's letters were not part of the original manuscripts, but were added by the collector or editor of the assembled letters. In order to specify the recipients of each letter, two words (in Greek) were placed above its opening line, e.g., *pros Galatas* (To Galatians). This pattern holds for all 13 letters (also for Hebrews), with the exception of those communities to whom two communications were identified. They were differentiated by an "A" and a "B". Thus the two letters to the Corinthian Christians were given the titles "To Corinthians A" and "To Corinthians B."

The original openings or salutations of Paul's letters on the whole remain intact. In general, they follow a common pattern: (1) name of sender, his credentials, and the name(s) of his companions, presumably beginning with the name of the scribe taking dictation; (2) recipient(s), i.e., a community or communities in a province or city—in one case (Philemon) an individual is named; (3) a greeting, "Grace to you and peace from God our Father and the Lord Jesus Christ." (NRSV) This greeting is found in all his letters except 1 Thessalonians, which has an abbreviated version, "Grace to you and peace."

The pattern of the whole salutation is based on a common Hellenistic letter format of the time. While the Hellenistic letter would normally have a brief salutation ending in "greetings" (*chairein*), Paul concludes the salutation with "grace" (*charis*) to which he adds *eirēnē*, the Greek version of the Hebrew *shalōm* ("peace"), thus creating his characteristic "grace and peace" formula. Here is an example of one of Paul's salutations:

Paul and Timothy, servants of Christ Jesus, to all the saints in Christ Jesus who are in Philippi, with the bishops and deacons: Grace to you and peace from God our Father and the Lord Jesus Christ."[400] (Philippians 1:1-2, NRSV)

Of course, a letter in which two or more of Paul's original communications have been combined no longer contains the openings to all the communications included in that writing. One opening would have been selected, or perhaps more than one combined, to cover all the contents of the new format.

The thanksgiving follows the opening address. Paul's letters show similarities to the common Hellenistic practice of presenting a thanksgiving to a deity, usually for deliverance from some danger such as sickness. Once again, Paul creates a distinctively Christian content. His thanksgivings normally play a dual role. First, they praise the faith and other positive elements of the community addressed, and refer to God's graciousness to them, in an almost liturgical fashion. Paul's thanksgivings may also rehearse the founding of the congregation addressed, and Paul's early relationship to them, especially his positive feelings about them.

Second, the thanksgivings often contain allusions to what follows in the main part of the letter. For example:

I thank my God every time I remember you, constantly praying with joy in every one of my prayers for all of you,

---

[400] "Bishops" and "deacons" had not yet become technical terms for church offices. The first (found only here in Paul's authentic letters) could be translated "supervisor" or "overseer" of a congregation, a function exercised by Paul himself in the early stages of the life of one of his congregations and perhaps passed on to a trusted convert when he left. Likewise, a deacon (*diakonos*) in Paul's usage is primarily a servant (of God or Christ), a term which Paul applies to himself (e.g., 1 Corinthians 3:5; 2 Corinthians 6:4; 11:23). The English word "servant" often translates the Greek *doulos* (slave), a term also used by Paul as a self-designation (Romans 1:1; 2 Corinthians 4:5; Galatians 1:10; Philippians 1:1).

because of your sharing in the gospel from the first day until now. (Philippians 1:3-5, NRSV)

Later, we learn more about the Philippians' "sharing in the gospel." They have repeatedly supported Paul financially in his mission after he left Philippi (4:15-16). Most recently, they sent one of their own, Epaphroditus, with some unspecified service to Paul in prison (2:25-30; 4:18). The church at Philippi had given Paul much for which to be thankful. His references to their "sharing" creates an amicable atmosphere at the outset.

Another example: in Philemon the thanksgiving exudes praise of the person being addressed:

When I remember you in my prayers, I always thank my God because I hear of your love for all the saints and your faith toward the Lord Jesus. I pray that the sharing of your faith may become effective when you perceive all the good that we may do for Christ. I have indeed received much joy and encouragement from your love, because the hearts of the saints have been refreshed through you, my brother. (Philemon 4-7, NRSV)

At this point, Philemon must have felt pretty good about the recognition being given his faith and good works. But the thanksgiving has been laying the foundation for a request, namely, that Philemon not only receive the runaway slave Onesimus back without recrimination, but send him back to Paul, and perhaps also grant him freedom. The thanksgiving does not stand in isolation, but prepares for what follows.

Two of Paul's letters do not contain a thanksgiving: 2 Corinthians and Galatians. However, as we observed earlier, while 2 Corinthians technically lacks a thanksgiving as such, it does contain a close substitute, a blessing. It is modelled on a typical Jewish blessing or *berakah* with which Paul would have been familiar from his own education as well as from family devotions and the synagogue service. Since 2 Corinthians is a collection of letters, we do not know what thanksgiving was found in each composition. However, the existing blessing fits well into its present setting.

The absence of a thanksgiving in Galatians is an entirely different matter; Paul does not replace it with a substitute. By omitting this normal feature of his letters (and letters in general), Paul immediately signals his readers in Galatia that they have given him little for which to be thankful. Instead of demonstrating that they are growing in the faith he has shared with them, they have questioned his teaching and his authority as an apostle of Christ. Indeed, he fears that they are abandoning his gospel in favor of "another gospel" which is not good news at all. It is understandable, therefore, that he skips over his usual thanksgiving.

Paul's thanksgivings always play an important role, but they may not always be as straightforward as in Philemon and Philippians. In 1 Corinthians one suspects a bit of irony in the formulation of the thanksgiving. The rich charismatic speech and wide-ranging knowledge of the recipients praised in the thanksgiving will later be shown to be not quite as desirable and valuable as the recipients think. Paul can offer both praise and criticism at the same time.

The third part of the letter is the longest and most varied in form and content. The body of the letter treats in detail its purpose. This section may begin with words like "I want you to know" (Romans 1:13, NRSV), or in the case of Galatians, "I am astonished." (1:6, NRSV) Sometimes, at or near the beginning of this section, Paul shares the latest news about himself. He may also respond to questions contained in a prior communication from the congregation addressed, or to issues within the congregation related to him by another person. Theological teaching and ethical exhortation are also common throughout this portion of the letter.

Paul's letters are closed in various ways. The readers may be informed of upcoming travel plans. Greetings from others present with Paul are often included, as are greetings to acquaintances in the church addressed. Paul may also commend certain persons for their deeds of service or as examples to be emulated.

The final element of the letter, the benediction, is another example of Paul's modification of the Hellenistic letter form. The latter may conclude with a repetition of the opening's wish for the health of the recipient and a "farewell." Paul does not always follow a set formula, but he incorporates certain key terms, especially "grace" and "love," as well as the divine names, into a closing benediction. Some examples:

The grace of the Lord Jesus Christ, the love of God, and the communion of the Holy Spirit be with all of you. (2 Corinthians 13:13, NRSV)

May the grace of our Lord Jesus Christ be with your spirit, brothers and sisters. Amen. (Galatians 6:18, NRSV)

The doxology[401] in Romans 16:25-27 is probably not original; it is certainly unlike any of the other endings of Paul's letters. It is not found in some ancient manuscripts of Romans. Paul does include doxologies in some of his letters, but always within the body of the letter, never at the conclusion.[402] There are three earlier benedictions in Romans. The first in 15:5-6 touches on important themes of the letter.[403] The second in 15:33 concludes the body of the letter proper, to which are added greetings to various individuals and groups in Rome and from believers with Paul. The third, to

---

[401] A doxology ("praise to God") should not be confused with a benediction ("blessing"). While both are prayers, the former directs honor to God, normally for blessings received and/or expected. The benediction normally expresses a hope for divine benefits to come to those addressed. However, benedictions may also praise God (e.g., Luke 1:68).

[402] E.g., Romans 11:33-36.

[403] Jewett, *Romans*, 883.

which some manuscripts add "all" (16:20b), completes the entire letter, and may originally have followed 16:23.[404]

Dating the Letters

The seven undisputed letters were all written relatively late in Paul's life, almost certainly during a period of less than a decade. Indeed, it is possible that only six or seven years elapsed between his first and last surviving letters. Scholars do not agree on the dating of all the letters and consensus is lacking even on their relative chronology. Their order in the NT is not an indication of when they were written. The letters are arranged in published Bibles according to descending length, with Romans, the longest of Paul's letters, at the beginning of the collection and the brief Philemon at the end. There is one exception—Ephesians is actually a little longer than Galatians which immediately precedes it. Trobisch believes that fact indicates that Ephesians was added to an earlier collection of Romans, 1 and 2 Corinthians, and Galatians.

Scholars generally agree that 1 Thessalonians is Paul's earliest letter, written from Corinth in ca. 49-50 CE. That date is determined by correlating the letter with a story found only in Acts. Luke connects Paul's first stay in Corinth to the tenure of the proconsul of the province of Achaia, Gallio (Acts 18:12-17). Gallio's time in Corinth has been dated May of 51 CE to May of 52 CE. Acts reports that Paul's stay of 18 months in that city overlapped Gallio's appointment there, but we do not know who arrived in Corinth first and who left first. Consequently, there is a range of up to two years for dating Paul's sojourn in Corinth and therefore for dating his letter to the Thessalonians.

---

[404] Scholarly analysis of 16:17-27 still has not reached agreement. Jewett, *Romans*, 985-1014.

402

Determining the date of the last of his letters depends on factors impossible to resolve definitively, such as whether Paul was imprisoned in Ephesus, and whether he wrote any letters when under house arrest in Rome. Philippians and Philemon (the "imprisonment epistles") could possibly have been written from Caesarea where Paul was detained before being sent to Rome under guard (Acts 23:31-26:32). More likely, they were written when Paul was either in Ephesus or Rome. If written from the latter location, they would be Paul's final letters. If written from Ephesus, Romans would be his last letter. The Corinthian letters precede Romans; all three can be dated to the mid-50s. If Philippians and Philemon were written from Rome, they would be dated in the early 60s. The substantially shorter distance of Philippi from Ephesus than from Rome favors Ephesus as the place from which Paul wrote Philippians. It is likely that Philemon was also written during Paul's Ephesian sojourn.

A wide range of dates have been posited for Galatians. Martyn argues that it is very early,[405] while others find the similarities between Galatians and Romans evidence that they were written within a short time of each other. Still others see significant development in Romans beyond Galatians, which suggests a substantial time lapse between them.

Although it is not possible to assign definite dates to most of Paul's letters, we can provisionally suggest a relative order with tentative dates. These dates are based on the assumption that 1 Thessalonians was Paul's first letter and Romans was his last.

---

[405] Martyn suggests that Galatians could have been Paul's first letter. Martyn's relative chronology of the letters is based on whether or not they mention the collection Paul was assembling for the poor in the church at Jerusalem. There is no reference to the collection in 1 Thessalonians, Philippians, or Galatians, but there is in 1 Corinthians, 2 Corinthians, and Romans. Therefore, Galatians must precede the other three. *Galatians,* 19-20.

Ca. 49-50 CE: 1 Thessalonians: written from Corinth after Timothy had returned from his trip to Thessalonica.

Ca. 53-56: Galatians: written from Ephesus during Paul's three years there, but possibly earlier.

Philippians: written while Paul was in prison, probably in Ephesus.

Philemon: written in prison, probably during Paul's Ephesian period.

1 Corinthians: written from Ephesus, probably during the middle of Paul's time there.

2 Corinthians: parts of it were written in Ephesus toward the end of Paul's time in that city, while the other parts were composed while Paul was in Macedonia en route to Corinth.

56-57 CE Romans: written from Corinth during the three months of winter that Paul stayed in that city.

Summary

There is general scholarly agreement that only seven of the thirteen letters attributed to Paul in the NT are indisputably authentic. There is considerable uncertainty about when and where some of them were written. This imposes restrictions on any attempt to compose a geographical chronology tracing Paul's life as a missionary. The best we can do is to propose probable dates for some of the letters and reasonable estimates for the others.

CHAPTER 15: The Acts of the Apostles

In earlier times, much of the data for a life of Paul was drawn from the Acts of the Apostles. This writing does contain much more information about Paul's activities than do his own letters. However, in recent decades, there has been a shift to the letters of Paul as the primary source material.[406] It is important to know some of the main reasons for that change. One should also be aware that, between the writing of the letters and the publication of Acts, two catastrophic events occurred: the slaughter of many of the Christians in Rome (64 CE), followed only a few years later by the human and material devastation in Judea resulting from the war between the Jews and the Romans (66-73 CE).

The book of Acts is the second part of a two-volume work, the first part being the Gospel According to Luke. Each may originally have occupied a separate papyrus scroll. While both parts are assigned to "Luke," neither contains the author's name. To be accepted as worthy of a place among the churches' scriptures, a writing had to be regarded as "apostolic," that is, written by an apostle or by a companion of an apostle. In Philemon 24, a Luke, identified as a "fellow worker," sends greetings. The same name also appears in two post-Pauline writings: Colossians 4:14, where Luke is identified as a "physician," and 2 Timothy 4:11, where Luke alone is Paul's companion. The tradition that Luke-Acts was written by Luke, the beloved physician and a fellow-worker with Paul, is largely based on these three references.

The actual title of Luke's Gospel was added when the four canonical Gospels were brought together into a single collection

---

[406] John Knox was an important figure in initiating this shift. See his seminal book, *Chapters in a Life of Paul,* 1950.

sometime before 150 CE.[407] The collector/editor(s) gave a name to each Gospel which he associated with an apostle. The same pattern was followed for each title, i.e., *kata Matthaion, kata Markon, kata Loukan, kata Iōannēn* ("According to Matthew," etc.), though the relative order differs in various manuscripts. This arrangement suggests that the overall title *hē Evangelion* ("The Gospel") was placed at the head of the collection. One consequence of inserting Luke's version into the collection of Gospels was the removal of Acts from its original position as the sequel to his Gospel. However, their respective prologues continue to provide a link between the two writings.

The first part of Luke's project begins with an introduction covering both volumes. Here the author dedicates to Theophilus his literary work (Luke 1:3b-4). Assuming that Theophilus ("lover of God") was a real person and not just a name in a fictional introduction, we know nothing more about his identity than what Luke tells us. His reference to the prior "instruction" of Theophilus may indicate that Theophilus was a convert who had undergone catechetical instruction and now wanted to learn more about the movement he was joining. The ambitious undertaking of the author suggests that Theophilus was a person of some note, and wealthy enough to finance the project. It has been conjectured that he was a Roman official, but there is no direct evidence of that, even though it is clear that the author maintains throughout a friendly attitude toward the Roman government. Of course, it is possible that "Theophilus" is anybody with an interest in Christian beginnings, particularly persons occupying leadership positions in the Jesus movement of Luke's time.

The second part begins with another reference to Theophilus and a one-sentence summary about the contents of the first book.

---

[407] Tatian, a Syrian Christian, published ca. 160 CE a Gospel harmony, known as the Diatessaron (literally, "through the four") in which he wove together into a single Gospel material from the four canonical Gospels, avoiding repetitions.

Luke then turns to the next phase of the movement, the beginnings of the church. The transitional event is the coming of the Holy Spirit, which empowers and guides the movement, a recurring theme underlying both parts of the work.[408] Jesus himself had been empowered by the Spirit, both in his conception (Luke 1:35) and at his baptism (3:21-22; 4:1). The Spirit stayed with him until his death at which time he delivered it back to God (23:46). The Spirit then comes again to make it possible for Jesus' followers to bear witness to the resurrected Christ and to extend the gospel to others (Acts 1:8; 2:1-4, 16-18). The central role of the Spirit is obviously an important element in Luke's story of Jesus and throughout the early church. In this, Luke continues Paul's emphasis on the church as a spiritual movement.

The title, The Acts of the Apostles ("Acts of Apostles" or "Apostolic Acts" in Greek), was probably supplied, as was the title of the first part, by a later editor. It is somewhat misleading, as the writing is really focused on only two persons, Peter in chapters 1-12, and Paul in chapters 13-28, with some overlap when Paul is introduced (7:58-8:1) and again when Peter supports Paul's Gentile mission at the apostolic conference (15:7-11). If Luke had assigned his writing a title, it might have been "The Acts of Peter and Paul." Other apostles are mentioned, but play little or no role in Luke's composition. Technically, Acts is concerned with the deeds of only one apostle, Peter, since the author limits the category of apostle to the twelve disciples, of which Peter, but not Paul, is a member. Paul is considered the star missionary to the Gentiles, but as we

---

[408] Various accounts of the coming of the Spirit are found in the NT, both in regard to Jesus and to believers. All four Gospels relate the descent of the Spirit to Jesus at his baptism (Mark 1:10; Matthew 3:16; Luke 3:22), though in the Fourth Gospel only John the Baptist testifies to the event (1:32-34). In addition, Matthew and Luke have birth stories in which the Holy Spirit generates a child for Jesus' mother. In John's Gospel, in which there is neither birth nor ascension story, the resurrected Jesus delivers the Holy Spirit to his disciples (20:22; see also 7:39) by breathing on them. Paul has no inaugurating story as such, but assumes the presence of the Spirit in and among believers.

have seen, he is not regarded as an apostle in the same sense as Peter.

While Paul is assigned more space in Acts than Peter, each is given more or less equitable treatment. Both live and act under the power of the Holy Spirit. Both are portrayed as prominent speakers and both are miracle workers. Both contribute to the Gentile mission; while it is Peter rather than Paul who initiates it (chapter 10) and who defends it against its critics (11:1-18), it is Paul who takes the gospel beyond the homeland and all the way to Rome. Peter and Paul are the complementary twins of the Way, never in competition with each other and always on congenial terms. Indeed, Peter comes to Paul's defense when the latter's practice of accepting Gentiles without circumcision is criticized by some in the Jerusalem church (15:6-11).

One of Luke's goals in Acts is to bring the followers of the principal players in the Jesus movement under a single umbrella. Those who look especially to Peter and those who follow Paul have no cause to suspect the members of the other party, for Peter and Paul recognized the ministry of each other. Paul's own writings reveal that relations between himself and Peter were not quite as harmonious as those represented in Acts.

Looking back on the time of Jesus and the first generation of missionaries, the author of Acts creates a pair of documents which could serve as a handbook for teachers, i.e., a resource for Christian catechists in the Gentile world.[409] His work focuses on three figures: Jesus, Peter, and Paul, all guided by the Spirit of God. From Galilee to Rome they pursue their own special callings. Luke-Acts thus provides a new generation with the necessary information and perspective to understand what God is doing, not only through Jesus but also through his two greatest earthly advocates.

---

[409] The Gospel According to Matthew could serve the same function, but for churches whose mission still included Jews. Luke-Acts clearly envisages an exclusively Gentile mission for the future.

The Sayings Source (Q) had already provided leaders in the Jesus movement with a compilation of Jesus' sayings,[410] and Mark's gospel had combined sayings with an early narrative of Jesus' life. Luke incorporated both Q and Mark in his gospel and went on to pioneer a sequel. Acts traces activities of Peter and Paul, and to a lesser degree, those of other first generation followers of Jesus. Traditions about them are imprinted with a definite theological perspective. Thus both traditions and their larger meaning are passed on to those called to teach; together, they show that the revelation in Jesus continued in his followers.

The relevant parts of Acts for this study of Paul are the narratives dealing with his travels and other activities, particularly his founding of churches. Surprisingly, Acts contains almost nothing about Paul's teachings, apart from his belief that he had been chosen to take the gospel to the non-Jewish world. Scholars regard the speeches attributed to Paul in Acts not as authentic reports of Paul's missionary preaching, but constructions by the author which follow conventional practices of "historians" of the time. That is, the author wrote speeches to fit the occasions faced by Paul as the narrative progresses, just as Peter speaks appropriately in the earlier part of Acts. In vocabulary, style, and message the Galilean fisherman and the former Pharisee sound suspiciously similar. The theology expressed in the speeches is neither Paul's nor Peter's, but Luke's. This view fits with the fact that Acts shows no indication that its author was prepared to recognize that Paul wrote letters, which is especially surprising in view of Luke's claim to have investigated "everything carefully from the very first. . . ." (Luke 1:3, NRSV).

No one can doubt that Luke has done substantial research. His gospel would have been greatly impoverished without Q and Mark. Acts could not have been written without relying on nu-

---

[410] The Gospel of Thomas likewise is a collection of sayings (in its present form, it contains 114 sayings). The date of its origin is uncertain. Some scholars would place it as early as Q in the mid-first century CE, others a century later.

merous traditions, probably mostly oral, from various churches. One written source is particularly obvious, the so-called "we-source" (also known as the Travel Document), found in the second half of Acts.[411] It is primarily a travel diary tracing some of Paul's trips, starting with his initial foray from Troas in Asia to Philippi in Macedonia, then resuming years later in Philippi when Paul was on his final trip to Jerusalem, and carrying on to Rome after his arrest. Any relevant documentation is welcome, even a travel itinerary, but it has limitations as a source for knowledge about Paul, partly because the author of Acts has redacted portions of it. Some of the stories associated with the Travel Document may have come from other sources, and some may have been composed by Luke.

These and other considerations prompt the question, how much credence should be accorded the portrait of Paul in Acts? There are often significant inconsistencies and sometimes outright contradictions between Luke and Paul when they both report the same event. There are occasions when Luke obviously is wrong. This raises suspicions about those events where we do not have a control supplied by Paul. The earlier practice of accepting everything in Acts as true or accurate is no longer possible. Consequently, caution might dictate that we follow Acts only on events or stories validated by Paul himself or some other reliable authority.

That course becomes even more attractive when we consider other aspects of Luke's agenda. Since Acts was written for churches of the late first or early second century Roman Empire, we would expect it to reflect that later situation. The Christians of Luke's time could never feel secure vis-à-vis the Roman government. A generation earlier the believers in Rome had undergone a severe persecution under Nero with many lives lost. The trauma of that event must have weighed heavily on other followers of Jesus and the fear of persecution could never be entirely laid to rest. Close to or during Luke's time, renewed hostility to the Christians appar-

---

[411] Found in Acts 16:10-17; 20:5-15; 21:1-17; 27:1-28:16 (with some insertions).

ently emerged during the reign of Domitian (81-96 CE), to which the writing we know as The Revelation to John is considered to be a Christian literary response.

Expecting his writing to be seen by Roman authorities, Luke molded it to show that the new faith was not a threat to public order; in the past, Roman governors, police, and magistrates had treated it favorably. Where Christians had been involved in public disorder, they did not initiate it. All the persecutions except one (Acts 19:23-41) faced by Paul are instigated by "the Jews," never by Roman authorities. Luke's default position is to blame the Jews for any trouble falling on Paul.[412] Thus Luke demonstrates that contemporary Roman officials had precedents for being favorably inclined toward Christians.

On the other hand, aware of the special privileges given to the Jewish people over the previous century and more,[413] Luke sets out to demonstrate that the new faith is actually a continuation of the Jewish religion and therefore should be given the same toleration in Roman law. Indeed, he presents it as the authentic Jewish faith since it alone recognizes the fulfillment of the ancient promises in Jesus.

A related matter is Luke's representation of Paul's missionary strategy. The missionary to the Gentiles repeatedly goes to the Jews first (in the local synagogue). When they reject his teaching, he goes to the Gentiles.[414] It is reasonable that Paul in fact did start

---

[412] The war between the Romans and the Jews left the latter in an unfavorable light following that event. Luke may be taking advantage of that prejudice in his portrayal of Paul's conflicts.

[413] Those privileges included exemption from military service, permission to raise money to send to Jerusalem for the Temple tax, to conduct their own court system, and to assemble.

[414] Paul himself knows this formula, "to the Jew first and also to the Greek." (Romans 1:16, NRSV; see also 2:9, 10) However, he is not describing his own missionary strategy as portrayed in Acts, but the historical fact that the gospel first came to the Jews (through Jesus and his disciples) and was then extended to the Greeks (through Paul and others).

in each city by going to the local synagogue, inasmuch as that was possible. In the synagogue he would have been able to direct his message not only to his fellow Jews but also to those Gentiles who regularly came there to learn more about Judaism. It is not entirely clear how that procedure cohered with the Jerusalem agreement that Peter, James and John would go to the Jews while Paul and Barnabas would evangelize among the Gentiles. In any case, Luke uses Paul's practice for his own purpose—to demonstrate that the expansion of the church among the Gentiles was due not only to the divine initiative but also to Jewish unbelief. As a form of Jewish religion, the message was offered first to Jews. But when they refused to accept it, the missionaries turned to the Gentiles to whom Luke was convinced God's favor was being transferred.

Another item in Luke's agenda is his geography of mission. Even though the Jerusalem church no longer existed, and the city itself had been razed by the Roman military decades earlier, Luke envisages Jerusalem as the original head office of the Jesus movement. It began there under the direction of the risen Jesus himself. While the Gospels of Mark, Matthew, and John all point to the disciples' returning to Galilee following the crucifixion, in Luke's schema the risen Christ explicitly directs the disciples to stay in Jerusalem.[415] Luke recognizes only one congregation as the source of the movement, the one led by the twelve apostles in Jerusalem, even though he is aware that churches also existed in Galilee, Samaria, and elsewhere in Judea (Acts 9:31). He is concerned to demonstrate that the leaders in Jerusalem were in control as the gospel moved westward,[416] until finally at the close of Acts, their

---

[415] Mark 16:7; Matthew 28:10, 16; John 21:1-14; Acts 1:4.

[416] In fact, the Jesus movement spread in all directions, not just to the west. Acts does not narrate the evangelization of Egypt or the eastern countries, though Peter's sermon at Pentecost is delivered to Jews "from every nation under heaven" from which Luke reports 3,000 conversions. (Acts 2:5, NRSV) Luke is aware of a much larger dispersion of the Jesus movement than he narrates. He selectively focuses on its singular progress from Jerusalem to Rome.

approved representative, Paul, carries it to Rome itself.[417] The final words of the risen Jesus prior to his ascension constitute a synopsis of the coming mission and a brief outline of Acts:

> But you will receive power when the Holy Spirit has come upon you; and you will be my witnesses in Jerusalem, in all Judea and Samaria, and to the ends of the earth. (Acts 1:8, NRSV)

Peter becomes the major witness to Jesus in Jerusalem, and monitors the work of other witnesses in Judea and Samaria, and Paul takes the gospel to the ends of the earth, i.e., progressively westward to Rome. The Jerusalem connection of both missionaries guarantees their legitimacy and that their gospel adheres to that of the leaders of the Jerusalem congregation.

These and other "tendencies" in Luke's theological history of the early church must be taken into account in determining the actual course of events in which Paul was involved. Where there is another witness to those events, it is relatively easy to make reasonable inferences. But what about those narratives in Acts where we do not have another account to validate it? For example, Luke places Paul at the stoning death of Stephen. Was he actually there? There are no other reports of that event. Many scholars today dismiss this part of Luke's account as his imaginative way of introducing Paul as a persecutor of the church and leading up to his conver-

---

[417] The actual founding of the Roman church is not described in Acts and may have been a topic that Luke had not researched or in which he was uninterested. Possibly, there was no apostolic involvement in the founding of the Roman church, similar to the beginning of the church in Syrian Antioch. When Paul arrives in Rome under arrest in the final chapter of Luke's story, there are already congregations there, as Paul's own letter to the Romans demonstrates. His apology for not visiting them earlier (15:22-29) suggests that they had been in existence a considerable time already.

sion near Damascus. However, we have no definitive evidence and Luke's account is as least as believable as modern alternatives.

Scholars can either accept or reject Luke's various stories according to "the weight of evidence," which on occasion may be a euphemistic way of stating their hunch. Inherent in this process is the matter of the burden of proof. One may require independent evidence to accept one of Luke's claims, or one may require external evidence to reject it. The latter approach tends to accept the accounts in Acts unless there is contrary evidence. The first requires evidence to overcome inherent skepticism about Luke's account. We are not always consistent in our choices, sometimes practicing skepticism here but not there.

My inclination is to accept the accounts in Acts except where there is demonstrable reason to conclude otherwise. Such a reason would certainly arise if a datum of Acts was contradicted by Paul or another credible source. A doubt would also be justified when a statement of the author appears to be determined by one of his own theological "tendencies" or subject to his agenda. With all the provisos previously mentioned, and with others as the occasions arise, Acts is to be considered an important source for the story of Paul's life. On particular points, however, one must always be open to healthy skepticism.

Summary

The Acts of the Apostles is an important secondary source to be employed, though cautiously, in writing a biography of Paul. Its author has his own agenda which impacts how Acts is to be used as a source, but the various aspects of that agenda are now well recognized. There is no general agreement on who composed Acts, when it was written,[418] or whether the travel itinerary which the author incorporated was his own.

My belief is that Acts was written a generation or two after Paul's death, but prior to the publication of a corpus of his letters. Acts is the earliest surviving written attempt to narrate the place of Paul in the developing Jesus movement. As a proponent of the faith, Luke writes a theological "history" in which the Spirit of God is the motivating and guiding factor. Peter and Paul are the two human characters inspired to carry the faith from Jerusalem into the wider world, but Paul emerges as the dominant missionary to the Gentiles. That scenario is consistent with Paul's own self-image.

Among the various purposes served in Luke's representation of the development of the early church, two stand out. First, the author wants to assure the Roman administrators that the Jesus movement was a legitimate religion and not a threat to the government or to public order. This may be a "soft" way of responding to hostility of the government toward the church. Second, Luke demonstrates to the various Christian parties that they should be pulling together in a single, united body. There should be no more squabbles between those who favor a particular missionary, and do not recognize that all were witnesses to the one Christ (a position earlier advanced by Paul). The writing of Acts is an attempt toward bringing all the streams of tradition and missionary activity together. Such an achievement would benefit the movement internally as well as externally vis-à-vis the government and the larger society.

---

[418] The most common dating for Luke-Acts is 80-100 CE, but an early 2nd century date cannot be ruled out.

ABBREVIATIONS

ABD	The Anchor Bible Dictionary
BCE	Before the Common Era (formerly, BC)
CE	The Common Era (formerly, AD)
IDB	The Interpreter's Dictionary of the Bible
NIB	The New Interpreter's Dictionary of the Bible
NT	New Testament
OT	Old Testament

WORKS CITED

Akenson, Donald Harman, *Saint Saul: A Skeleton Key to the Historical Jesus.* Montreal & Kingston: McGill-Queen's University Press, 2000.

Betz, Hans Dieter, "Corinthians, Second Epistle to the," *The Anchor Bible Dictionary* 1:1148-1154. New York, London, Toronto, Sydney, Auckland: Doubleday, 1992.

Betz, Hans Dieter, *Galatians, A Commentary on Paul's Letter to the Churches in Galatia.* Philadelphia: Fortress Press, 1979. (Hermeneia Series)

Betz, Hans Dieter, "Paul," *The Anchor Bible Dictionary* 4: 186-201. New York, London, Toronto, Sydney, Auckland: Doubleday, 1992.

Betz, Hans Dieter, *The Sermon on the Mount.* Minneapolis: Fortress Press, 1995. (Hermeneia Series)

Betz, Hans Dieter, *2 Corinthians 8 and 9, A Commentary on Two Administrative Letters of the Apostle Paul.* Philadelphia: Fortress Press, 1985. (Hermeneia Series)

Blumell, Lincoln H., "Travel and Communication in the NT," *The New Interpreter's Dictionary of the Bible* 5:652-656. Nashville: Abingdon Press, 2009.

Borg, Marcus J., *Speaking Christian; Why Christian Words Have Lost Their Meaning and Power—And How They Can Be Restored.* New York: HarperCollins Publishers, 2011.

Borg, Marcus J., and John Dominic Crossan, *The First Paul, Reclaiming the Radical Visionary Behind the Church's Conservative Icon.* New York: HarperCollins Publishers, 2009.

Brown, Raymond E., and John P. Meier, *Antioch and Rome, New Testament Cradles of Catholic Christianity.* New York/Ramsey: Paulist Press, 1983.

Charles, R. H., *The Apocrypha and Pseudepigrapha of the Old Testament.* Oxford: At the Clarendon Press, 1968. Available online.

Church, Alfred John and William Jackson Brodribb, *The Annals of Tacitus.* London: Macmillan and Co., 1876. Available online.

Conzelmann, Hans, *Acts of the Apostles, A Commentary on the Acts of the Apostles.* Translated by James Limburg, A. Thomas Kraabel, and Donald H. Juel. Edited by Eldon Jay Epp with Christopher R. Matthews. Philadelphia: Fortress Press, 1987. (Hermeneia Series)

Conzelmann, Hans, *1 Corinthians, A Commentary on the First Epistle to the Corinthians.* Translated by James W. Leitch. Edited by George W. MacRae, S.J. Philadelphia: Fortress Press, 1975. (Hermeneia Series)

Danby, Herbert, *The Mishnah Translated from the Hebrew with Introduction and Brief Explanatory Notes.* London: Oxford University Press, 1933.

Dibelius, Martin and Hans Conzelmann, *The Pastoral Epistles.* Translated by Helmut Koester. Philadelphia: Fortress Press, 1972. (Hermeneia Series)

Fitzgerald, John T., "Philippians, Epistle to the," *The Anchor Bible Dictionary* 5:318-326. New York, London, Toronto, Sydney, Auckland: Doubleday, 1992.

Funk, Robert W., Roy W. Hoover, and The Jesus Seminar, *The Five Gospels, The Search for the Authentic Words of Jesus.* New York: Macmillan Publishing Company, 1993.

Gamble, Harry Y., *Books and Readers in the Early Church, A History of Early Christian Texts.* New Haven and London: Yale University Press, 1995.

Gasque, W. Ward, "Perga," *The Anchor Bible Dictionary* 5:228. New York, London, Toronto, Sydney, Auckland: Doubleday, 1992.

Georgi, Dieter, "Corinthians, Second Letter to the," *The Interpreter's Dictionary of the Bible (Supplementary Volume)*: 183-186. Nashville: Abingdon, 1976.

Haenchen, Ernst, *The Acts of the Apostles, A Commentary.* Translated by Bernard Noble and Gerald Shinn, revised by R. McL. Wilson. Oxford: Basil Blackwell, 1971.

Hardin, Michael, ed., *Reading the Bible with René Girard: Conversations with Steven E. Berry.* Lancaster, PA, 2015. Kindle version.

Harrill, J. Albert, "Slavery," *The New Interpreter's Dictionary of the Bible* 5:299-308. Nashville: Abingdon Press, 2009.

Hays, Richard B., *Echoes of Scripture in the Letters of Paul*. New Haven: Yale University Press, 1989.

Hock, Ronald E., *The Social Context of Paul's Ministry, Tentmaking and Apostleship*. Philadelphia: Fortress Press, 1980.

Jeremias, Joachim, *Jerusalem in the Time of Jesus; An Investigation into Economic and Social Conditions during the New Testament Period*. Philadelphia: Fortress Press, 1969.

Jeremias, Joachim, *The Prayers of Jesus*. London: SCM Press LTD, 1967.

Jewett, Robert, *A Chronology of Paul's Life*. Philadelphia: Fortress Press, 1979.

Jewett, Robert, *Romans, A Commentary*. Minneapolis: Fortress Press, 2007. (Hermeneia Series)

Josephus, *Against Apion*. London: William Heinemann Ltd, Cambridge, Massachusetts: Harvard University Press, 1965. (Loeb Classical Library). Text also available online.

Josephus, *Jewish Antiquities*. London: William Heinemann Ltd, Cambridge, Massachusetts: Harvard University Press, 1965. (Loeb Classical Library). Text also available online.

Josephus, *The Jewish War*. Cambridge, Massachusetts: Harvard University Press, London: William Heinemann Ltd, 1961. (Loeb Classical Library). Text also available online.

Josephus, The *Life*. London: William Heinemann Ltd, Cambridge, Massachusetts: Harvard University Press, 1961. (Loeb Classical Library). Text also available online.

Kearney, Richard, *On Stories.* London and New York: Routledge Taylor & Francis Group, 2002.

Knox, John, *Chapters in a Life of Paul.* New York: Abingdon-Cokesbury Press, 1950. Revised by the author, and edited with introduction by Douglas R. A. Hare, Mercer University Press, 1987.

Knox, John. *The Death of Christ, The Cross in New Testament History and Faith.* New York and Nashville: Abingdon Press, 1958.

Malina, Bruce J. and Jerome H. Neyrey, *Portraits of Paul, An Archaeology of Ancient Personality.* Louisville, Kentucky: Westminster John Knox Press, 1996.

Martyn, J. Louis, *Galatians, A New Translation with Introduction and Commentary.* New Haven and London: Yale University Press, 1997. (The Anchor Yale Bible)

Meeks, Wayne A., *The First Urban Christians; the Social World of the Apostle Paul.* New Haven and London: Yale University Press, 1983.

Murphy-O'Connor, Jerome, *Paul: A Critical Life.* Oxford & New York: Oxford University Press, 1997.
Neusner, Jacob, *From Politics to Piety, The Emergence of Pharisaic Judaism.* Englewood Cliffs, New Jersey: Prentice-Hall, 1973.

Philo, *On the Contemplative Life.* Cambridge, Massachusetts: Harvard University Press, 1989. (Loeb Classical Library). Text also available online.

Philo, *On the Creation*. Cambridge, Massachusetts: Harvard University Press, London: William Heinemann Ltd, 1929. (Loeb Classical Library). Text also available online.

Richardson, Cyril C., Translator and Editor, *Early Christian Fathers*. Philadelphia: The Westminster Press, 1953. (Volume One of The Library of Christian Classics). Texts also available online.

Roetzel, Calvin J., "Paul, the Apostle," *The New Interpreter's Dictionary of the Bible* 4:404-421. Nashville: Abingdon Press, 2009.

Roetzel, Calvin J., *The Letters of Paul, Conversations in Context*. Louisville, Kentucky: Westminster John Knox Press, 2009 (Fifth Edition).

Saldarini, Anthony J., "Pharisees," *The Anchor Bible Dictionary* 4:289-303.

Stendahl, Krister, *Paul Among Jews and Gentiles and Other Essays*. Philadelphia: Fortress Press, 1976.

Towner, Philip, "Corinthians, Second Letter To", *The New Interpreter's Dictionary of the Bible* 1:744-751. Nashville: Abingdon Press, 2006.

Townsley, Jeramy, "Paul, the Goddess Religions, and Queer Sects: Romans 1:23-28," *Journal of Biblical Literature* (Winter 2011) 130:707-728.

Trobisch, David, *Paul's Letter Collection, Tracing the Origins*. Augsburg Fortress Press, 1994. E-book edition 2001.

DICTIONARIES

The Anchor Bible Dictionary (6 Volumes). David Noel Freedman, Editor-in- Chief. New York, London, Toronto, Sydney, Auckland: Doubleday, 1992.

The Interpreter's Dictionary of the Bible, An Illustrated Encyclopedia (4 Volumes). George Arthur Buttrick, Dictionary Editor. New York and Nashville: Abingdon Press, 1962. Supplementary Volume, Keith Crim, General Editor, Nashville: Abingdon, 1976.

The New Interpreter's Dictionary of the Bible (5 Volumes). Katharine Doob Sakenfeld, General Editor. Nashville: Abingdon Press, 2006-2009.

BIBLES

The Access Bible, New Revised Standard Version with the Apocryphal/Deuterocanonical Books. Gail R. O'Day and David Petersen, General Editors. New York: Oxford University Press, 1999.

The Greek New Testament. Edited by Kurt Aland, Matthew Black, Carlo M Martini, Bruce M. Metzger, and Allen Wikgren. Third Edition (Corrected). United Bible Societies, 1983.

The Jewish Annotated New Testament, New Revised Standard Version Bible Translation. Amy-Jill Levine and Marc Zvi Brettler, Editors. New York and others: Oxford University Press, 2011.

The Septuagint Version of the Old Testament, with and English Translation and with Various Readings and Critical Notes. Grand Rapids, Michigan: Zondervan Publishing House, 1970.

CONCORDANCES

Morrison, Clinton, *An Analytical Concordance to the Revised Standard Version of the New Testament.* Philadelphia: The Westminster Press, 1979.

Moulton, W. F., and A. S. Geden, *A Concordance to the Greek Testament.* Edinburgh: T. & T. Clark, 1897; reprinted 1975.

Hatch, Edwin, and Henry A. Redpath, *A Concordance to the Septuagint and the Other Greek Versions of the Old Testament (Including the Apocryphal Books)* in Three Volumes. Grand Rapids, Michigan: Baker Book House, Reprinted 1983.

INDEX

Thessalonica, 192, 231, 236, 237, 238, 239, 242, 243, 245, 250, 255, 256, 289, 295, 301, 306, 321, 330, 341, 369, 403

Three Taverns, 344

Timothy, 14, 107, 212, 226, 227, 231, 233, 242, 243, 244, 245, 247, 249, 256, 260, 277, 279, 286, 287, 291, 302, 308, 318, 323, 336, 337, 349, 393, 394, 397, 403, 404

tithe, 43

tithing, 40, 42, 43, 44, 47

Titus, 210, 212, 227, 286, 302, 308, 317, 319, 321, 322, 323, 326, 327, 328, 340, 350

tongues, 70, 79, 80, 81, 85, 282, 284, 286, 330, 366, 379, 380

Torah, 29, 30, 34, 39, 41, 42, 46, 47, 54, 55, 75, 97, 99, 100, 202, 214, 309, 319, 325, 339, 394

transformation, 83, 84, 92, 147, 159, 177, 184, 187, 188, 195, 291, 356, 372, 375, 376, 383, 384, 385

transgression, 104, 107, 135, 148, 265

Travel Document, 60, 61, 233, 235, 249, 321, 337, 338, 341, 342, 409

trespass, 136, 174

tribune, 26, 341

Troas, 228, 231, 233, 249, 321, 322, 337, 409

Trophimus, 340

truth, 55, 63, 64, 72, 78, 97, 115, 116, 127, 137, 163, 168, 211, 212, 219, 220, 224, 233, 275, 283, 295, 296, 356, 387

Tryphaena, 332

Tryphosa, 332

type, 104, 105, 135, 136, 172, 174, 355, 393

unbelievers, 262, 272, 273, 274, 285, 289

Urbanus, 332

Vengeance, 358, 363

vision, 10, 13, 15, 46, 57, 58, 59, 61, 65, 69, 70, 71, 72, 82, 83, 84, 88, 130, 233, 364, 367, 368, 375, 384, 385

Way, 22, 49, 50, 56, 196, 252, 407

weak, 31, 71, 217, 259, 311, 314, 334, 372, 384

weakness, 25, 33, 70, 128, 204, 310, 315

weaknesses, 71, 309, 312, 315, 381

wife, 53, 102, 108, 121, 260, 263, 269, 270, 278, 287, 292, 302, 341, 382

wilderness, 37, 132, 134, 188, 314

wisdom, 31, 82, 94, 107, 312, 315, 360, 379

93911478R10237

Made in the USA
Columbia, SC
20 April 2018